Detours

Det

HŌKŪLANI K. AIKAU AND
VERNADETTE VICUÑA GONZALEZ, EDITORS

ours

▶▶▶ A Decolonial
Guide to Hawai'i

Duke University Press · Durham and London · 2019

Printed in the United States of America on acid-free paper ∞
Designed by Courtney Leigh Baker and typeset in
Fira Sans and Fira Sans Condensed by Westchester Publishing Services

The Cataloging-in-Publication Data is available at the Library of Congress.
ISBN 978-1-4780-0720-3 (ebook)
ISBN 978-1-4780-0583-4 (hardcover)
ISBN 978-1-4780-0649-7 (paperback)

Cover art: View of Waikīkī from the ruins of the Waikīkī Natatorium War Memorial, 2018. Courtesy of the authors.

Duke University Press gratefully acknowledges the Office of Undergraduate Education at the University of Hawaiʻi at Mānoa, which provided funds toward the publication of this book.

Duke University Press gratefully acknowledges the American Studies Program at the University of Hawaiʻi at Mānoa, which provided funds toward the publication of this book.

Duke University Press gratefully acknowledges the Center for Philippine Studies at the University of Hawaiʻi at Mānoa, which provided funds toward the publication of this book.

Duke University Press gratefully acknowledges an anonymous gift, which provided funds toward the publication of this book.

Duke University Press gratefully acknowledges the School for Cultural and Social Transformation at the University of Utah, which provided funds toward the publication of this book.

Duke University Press gratefully acknowledges the George and Marguerite Simson Biographical Research Center, which provided funds toward the publication of this book through a grant from the Hawaiʻi Council for the Humanities.

To our ʻohana, and ka lāhui Hawaiʻi

Contents

Conclusion: 'A'ole I Pau (Not Yet Finished) · 391
Hōkūlani K. Aikau and Vernadette Vicuña Gonzalez

Acknowledgments

This book owes everything to its contributors and their community and ʻāina relationships who have breathed life into its pages and entrusted us with the work of their minds, hearts, and hands. We want to thank the Hawaiʻi chapter of the American Studies Association and the American Studies Association Chapter Grants for seed funding that allowed us to host writing workshops early on in the process. These workshops were a place where contributors shared their work, received insights from others, and raised critical questions about the purpose and objectives of this decolonial guide. Nanea Kastner, an ʻŌiwi Undergraduate Research Fellow from the University of Hawaiʻi at Mānoa's Native Hawaiian Student Services, worked as our research assistant during the first year of this project. Her enthusiasm and organizational skills gave shape to the project when it was amorphous and unruly. We also want to thank Craig Howes and the George and Marguerite Simson Biographical Research Center for providing us with administrative support. Finally, mahalo to Kenneth Wissoker, who saw promise in the project early on, and the Duke University Press team, who helped us actualize our vision.

Mahalo nui.

Hōkūlani K. Aikau and
Vernadette Vicuña Gonzalez

Introduction

Many people first encounter Hawaiʻi through their imagination. A postcard imaginary of the Hawaiian Islands is steeped in a history of discovery, from the unfortunate Captain Cook, to the missionaries who followed, the military that rests and re-creates, and the hordes of tourists arriving with every flight. Travel writing, followed by photography and movies, have shaped the way Hawaiʻi is perceived. Guidebooks are one of the most popular genres depicting the islands. They offer up Hawaiʻi for easy consumption, tantalizingly reveal its secrets, and suggest the most efficient ways to make the most of one's holiday. Tour guides are part of the machinery of tourism that has come to define Hawaiʻi. Residents and visitors alike are inundated with the notion of Hawaiʻi's "aloha spirit," which supposedly makes Hawaiʻi paradise on earth. Hawaiʻi's economy revolves around tourism and the tropical image that beckons so many. This dominant sector of the economy has a heavy influence on the social and political values of many of Hawaiʻi's residents.

We titled this book *Detours* because it is meant to redirect you from the fantasy of Hawaiʻi as a tropical paradise toward an engagement with Hawaiʻi that is pono (just, fitting).[1] Hawaiʻi, like many places that have been deemed tourist destinations, is so much more than how the guidebooks depict it—a series of "must-do" and "must-see" attractions; a list of the most accommodating, affordable restaurants and hotels; beaches and forest trails waiting to be discovered; a reputation as a multicultural paradise adding color to a holiday experience; and a geography and climate marshalled for the pleasure of visitors. While this place is indeed beautiful, it is not an exotic postcard or a tropical playground with happy hosts. People here struggle with the problems brought about by colonialism, military occupation, tourism, food insecurity, high costs of living, and the effects of a changing climate. This book is a guide to Hawai'i that does not put tourist desires at the center. It will not help re-create the discovery narrative. It will not help people find paradise. It does not offer solace in a multicultural Eden where difference is dressed in aloha shirts and grass skirts. This book is meant to unsettle, to disquiet, and to disturb the "fact" of Hawai'i as a place for tourists. It is intended to guide readers toward practices that disrupt tourist paradise.

This guide considers the different ways that communities and other groups work together toward restoring ea (the breath and sovereignty of the lāhui, 'āina, and its people). The lāhui Hawai'i (Hawaiian nation) has tactically, strategically, and persistently resisted dismemberment and military occupation. What we offer here are unfamiliar and alternative narratives, tours, itineraries, mappings, and images of the Hawaiian Islands that present a decolonial understanding of Hawai'i that goes beyond global tourism's marketing. They show how people have disrupted and transformed life here in order to continue the tradition of refusal and resistance. The stories, poetry, and art gathered in this book include concrete examples of how we move from metaphors of decolonization to material practices and everyday acts of resurgence that bring about real change in people's lives, transforming our relationships with land as 'āina so it can better feed us once again.

While this is a guide, it should not be construed as a blanket invitation. Not everyone who reads this book will be invited or allowed to go to all of the places that are described. Some places and knowledge have been left out altogether because they are not meant for outsiders. We honor the wishes of the community that has asked that this book not be an invitation to visitors. We ask that you respect their wishes and follow their protocol for how to engage—or not. Sometimes the best way to support decolonization and Kanaka 'Ōiwi resurgence is to not come as a tourist to our home. The *our* in this sentence recognizes that Kanaka and non-Kanaka call this place home and that we all need to (re)learn how to live here in radically different ways if the 'āina and wai (land and water) are going to be able to support po'e (peoples, beings) into the future. Thus, an important underlying assumption of this book is that not all knowledge, information, or access to places is open and available to everyone. We understand that within a touristic framework, this is a radically audacious idea. But we ask that you proceed with caution and restraint.

We also recognize that this un-invitation might be disconcerting, and it should be. Hawai'i as ideal tourist destination is made possible by an infrastructure built for and around visitors' comfort, safety, and pleasure. That infrastructure and the ideas, values, and decisions that support it were and are built on the historical and present-day dispossession of Kanaka ʻŌiwi—Native Hawaiians. Unless we actively work to dismantle this infrastructure and refuse the tourist imaginary, we will (wittingly or unwittingly) contribute to reproducing the occupation and colonization of these places, people, and practices. This bleak picture of the contemporary moment will also be our future—but that is yet to be determined. If you want to contribute to preparing for a different future, and if this knowledge makes you at all uneasy and you want to approach and engage Hawaiʻi differently—with a sense of pono and kuleana (responsibility, obligation, authority)—then come with us on this huakaʻi, this transformative journey. Instead of looking at what Hawaiʻi can offer you (and it has much to offer beyond sun and sand), you might think instead of how you can learn from and contribute to ongoing efforts toward sustaining ea.

This book is important for at least two reasons. First, it affirms that the ala loa—the long path—of decolonization is one worth following, and that anyone with a commitment to do the work can walk this path. Second, the contributors and their work remind us that we are all following in the footsteps of people who came before us and that we are moving the cause forward in diverse ways according to our individual gifts, relationships, perspectives, and efforts. This is important because just as colonization, capitalism, and heteropatriarchy continue to evolve and shape-shift, appropriating our efforts, co-opting our people, and slowly killing us, we need decolonizing practices that are creative, adaptive, innovative, and ongoing if Indigenous peoples are going to get out in front of the colonizing machines and hold firm to "the chattering winds of hope."[2]

Cultivating Ea

We intentionally use the words *decolonize* and *decolonial* to identify the main goal of this book: to restore the ea of Hawaiʻi. Kanaka ʻŌiwi scholar and activist Noelani Goodyear-Kaʻōpua describes "ea as both a concept and a diverse set of practices. . . . Ea refers to political independence and is often translated as 'sovereignty.' It also carries the meaning of 'life' and 'breath,' among other things. . . . *Ea is based on the experiences of people on the land, relationships forged through the process of remembering and caring for wahi pana, storied places . . . Ea is an active state of being . . . Ea cannot be achieved or possessed; it requires constant action day after day, generation after generation."*[3] Ea is a political orientation and a set of intentional practices that must be done day after day, generation after generation. During

Cultivating ea, block print. *Photograph by Pekuna Hong.*

ka wā ʻŌiwi walo nō (the era that was indeed Native), ea was the way of life. Ea was for kanaka as water is for fish. It is the air we breathe.[4] Today, ea must be cultivated by Kanaka and non-Kanaka alike if it is going to persist into the future.

To be sure, resistance and decolonization, the companions of ea, have been around since Europeans "discovered" lands and people on far-distant shores and exerted control over the natural and human resources they found: colonization sparked decolonization. European exploration marked the dawn of an age of imperialism and colonialism—the process of creating European settlements in colonial outposts in order to assert direct control over land, labor, markets, resources, and the flow of capital, commodities, and ideas. Settler colonialism is the particular form colonialism has taken in places such as the United States, Canada, Aotearoa/New Zealand, and Australia. Settler colonialism describes the process by which settlers came, stayed, and formed new governmental structures, laws, and ideas intended to affirm their ownership of land and labor. These global shifts also marked the emergence of resistance to empire and colonization. Decolonization describes material practices that have arisen in response to the myriad forms imperialism and colonization have taken over five centuries. It includes, but is not limited to, the processes and practices of resistance, refusal, and dismantling of the political, economic, social, and spiritual structures constructed by colonizers.[5]

When we describe the aim of this book as to contribute to the decolonization of Hawai'i, we are also committed to the return of Hawaiian lands to the Hawaiian people and the removal of the kinds of institutions, such as the U.S. military and its governmental structures, that occupy and abuse this place. To achieve this, a process of decolonization must work at all levels at which imperialism and settler colonialism operate. This book works on the level of ideas and practices, reminding people, both Indigenous and not Indigenous, that there was a time in the not-so-distant past when Kanaka 'Ōiwi "were born into and lived in a universe which was entirely of our making."[6] A vision of a future where Indigenous people are sovereign is a commitment to understanding the process by which colonization and occupation occurred. Deoccupation, which is devoted to demilitarization and the repatriation of Kanaka land, is a crucial part of the broader project of decolonization.

Frantz Fanon, a writer and freedom fighter who sought the decolonization of Algeria from France, better explains the challenge to which we are responding. He charged Native intellectuals to write for the people, toward political ends—to write about the past and present "with the intention of opening up the future, of spurring them into action and fostering hope."[7] We asked our contributors to write, craft, create, and imagine a present that plans and prepares for a future built from action and hope. We asked them to relate stories that foster decolonial approaches and imaginaries of Hawai'i. Fanon also says that, in addition to writing, we must take action: "But in order to *secure* hope, in order to give it substance, [we] must *take part in the action and commit [our] body and soul* to the national struggle. You can talk about anything you like, but when it comes to talking about that one thing in a life that involves opening up new horizons . . . then *muscle power* is required."[8] The contributors to *Detours* are intellectuals putting "muscle power" toward opening up the future we desire. If we are going to (re)shape the future, we must actively prepare now. Many of the contributors share the work they do in relation to places and community. The kinds of practices, imaginations, and stories they are nurturing—all of which are putting decolonization into practice. These are not just words in a book, but a set of actions that must be done on a regular basis if decolonization is to be more than a metaphor and if we are to cultivate ea. No one project is like another, even though they all share similar themes, values, and commitments.

Modeling Kuleana

While we—the editors of this book—come from different places, we are both committed to the project of decolonizing Hawai'i—restoring and strengthening the ea of the people and the land. Hōkūlani is a Kanaka 'Ōiwi who was born in Hawai'i but whose family emigrated when she was three years old. She did not return until she was twenty-five, as a tourist. Hōkūlani's first trip back to her one hānau (her birth sands, the place of her birth) contrasted nostalgic family memories with images, smells, sounds, and representations of a Hawai'i made available to tourists, outsiders, malihini (strangers). Vernadette is a Filipina born in the Philippines whose family settled on the U.S. continent when she was eleven. She came to Hawai'i as a graduate student, then again in her thirties, as a professor. She first came to Hawai'i to study tourism from a critical angle, having encountered that prevalent idea of the islands as paradise.

We met as colleagues at the University of Hawai'i at Mānoa, both experiencing a broader process of connecting and reconnecting with places and people. For Hōkūlani, this meant learning the practices she had only heard described by her kūpuna (grandparents). These lands had not fed her for nearly thirty years. She had to reestablish her relationship with people, places, and practices in order to remember how she is of Hawai'i. For Vernadette, this meant learning the sometimes uncomfortable place, protocols, and responsibilities of someone who is a settler and an ally for decolonization in Hawai'i. As a settler on occupied lands, Vernadette navigates every day what it means to live and raise a family here and the kuleana that comes from being nourished by this place. On one level, our huaka'i are not all that different, yet our positions as Kanaka 'Ōiwi and settler afford us fundamentally different relationships to this place. Despite these differences, we both work diligently every day to carry our respective kuleana in pono ways. We hope that the contributions in this volume will demonstrate that not everyone carries the same kuleana. We must, however, support each other, and we need to hold each other lovingly accountable for our respective kuleana.

A History of Bad Guests

Given our similar yet distinct relationships to Hawai'i nei, it might seem strange for us to offer a guide to this place. We wrestled with this, but we felt that our unique stories give us insight into the struggles that many people might have who want to engage with Hawai'i and Kanaka 'Ōiwi initiatives of decolonization. A guide about Hawai'i was the best way for us to show how we and others—Kanaka 'Ōiwi and settlers in Hawai'i, Kanaka 'Ōiwi who have settled elsewhere—can live ethically and justly. This has not always been the case.

A gloss of Hawaiian history illuminates the tensions of an archipelago caught between Kanaka ʻŌiwi sovereignty and Western imperial maneuvers. The results were ugly for Native Hawaiians and others ensnared in the colonial land grab, belying the pretty postcard images of Hawaiʻi today. What we want to make clear in this history is that the myth of Native hospitality has supported this pattern of material dispossession.[9] Against colonialism's distortion of ideas and theft of land, Native resistance was born from the first moment of Western contact.

One could argue that the best known early "visitors" to encounter the Hawaiian Islands were Captain James Cook and his crew. By the time he sailed into the blue waters of the archipelago, a vibrant, prosperous, and complex society had established itself, having inaugurated the so-called Age of Exploration more than a millenium before the Europeans discovered Moananuiākea (the Pacific Ocean). Cook was a British explorer who in 1779 repaid the gift of being able to resupply and repair his ships on Hawaiʻi Island with an attempt to kidnap its chief. His "discovery" initiated a series of ill-behaved guests. Despite the dismal decision making that resulted in his death, he was given full honors at burial, and his remains were returned to his crew. Cook and his sailors left the worst of keepsakes: contagious diseases such as cholera, measles, and gonnorhea laid waste to a population that had no immunities.

Whalers and missionaries were the next set of arrivals to the islands in the 1820s. Whalers were drawn to the islands' salubrious climate, which beckoned them after months spent on cramped ships. Honolulu and Lahaina became ports of call for ships to resupply fresh provisions. These were also sites where sailors disembarked for local entertainments, misconstruing Indigenous practices of sexual exchange as prostitution or evidence of Native moral decay (charges they were somehow exempt from). Disease spread further, and the Native Hawaiian population continued to decline. Protestant missionaries also set sail for the islands, and upon their arrival transformed its social structure. The first generation of missionaries imposed their religious strictures on Kanaka ʻŌiwi, frowning on the "lascivious" movements of hula and encouraging practices of Western dress and domesticity. Their children and grandchildren went beyond harvesting souls for God to harvesting Hawaiian land for profit.

A generation after missionaries arrived, the Māhele, or Division of Land, that began in 1848 formalized a system of private property ownership that had not existed in the islands before then. Such a shift was induced by sweet dreams of sugar, which brought with them a new labor system using Asian contract laborers to work the plantations. The impact of Hawaiʻi's early visitors was grim, particularly for Native Hawaiians, who were increasingly marginalized from political power. Descendants of missionaries, entrenched in advisory positions to the Mōʻī (kings and queens) and consolidating their sugar wealth, essentially lobbied for most-favored guest status with the emerging superpower in the region, the United States. The Reciprocity Treaty of 1876 guaranteed Hawaiʻi's economic reliance on sugar and the ascendance of the Big Five (Castle and Cooke, C. Brewer, American Factors, Theo H. Davies, Alexander and Baldwin) as the economic players in the islands. Ten years later, the renewal of the treaty granted a new but insistent visitor—the U.S. military—exclusive rights to what would become Pearl Harbor.

These guests to the kingdom—for that is what they were: settlers who had been granted residency by virtue of royal tolerance—were unsatisfied with the concessions that made more and more Native Hawaiians uneasy. On June 30, 1887, a group of white American settlers—planters and businessmen who had made their fortunes in Hawaiʻi—put a gun to King Kalākaua, threatening him with death unless he signed a new constitution that removed powers from the monarch. When his sister, Liliʻuokalani, became Mōʻī and moved to create a new constitution in response to the pleas of her subjects, the white oligarchy, supported by U.S. Marines from the USS *Boston*, overthrew her and imprisoned her in her own home. Her crimes: refusal to recognize the Bayonet Constitution as the law and her intention to institute a new constitution that would reestablish Native Hawaiian sovereign rule of the kingdom and re-enfranchise those, including Asian settlers, who had been disenfranchised by race and class exclusions by the Bayonet Constitution. In other words, as leader of the lāhui, she moved to reestablish authority over her own home, and for this she and her people were punished.

Colonialism is the ultimate breach of guest protocol. It violates a welcome, one that was never actually extended, in order to fulfill a desire to take and possess land that is not one's own. Colonialism was not met with consent or passivity: in response to the Bayonet Constitution, Hawaiian nationalists planned armed uprisings; Robert Wilcox tried twice. Men and women across the islands submitted petitions urging the queen to rewrite the constitution and reestablish ʻŌiwi sovereignty. The imprisoned queen composed mele (chants) for her people, smuggling them out of her home to be published in Hawaiian-language newspapers.

In the face of the white oligarchy that was now in political power, and its machinations to annex the islands to the United States, Hui Aloha ʻĀina, also known as the Hawaiian Patriotic League, along with other political organizations amassed more than 38,000 signatures protesting such a move. Queen

Liliʻuokalani and her loyal subjects went to Washington, DC, to express their resistance (always following proper protocol as guests). And their political maneuvers worked. In 1897, the U.S. Congress voted against the annexation of Hawaiʻi.

When the Spanish-American War broke out in 1898 and the reality of Hawaiʻi's strategic position in the Pacific became essential, the U.S. Congress passed a Joint Resolution that annexed Hawaiʻi to the United States. This illegal maneuver bypassed international treaty law and unilaterally attached the islands to the continent by fiat, not democratic process. Today, this story of treason, overthrow, illegal occupation, and annexation is remembered by the United States as "the end of a lengthy internal struggle between native Hawaiians and white American business men for control of the Hawaiian government."[10] As David Uahikeaikaleiʻohu Maile writes in his contribution to this guide, "'Aʻole Is Our Refusal"; the struggle between Native Hawaiians and the United States is not over. Indeed, Kanaka ʻŌiwi evoke a history of refusal when they gathered at public hearings organized by the U.S. Department of the Interior across the pae ʻāina to say, "'aʻole, we do not now nor did we in the past consent to U.S. occupation."

This cursory history of overstaying, ill-behaved, and overreaching "visitors" illuminates the pattern of violations committed against the people, nation, and lands of Hawaiʻi. U.S. national historians would have us believe that this story was inevitable, a product and outcome of structural forces beyond anyone's control. But let us be clear: Kanaka ʻŌiwi and other subjects loyal to the Mōʻī have steadfastly refused the "gift" of recognition. We would much rather ʻai pohaku (eat stones, the fruit of the land) than be part of the United States of America. We refuse the marketing and prostitution of Hawaiian culture, land, and labor for tourist consumption. We rage against the U.S. military occupation of kingdom lands at the lowest rental rates in the country: $1.00 per year. Behind the image of the smiling, gentle, seductively beckoning icon of the hula girl—meant to invite, reassure, welcome—is a Hawaiʻi that has always been clear about its expressions of aloha ʻāina (love for our lands) and ʻaʻole (refusal). It has learned from its history that visitors do not always come with the best intentions, nor do they understand practices of true reciprocity as crucial to the extension of aloha. And many never leave.

A Map of the Way Forward

This book is arranged around several themes that are distinctly place-based. Unlike a travel guidebook, *Detours* does not offer comprehensive coverage of all the sites and sights in Hawaiʻi. What we have here is a selection of visual and written work that come together to shift conceptions and perceptions of Hawai'i, highlight different ways of moving through its spaces, and, when appropriate, invite people to work toward a decolonial future alongside others committed to the same goals.

We want to highlight two words that capture the tensions of this book: aloha, a term whose meaning incorporates notions of compassion, regard, fondness, and many other sentiments for mutual affection and reciprocity; and 'a'ole, which means "no, never, no!" We draw your attention to these key terms because they remind us that we must take heed and proceed with caution. Aloha is the Kanaka term most identified with the tourism industry, which, as noted above, uses the term to represent, market, and promote Hawai'i and Native Hawaiians as naturally hospitable and welcoming. It has also been widely appropriated to advertise ski and snowboard rentals in Park City, Utah, and poke bowls in Chicago (only two of thousands of examples). Such representations have contributed to how colonial powers— the United States foremost among them—have translated this to mean an unconditional open door. The word 'a'ole is a demand that has not been as equally heard, although it too has been uttered since the earliest instances of overreaching and overstaying in this place. Juxtaposing these two terms is meant to provoke, to frame this "guide" as an unsettling assertion of sovereignty and a demand to think critically about your relationship with Hawai'i.

Part I, "Wahi Pana/Storied Places," lingers on a number of places whose histories have been forgotten, buried, or misrepresented. Tourism and its sibling, urban and suburban construction, have had a lot to do with how the deep histories of these sites have faded from contemporary view or from human memory. The places described here include popular tourist attractions and lesser-known neighborhoods, as well as sites that do not make their way into tourist guidebooks because they are not deemed worthy destinations. Part II, "Hana Lima/Decolonial Representations and Projects," explores practices that restore or establish people's connections to places or the practices that are connected to places. These include community-based and place-based efforts focused on reviving cultural practices as well as ongoing struggles against and alongside tourism as a dominant economic engine of Hawai'i. Part III, "Huaka'i/Tours for Transformation," features actual tours that address geographic, environmental, social, and political issues on the islands; transformative practices of journeying that have been revived in the islands; or imaginative itineraries that unsettle tourists' and residents' expectations. They may be regular offerings, community-based tours intended to raise consciousness about a place, or unique mappings of commonly traversed areas that offer layered histories. Part IV, "Hawaiʻi beyond the 'Big Eight'/New Mappings," offers cartographies of Hawaiʻi that disrupt the notion that Hawaiʻi is geographically bounded by the eight main islands. Most guidebooks determine geographic location to be the limit of their authority, but this one considers how Kānaka ʻŌiwi have traveled, explored, and settled far beyond these shores, and how Hawaiʻi contends with the transformations brought by other Pacific migrations. Some of these dislocations have been by choice, others through force.

Our contributors use ʻōlelo Hawaiʻi (Hawaiian language) generously and at times without translation. In general, we asked authors to include their preferred English translations of Hawaiian terms upon their first use in an essay. For longer quotes we have included adjacent translations of the text. We also provide a glossary of terms commonly used throughout the volume, and we have honored the wishes of those contributors who asked that their work not be translated into English. We do so because we recognize that translation is political. As Noenoe Silva explains, "translation is unsatisfactory . . . because it is impossible to convey all of the cultural coding that English strips away and equally impossible to avoid the Western cultural coding that English adds."[11] By limiting the multiplicity of meaning and attaching unintended meaning to terms, translation also does violence to ʻike Hawaiʻi.

Given the signficance of ʻōlelo Hawaiʻi for restoring ea, we ask readers to approach translations for what they are: provisional interpretations of texts. The translations in this volume should not be treated as literal, one-to-one representations of the original; definitions vary from piece to piece and within a single essay. The glossary honors the multiplicity of meaning so valued in ʻike Hawaiʻi. We include the ʻōlelo Hawaiʻi source text in order to provide readers of ʻōlelo Hawaiʻi an opportunity to engage with the material in its original form. In sum, even when a translation is provided, it should not be construed as the final word on the interpretation of the primary source. Rather, we encourage you to learn ʻōlelo Hawaiʻi if you do not know it; if you do, we ask that you interact with the primary text in your own analytical and relational way.

A Conditional Invitation to Enter

According to Hawaiian protocol, a guest would present a mele kāhea, or a chant petitioning for entry or welcome, to ask permission to enter or pass through a place. One waits for the response, the mele komo, which grants entry and establishes the expectations of pono behavior, gifts, and other forms of reciprocity. Mele kāhea and mele komo continue to be protocol in the practice of hula and in other rituals involving learning.

A common mele kāhea, Kūnihi ka Mauna, describes the journey of Hiʻiakaikapoliopele, the younger sister of Pele, who traveled to Kauaʻi to fetch Lohiʻau, Pele's lover. As Hiʻiaka travels across Kauaʻi, she encounters many obstacles, including a missing bridge over the Wailua River. A particular version of this story describes Hiʻiaka arriving at the home of a seer and his relative. She asked permission to enter, but her chant was ignored by the seer's wife, who was beating her kapa cloth. Hiʻiaka must receive permission from the seer himself, who is down by the ocean. She would not be allowed to cross the river until the person with the kuleana (authority) to grant permission did so. So, she waited until his return then performed the mele kāhea again. The seer responded in the affirmative, and she was allowed to pass.

What we want to highlight from this story of Hiʻiaka's journey is that everyone—even a deity—must follow the understood protocols of each place and request permission to enter before passing through. This mele kāhea describes Hiʻiaka's journey across the islands and her various encounters with people and places. They transform her, just as she transforms them. Her huakaʻi is an active and involved one. It demands an openness to what the encounters have to teach her, a deference to the depth and authority of local knowledge, and a willingness to be changed by the journey itself. It is with this understanding that encounters effect change that we have oriented this book toward people who want to be changed by experience and contribute toward ea and a decolonized future.

We offer these detours as a reminder that Kanaka ʻŌiwi are voyaging people. We travel across our islands and around the earth. We invite you to join us on this huakaʻi.

Notes

1 We thank Aunty Terri Kekoʻolani and Kyle Kajihiro for permission to use the name of their established demilitarization DeTours for our book title.
2 Brandy Nālani McDougall, "The Second Gift," in *The Value of Hawaiʻi 2: Ancestral Roots, Oceanic Visions*, ed. Aiko Yamashiro and Noelani Goodyear-Kaʻōpua (Honolulu: University of Hawaiʻi Press, 2014), 250–53.
3 Noelani Goodyear-Kaʻōpua, Ikaika Hussey, and Erin Kahunawaikaʻala Wright, eds., *A Nation Rising: Hawaiian Movements for Life, Land, and Sovereignty* (Durham: Duke University Press, 2014), 3–4. Emphasis added.
4 Brian Kamaoli Kuwada, "'Na Moolelo o Kou Aina Makuahine': Our Kūpuna on Sovereignty and the Overthrow," *KE KAUPU HEHI ALE* (blog), January 17, 2017,

https://hehiale.wordpress.com/2017/01/17/na-moolelo-o-kou-aina-makuahine-our -kupuna-on-sovereignty-and-the-overthrow/.

5   Linda Tuhiwai Smith, *Decolonizing Methodologies: Research and Indigenous Peoples*, 2nd ed. (London: Zed, 2012), 20–22.

6   Smith, *Decolonizing Methodologies*, 24.

7   Frantz Fanon, *The Wretched of the Earth* (New York: Grove Press, 1963), 167.

8   Fanon, *Wretched of the Earth*, 167; emphasis added.

9   Paige West, *Dispossession and the Environment: Rhetoric and Inequality in Papua New Guinea*, repr. ed. (New York: Columbia University Press, 2016).

10 "The 1897 Petition Against the Annexation of Hawaii," National Archives, accessed September 7, 2017, https://www.archives.gov/education/lessons/hawaii-petition.

11 Noenoe Silva, *Aloha Betrayed: Native Hawaiian Resistance to American Colonialism* (Durham, NC: Duke University Press, 2004), 12.

PART I. Wahi Pana / Storied Places

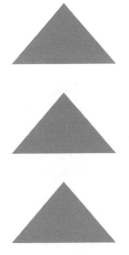

As a place, Hawai'i's value is often defined through its attractiveness as a tourist destination, the productivity of its land for industries such as sugar, coffee, or pineapple (none of which are native crops), or its geostrategic utility as a military site. In contrast to this value system, Kanaka 'Ōiwi have a familial relationship to the 'āina that requires interaction based on mālama 'āina (mutual care) and kuleana (responsibility).

In Hawai'i, wahi pana is the term used to designate a place as sacred or "legendary." The names of places and people alike "act as mnemonic devices for the remembrance of stories and particular events."[1] In this section, and throughout this volume, contributors use 'Ōiwi place-names to remember and honor the mana, the spiritual and cultural power, that resides in places and the persons (humans, other-than-humans, and celestial beings) associated with those places. We approach wahi pana in two registers. First, we honor the familial and genealogical relationship between Kanaka and 'āina by acknowledging all places as sacred. We recognize that stories live in places, and when we learn a place's name, we call forth the stories, great and small, that live there. Second, we recognize that some places are "more" sacred than others because of their profound genealogical importance or the cultural practices associated with them over generations. We believe that telling the 'Ōiwi stories of wahi pana is a decolonial practice of restoring the relationship between people and places. In remembering the wahi pana across the pae 'āina (archipelago), contributors often contrast the 'Ōiwi understandings of place with how those places are used, treated, and remembered today.

We begin this section with essays and images from Hawaiʻi Island that are firmly grounded within an ʻŌiwi sensibility. Kamanamaikalani Beamer reflects on Hawaiian ways of mapping by decentering tourist understandings of distance and destination, instead indigenizing our orientation to place. This reorientation continues with Haley Kailiehu's and Noʻeau Peralto's visual and written tributes to an old plantation town in Hāmākua; their works illustrate how stories—ʻŌiwi and settler alike—are deeply rooted in places. Our ʻŌiwi sense of place is disturbed by the next set of essays, which juxtapose wahi pana with various destructive practices taking place across the pae ʻāina. Focused on Maui Island, Kapulani Landgraf uses photography to draw our attention to ke one hānau and ke kulaiwi (the birth sands and burial sites of generations of ʻŌiwi ancestors) that have been desecrated by construction on both Maui and Oʻahu. Concrete does more than hide ʻŌiwi wahi pana; the sand used to make the concrete may include the crushed bones of our ancestors. Katrina-Ann R. Kapāʻanaokalāokeola Nākoa Oliveira contrasts Kanaka ʻŌiwi notions of sacred places with the value of place for science and tourism, whereas Dean Itsuji Saranillio focuses on the discursive violence of place-making when the intended audience is visitors, not the people who live on the islands. Brandy Nālani McDougall's poems take issue with a contemporary mapping technology, noting how the directions given by Google Maps are emptied of history. Her poems, along with the other contributions in this section, remind us that giving and receiving directions in Hawaiʻi is relational, based on the spatial relationships of the person giving directions to the place to which they are giving the direction, and their relationships to the places from which they are departing and the places to which they are going.

Stephanie Nohelani Teves, remembering the places of importance to Princess Kaʻiulani, and Uncle Joe Estores and Ty Kāwika Tengan, who remember the lifeways at Āhua Point before the land and waters were polluted by U.S. military occupation, use moʻolelo of the past to help us dream of a future where the land and water can again sustain life. Laura E. Lyons interrogates the conflicted history of Lānaʻi (one of two islands owned by individuals). Lianne Marie Leda Charlie and a group led by Mehana Blaich Vaughan focus on Anini and Kahaleʻala on the island of Kauaʻi in order to disrupt the ways that tourists and real estate agents describe and interact with these places. They remind us that some of the most touristic or exclusive sites on the islands are and will always be ʻŌiwi wale nō!

In the age-old tradition of composing mele (song) to honor places, Halena Kapuni-Reynolds and Wendy Mapuana Waipā begin their essay with an original mele to honor the wahi pana of Keaukaha on Hawaiʻi Island. With each stanza they remember the beauty of the place and the historical and contemporary stories that keep it alive in our minds and our hearts.

The essays in Part I and throughout this guidebook highlight how contemporary kānaka, both ʻŌiwi and their allies, continue to rejoice and celebrate the love they have for wahi pana.

Note

1   Noelani Arista, "Listening to Leoiki: Engaging Sources in Hawaiian History," *Biography* 32, no. 1 (winter 2009): 66–73.

Kamanamaikalani Beamer

Only Twenty Ahupuaʻa Away

I had just about made it to the showers with my two youngest keiki clinging to opposing limbs of my body. My eldest had already immersed herself in the shower, barely noticing the tourist couple who were rapidly approaching what we were about to claim as our ʻohana shower space. All at once the sound of a brash East Coast American accent pierced our Native ears: "How far is the airport from here?" This was not an unusual question to hear from a tourist at Wailea Beach, which is in South Kohala in the ahupuaʻa of Waimea on Hawaiʻi Island.[1] Since the 1960s, when, after spending some time playing on our shores, Laurance S. Rockefeller developed the Mauna Kea Beach Hotel—the first on our coast—our beaches and the spaces between them have been transformed into a playground for visitors.

Having spent the day with my young keiki in the arms of Kanaloa, sliding in waves, constructing what we effectively term *punakai*,[2] and variously pursuing unlucky sand crabs, I was now washing the sand from my sons' shorts but still close enough to my Hawaiian state of Zen to reflect before responding to the urgent cry for help issued by our uninvited guests. In that moment, I understood that they probably wanted me to give them a distance in miles from our location to the international airport in Kona, or perhaps the approximate amount of time it would take to drive there by car, but I had a much better answer.

"The airport is just about twenty ahupuaʻa to the south," I uttered while trying to conceal my smirk.

Their expectant facial expressions morphed into puzzled stares that reminded me of the look of a confused child trying to comprehend what they were just told. Holding back my grin with less success, I continued, "You will see the planes landing in what looks to be the middle of the lava when you get close, but there are about twenty ahupuaʻa between Waimea and the airport."

In truth, at that particular moment, I wasn't sure if twenty-two or perhaps eighteen ahupuaʻa were between the showers at Wailea and the Kona International Airport. My retort to my new American East Coast "friends" was also influenced by the fact that I had spent the evening before reviewing materials for an ahupuaʻa lecture I was scheduled to give the following week, and thus my mind was probably more focused on palena (place boundaries) and ahupuaʻa boundaries than it might be on another day. Neither of these factors seemed of much significance to the East Coast couple, as they left our interaction perhaps feeling less certainty about their pending voyage than they had before it. The last thing I recall hearing was, "OK, thanks," as they scurried to find another person who might give them an answer that was more aligned with their conceptions of place, boundaries, and the geography of Hawaiʻi.

I have come to be thankful for that chance encounter, not merely because it allowed me an opportunity to express my poor sense of humor, but because it made me reflect on the ways that people traverse our places unaware of the uniqueness of our geography and systems of palena. Rather than traveling across a landscape mapped and organized by mile markers between points of departure and destination, how might one experience that movement with a more intimate knowledge of Hawaiian geography and place? The landscape between Wailea and Kalaoa ahupuaʻa in Kona appears somewhat vast on the map distributed by flight attendants on airplanes before landing or by car rental companies. In contrast, while traveling the ma kai road, one becomes an eyewitness to the differing flows of pahoehoe and ʻāʻā lava that have been laid by Tūtū Pele in years prior. Driving long sections of highway one can see along the coastline the Ala Loa trail as it runs between the multiple gated communities that have developed. To the untrained eye it may appear somewhat empty as one drives through large stretches of what some refer to as "barren lava fields." We, however, know that these stones carry the stories of our kūpuna—they speak of our place, the diverse environments of our people, and of our palena. In the midst of the rapid changes Hawaiʻi has faced in the past two hundred years, how do we restore and share our palena, our knowledge of place boundaries?

Palena were established scores of generations before Europeans arrived in Hawaiʻi. Lands were bounded and defined in ways that made sense to the ʻŌiwi of old. What is commonly referred to as the moku or ahupuaʻa system is a result of firmly established palena. When attempting to translate the word *palena*, I use "place boundaries" in order to signify that I am speaking of a particular kind of boundary. Palena might be also translated as a "protected place." Palena is a boundary specific to the ʻŌiwi system of land tenure. These types of boundaries were not impenetrable fences, as people had the ability to move from one place to another. Instead, palena bound the material and spiritual resources of a place for community access and control while enabling chiefly leadership to regulate resources on the larger scale of the island. Aliʻi (ʻŌiwi chiefly leadership) who accomplished the task of clearly bounding the land and defining palena were often famous for their works, as was Māʻilikūkahi on Oʻahu Island. The Hawaiian historian Samuel Kamakau had this to say about Māʻilikūkahi's planning work on Oʻahu: "When the kingdom passed to Māʻilikūkahi, the land divisions were in a state of confusion; the ahupuaʻa, the kū, the ʻili ʻāina, the moʻo ʻāina, the pauku ʻāina, and the kīhāpai were not clearly defined. Therefore Māʻilikūkahi ordered the chiefs, aliʻi, the lesser chiefs, kaukau aliʻi, the warrior chiefs, pūʻali aliʻi, and the overseers, luna[,] to divided [*sic*] all of Oʻahu into moku, ahupuaʻa, ʻili kupono, ʻili ʻāina, and moʻo ʻāina."[3]

The establishment of palena on these geographical scales brought greater productivity to the lands. It would also be a means of settling land disputes among aliʻi who would control the bounded lands. Palena enabled konohiki (ahupuaʻa-based resource managers) to know the limits of the resources to be managed. Important archival sources often tell us that people knew the palena of their ahupuaʻa so they would not extend their resource gathering across their palena and into an adjoining ahupuaʻa.[4] Other archival materials state that palena were established because "in old times the people used to fight over cultivating grounds, and so we used to keep the run of the boundaries of our lands."[5]

Palena also played a critical role in the annual makahiki procession (a religious ceremony conducted once a year in which people traversed the entire island). It was at the makai palena of the ahupuaʻa that hoʻokupu (material gifts in a ceremony) would be collected for the aliʻi nui (head chief) and akua (god). Near the ahu (mound, shrine) that marked the makai portion of the palena, ālia sticks were placed to mark the boundary of the place that was kapu (prohibited). This was a ridged boundary, one that if crossed by a person without kuleana (right to access) would likely result in death. Palena that marked the area where hoʻokupu would be collected represent an ordering of the land and resources that allowed the early governments of Hawaiʻi to manage resources across an entire island. Collecting hoʻokupu at the makai portion of each ahupua'a enabled the government to exercise some measure of control over diverse place-specific resources. For an island nation entirely dependent on local marine and terrestrial resources for survival, palena were critical toward establishing manageable units that allowed generations of communities to survive and thrive in what many today might call a sustainable fashion. When it worked well, this delicate balance of top-down oversight of finite resources, coupled with a fully empowered and engaged community with the ability to intergenerationally self-regulate place-based resources, enabled 'Ōiwi society to flourish for centuries.

Palena and Place

To understand the palena of an area (moku, ahupua'a, 'ili) like the ancestors did, one must have a much more intimate sense of that place. One might be able to draw imaginary lines over a "space"; however, "place is not a purely formal operator empty of content, but is always contentful, always specifiable as this particular place or that one."[6] This is the lesson that Aunty Lady taught me. When I spoke with Aunty Lady, a kupuna whom I thought had been born in Wai'āpuka ahupua'a in North Kohala, I found that she had actually been born in the ahupua'a of Niuli'i (an ahupua'a bordering Wai'āpuka). One of the first questions I asked her was whether she had been born in Wai'āpuka. Her answer was immediate: "No, I was born in Halilipalala!" I was confused at first, but after further research into the place names of Wai'āpuka and their adjoining ahupua'a, I found that Halilipalala was actually an 'ili in Niuli'i, several hundred feet from Wai'āpuka. I am sure Aunty Lady knew I would be confused by her answer: you cannot find Halilipalala on any modern map, nor is it a name that one is likely to ever hear today. Perhaps she wanted to see how much I already knew and my intellectual capacity. The sense of place that Aunty Lady conveyed to me was of a much more traditional nature than I had initially realized. Halilipalala, though very close to Wai'āpuka in actual measured distance, and indistinguishable on almost any modern map, was a distinctly different place in the eyes of this kupuna.

Often, when you ask a Hawaiian in their forties or fifties, "Where you from?" you are likely to get an answer that is island based, such as Kaua'i, or Maui, or perhaps a moku district such as Hilo. Sometimes you might get an answer that refers to a more specific place, possibly an ahupua'a such as Hakipu'u, Waimea, or Wailua. People my age rarely refer to their places of origin in terms of 'ili. Perhaps it is because most of us were born in area hospitals rather than at home, as most kūpuna were. Or it could be because today many of us do not relate to the land in 'ili terms. We definitely live in a different time, and it has indeed changed our perceptions of place. Gregory Cajete states that "Indigenous people are people of place, and the nature of place is embedded in their language[;] the physical, cognitive, and emotional orientation of a people is a kind of map they carry in their heads and transfer from generation to generation."[7]

Cajete's ideas, together with my own personal feelings and experience, have led me to a deeper understanding that one cannot know the palena of an ahupuaʻa or ʻili without "knowing the place much more intimately" or having information passed down by someone who does. Any inquiry into the nature of palena must be a place-based inquiry. Traditionally, knowledge of boundaries was held in the memories of people who were intimate with their place, geography, and historical land use. In fact, knowledge of palena often included references to other realms of information, such as that contained in oli, kaʻao, mele, and moʻolelo (different types of chants and stories) concerning personages such as menehune, moʻo, kupua, or akua (various legendary or godlike figures). Therefore, place names themselves denote stories and people's relationships with the natural, physical, and spiritual environment. Places—and even elements and natural processes specific to a particular place—were given specific names.

One need only open a Hawaiian language dictionary to the page that lists the English word *wind* to see how this generic term fails to capture the complexity and intimacy of air currents when they connect to specific places or seasons. For that one English word over three hundred options are available in Hawaiian. *One could repeat this exercise using the words* rain, cloud, sea, sky *and see a pattern of* Hawaiian descriptions of place-based observations and descriptions of natural systems that are as varied and diverse as our genealogies. For a people to be able to give such detailed descriptions for different states of ʻāina, the ancestors also must have had extensive knowledge of place and the boundaries that gave each its unique identity. The boundaries did not necessarily manifest as lines on a map, but palena associated distinctive characteristics with each place. Many ahupuaʻa and ʻili have distinct rain names. For instance, a rain name associated almost exclusively with Mānoa is **Tuahine**, whereas its neighboring valley Pālolo is famous for its **Līlīlehua** rain. Knowledge of palena would enable a person to know which of the two rains one was experiencing.

Imagine place-specific mental maps that organize and categorize orographic rainfall by place, known and understood by the hundreds of thousands of ʻŌiwi who were dependent on these springs and streams for life. What kinds of relationships must they have had with these places and their resources? Surely, we possess a pair of eyes that should function like those of our ancestors, but what would it be like to see Hawaiian geography as they did? What would it take on our part? Imagine the links between unique microclimates, wind patterns, and cultivation of place-specific agriculture that we might rediscover!

In the modern era, insatiable human consumption and combustion of resources continue to profoundly affect our planet's climate and its potential to support life for future generations. In some ways, global climate change is enhanced because modern societies have lost an intimate connection to place and the resources that feed them. We modern humans must change our behavior and our relationships with the environment and the things we consume. We must bring our social systems and cultures into alignment with the unique ecosystems within which we reside. We must find ways to live and develop intimate relationships with our natural world and food systems that are not simply built around extraction and profit, but rather around maintaining abundance and the health of our natural world. In Hawai'i, we have an Indigenous knowledge system that developed in relation to the unique and diverse ecosystems of our islands, which enabled 'Ōiwi society to survive and thrive for centuries on the most physically isolated islands on the planet. While some of that knowledge has been lost as a result of American imperialism, most of it has endured through our cultural practices and the vast Indigenous print and oral archive. There probably remains a few generations of work for us to do in order to recover our ancestral understandings of Hawaiian geography and resource management—an extensive knowlege system that is critical for the sustainable future of our islands. This future could seem far away from us in distance, when in reality it is perhaps as few as twenty ahupua'a away.

Notes

1   I define *ahupua'a* as a "culturally appropriate, ecologically aligned, and place specific unit with access to diverse resources." Quoted from Lorenz Gonschor and Kamana-maikalani Beamer, "Toward in [*sic*] Inventory of Ahupua'a in the Hawaiian Kingdom: A Survey of Nineteenth- and Early Twentieth-Century Cartographic and Archival Records of the Island of Hawai'i," *Hawaiian Journal of History* 48 (2014): 71.

2   This is a word my daughter, Halialoha Kawahinekapuanolani Kapuailohamanonokalani Leipuanala Beamer, created when she was still quite young and we would play together ma kai. It is a playful word for a pit dug in the sand to fill with ocean water. Puna translates to spring and kai translates to salt water. A punakai is a saltwater spring. One day, when my daughter was about two years old, after my digging the sand to create a

place for her to play she told me, "'E eli punakai makua" ("Dig a punakai Daddy"). The word has stuck with us ever since.

3   Samuel Mānaiakalani Kamakau, *Tales and Traditions of the People of Old: Nā Mo'olelo a ka po'e Kahiko* (Honolulu: Bishop Museum Press, 1991), 53.

4   Boundary Commission no. 8, Ahupua'a of Malanahae, April 19, 1871. Boundary Commission Report Keauhou 2nd Kona, Island of Hawai'i, vol. A, no. 1: 256–72. Boundary Commission Ahupua'a of Waika District of North Kohala, Island of Hawai'i, Hawai'i, vol. A, no. 1: 170–74.

5   Boundary Commission Ahupua'a of Waika District of North Kohala, 170–74.

6   Edward Casey, "How to Get from Space to Place in a Fairly Short Stretch of Time: Phenomenological Prolegomena," in *Senses of Places*, ed. Steven Feld and Keith Basso (Santa Fe, NM: School of American Research, 1996), 13–52.

7   Gregory Cajete, *Native Science: Natural Laws of Interdependence* (Santa Fe, NM: Clear Light Publishers, 2000), 74.

Haley Kailiehu

_____

Hā-mākua

ʻO Hāmākua kihi loa ia, mai Kaʻula a i Honokeʻā. It is Hāmākua of the "long corner," from Kaʻula to Honokeʻā. Hāmākua is one of the largest moku, or districts, on the island of Hawaiʻi. It spans the island's precipitous northeast coast, from Kaʻula Gulch to Honokeʻā Valley, and stretches inland from the coast, over the summit of Maunakea to Pōhaku o Hanalei at the summit of Maunaloa. The moku's name can be interpreted as the "parent stalk." Likening the island itself to an ʻohana kalo (kalo family), the moku of Hāmākua embodies the hā (stalk) of the mākua (parent) plant. As the eldest mountains on the island, Mauna a Wākea (Maunakea) and Maunaloa are the mākua mountains and the piko from which life constantly flows, sustaining the rest of the island. At their base, the foundation of this moku is Papa—generation upon generation of ʻāina, layered upon each other, forming the pali (cliffs), our Palikū ancestors. As a whole, this ʻāina embodies the convergence of genealogies that connect us Kanaka ʻŌiwi with our ancestral "mākua," Papahānaumoku, Wākea, and Hāloa. And she exemplifies the kuleana (responsibility) carried by mākua to feed their keiki (offspring) physically, intellectually, and spiritually.

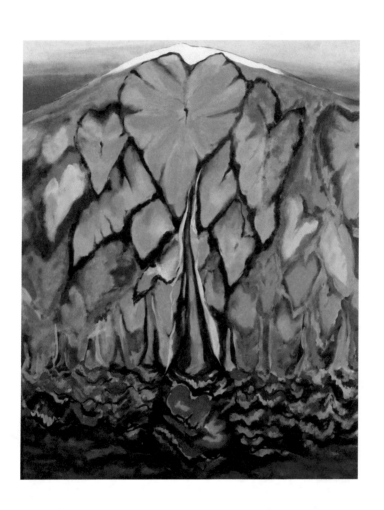

No'eau Peralto

He Mo'olelo no Pa'auilo
Restor(y)ing 'Āina in a Quiet, Old Plantation Town in Hāmākua

The Hawaiians of old were a people who focused much of their thinking on the nature that surrounded them, and an important way to do this was to name and thus cherish even the tiniest spots. —*Mary Kawena Pukui*

Every place has a name, and every name has a story. Here is one short story (of many untold) of a cherished place whose name is familiar to many, but whose stories are known by few. Here is a story of a quiet, old plantation town in Hāmākua.

Whether you are a diehard Pa'auilo School Tiger or an occasional passerby, and definitely if you're a born-and-raised kama'āina, there's a good chance that Pa'auilo has influenced your life in some way.[1] No joke. You might be thinking to yourself, "That small country town?!" Yeah. It doesn't look like much to most, but I can assure you that if you are Kanaka and/or a kama'āina of Hawai'i Island, this place—now recognized as a "town," whose name is derived from the ahupua'a (ancestral land division) in which it is located— has played some sort of role in your past, present (and if not, then future) experience of Hawai'i. So if you're not from Pa'auilo, or Hāmākua, then let's begin at the most basic, surface level: Earl's Pa'auilo Store.

Chances are, if you've driven through Hāmākua on your way to Hilo or Waimea, you've stopped at Pa'auilo Store and bought a bento roll made by Earl's. If you haven't, pua ting you! Well, maybe you didn't happen to have cash on you when you stopped, so you just took the opportunity to use the porta potty outside the store. Either way, Pa'auilo is generally a midway stop for commuters, cruising locals, or tourists, and a central hub for kama'āina of

Earl's Pa'auilo Store. *Photo by John C. Wright, December 1973. Bishop Museum Archives.*

the area. It's about forty minutes from Hilo, and about twenty-five minutes from Waimea. So, if nothing else, your belly and bladder can probably thank Pa'auilo for tiding you over on your long journeys.

OK, let's kick it up a notch. Until the early 1990s, Pa'auilo was smack-dab in the middle of the island's century-old sugarcane industry. Pa'auilo was a bustling plantation town made up of various "camps"—Old Camp, New Camp, Japanese Camp, Haole Camp, Nakalei—a school (home of the Pa'auilo Tigers), stores, a post office, a few churches, a ball park, and a couple generations of kama'āina, most of whom led humble lives shaped by the cultivation of sugar or cattle. A handful of my ancestors experienced Pa'auilo in this way and developed a deep love and respect for this 'āina, like many others. Those memories, however, remain beyond the realm of what my eyes have seen, and would best be shared by those whose eyes have. So let's continue on this path and talk a little more about what most do not see about this place.

Paʻauilo, called "Pauilo," or something close to "Pawilo" by most people today, is one of over 130 ahupuaʻa located in the district of Hāmākua. The name of this ahupuaʻa, Paʻau-ilo, could be thought of as describing the "worm-filled skin of a banana stalk," suggesting, perhaps, an abundance of fruit-bearing banana groves in ancestral times. Paʻa-uilo could also describe a fastened "square-shaped braid, as in lei palaoa cord," suggesting, perhaps, the place's relationship to the chiefs of the region, who would have worn such whale-tooth pendant adornments. In the early 1800s, this ahupuaʻa was the kuleana (responsibility) of an aliʻi wahine (chiefess) by the name of Mikahela Kekauonohi. She was a high-ranking chiefly grandchild of Kamehameha I and kiaʻāina (governor) of Kauaʻi. As part of her "payment" to the government for lands received during the Māhele of 1848, Kekauonohi relinquished Paʻauilo to Kamehameha III (Kauikeaouli), who later set the ahupuaʻa aside as part of the Government Lands of the Kingdom. Not long after, George S. Kenway and Robert Robinson, two haole men, purchased most of the ʻāina in this ahupuaʻa from the kingdom government as Royal Patent Grants 2221, 2222, and 663—"Koe naʻe ke kuleana o nā kānaka" (Subject to the rights of Native tenants). These land sales would eventually plow the way for the establishment of large-scale sugar cultivation in the area.

Before the Māhele, Paʻauilo, like other relatively small ahupuaʻa in Hāmākua Hikina (East Hāmākua), was home to about 150 to 200 Kānaka. Early European explorers and American missionaries described the area as fertile and highly cultivated, dissected by a multitude of streams that, now mostly dry, once cascaded off the edge of Hāmākua's sheer cliffs. One of these streams, Waipunalau, which forms the Kohala-side boundary of Paʻauilo (adjoining the ahupuaʻa of Pahukiʻi), is fed by a spring named Waihalulu. Once favored by the kamaʻāina of Hāmākua Hikina for its "wai māpuna ʻono huʻihuʻi" (deliciously cold fresh spring water), Waihalulu was visited by Kamehameha I and his koa when they retired from the battle of Koapāpaʻa. Koapāpaʻa, located in the ahupuaʻa of Kūkaʻiau (just over a mile from Paʻauilo) was the site of the last battle fought by Kamehameha on Hawaiʻi Island in his campaign of unification.[2]

The 1791 battle ended with Keōua-kūʻahuʻula, the reigning chief of Kaʻū, seeking refuge under a large stone in Kainehe, which later came to bear his

> **Royal Patent Grants**

Royal patent grants were parcels of government-owned land purchased directly from the Hawaiian Kingdom Government under the Kuleana Act of 1850. These parcels were granted with fee simple title that was "subject to the rights of Native tenants." These kuleana, or rights, were derived from the Kuleana Act itself, and they are still drawn upon today in community organizing and legal proceedings seeking the protection and reclamation of ʻāina for ʻŌiwi and other descendants of Hawaiian Kingdom citizens.

Pa'auilo, Hāmākua, in the 1880s. *Photograph by H. L. Chase, n.d. Bishop Museum Archives.*

name: Pōhaku o Keōua. The battle proved to be a decisive victory for Kamehameha, as he soon gained control over the entire island.

But what was Kamehameha doing in Pa'auilo? Kamehameha was not
the chief of Hāmākua. Kamehameha was from Kohala, and his primary alliances were formed with other Kohala and Kona
chiefs. When Kamehameha rose to power the ali'i
'ai moku (district chiefs) of Hāmākua were Kānekoa
and Kaha'i, two chiefly brothers and Kamehameha's uncles. Both Kānekoa and Kaha'i had actually
fought against Kamehameha in the famous battle
of Moku'ōhai (in 1782, near Ke'ei, Kona), defending
Kīwala'ō and his kālai'āina (chiefly redistribution
of 'āina). After Moku'ōhai, Hāmākua came under the
control of Keawemauhili, the highest-ranking chief of
the "house of 'Ī" alive at the time.

Under his protection, Kānekoa and Kaha'i remained until a disagreement forced them to flee the

▶ 'Ī

'Ī was a famous ruling chief of
Hawai'i Island approximately
thirteen or fourteen generations before the present. The
chiefly descendants of 'Ī, ref-
ered to poetically as "ka hālau
a 'Ī" (the house of 'Ī), ruled
the east side of Hawai'i Island
from Hāmākua to Ka'ū until
the time of Keōuakū'ahu'ula.

Hilo chief and go live under the Ka'ū chief, Keōua-kū'ahu'ula. The Hāmākua chiefs must have been quite independent in their thoughts and actions, because not long after settling in with Keōua, another fight ensued between the chiefs, leaving Kānekoa dead and his brother grieving.

While he mourned, Kaha'i sought refuge with his nephew, Kamehameha. Kamehameha showed aloha for his uncles, recalling days when he was carried on their backs, and he vowed to put an end to the Hilo and Ka'ū chiefs. These events, among others, eventually brought the decisive battle to Hāmākua Hikina. It should be noted, however, that in his flight of defeat, Keōua was hidden and protected in Kainehe, by a kahuna (priest) of the area, presumably with the support of the people in the area. Keōua represented the last of the ruling ali'i of the powerful 'Ī line that had kuleana over east Hawai'i (from Hāmākua to Ka'ū) since the time of 'Ī, the great-grandson of the famous 'Umi-a-Līloa. The people of east Hawai'i were fiercely loyal to the chiefs of the house of 'Ī, whereas those of the west held tightly to the Keawe clan. This battle between lineages was not a new one. It stemmed back to the generations that followed Umi's unification of the island (about sixteen or seventeen generations before the present). It seems only fitting, then, that the last battle in Kamehameha's unification of our island would take place in the 'āina hānau (birthplace) of 'Umi, the great unifying ancestor from whom both Keōua and Kamehameha descended. Hāmākua, then, was the "parent stalk" that held together the 'ohana of moku on Hawai'i Island.

Fast forward a few generations to another time of vast political upheaval in Hawai'i. Following the unlawful overthrow of the beloved reigning monarch of the Hawaiian Kingdom, Lili'uokalani, in Honolulu, and the onset of the United States' prolonged occupation of our islands, Kanaka and other loyal subjects of the kingdom fought fiercely to restore our country's independence. In addition to organizing the Hui Aloha 'Āina and Hui Kālai'āina, which effectively defeated an impending treaty of annexation forced upon Hawai'i by those with imperialistic interests, Kanaka leaders in the struggle for independence from both Hui also formed the Independent Home Rule Party, nā Home Rula Kū'oko'a. Founded in 1900 by po'e aloha 'āina 'oia'i'o (people truly loyal to this 'āina)—Robert Wilcox, David Kalauokalani, and James Kaulia—the Independent Home Rule

Party, as its name suggests, stood for the restored independence of the Hawaiian Kingdom. And its battle cry was one rooted in unification.

As part of its campaign of unification, the party published two newspapers: first *Ka Naʻi Aupuni* (*The Conqueror*), and then *Kuokoa Home Rula* (*Independent Home Rule*). *Ka Naʻi Aupuni* made clear whose responsibility it was to remedy the dire situation the lāhui had found itself in: "Na Hawaii e Hooponopono ia Hawaii" (It is Hawaiʻi/Hawaiians who will bring pono to Hawaiʻi once again). The second paper, *Kuokoa Home Rula*, went further to remind us of the means by which we could fulfill this responsibility: "Ma ka Lokahi ka Lahui e Loaa ai ka Ikaika" (It is in Unity that the Lāhui obtains its Strength). Without consciously enacting the hui in lāhui—uniting together—we would cease to exist as a lāhui, a nation.

This brings us back home to the place that this story began. The owner of both papers, and later the president of the Independent Home Rule Party, was Charles Kahiliaulani Notley, a home-grown kamaʻāina of no place other than Paʻauilo, Hāmākua, Hawaiʻi. Kahiliaulani was the son of Charles Notley Sr. and Mele Kaluahine, a chiefly descendant of Keōua-kūʻahuʻula. In 1906, while running as the Home Rule candidate for "territorial" delegate to the U.S. Congress, Kahiliaulani gave a rousing speech before supporters of Home Rule and Hawaiian independence, encouraging Kānaka to unite "no ka Pono, ka Pomaikai, ka Holomua, ka Lanakila, a me ka Hanohano o ka Lahui" (for the pono, the prosperity, the advancement, the victory, and the dignity of the nation). In closing his speech, Kahiliaulani, like many of our contemporary Kanaka leaders, likened the path ahead for the nation to that of a voyage on rough seas. As was printed in *Ka Naʻi Aupuni* on November 5, 1906, this part of his speech went as follows:

E hookele kakou i ke kai hoee e nee mai nei a popoʻi iho ma luna o ka lahuikanaka oiwi o Hawaii. Nolaila, i hookahi puuwai, hookahi ka manao, moe a ka umauma imua, paa like na lima i ke kaulako-waa o Halaualiiokalani, a e kahea aku au ia oukou:

    I-ku-mau-mau!
E hooho mai oukou:
    I-ku wa!
I hea aku au ia oukou:
    I ku mau mau! I ku huluhulu! I ka lanawao!!
E pane mai like oukou: I ku wa!
I kahea aku au ia oukou: I ku lanawao!
Alaila, moe like na poo imua, hoomolo like na lima, a kahea aku au:
    I ku mau mau—e! Ko!

Alaila e huki like oukou apau i ke koho balota ana no ka oukou Elele nei,
me ka puana ana i na olelo a ko kakou mau kupuna:
I ku wa!
I ku wa! Ko!
E huki—e! Ko!
Umia ka hanu! Ko!
A lau i ka waa—e
Lanakila! Ua ko![3]

Let us navigate forth into the rising seas that approach, soon to break
upon our native nation of Hawai'i. Let us, therefore, be of one heart and
one mind. Face our chests forward, and together our hands grasp and
pull the canoe of Hālauali'iokalani. And I call out to you all:

I-ku-mau-mau!
And you call out:
I-ku wa!
Then I call out to you all:
I ku mau! I ku huluhulu! I ka lanawao!!
And you all respond together: I ku wa!
I call out to you all: I ku lanawao!

And then, face your heads forward, interweave your hands, and I call out
again:

I ku mau mau—e! Ko!

And then all of you pull together in voting for your representative here,
as we call out the words of our ancestors:

I ku wa!
I ku wa! Ko!
E huki—e! Ko!
Umia ka hanu! Ko!
A lau i ka waa—e
Lanakila! Ua ko!

Now a commonly heard chant at Hawaiian gatherings of all sorts, "I Kū Mau"
was primarily invoked by our ancestors to inspire collective action when
pulling a large felled tree down from the uplands (such as those on the
slopes of Maunakea in Hāmākua), to be carved as a canoe or a ki'i (carved

wooden image). Kahiliaulani's invocation of this chant in his speech may be the first recorded usage of it in the context of contemporary Hawaiian politics. Although never successful in his campaigns to become a delegate to the U.S. Congress, Kahiliaulani remained a fervently loyal Home Rula and Aloha ʻĀina, encouraging our people to "pull together" until the end. In fact, in a 1912 hearing regarding the conditions of Native Hawaiians, Kahiliaulani was quoted as having testified before then U.S. Secretary of the Department of the Interior, Walter L. Fisher, that the U.S. should "give all the lands back to the Hawaiians."[4] According to the reporter from the *Pacific Commercial Advertiser*, many of those present in the room chuckled at what seemed to be an unrealistic proposition. But Kahiliaulani did not waver in his conviction. Not only should all the lands be returned to Hawaiians, he insisted, but the government should also appropriate sufficient funds to support Hawaiians living and remaining on those lands. *Imagine that.* And just a little over a hundred years later, not only are the brilliant aloha ʻāina of this place still giving the U.S. Department of the Interior an earful, they are restoring and re-storying to Paʻauilo and other ʻāina throughout Hāmākua the abundance of food and stories that sustained our ancestors here for generations.

Surely Kahiliaulani is not the only historical figure from this ʻāina who deserves our praise and remembrance. He is but one of many who has been selectively honored in this moʻolelo—a moʻolelo that serves, really, to honor this ʻāina. After all, they are one and the same. And as is the responsibility of any storyteller, I will now conclude this moʻolelo back home where it began: in a quiet, old plantation town in Hāmākua. So the next time you pass by or stop at Paʻauilo Store, look across the street ma kai (toward the ocean) and imagine Kahiliaulani once living there. And then look toward Hilo and imagine the abundant days of ʻUmi-a-Līloa's youth or the awesome scene of over thirty thousand koa converging in battle at Koapāpaʻa. Then look ma uka (toward the mountain) and see the sacred summit of Mauna a Wākea, the highest peak in all of Oceania. Then look toward Kohala, toward the sacred valleys of Waipiʻo and Waimanu, where generations of our most powerful chiefs once ruled. Remember why this place is called Hāmākua, "the parent stalk" of this island. And back here in the middle of it all you will find yourself, in a quiet, old plantation town, sitting calmly upon the storied ʻāina of Paʻauilo.

(Aole i pau)

Resources

Hui Mālama i ke Ala ʻŪlili: www.alaulili.com. Hui Mālama i ke Ala ʻŪlili (huiMAU) is a community-based, nonprofit organization of ʻohana from Hāmākua Hikina (East Hāmākua) based in Paʻauilo, of which the author is a founding member. Founded in 2011, huiMAU is committed to cultivating kīpuka (safe spaces) that foster and regenerate the growth of place-based ancestral knowledge, healthy food systems and ecosystems, and strong ʻohana with the capability to live and thrive in Hāmākua for generations. huiMAU's mission is to reestablish the systems that sustain our community through educational initiatives and land-based practices that cultivate abundance, regenerate responsibilities, and promote collective health and well-being.

To learn more about the moʻolelo of ʻUmi-a-Līloa, see huiMAU's blog "Moʻolelo no ʻUmi," http://www.alaulili.com/moolelo-no-umi-blog/.

To learn more about the moʻolelo of Kamehameha I, see "Ka Moolelo o Kamehameha I," authored by Hooulumahiehie in the Hawaiian-language newspaper *Ka Naʻi Aupuni*, November 27, 1905 to November 16, 1906. An English translation of the moʻolelo of Kamehameha can be found in Stephen L. Desha's *Kamehameha and His Warrior Kekuhaupiʻo*, trans. Frances Frazier (Honolulu: Kamehameha Schools Press, 2000).

Notes

1   Kamaʻāina literally means "child of the land" or "familiar." Here I use the term *kamaʻāina* to refer to ʻŌiwi and others who were born and raised in Paʻauilo.
2   Pukui and Elbert (1986) define koa as "1. nvs. Brave, bold, fearless, valiant; bravery, courage; 2. nvs. soldier, warrior, fighter; 3. n. The largest of native forest trees (Acacia koa), with light-gray bark, crescent-shaped leaves, and white flowers in small, round heads." I intentionally choose not to translate this term in text here in order to elevate an ʻŌiwi understanding of battle and "warriorhood." Mary Kawena Pukui and Samuel H. Elbert, *Hawaiian Dictionary* (Honolulu: University of Hawaiʻi Press, 1986), 156.
3   "Ka Haiolelo a Chas. Kahiliaulani ma ka Aala Paka," *Ka Naʻi Aupuni*, vol. II, no. 132 (November 5, 1906), 2. Translation by the author.
4   "Give All Lands Back, Says Notley," *Hawaiian Gazette*, September 20, 1912, 7.

Bibliography

Hooulumahiehie. "Ka Moolelo o Kamehameha I. Ka Naʻi Aupuni O Hawaiʻi: Ka Liona O Ka Moana Pakipika." *Ka Nai Aupuni*. November 27, 1905–November 16, 1906.
Silva, Noenoe K. "I Kū Mau Mau: How Kanaka Maoli Tried to Sustain National Identity within the United States Political System." *American Studies* 45, no. 3 (2004): 9–31.

Kapulani Landgraf

Ponoiwi

In 1907, the Hawaiian Commercial & Sugar Company (HC&S) constructed the Pā'ia lime kiln on the island of Maui. HC&S, run by Alexander and Baldwin, mined the coral sands from the beaches of Keonekapo'o to Pā'ia for seven decades. They manufactured hydrated lime for use in processing sugar cane, and they used the sand to construct roads and buildings. In the mid-1940s, the U.S. Navy destroyed both Pu'u Hele and Pu'u Nēnē.[1] Their cinders were quarried extensively to build roads and the air base at Pu'unēnē.[2]

Historically in Hawai'i, sand for use in the construction industry was often taken from beaches statewide. Pāpōhaku Beach on Moloka'i was the location of the largest sand mining operation in Hawai'i. Honolulu Construction and Draying Company, Ltd., began taking sand from Pāpōhaku in the early 1960s, shipping it to O'ahu. During the 1970s, Hawai'i experienced a construction boom. The two concrete supply companies, Ameron HC&D, which bought Concrete Industries, and Maui Concrete and Aggregate, which became Hawaiian Cement, used 48,000 tons of sand a year.

In 1972, the Hawai'i state legislature banned sand mining operations below the high-water mark. The construction companies had until 1975 to comply with the law. Concrete companies on O'ahu began using "mansand"—crushed basaltic rock. It was expensive and more difficult to work with because of its angular nature. But they soon found a cheaper alternative: Maui dune sand. In 1985, the Leisure Estates were built on the sand dune Waiehu. Sand was stockpiled until Ameron bought the sand and transported it by barge to O'ahu. This was the beginning of the method of carrying Maui sand to Honolulu, and it continues to this day.

In 2006, the Maui Inland Sand Resource Quantification Study reported that over 4 million tons—or 130,000 semitruck loads—of Maui sand was used for concrete. The report noted that Ameron and Hawaiian Cement together transported by barge 244,000 tons of sand per year, whereas 74,000 tons of sand were used on Maui. In 2007, Hawaiian Cement began importing sand from British Columbia because it was restricted from shipping Maui sand to Oʻahu (the grayish silica granules of sand cannot be used for restoring beaches or creating golf courses). Ameron continues to export Maui sand to Oʻahu.

Native Hawaiians buried the iwi (bones) of their ancestors within the sand dunes throughout Hawaiʻi. They believed a person's mana lived in the bones. Ola nā iwi. The bones live. At Honokahua, Maui, in 1989, over one thousand Native Hawaiian remains were removed to build the Ritz-Carlton Kapalua resort. As a result, in 1990, the Hawaiʻi state legislature passed Act 306, a bill that provides a process for protecting Hawaiian burial grounds and established burial councils for each island. Despite this law, however, pressure continues to develop Hawaiian ʻāina (land and its natural resources), and Hawaiian iwi are constantly threatened. Na wai e hoʻola i nā iwi? (Who will protect our bones?)

Notes

1   Puʻu Hele was once a hill located in Maʻalaea, Maui—now it's a cinder pit. Puʻu Nēnē was a hill near Keonekapoʻo, Maui—now it's flattened.

2   Puʻu Nēnē and Puʻunēnē are two different places on Maui.

Pu'u Nēnē.

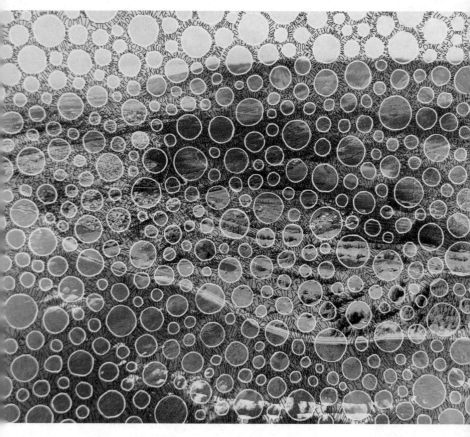

Hono a Pi'ikea.

Kapukaulua.

Waiʻale.

Pu'u Hele.

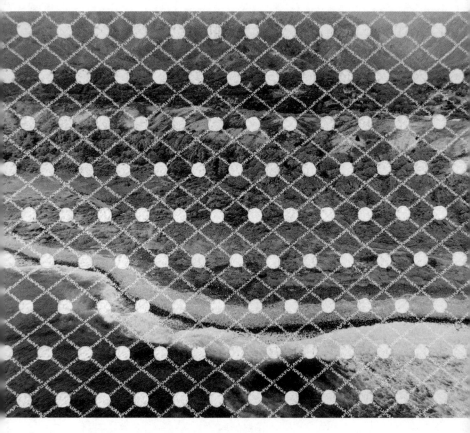

Waiheʻe.

Katrina-Ann R. Kapāʻanaokalāokeola Nākoa Oliveira

Wehe aʻela ka ʻĪao ma Haleakalā

"Wehe aʻela ka ʻĪao ma Haleakalā" explores the ancestral histories of two places on the island of Maui—Haleakalā and ʻĪao. I juxtapose the intimate relationships of Kanaka (Native Hawaiians) to the ʻāina (land, that which feeds) with the fleeting affairs of tourists who interact with the land as a commodity of pleasure. For both of the places visited, I take the reader on a tour of the current efforts of Kānaka to maintain the sacredness of these places and to ensure that the histories of these wahi pana (storied places) continue to be passed down to succeeding generations.

Haleakalā

E ala ē ka lā i kahikina,
i ka moana, ka moana hohonu
piʻi ka lewa, ka lewa nuʻu
i kahikina aia ka lā
E ala ē!
(Pualani Kanahele)

Awaken the sun in the east,
in the ocean, the deep ocean
the heavens rise, the high heavens
in the east there is the sun
Awaken!

Haleakalā, "the house of the sun," is world-renowned for its stunning sunrises and beautiful, though less commonly appreciated, sunsets. Haleakalā is also known for its spectacular panoramic views of Maui. An alternative name for Haleakalā is ʻAheleakalā (rays of the sun).

Haleakalā is a dominant feature of the physical landscape of Maui. In fact, it can be seen with the naked eye from neighboring islands. Most places in ka pae ʻāina Hawaiʻi (the Hawaiian archipelago) are located within a single moku (large land division). Haleakalā, however, extends to eight of the twelve moku of Maui, emanating from a single stone on Haleakalā known as Pōhaku o Haleakalā.

Each year, 2.2 million visitors make their way ten thousand feet up the slopes of Haleakalā to its summit to view the sun. Many of these tourists do so under the darkness of night, hours before sunrise, in search of the perfect vantage point to watch the dawning sun. At first light, tourists can be seen taking selfies against the picturesque backdrop. Shortly after sunrise, packs of visitors engage in one of the most popular tourist activities on Maui—riding a bicycle thirty-eight miles down the jagged Haleakalā Highway under extreme weather conditions. In spite of the popularity of this activity, most of the ninety thousand cyclists who ride down the dormant volcano annually probably do not truly understand how dangerous their downhill adventure could be. After all, tragedies are common among these thrill-seeking adventurists—so much so that in 2007, commercial bicycle tours were temporarily suspended after three fatalities and other serious injuries occurred.

While many tourists may appreciate Haleakalā for its splendor and its entertainment value, few tourists probably realize that the Haleakalā National Park is considered by many Kānaka to be a sacred place. Located in the wao akua, a remote upland region reserved for the gods, the summit of Haleakalā was generally not frequented by Kānaka in ancestral times, although some Kānaka may have sometimes braved the frigid temperatures to study the stars.

Kanaka have rich oral traditions related to our wahi pana. Since time immemorial, these moʻolelo (historical accounts) have been passed down from generation to generation. Ironically, tourists have come to better understand some of the Hawaiian moʻolelo associated with Haleakalā, including the moʻolelo about how the demigod Māui left his mark on the island named after him, because of the 2016 Disney film *Moana*. According to one such moʻolelo, Māui was saddened that the sun rose and set so quickly that his mother was unable to dry her kapa (bark cloth) in a single day. Therefore, he devised a plan to snare the sun in order to slow its movement. Māui went to Peʻeloko (also known as Paeloko) in Waiheʻe to gather the coconut fibers he needed to fashion sennit, which he would use to lasso the sun. Moemoe, the name given to the sun's rays, taunted Māui as he attempted to lasso them. Māui warned that when he successfully captured Moemoe, he would take revenge on the sun for traveling so quickly by killing it. Once Māui secured Moemoe, he broke off the rays with his lasso. The sun pleaded with Māui, promising to slow its pace if Māui spared its life. Thus, the sun slowed its transit so that kapa could be dried in a single day.

The quest to harness the sun did not end with Māui's feat. Researchers harness the sun through the use of telescopes atop Haleakalā. Haleakalā provides a unique vantage point for observing the sun, moon, land, and sea. Today, the summit of Haleakalā is one of the most sought-after locations in the world for ground-based telescopes. While the modern scientific community may welcome construction of the world's largest solar telescope, hundreds of Kanaka activists have denounced the building of the Daniel K. Inouye Solar Telescope because of our opposition to the desecration of Hawaiian national lands and sacred places. Hundreds of protectors lined the streets at various places around Maui, marching back and forth, waving Hawaiian flags, chanting, praying, and locking arms to prevent the transport of convoys of equipment and contruction materials for the new solar telescope. Dozens of activists were arrested after engaging in civil disobedience to protect the 'āina from further desecration. Many of the protectors argued that they are not against science or even against the telescope; rather, they are against development on sacred Hawaiian national lands. Furthermore, they recount the rich history of Kanaka scientific breakthroughs (e.g., navigation without instruments, lo'i [wetland taro systems], and fishponds), which were made without using any type of invasive machinery.

Haleakalā's scientific contributions to our understanding of the world are not limited to solar observations. In fact, Haleakalā is one of the few places in the world that people may visit on land to see firsthand turbulence in action. For most of us, our understanding of turbulence is limited to experiences on airplanes. While ancestral Kānaka did not travel by air, they understood the scientific principles of atmospheric pressure through their interactions with and observations of the natural environment on Haleakalā. As the Nāulu (the name of a particular shower cloud) and 'Ūkiukiu (a chilly wind that blows from the north) wind clouds tango, they create turbulence that may be simultaneously seen, heard, and felt—a phenomenon that is rarely experienced from the window of an aircraft.

Most tourists come and go as if they are clouds appearing then disappearing atop Haleakalā. While many visitors may appreciate Haleakalā for its breathtaking scenery and gorgeous views of sunrises and sunsets, few recognize the sanctity of this wahi pana. Absent from tourist magazines are images of the rising stars of the Kanaka protector movement. Tour guides sanitize the turbulent struggles of Kānaka to preserve our pristine landscapes and sacred places for the generations yet to come.

ʻĪao

Like Haleakalā, ʻĪao is considered to be a very sacred place. In fact, it is arguably the most sacred place on the island of Maui, as evidenced by the number of chiefs that were buried there. The bones of aliʻi nui (high-ranking chiefs) who resided at various places on Maui were brought to ʻĪao and hidden deep within the valley.

For Kanaka, our connection to place is foundational. Kānaka often bury the piko (umbilical cords) of our children in our kulāiwi (ancestral homelands). It was once common practice for Kānaka to bury our dead in our kulāiwi, often near our house lots. Taking this into consideration, it may come as no surprise that Kānaka are very deliberate when selecting the final resting grounds of our deceased loved ones. In ancestral times, Kānaka went to great lengths to prevent anyone from finding the remains of high-ranking individuals. Thus, the remains of aliʻi nui were buried by trusted companions at places that reflected the person's mana (spiritual power). The higher the individual's rank, the more remote that person's final resting place would be.

ʻĪao is also the final resting place of countless Kānaka because of the famous battle of Kepaniwai. Before his battle in ʻĪao with the aliʻi (chief) of Maui, Kamehameha I, the first aliʻi purported to unite the pae ʻāina (archipelago) under a single ruler, instructed his warriors to disassemble all of their battle canoes. He then uttered the following phrase before going to battle: "I mua e nā pōkiʻi a inu i ka wai ʻawaʻawa, ʻaʻohe hope e hoʻi aku ai" (Go forth my siblings, drink the bitter waters, there is nowhere to flee). Kamehameha's statement was calculated. Kamehameha made it clear to his warriors, who had no canoes to escape in, that he intended to win the battle no matter how fierce it might be; his forces were expected to fight to the bitter end. As a result of the bloody battle, thousands of warriors lost their lives in ʻĪao. The bloodshed was so great that the corpses dammed the stream; thus the battle was given the name Kepaniwai.

Kamehameha's statement continues to inspire modern Kānaka as we fight for justice in our ancestral lands today. Kamehameha's declaration is indelibly etched in Kanaka collective memory—through t-shirt designs and speeches that incorporate these profound words. In challenging times,

Kānaka are encouraged to continue to fight for what is right and to persevere in the face of adversity and uncertainty.

In spite of signage and tour guides that recall the bloody history of the valley, many tourists continue to gather at ʻĪao to enjoy family picnics or stroll through the Kepaniwai Heritage Gardens. Still others are married at the park. Obscured from the landscape are the thousands of corpses buried throughout the valley.

Today, Kānaka and environmental interest groups are monitoring clean-up efforts after a deluge and flooding in ʻĪao in 2016 to ensure that the debris is managed in culturally and environmentally responsible ways. Because ʻĪao is a place known to be an extensive burial ground, Kanaka groups are not only interested in the environmental impact that massive dredging and dumping of material will have on the ʻāina and the ocean. Equally important is maintaining the sanctity of ʻĪao as a massive burial site and handling with the utmost respect any human remains recovered in the aftermath of the storm.

Conclusion

Haleakalā and ʻĪao are two wahi pana on the island of Maui that many Kānaka consider sacred. Whereas in the past, the remoteness of these places protected them from desecration, today the seclusion of these places attracts inquisitive visitors. With each passing generation, the landscape changes through the effects of both natural and human forces. It is my hope, however, that the rich moʻolelo of these wahi pana will stand the test of time. Inasmuch as we as Kanaka must protect physical places throughout the landscape, we must also teach the traditional moʻolelo of these sacred sites to succeeding generations so that our descendants may enjoy the same intimate familial relationship to the ʻāina as our ancestors.

Dean Itsuji Saranillio

———————————

(Locals Will) Remove All Valuables
from Your Vehicle

The Kepaniwai Heritage Gardens and
the Damming of the Waters

At the ʻĪao State Park on the island of Maui, a sign warns tourists not to leave valuables in their rental cars, lest they risk having them stolen while they venture into the park. One such sign was defaced by adding "LOCALS WILL," boldly stating just *who* will remove these valuables. While the sign's defacement reveals the underlying animosity that many in Hawaiʻi feel toward tourists, the location of the sign in ʻĪao Valley also reveals an inconsistency in just what kinds of thefts are criminalized. Property crimes against tourists are often taken most seriously. Yet crimes against Kānaka ʻŌiwi (Native Hawaiians), such as the desecration of sacred burials; the continued seizure of water leading to the death of rivers, forcing people to change their way of life; and not least the theft of an entire nation, are all forms of violence often considered natural and a normal part of American history.

Located just down the road from ʻĪao State Park, the Kepaniwai Park Heritage Gardens is a popular site for tourists celebrating Hawaiʻi as a racial paradise. Construction began in 1968, and the Kepaniwai Heritage Gardens (as it is more commonly known) eventually came to comprise eight diverse structures among six gardens. These structures represent different communities in Hawaiʻi—a Japanese teahouse, a Filipino nipa hut, a Chinese pavilion with a moon gate, a New England saltbox house (missionary house), a Portuguese home with a cement oven, a Puerto Rican monument, a Korean pavilion replete with pots for kimchi, and different Kanaka ʻŌiwi structures.

Flowing through ʻĪao Valley is beautiful Wailuku River, one of four rivers and streams that run through four separate valleys and are together referred

State sign at the ʻĪao State Park parking lot. *Photograph by Dean Itsuji Saranillio.*

to as Nā Wai ʻEhā (the Four Great Waters). "Kaulana Nā Wai ʻEhā" (Famous are the Four Great Waters) are made up of four streams—Waikapū (water of the conch), Wailuku (water of destruction), Waiʻehu (water spray), and Waiheʻe (squid liquid)—that irrigated the largest continuous area of loʻi kalo (taro) in all of Hawaiʻi, considered the pinnacle of Hawaiian agriculture. Loʻi kalo is a renewable and sustainable mode of Hawaiian farming that makes use of intricate ʻauwai (irrigation canals) to irrigate a diversity of kalo and an array of other plants and animals and then return the water back to the stream or river. This fresh water, rich with nutrients after traveling through the loʻi, then flows to the shoreline, where it mixes with saltwater to create brackish water essential to the health of fisheries and reefs. Centuries of such foodways and creative practices have shaped knowledge of the specific environmental features of Nā Wai ʻEhā. This holds positive implications for the overall ecology of the island, from mountain to ocean. For more than ten centuries, the vast cultivation of varieties of taro—the food staple and genealogical ancestor of Kanaka ʻŌiwi—nourished one of the largest and densest populations on the island.[1]

In the latter half of the nineteenth and early twentieth centuries, however, sugar plantations claimed ownership of these rivers. Water was diverted away from Kanaka ʻŌiwi communities to arid areas of the island in order to expand the industrial production of sugar sold to the United States. These water diversions had devastating genocidal effects for Kānaka ʻŌiwi, who were no longer able to access the water necessary for loʻi kalo and Hawaiian foodways to continue.

Yet, although their way of life was stolen, local residents' did not forget the memory of Nā Wai ʻEhā. In 2004, taro farmers calling themselves the Hui o Nā Wai ʻEhā and environmentalists of Maui Tomorrow, both supported by the nonprofit, public interest environmental law firm Earth Justice, petitioned for these four streams to be restored in order to counter environmental degradation, to recharge rapidly depleting groundwater sources, and to support local nonindustrial agriculture. In 2014, these water protectors were successful in restoring 25 million gallons of water a day to these four rivers and streams. This was the first time water had flowed from mountain to ocean in 150 years.

Although the Kepaniwai Heritage Gardens and the diversion of water away from Nā Wai ʻEhā seem to have nothing to do with each other, the Gardens facilitate and naturalize the diversion of water by portraying Kanaka ʻŌiwi ways of life as dead and in the past. Although the park offers visitors a view of different sites within a six-acre stretch of land, the park limits visitors' view of the largest water diversion from ʻĪao Valley. Visitors are unable to view the park's obstruction of a Hawaiian *way of life*, one that has historically been and is currently hindered by the expropriation of water just behind the Kepaniwai Heritage Gardens. By portraying Kanaka ʻŌiwi ways of life as dead, while foreclosing the ability of visitors to see the environmental and social impact of these water diversions, the Kepaniwai Heritage Gardens exhibits the same Hawaiian ways of life that it itself makes impossible.

When the area for the Kepaniwai Heritage Gardens was first being cleared, a Kanaka ʻŌiwi bulldozer operator came across a giant pōhaku (boulder) that he was unable to move. Believing the boulder could not be moved because it had mana (spiritual or divine power), he asked a Kanaka ʻŌiwi family living in the valley about the boulder. The family supposedly told him that the boulder's name was Kapiliokakae, the companion of Kakae, who governed Maui in the fifteenth century. The next day the bulldozer operator approached the boulder and prayed to it. He called Kapiliokakae by name and asked it to move to safety or others would use dynamite. Only then was he able to use the bulldozer to move Kapiliokakae into the middle of Kapela stream. Soon after this, however, a flash flood destroyed the park grounds and washed out Kinihapai Bridge, and the boulder is said to have disappeared.[2] Today, only a few residents know the location of Kapiliokakae. That such instances of the "supernatural" (for lack of a better word) are commonly linked to this valley is well known to most Maui residents.

Placing the valley within a broader ʻŌiwi history, many Kānaka ʻŌiwi view the valley as being rooted in deep historical significance and spiritual meaning. ʻĪao Valley has long been revered as a sacred site where twenty-four generations of ali'i (royalty) were buried alongside those deemed to possess mana.[3] Kapiliokakae was a part of the preparation for those entombed in 'Īao Valley. Their bones were placed in burial caves that remain hidden in 'Īao. The Kepaniwai Heritage Gardens was built on the exact site of a 1790 battle between Kamehameha and Kalanikupule, during which Kamehameha from the island of Hawai'i, armed with cannons and muskets, slaughtered Maui warriors who in previous battles had outmatched the Hawai'i Island forces. Named after this battle, Kepaniwai translates as the "damming of the waters" caused by the bodies of thousands who died in the river.

For some of these reasons, in 1960 the Central Maui Hawaiian Civic Club opposed the construction of a Japanese tea garden, which became the basis for the Heritage Gardens. The civic club argued that it would only be appropriate for a Kanaka 'Ōiwi garden to exist there. In letters to the *Maui News* newspaper, the Hawaiian Civic Club explained that "everything in the valley and all of the names are sacred to the people who know its history."[4] The Club appealed to the general public to reconsider building the Japanese tea garden: "We do not feel that anything but a Hawaiian Garden would be appropriate in a Hawaiian Temple of the Dead!" Maintaining Kanaka 'Ōiwi historical and cultural continuity with this sacred valley was denied, however, as these aims conflicted with the county's ostensible celebration of the heritage of all groups.

The celebration of Hawai'i's racial diversity was often used as propaganda during the Cold War. For the majority of the first half of the twentieth century, as Hawai'i business and government leaders rallied for statehood, Congress deemed Hawai'i to be unqualified because it was considered a largely "Asiatic" territory. To make Hawai'i statehood more attractive to Congress, proponents strategized how to use Hawai'i's racial diversity in the service of Cold War politics. After World War II, decolonization of nations in Asia, Oceania, Latin America, Africa, and Europe transformed global politics, and criticism of Western imperialism was the dominant international sentiment. In this way, Cold Warrior ideologues realized that Hawai'i's multiracial population could be used to capture the "hearts and minds" of newly decolonized nations—an opinion campaign developed by the "father of public relations," Edward L. Bernays.[5] This "nation of immigrants" story helped achieve seemingly permanent control of Hawai'i through statehood while creating a multicultural image of the United States that aided the establishment and maintenance of U.S. military bases throughout much of Asia and the Pacific.

Located just above the Kepaniwai Heritage Gardens is an example of how tourist sites in 'Īao are entangled with the Cold War. In 1970, an outcropping rock profile of what was argued to be Cold warrior president John F. Kennedy was dedicated as a popular tourist attraction. This rock profile, however, is that of a kahuna (priest) named Kaukaiwai, who lived in the fifteenth century and is said to protect the sacred burial sites in the valley. In June 1963, Kennedy spoke from Hawai'i, viewing the islands as an appropriate "intra-racial backdrop" for his civil rights message challenging Alabama governor George Wallace's refusal to desegregate the University of Alabama.[6] Kennedy often made mention of Hawai'i's racial diversity, going so far as to state that "Hawai'i is what the United States is striving to be."[7] Kennedy is present in the Heritage Gardens, not only because the Gardens can be seen as a symbol of racial diversity, but also because they can be considered an international garden framed by U.S. global hegemony.[8]

In the move to renarrate 'Īao Valley from a sacred site of reverence to one that propagates an image of the United States as bringing harmony to the islands, Hawaiian ways of life and self-governance were marked as primitive. In the book *Maui Remembers*, the authors write, "As in ancient times, Wailuku retains much of its status as a population and government center and upholds its reputation as a combat site. The only difference is that, today, legal battles in Wailuku's courthouse replace the bloodshed of old."[9] The peaceful racial diversity represented in the Heritage Gardens is thus defined against a portrayal of Hawai'i as savage, reducing Kānaka 'Ōiwi to a caricatured people who solved their differences through bloodshed. As such, Kānaka 'Ōiwi are, unlike the United States, seen to lack the capacity to create harmonious and peaceful relations. U.S. control over Hawai'i is made evident in the Heritage Garden's location: where once was war now exists peace, and a seemingly nonviolent approach to resolving conflict through mutual understanding has replaced the "bloodshed of old."

The irony of such framings is that if one were to read the Heritage Gardens against the grain, each national/ethnic structure also represents imperial relations that were initially established through the militarized violence of U.S. empire. The Filipino nipa hut reminds one of the upward of 2 million Filipinos who died as a result of a genocidal U.S. military campaign for occupation of the Philippines; this campaign, beginning in 1899, made Filipinos into U.S. nationals from a war-torn country who were available as exploitable labor for Hawai'i's sugar plantations. The Japanese Tea Garden highlights the forced opening of Japan by U.S. Commodore Matthew Perry in 1854, setting in motion the Meiji Restoration that displaced many Japanese to Hawai'i. And one cannot forget the firebombing of major cities and the atomic bombs that targeted Japanese civilians during World War II. Indeed, the Korean pavilion is reminiscent of the Korean War, often referred to as "the Forgotten War," which resulted in over 3 million Korean civilian casualties, 2 million missing or wounded, and almost 10 million Koreans separated from friends and relatives—with fewer than ten thousand subsequently reunited.

The most recent addition to the Heritage Gardens speaks directly to such alternative ways of viewing them. On January 16, 2013, the eve of the anniversary of the 1893 U.S. military–backed overthrow of the Hawaiian Kingdom, a group called Puʻuhonua o Iao created an altar in the Kepaniwai Heritage Gardens using an uncut stone that was strategically placed to represent the Kūʻē petitions. These petitions, signed in 1897, include over 90 percent of the eligible Hawaiian national population that opposed U.S. citizenship.

While the Heritage Gardens represent a U.S. presence in Hawaiʻi as bringing peace to both Hawaiʻi and the world—in opposition to Hawaiians' "bloodshed of old"—many of Maui's diverse residents have lost their lives in service to the United States. The War Memorial Stadium and Gym, listing the names of the hundreds of Maui residents who died in World War I, World War II, the Korean War, the Vietnam War, and the Gulf War, currently stands on the road leading to the Gardens. Down the road from this memorial, at the Kaʻahumanu Shopping Center in the "Plantation Section," exist the recruitment stations for the U.S. Army, Marines, Navy, and Air Force.

Not only have Maui residents lost their lives in U.S. wars; the U.S. military presence in the islands made it a target for other imperialist nations. Although Pearl Harbor is hailed in U.S. national public memory as the one site attacked by the Japanese military, the fact that Maui was the site of three other attacks is all but forgotten. On December 15, 1941, and again on December 31, Japanese military submarines fired torpedoes onto the island, missing their primary targets, one of which was the town of Puʻunēnē. In 1942, however, a Japanese submarine off Maui successfully sank an army transport, killing twenty-four men. Such attacks were cause to occupy the island with more than 200,000 soldiers from the Marines, Navy, Army, and Air Force. With more than fifty military training sites on the island, Maui residents were eventually outnumbered by military personnel, four to one. In preparation for fighting in the sugar fields of Saipan and Tinian, Maui plantation workers were made to teach marines how to maneuver through dense and sharp sugarcane and how to set cane fires. The key training site, however, was on the nearby island of Kahoʻolawe. Controlled by the Navy, Kahoʻolawe was used for live-fire training exercises through which seamen rehearsed taking over islands in the Pacific from the Japanese. In fact, marines in the Fourth Division who fought in Iwo Jima named the first street rebuilt after U.S. occupation "Maui Boulevard."[10]

The seemingly pristine Wailuku River that flows through ʻĪao Valley does not entirely continue out of the valley. Huge grates that extend the width of the river divert its water to irrigate sugarcane, golf courses, resorts, and new real estate subdivisions. Tourists who visit ʻĪao probably marvel at the natural beauty of both the valley and the Wailuku River. At the opposite end of Wailuku River, however, they would find only a trickle flowing over concrete. Many of the fish, shrimp, and snails in Maui's streams and rivers are diadromous, which means they live in both fresh water and salt water during their life cycles but often die because they are unable to make their way back upstream. After storms, however, Skippy Hau, a member of the Hui o Nā Wai ʻEhā, scoops them up and drives five miles upstream, where he releases them into the fresh water.

The project of returning water to streams and rivers poses the very real threat that these planters could be able to produce food in ways that both precede and exceed the current system, serving as a foundation on which an alternative way of life to the settler state could materialize—one that would radically challenge the current system. As is often noted, *water* is *wai* in the Hawaiian language and *wealth* translates as *waiwai*. During a period when water wells on the island of Maui are drying up at the same time that the number of residential areas and their need for water is increasing, this shift in thinking tells us that nature, not profit, needs to determine the conditions of possibility for Maui.

▶ **A Brief History of Water on Kahoʻolawe and Maui**

Kahoʻolawe is an island only eight miles to the south of Maui, and the hydrology of both islands are interdependent. In the last half of the nineteenth century, the island of Kahoʻolawe was used as pasture for sheep. By World War II, the U.S. Armed Forces were using the island as a training ground and missile range. Each contributed to the elimination of once dense forests on both islands.[1] In 1909 an unnamed Kanaka ʻŌiwi woman from ʻUlupalakua on

Maui explained that forests on Kahoʻolawe previously attracted clouds to the island in the morning. By the afternoon, these clouds, laden with moisture, would travel across the channel and rain over ʻUlupalakua, an area on the leeward slopes of Maui. When both ranchers and the U.S. military eliminated the forests on Kahoʻolawe, the clouds no longer gathered there, and thus the climate of South Maui went from wet to dry. These factors, combined with earlier deforestation of sandalwood, contributed to rapid deforestation such

that only 5 percent of the Native forests in South Maui remain.[2]

In a 1959 master plan for the economic development of Maui, lack of water sources in South Maui was considered an obstacle to development. As South Maui became targeted for the development of luxury resorts, the demand for water increased, but no adequate water sources could be found. In 1975 development companies building large-scale resorts struck a deal with the Maui County Board of Water Supply. Four companies, including one

Notes

1 E. S. C. Handy and E. G. Handy, *Native Planters in Old Hawaii: Their Life, Lore, and Environment* (Honolulu: Bishop Museum Press, 1972), 272.

2 "Ghost Picture Excites Japanese," *Maui News*, April 18, 1919; "Work Starts on Picnic Grounds in Iao Valley," *Maui News*, November 3, 1951; Inez Ashdown, "The Valley Worthy of Kings," *Sunday Star-Bulletin*, July 24, 1960.

3 Samuel Kamakau, *Hawaiian Annual* (Honolulu: Thomas G. Thrum, 1932).

4 "Development of Iao Is Aim of Civic Club," *Maui News*, July 9, 1960.

5 Dean Itsuji Saranillio, "Colliding Histories: Hawai'i Statehood at the Intersection of Asians 'Ineligible to Citizenship' and Hawaiians 'Unfit for Self-Government,'" *Journal of Asian American Studies* 13, no. 3 (October 2010): 283–309.

6 Chuck Frankel, "Isles Called Appropriate for Kennedy Rights Talk," *Honolulu Star Bulletin*, June 6, 1963; "Text of Kennedy's Speech to Mayors," *Honolulu Star Bulletin*, June 10, 1963.

7 As cited in Tom Coffman, *The Island Edge of America: A Political History of Hawai'i* (Honolulu: University of Hawai'i Press, 2003), 2.

8 Kennedy's posthumously released book, *A Nation of Immigrants*, popularized the term in the national lexicon. John F. Kennedy, *A Nation of Immigrants* (New York: Harper Perennial, 2008).

9 Gail Batholomew (text) and Bren Bailey (photo research), *Maui Remembers: A Local History* (Taiwan: Mutual, 1994), 128.

10 Batholomew and Bailey, *Maui Remembers*, 146–47.

from Japan, were permitted to jointly finance a multimillion-dollar project to drill new wells into the 'Iao aquifer, twenty-five miles from South Maui. The 'Iao aquifer was intended to support a renewable withdrawal of 36 million gallons per day (mgd), and consequently the County of Maui offered to construct the infrastructure necessary to transport 19 mgd of water from Nā Wai 'Ehā to the luxury resorts in South Maui. The estimate of 36 mgd, however, was much higher than the actual 20 mgd that the aquifer could sustainably yield.

This did not sway further development, however, and as tourism slumped, future developments were deemed necessary. Water extraction from the 'Iao aquifer rose to 20.5 mgd, and by 1985 salinity levels had increased and the state water commission threatened to seize control of the aquifer from the county by designating it a water management area. Determining that the water resources were in jeopardy in 2008, the state of Hawai'i designated the 'Iao aquifer a water management area, taking control away from the county.

Notes

1 Matthew Spriggs, "'Preceded by Forest': Changing Interpretations of Landscape Change on Kaho'olawe," *Asian Perspectives* 30, no. 1 (1991): 71–116.

2 "1909 Article Tells Why Ulupalakua Dried up," *Maui News*, November 9, 1977; *Noho Hewa: The Wrongful Occupation of Hawai'i*, dir. Anne Keala Kelly, DVD (Honolulu: Kuleana Works, 2009).

Brandy Nālani McDougall

Finding Direction

Google Mapping the Sacred, Moʻolelo
Mapping Wahi Pana in Five Poems

These poems offer an alternative mapping of wahi pana (storied, sacred places) on Maui and Oʻahu. They were created by using two very different mapping technologies—moʻolelo (stories, history) and Google Maps. I am interested in exposing the kind of rhetoric of directions and orientation used by Google Maps, whether in map, satellite, or street-view mode, that assures its users of its knowledge and familiarity with a place. This kind of rhetoric can be erroneously taken for granted as a universal means of giving directions and helping people locate and situate themselves, when directionality and senses of orientation are always culturally and politically bound. Juxtaposing moʻolelo of wahi pana in Hawaiʻi with Google Maps destabilizes its rhetoric of directions, exposing this knowledge as foreign and superficial, while also demonstrating how moʻolelo are a rich and valuable Indigenous compass to help determine where one is, has been, can be, or wants to go.

In these poems, I also want to uncover how surveillance by Google Maps (and its seeming lack of caution or apprehension in surveilling) within colonized spaces like Hawaiʻi gives its users a sense of entitlement to all places—even those considered to be most sacred or ecologically vulnerable—as they are shown to be free and open for all to visit. My intention through these poems is to make the moʻolelo of these places more visible, even when the moʻolelo are not completely revealed and only hint at a deeper history and meaning. In being made to experience the tensions arising from the use of both mapping technologies, I hope readers can reflect on the colonial directionality of Google Maps, while being guided by the moʻolelo of our wahi pana toward a decolonial orientation.

Haleakalā on Google Maps (Satellite View)

You need a reservation now.
Go online and schedule
this trip several days
in advance.
Head south on Haleakalā
Highway (State Hwy 377)
and turn before
it becomes Kekaulike
(State Hwy 378).
You will need warm
clothes and a blanket,
a working heater
in your car.
There are thirty-one turns over
the ten miles up
to the summit entrance.
Follow the long line
of cars ahead.
Answer the haole man
or woman with nps
when they ask
for confirmation
of your
reservation.
Tell him/her you are
Kanaka
and are here
for spiritual reasons.
You will need to answer
when you are asked
what kind of cultural
protocol you will be
following.
You will need to pay
the nps fee anyway
because he/she could
not recognize you.
Quietly seethe and pass

Puʻunianiau
and look down toward
the lights descending
from mountain to ocean,
the coil of cars snaking
behind you. Feel yourself
climb higher and higher
over cinders, silversword,
and tufts of sharp grass.
Ten more turns before
reaching
the observatory
at the summit.
There are
telescopes here, too,
a new one just built,
astronomers who
only look up,
beyond even the sun,
and don't need
or have reservations.
Remember Maui
crouching in the dark,
waiting for the sun.
Remember Pele
hoping to find a home,
digging into the earth
for fire, waiting for
her sister. Remember
the aloha ʻāina laying
down to block the trucks,
arms linked in pvc,
waiting for the police
saws to cut through.
Park your car and walk
across the parking lot.
Pass tour buses and rental
cars and find some space
within the crowd along

the railing at the edge.
Wait for your voice
to rise with the light.

**Honokahua on Google Maps
(Satellite then Street then Satellite View)**
Your first attempt to find
Honokahua seems wrong.
You know it should be
in Lahaina, but you are placed
amid the cinder cones
of Haleakalā.
Wonder if Google knows
Honokahua is an 'ahupua'a.

Your second attempt leads
to choices:
Honokahua Bay, Maui County, HI
Honokahua Burial Site, Lahaina, HI
Kapalua, HI
Honokahua Stream, Maui County, HI
Honokahua Street, Honolulu, HI

The last of these is not your destination.
You satellite view the bay,
see Honoapi'ilani Highway
(State Hwy 30)
flank the coastline
then run mauka away
from Plantation Estates Drive
and Plantation Club Drive.
See the wide roofs
of multimillion-dollar
houses, fenced and gated,
with pools and ocean views,
flanking the evenly
green golf course.

Switch to street view and insist
on taking Lower Honoapi'ilani Road.

You want to see what was here
before the asphalt, the manicured
hau and bougainvillea bushes.
The well-placed coconut-less palms.
Wonder, instead, if there is just one big
golf course or several in a cluster.
See more multimillion-dollar
houses that look like all the others.

A crossed steeple rises
on your right—a church.
You cannot go further.
Turn left to park.
A sign reads:
Honokahua Burial Site
Registered as a State Historic Place
Deeded to the State of Hawaii
Public entry is prohibited
Please kokua

Your street view ends, so
you zoom out. You need
to walk 0.6 miles (about 10 min.)
past the Napili Wing
and crucifix-shaped pool
of the five-diamond hotel
honoring the beauty and traditions
of Hawaii—the Ritz Carlton.

Look past the men
setting up the white chairs,
the plumeria walkway,
the arch swirled in chiffon to frame
the sunset ocean wedding.

Try to see what was here
before the landscaped naupaka
boundary, the evenly green grass
over the sand, before there was
Honokahua Preservation.

Try to see what was here
when the dunes were dug up
then sliced into tiers. See
our kūpuna laid bare. Uē.

See our people holding signs:
Na wai e hoʻola i nā iwi?
Stop Digging Hawaiian Bones
Kapu the Bones
Leave our Ancestors Alone
Mai kaulaʻi wale i nā iwi kupuna

See our people stopping
bulldozers, then archaeologists.
See our people relearning
to kuʻi kapa to wrap hundreds.
See us waiting for the aumoe
to replant the bones of our kūpuna
in the maluhia of darkness.

See the koholā's fin slapping
the ocean's surface, the pueo
circling overhead, the moonlit
hōʻailona showing you the way.

Waikīkī on Google Maps (Satellite View)

In Waikīkī
Liliʻuokalani is just
a few blocks
from the
Royal Hawaiian
Shopping Center
and runs mauka
from Kalākaua
to the Ala Wai.

Kūhiō meets with her
amidst vacation condos,
hotels, fenced empty lots
with tarped shopping carts,

overpriced apartments
and abc stores

as does Koa,
Prince Edward,
Cleghorn, and
Paoakalani.

Ka'iulani runs alongside
her, but turns mauka
and has a much
shorter life
before becoming
Kanekapolei.

From Lili'uokalani,
take Kūhiō
or Prince Edward
to the Princess Ka'iulani
Hotel.

When you get
to the King's Village
you must run
mauka with them
(but only to the Ala Wai).

Search the brown
canal water
that once fed
the marshes
for any part of us
that is still ours,

whatever remains
after even the names
of our kings and queens
have been taken,
left roaming the streets.

Kūka'ō'ō Heiau on Google Maps (Satellite View)
University meets Dole
at Bachman Lawn

Metcalf runs parallel
to Dole and intersects
University just one block
mauka across Sinclair

Up farther
Vancouver
connects University
to McKinley,
which you can take
to Beckwith

If you go up
even farther
University
becomes
Oʻahu

and runs past
Kūkaʻōʻō Heiau
(Mānoa Heritage Center)
which can only
be accessed
via one
of the Cooke houses,
which they named
Kūaliʻi. Tours
run for $7 by
appointment only.

Heading mauka
from Oʻahu, take
a left on Cooper
to get to Mānoa
to get to Kūaliʻi
to get to Kūkaʻōʻō

there, in the piko
of foreign trees
and multimillion-
dollar homes
that still, or once,

belonged
to missionaries,
on land that still
belongs to Lono.

You pass it everyday
without knowing.

The King Kamehameha Statue on Google Maps (Map View)

The King Kamehameha statue
looks smaller than you think.

To his left,
Mililani
runs two ways.
To his right,
Punchbowl
moves only makai.

He stands,
his back to Ali'iolani
and Queen.
He faces South King Street
heading Diamond Head,
his arm still
extending toward
a beige box
in an open
gray field
named 'Iolani Palace.

It is just beyond reach.

Stephanie Nohelani Teves

Princess Kaʻiulani Haunts
Empire in Waikīkī

Kaʻiulani is haunted. Someone fell from the balcony of the Sheraton Princess Kaʻiulani Hotel and on another occasion a hotel room caught on fire from a cigarette. The 2008 production of the film *Princess Kaʻiulani* was cursed. Some of the production assistants heard voices and saw unexplainable shadows during filming at ʻIolani Palace. The film was already shrouded in controversy as Kānaka questioned the film's historical accuracy and protested its production. In an ominous turn of events, one of the production managers working on the film died in a tragic accident at the Sheraton Princess Kaʻiulani Hotel during preproduction.[1] Were these "accidents"? Was it just their imaginations? Was it simply bad luck? An omen? Something else? Or are they a reminder of the contested histories in Hawaiʻi and claims to power that include the spirits of those no longer living. One thing is clear—the ongoing existence of the lāhui Hawaiʻi (Hawaiian nation) haunts Waikīkī, especially in the public memorials of the Hawaiian Kingdom's heir apparent at the time of the overthrow, Princess Kaʻiulani.

Princess Victoria Kawēkiu Kaʻiulani Kalaninuiahilapalapa Cleghorn was born October 16, 1875. Her death on March 6, 1899, is also shrouded in controversy. Some say she died of pneumonia brought on by inflammatory rheumatism. Was her death a result of horseback riding in the rain in Waimea on the big island of Hawaiʻi, or did she die of a broken heart, as the San Francisco *Morning Call* reported? What we know for sure is that Kaʻiulani perished less than two years after she had returned home to Hawaiʻi, a year into her engagement to Prince David Laʻamea Kawananakoa, eight months after Hawaiʻi was annexed by the United States through the Newlands Resolution, six years after the U.S. military backed an illegal overthrow of the Hawaiian

Kingdom, and eight years after she had been declared heir to the throne. The unexpected loss of "the hope of Hawai'i"—as Ka'iulani has been called—seemed to foreclose the future of the Hawaiian Kingdom, making way for the ascendancy of American empire. She continues to haunt both, refusing to be engulfed by forces of history beyond her control.

Princess Ka'iulani was named Crown Princess by her aunt, Queen Lydia Lili'uokalani, on March 9, 1891. In 1875, her birth was celebrated widely as the highest ranking royal birth of the Kalākaua dynasty. Educated in England, she traveled across Europe and the U.S. in her early twenties, spreading awareness about the overthrow. Since her death in 1899, she has continued to be memorialized in hula, mele (song), film, and other performances in Hawai'i and around the globe. An elementary school in Nu'uanu, Honolulu, is named after her. She is memorialized with an annual keiki hula festival in October, usually around the time of her birthday. The event is hosted by the Sheraton Princess Ka'iulani Hotel and involves a reenactment of the royal court of the Hawaiian Kingdom. The Sheraton Princess Ka'iulani Hotel sits on the site of her former home at 'Āinahau. In 1999 a statue of her was built at the quadrangle of Kuhio Avenue (which later intersects with Ka'iulani Avenue) and Kanekapolei Street in Waikīkī. The statue was commissed by Outrigger Enterprises (Outrigger Hotels) to demonstrate their committment to Hawai'i's past. A small park sits adjacent to the statue.

A ghost tour of Waikīkī invokes Ka'iulani's memory at the hotel named after her, but I will not tell you any of these ghost stories. Cultural practitioners and tour guides hold them and have the oratorical and cultural skills to transfer this knowledge, which I encourage you to seek out if it interests you. But the existence of these tours should give us all pause. Being haunted in a certain place represents uneasy feelings, reminding us that something important, uncanny, or unresolved happened there. These feelings are common in Hawai'i. Hawaiian history, culture, and governmental politics haunt the public sphere in Hawai'i: something remains unfinished. What has been concealed is alive and present, and what is hidden cannot be fully repressed or contained. If we are open to listening, we might hear these stories. The ghostly presence of Ka'iulani gestures to how Hawai'i came to be part of the U.S. and how it also became a tourist destination. It reminds us that someone or something is lingering because of an injustice or unfinished business. If we ignore the ghost, we become complicit. So, in this spirit, my thoughts here attempt to get us to open our senses, to be aware of what came before.

Victoria

As a royal woman in the late nineteenth century, Kaʻiulani was subject to constant surveillance by the global press, in Hawaiʻi, on the U.S. continent, and across Europe. Kaʻiulani was known around the world for her intelligence and attractiveness; American newspapers consistently ran stories about her—or rather, her looks. On March 2, 1893, the San Francisco *Morning Call* described her as a "beautiful young woman of sweet face and slender figure," remarking on her dark skin and soft eyes, which are "common" among the Hawaiians.[2] While this was a typical characterization of her, other descriptions seemed to be shocked by her "intelligence," attributing her education to her royal status and her father's Scottish bloodline, instead of a valued Kanaka characteristic. In an interview with the *Morning Call* shortly after Kaʻiulani's death, Colonel Macfarlane, a close family friend, described her as having "the dignity of an English aristocrat and the grace of a creole." He describes her as a "pure half-caste," explaining that her early seclusion from other Hawaiians and English schooling made her thoroughly English in her manners and ambitions, with no trace of "native superstition" left.[3] Macfarlane attributes Kaʻiulani's civilized and dignified demeanor to her Englishness and her colonial training, in spite of her Nativeness. Although seemingly intended as a compliment, Macfarlane's own perceptions reflect the racial logics of the time.

Today, Kaʻiulani's story is easily packaged for feminist audiences of all ages and backgrounds. The film *Princess Kaʻiulani* portrays her as a princess from a romantic faraway place who falls for the son of a wealthy Scottish businessman. But in a feminist twist, she does not give up her country for love, which the film affirms in a crucial scene: "Do you think I love you more than my country?" Kaʻiulani was not seduced by empire; she in fact turns away from it, remaining loyal to her kingdom. Couched in a universal feminist narrative of a young, intelligent, beautiful princess that young women, anglophiles, and Kānaka Maoli can latch onto, Kaʻiulani's story still cannot be fully managed by historical accounts. Kaʻiulani defied perceptions and expectations of women of her generation, class, and race. European travelogues notably represented Pacific women as sexually available, with no mores or rationality.

In contrast, Hawaiian-language newspapers wrote about Kaʻiulani with the utmost respect, expressing deep aloha (affection) toward her. Notably, in the published mele Hawaiian-language newspapers featured in the 1890s, Kaʻiulani is honored in name songs: "He inoa no Kaʻiulani," written by Queen Liliʻuokalani, and "He inoa no Kalaninuiahilapalapa," written by Eleanor

Kekoahoiwaikalani Prendergast. The latter celebrates Kaʻiulani as representing the proud ancestry of the flag of Hawaiʻi, writing "welo haaheo e ka hae Hawaii" and later, "ua nani hiehie oe e kahiwa, e ka wohi kukahi a o Hawaiʻi." These lines compare Kaʻiulani to the most sacred vines, noting that her voice and presence brings joy to Hawaiʻi. Outsiders might remember Kaʻiulani only for her beauty; we remember her for political resistance and her commitment to the Hawaiian people.

As an emergent head of state, Kaʻiulani carried her kuleana (responsibility) boldly, protesting the overthrow of the kingdom by writing letters to American newspapers, taking on Lorrin A. Thurston, one of the architects of the overthrow. She accused him of conspiring to keep her away from Hawaiʻi so that he and other annexationists could steal the throne. Kaʻiulani and her contemporaries all fought to save the kingdom. They were responsible for the anti-annexation petitions that are today known as the Kūʻē Petitions. These wāhine koa (women warriors) traveled from island to island and village to village collecting signatures from Kānaka Maoli (and non-Kanaka subjects of the Hawaiian Kingdom) who were opposed to annexation. Mainstream history fails to document the resistance of Kānaka Maoli, who organized 38,000 signatures opposing annexation, and that women were responsible for much of this resistance. Women like Emma Nawahī and Abigail Kuaihelani Campbell of Aloha ʻĀina o Nā Wahine (Hawaiian Women's Patriotic League) rejected Western social conventions that said women should stay home and out of politics. They were key figures in Hawaiian resistance. The erasure of this history represents the ways in which Hawaiian women's labor, their politically astute activism, and their loyalty to lāhui is rendered invisible in history and occluded by hotels, hula competitions, and even street names. These events and signs are hauntings of what was and a future that could have been. They are mnemonic devices that remind us of the story of women's organizing. The emphasis on Kaʻiulani marks ongoing non-Hawaiian fascination with images of Hawaiian women and stories about Hawaiʻi, but these non-Hawaiians are not interested in Hawaiʻi's complex political history.

From Royal Estate to Hotel

Near the corner of Kalākaua Avenue and Kaʻiulani Avenue, the Sheraton Princess Kaʻiulani Hotel allegedly sits at the entrance to Kaʻiulani's estate, ʻĀinahau. Princess Ruth Keʻelikolani, Kaʻiulani's aunt, gifted the estate to her (and her family) on the occation of her birth in 1875. ʻĀinahau was a beautiful estate known for its gardens, lily ponds, coconut trees, varieties of hibiscus, mango trees, and a giant banyan tree Kaʻiulani's father brought from India.

Kaʻiulani, Princess of Hawaii (1875–99), at her home in Waikīkī, Ainahau, circa 1898.
Courtesy Hawaiʻi State Archives.

During Kaʻiulani's youth and adulthood, her family hosted many high society functions. Her mother, Miriam Likelike, sister to King David Kalākaua, died young, leaving Kaʻiulani and the estate in her father's care. The residence included several bungalows and a two-story Victorian home. Kaʻiulani was often pictured at ʻĀinahau with her exotic peacocks.

After her death in 1899, hundreds of Hawaiians gathered under the family's banyan tree to perform kanikau (laments) and mourn their loss and the devastating blow for the lāhui. Upon Kaʻiulani's passing, her father managed ʻĀinahau and bestowed the land to the Territory of Hawaiʻi with the intention to create Kaʻiulani Park. When Cleghorn died in 1910, the land was divided up and sold. The Moana Hotel, located on the ocean side of Kalākaua Avenue, had been in operation since 1901 and had built small bungalows on the land. The old Victorian mansion that was once Kaʻiulani's childhood home was converted into a small hotel and operated from 1913 to 1917. It burned down in 1921.

This is a densely populated area full of hotels, apartments, restaurants, and stores. Despite the transformations that have taken place in Waikīkī, remnants of what was Kaʻiulani and other nā aliʻi presence—indicated by streets named for Kaʻiulani; her father, Archibald Cleghorn; Queen Liliʻuokalani; and Prince Jonah Kūhiō Kalanianaʻole—are still evident. The Moana Hotel (Moana

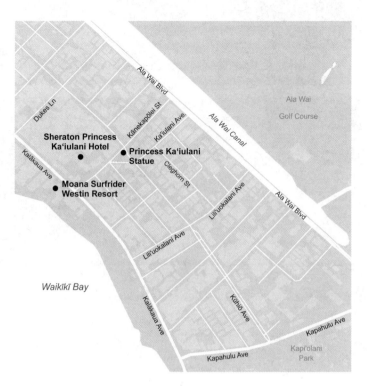

Ka'iulani in Waikīkī. *Cartography by University of Oregon InfoGraphics Lab.*

Surfrider Westin Resort on map) was the first hotel operating in Waikīkī. Ka'iulani Drive was eventually renamed Ka'iulani Avenue; this road runs from Kalākaua Avenue to the Ala Wai Canal after splitting off onto Kanekapolei Street at a quadrangle where Princess Ka'iulani Triangle Park and a statue are today (not to be confused with Ainahau Triangle, which exists today between Kalia and Maluhia Roads near the Fort DeRussy military installation). Apukehau, Kukaunahi, and Piianaio are original streams that were connected to Pālolo and Mānoa Valleys as part of the ahupua'a system, which moved water from the mountain to the sea, but these streams no longer exist. They were rerouted to build the Ala Wai Canal in 1928. Small bungalows that the Moana Hotel operated were demolished in 1953. The Matson Line constructed the Princess Ka'iulani Hotel in June 1955; in 1959 it was sold to Sheraton Hotels. A second wing was built in 1960 and another in 1970. The Japanese company Kyo-Ya purchased it in 1963 and continues to own it and a slew of other Waikīkī hotels—the Moana Surfrider, the Royal Hawaiian, the Westin, the Sheraton Maui. Consisting of two towers, the Princess Ka'iulani

Princess Kaʻiulani statue, Waikīkī. *Photograph by Jesse Stephen.*

Hotel boasts a thousand rooms. Today, the hotel lobby displays a life-sized portrait of Kaʻiulani, and a collage of images of Kaʻiulani serve as the backdrop of the concierge area. The tourists who pass these large portraits daily are presented with imagery of the Hawaiian Kingdom as a thing of the past, one whose majesty and royal magnitude has cultural value but no political relevance today, erasing Hawaiʻi's history as a kingdom, a nation. Waikīkī is not just a place for tourists; hotels are not off-limits to residents. Go there. Walk around. Listen for the stories alive in the portraits and images of Kaʻiulani and the lāhui.

Princess Kaʻiulani Statue

The Princess Kaʻiulani statue was dedicated in 1999 on the 124th anniversary of the princess's birth. The seven-foot bronze sculpture by Jan Gordon Fisher stands in Waikīkī's Kaʻiulani Triangle Park. Every year the Princess Kaʻiulani Hotel hosts a birthday party to honor the late princess. This involves a lei-giving ceremony in front of the Princess Kaʻiulani statue. A weeklong tribute of events includes workshops by cultural practitioners, presentations by historians, and tributes from hālau hula (hula schools). The statue depicts Kaʻiulani with a peacock, something she was famous for. The small grassy area is far from a park, but it does have a bus stop. When I was there, a home-less person was sleeping on it. This small Kaʻiulani Triangle Park smelled of dog poop. It made me terribly sad that one of our most cherished aliʻi wahine (female royalty), who was known around the world for her beauty and intel-ligence, would be memorialized with such a small area in what used to be the location of her royal estate. Just across the way is a tattoo and piercing shop, a small convenience store, and a laundromat.

The transformation of ʻĀinahau from estate to hotel is part of a larger violent transformation of Waikīkī from a place of spouting water, with taro patches, rice paddies, and small fishing areas, to a world-reknowned tourist destination. The dredging of the Ala Wai Canal rerouted streams; commercial development filled in the loʻi to build hotels, shopping malls, restaurants, movie theaters, and bars. Street signs are all that remain of our aliʻi. The fabrication of "Hawaiianness" throughout Waikīkī in Hawaiian motifs, street names, and so-called Hawaiian cultural performances, caters to tourists' fan-tasized image of Hawaiʻi, a simulation of a Native presence which, in fact, signals Native absence.[4] The Sheraton Princess Kaʻiulani Hotel memorializes the former glory and power of the Hawaiian Kingdom throughout its interior design, dining room performances, and even educational cultural activities intended to craft a more nuanced tale of Hawaiian history, but such cele-brations foreclose the possibilities of and a desire for decolonization and a contemporary/future independent Hawaiʻi.

Kānaka Maoli take very seriously our history as a lāhui. Remembering our aliʻi and the Hawaiian Kingdom anchors our ongoing political claims, so you understand my frustration when these histories are domesticated and man-aged to fulfill a touristic version. Remembering aliʻi connects Kanaka to our culture, our ancestors, and the essence of who we believe we are as Kanaka Maoli people, which always contains a future projection of who we could be again. This remembering plays a crucial role in decolonization because it al-lows us to bring our aliʻi back to life, to bring Kanaka Maoli independence back to life.

This is also an act of mourning. Rather than focusing solely on our past, as tourism constantly encourages us to do (especially when talking about the kingdom or aliʻi), remembering our aliʻi is part of our shared sense of self; it is how we know who we are, and it is built into every understanding of what it means to be Kanaka Maoli. We refuse to be ghosts, but we still haunt. While the outside world tells us (Hawaiʻi and Hawaiians) that we are just their play-ground, a sexy culture, a military landing and staging site, Kaʻiulani's memory haunts all of us, reminding Kānaka Maoli that we were a royal, civilized people whose love for our nation never died. The story of Princess Kaʻiulani is haunted by ghosts, memory, history, fears, and desires for control over the meaning of the past and how it informs the future. The curated history packaged for tourists will not disrupt their vacation in paradise. But as all hauntings go, the spirit of the past reminds people that something is wrong, amiss, unfinished. That unsettling feeling reminds us in the present that the past remains a terrain of contestation. The sovereignty of the Hawaiian Kingdom lives and ka lāhui Hawaiʻi persists.

Notes

1   Dennis Shaughnessey, "She Lived, and Worked, Behind the Scenes," *Lowell Sun*, March 17, 2008, http://www.lowellsun.com/ci_8602523.

2   "Her Only Plaint," *Morning Call* (San Francisco), March 2, 1893, http:// chroniclingamerica.loc.gov/lccn/sn94052989/1893-03-02/ed-1/seq-1/.

3   "The Princess Died of a Broken Heart, Says Colonel Macfarlane," *Morning Call* (San Francisco), April 9, 1899, http://cdnc.ucr.edu/cgi-bin/cdnc?a=d&d=SFC18990409.2.209.3#.

4   Gerald Vizenor, "Aesthetics of Survivance: Literary Theory and Practice," in *Survivance: Narratives of Native Presence*, ed. Gerald Vizenor, 1–24 (Lincoln: University of Nebraska Press, 2008).

Resources

Bergland, Renée L. *The National Uncanny: Indian Ghosts and American Subjects.* Reencounters with Colonialism: New Perspectives on the Americas. Hanover, NH: Dartmouth College, 2000.

Gordon, Avery. *Ghostly Matters: Haunting and the Sociological Imagination.* Minneapolis: University of Minnesota Press, 1997.

Herman, Doug. "Kalaʻaina—Carving the Land: Geography, Desire and Possession in the Hawaiian Islands." PhD diss., University of Hawaiʻi, 1995.

Kam, Ralph Thomas, "The Legacy of ʻĀinahau: The Genealogy of Kaʻiulani's Banyan." *Hawaiʻi Journal of History* 45 (2011): 49–68.

Kosasa, Karen. "Critical Sights/Sites: Art Pedagogy and Settler Colonialism in Hawaiʻi." PhD diss., University of Rochester, 2002.

"Letters of Congratulations," *Pacific Commercial Advertiser* Vol. XX, no. 18 (1875). Accessed March 18, 2019. https://nupepa-hawaii.com//2014/10/16/more-on-the-birth-of -princess-kaiulani-1875/.

Marek, Serge. "Waikiki Virtual Reality: Space, Place and Representation in the Waikiki Master Plan." MA thesis, University of Hawaiʻi, 1997.

"Miss Kekoaohiwaikalani, He Inoa No Kalaninuiahilapalapa," *Leo o ka Lahui*, March 21, 1893, http://nupepa-hawaii.com/2015/03/05/ellen-prendergasts-mele-inoa-for -princess-kaiulani-1893/.

"Princess Kaiulani Protests," *Wichita Daily Eagle* XVIII, February 19, 1893, 2, https://nupepa-hawaii.com/2015/03/02/princess-kaiulani-protests-1893/.

"Princess Kaiulani Proclaimed Heir of the Crown," *Hawaiian Gazette*, March 17, 1891, http://nupepa-hawaii.com/2014/02/06/kaiulani-the-heir-to-the-throne-1891/#more-11897.

Silva, Noenoe. *Aloha Betrayed: Native Hawaiian Resistance to American Colonialism*. Durham, NC: Duke University Press, 2004.

S. Joe Estores and Ty P. Kāwika Tengan

Sources of Sustainment
Fort Kamehameha and ʻĀhua Point

Preface

In 2016, the 5.5 million visitors who landed at Honolulu International Airport flew directly over the largely forgotten Army Coast Artillery Corps base of Fort Kamehameha, established in 1907 in response to the Taft Board's recommendations that the U.S. fortify the harbors of its new island colonies. By 1920, the Army Corps of Engineers had built five batteries with long-range cannons at Fort Kamehameha to defend the adjacent Pearl Harbor against naval assault. These guns proved useless when military personnel at both the fort and nearby Hickam Air Field suffered casualties in the December 7, 1941, attack that forever transformed this site. The obsolete batteries were dismantled after the war, and Fort Kamehameha ceased operations in 1949.[1] The reef off of ʻĀhua Point on the eastern end of Fort Kamehameha was dredged in the 1970s; the material was used as fill while constructing Honolulu Airport's twelve-thousand-foot Reef Runway, which still receives millions of visitors today.[2] In the seventies, the Navy built a wastewater treatment plant on the fort's western end; expansion of the plant in the 1990s led to the disinterment of almost one hundred sets of Native Hawaiian remains that were eventually reburied in a stone vault next to the old officers houses in the area designated as the Fort Kamehameha Historic District.[3] In 1992, Fort Kamehameha was absorbed into Hickam Air Force Base (which itself became the Joint Base Pearl Harbor–Hickam in 2010).

While the U.S. military and global tourism have left indelible prints on these land- and seascapes, deeper histories of family and abundance survive in the stories of Uncle Joe Estores, a kupuna (elder) and Army veteran born in 1933 who lived there before and at the dawn of World War II. Uncle

Hawaiian Airlines flight descending above Fort Kamehameha Wastewater Treatment Facility as it comes in for a landing at Honolulu International Airport, October 28, 2017. *Photograph by Jesse Stephen.*

Joe leads his own personal (de)tours of Fort Kamehameha by taking small groups on base and showing them the places he, as a young boy, played and fished with his 'ohana (immediate and extended family). Much like the elderly women who decades earlier had sought to protect the nearby Hālawa Valley from desecration by the military highway H-3, Uncle Joe uses embodied storytelling as a way of "authorizing an indigenous genealogy of the land."[4] Uncle Joe's retelling of the history of Fort Kamehameha and 'Āhua Point asks readers to remember not only the deaths that came with America's entrance into World War II, but also (or even, rather) the loss of cultural and ecological life that followed Hawai'i's transformation under U.S. occupation, and what might be restored if the Hawaiian people could return to the land.

This essay is told from the first-person perspective of the lead author, Uncle Joe Estores. Coauthor Ty Tengan met Uncle Joe in 2010 while carrying out research on Hawaiian veterans. Tengan has written the preface and postscript; Uncle Joe has written the primary essay that retells his personal, familial, and cultural connections to the place. Hawaiian words have been translated and generally produced with correct modern diacritics and spelling, with some exceptions (in pluralization and capitalization) that pre-serve Uncle Joe's style of using Hawaiian.

Uncle Joe's Moʻolelo (Stories)

ʻĀhua Point and Fort Kamehameha are places once vibrant with life. To talk about these places, one must look at them as segments of the larger complex of land, estuaries, former fishponds, wetlands, and the coastline of ahupuaʻa (land divisions) emanating from the summits of the Koʻolau and Kaʻala mountain ranges. The area falls between Keʻehi Lagoon on the east and the entrance to Pearl Harbor on the west. Herein lies the context in which these two places gain their full meaning as sources of sustainment for people of the past and into the future.

As a child I grew up with seven siblings. ʻĀhua Point was where our mili-tary residence was located, along with those of other military families. Father was in the U.S. Army, stationed at Fort Kamehameha. ʻĀhua Point was wilder-ness, with a long sandy beach controlled by the Army, so we had exclusive access to all that was at this place. The wetland area gave us patches of sea salt and served as our playground full of native fauna and flora. The sandy beach was full of shells of all colors and shapes, large ʻōhiki (sand crabs), and glass balls of different sizes, sometimes covered with netting. This beach was like a long private sandbox, alive and always changing, the tides and waves bringing ashore artifacts of the ocean.

Across the shoreline lay our aquatic garden. From the shallow, clear waters and sandy bottoms, we gathered large clams that we felt for with our bare feet. Along the areas where there were outcroppings of volcanic rock forma-tions, we picked all the pipipi (small mollusks) and ʻopihi (limpets) we wanted, and plenty of ʻalamihi and ʻaʻama (two types of black crabs). Here, our Tūtūs (grandparents) taught us how to take only what was needed to ensure more would come. The coral reef extended out waist-deep for five hundred yards to the breakers, where all the manini (surgeonfish), weke (goatfish), ʻōpakapaka (blue snappers), pālau (wrasse), and other large fish were abundant. Father had a skiff and took us pole fishing, spear fishing, laying long nets day and night over the weekends. We learned of the Kona winds, the tides, and the behavior of all that lived and flowed through this place.

On weekends father brought uncles, aunts, cousins, and Tūtūs through the military gates to stay with us and enjoy the bountiful pleasures of old Hawaiʻi. We did the hukilau (communal seine net fishing) the old way; we went crabbing, using scoop nets to gather the plentiful large white and blue crabs. We gathered all the different types of limu (seaweed). In the brackish waters of the streams and along the mangroves, we caught 'o'opu (goby fish), crayfish, 'ōpae (shrimp), and all the large Samoan crabs we wanted. Using our spears and an uncle's glass box, we poked *he'e* (octopus) and sometimes different eels. We harvested large oysters from the numerous oyster beds throughout the area. Uncles would dive for lobsters, which were a treat. At night, we went torch fishing, laid our nets and went pa'ipa'i (slapping the water) to drive the fish into the nets. We learned when the great schools of migrating halalū (young scad), 'oama (young goatfish), and small 'ōpelu (mackerel) were leaving Pearl Harbor and harvested from them. There was also an abundance of nehu (anchovy) that thrived throughout the harbor's protective shores and lagoons. The occasional sea turtle was a prized catch, adding to the bountiful seafood that supplemented the Hawaiian diet of this military family.

From this bounty and more, we learned the different ways of cooking, preserving by salting or drying in the sun, or using sea salt and limu to preserve the variety of poke (cubed) fish and the spiny crustaceans that were all over the place. We spent Saturday nights sitting on the floor, newspaper spread out to hold the abundance of crabs, oysters, and clams, hot rice in the middle. We ate and then listened to spooky stories told by the Kupunas. This was home, a life-start at 'Āhua Point. This was Paradise, lost forever in the December 7, 1941, attack, when this Hawaiian family, living as Hawaiians, could not go back, could not live and mālama (care for) the 'Āina (air, land, and sea in all physical and spiritual dimensions) as it should be. Sadness fills my Hawaiian heart when I am back in the islands and go to this place that lingers only in memory. Why?

Fort Kamehameha had its heyday before the war. The scope of its military mission was very limited. So limited that it was not effective against aerial bombardment. Its only usefulness was its huge, long-range guns that protected against naval intrusion into Pearl Harbor. On that fateful day, the "Day of Infamy," its guns were silent, unable to be any threat to the aerial slaughter of the only assets that were available to counter the attack—those sitting on the tarmac at Hickam Air Field. The guns remained silent throughout World War II, other than occasional test firing and crew training. Therefore, this big investment in weaponry, manpower, encroachment, and in some aspects desecration of the 'Āina causes one to ask why must this continue.

This fort, this place, has gone through many changes over the years. The area was once a breadbasket of the full spectrum of foods that supported a large portion of the population on O'ahu. In the past, this basin was a confluence of pristine rivers and streams, a natural ecology of sustainment. In the 1880s, the dowager Queen Emma had a home along the shoreline on which Fort Kamehameha was built. After World War II, the U.S. Army continued to

Woman fishing on a dock in front of the U.S. Army Logistics Support Vessel watercraft anchored off Bishop Point at the entrance of Puʻuloa (Pearl Harbor), October 28, 2017. *Photograph by Jesse Stephen.*

control the installation as military housing while dismantling the heavy guns. They began to share the landscape with the U.S. Army Air Corps, which later became the U.S. Air Force. The Hawaiian Air National Guard was eventually added, and major changes came with the construction of new hangars and the maintenance of administrative structures. Roads were rerouted within the massive fenced area. New asphalt, concrete, and housing covered more of the land, and old structures were renovated with modern features including solar technologies. Management and control of Fort Kamehameha were then turned over to the U.S. Air Force, which soon after condemned the former U.S. Army Officers quarters because of their location within the flight approach into Honolulu International Airport. All geological and ecological features of Mamala Bay, including inland areas of Pearl Harbor, were so altered that the great migration of various fish was no longer supported. The coral reef—once full of life, full of sustenance—is now barren and in some places continues to be polluted. Care of this land and access to shoreline resources are denied for military security reasons.

ʻĀhua Point lies beneath concrete and is no longer shown on maps. Mamala Bay is altered by the Reef Runway. The shoreline is no longer a habitat for the fish, crustaceans, or sea and land birds. The Pueo, the owl, is silent, no longer there. The great flocks of beautiful pheasants, kolea (plovers), 'iwa (frigate bird), bright red Cardinals, and albatross are no more. The once-great patches of mangroves full of Samoan crabs are gone. The salt works and marshes have been bulldozed over. Stewards of this land are no longer present. Machine guns, rifles, and heavy guns, once fired day and night, have gone away. Silence is noticeable, except for the occasional landing and takeoff of commercial and military aircraft. Instead of mālama the 'Āina for its purpose to sustain our people, signs of warning are posted: Do not eat the fish. No crabbing. Polluted waters. Stewardship is in the hands of those who control the land and the waters. The coral reef is mostly gone because of construction. What is left is now bare, like a desert under water. There, too, is a strange, eerie silence; no living movement, only the polluted waters oscillated by the currents that still are there but that have been changed by the altered underwater landscape, continually mixing as the tides rise and recede. Where is the threat that keeps this place hidden from the people who would be happy to mālama this 'Āina? The threat, real or imagined, keeps Fort Kamehameha in the hands of the U.S. military, which continually searches for reasons to hold on to it, despite its strategic irrelevance in the past and its uselessness in the war of terror in the future.

Transformation continues, now seventy-five years later. In fact, the design and operations at all three of these major targets—Pearl Harbor, Hickam, and Fort Kamehameha—have been radically reconfigured and upgraded, which more seriously impacts the land, water, and shoreline ecologies. The once-rich source of highly productive fishponds, wetland habitat, coral reef, and other natural geological features have been so altered as to require hundreds, if not thousands, of years for the area to fully recover to its historical significance for sustainment and recreation. Tragically, this treasure trove of resources continues to be polluted in spite of all the technological and intellectual advancements of our time. This is not the kind of legacy of war that should exist in a nation-state that had declared itself neutral among its international neighbors. It is time to reassess the justification of such erosive effects on the 'Āina and to heal the wounds and scars of the past for the sake and sustainment for future peaceful generations.

Postscript

I begin where Uncle Joe ended his mo'olelo—with a commitment to sustaining the next generations. I was privileged to meet Uncle Joe and to tour Fort Kamehameha and 'Āhua Point through our respective writing projects—his a

Uncle Joe Estores sharing his moʻolelo (stories) on the beach of Kapuaʻikaula at Fort Kamehameha, October 28, 2017. *Photograph by Jesse Stephen.*

personal telling of his story, and mine a research project on the experiences of Native Hawaiian veterans. Generationally, I stand as keiki (child) to Uncle Joe, who fulfilled his kuleana (relational responsibility) as a kupuna to pass on knowledge and moʻolelo of the ʻĀina, which I in turn have a kuleana to pass on to those who come after me. I have partly been able to do that by inviting him to speak in my classes and by involving two undergraduates (Kamōʻīokalani Sausen and Mahealani Wilson) and one graduate student (Mahiʻai Dochin) in this project (with the support of Native Hawaiian Student Services). Mahiʻai Dochin's research into the vast Hawaiian-language archive that remains neglected by mainstream scholars gives lie to the statement that Kapuaʻikaula (the land Fort Kamehameha sits upon) was "little more than a wasteland" that "was of dubious value to anyone but the military and a few natives" when the U.S. federal government condemned and purchased it in 1907.[5] Instead, as stories of Uncle Joe's childhood in the 1930s attest, the traditions of this place highlight its "'ano waiwai maoli" (truly rich nature).[6]

Whereas Uncle Joe's stories convey a deep sense of loss and despair, I find in them a cause for hope. In the past, our people had seen in Fort Kamehameha and 'Āhua Point only military fences, concrete runways, and spaces that were generally off-limits to Kanaka (Hawaiians). We now know of a deeper history of Native presence, one that reemerges each time we step onto those grounds and recall the kūpuna that came before us. Although we recognize the perils of eating contaminated fish, we dare to imagine the possibilities of making the land abundant again. We may take solace in the fact that the land has a way of outlasting people and their constructions. But even if that nourishment has less to do with our bodies than it does our minds and our souls, it is (as Uncle Joe puts it) "sustainment" nonetheless.

The term 'Āhua (derived from *ahu*) means "heap."[7] This term points us to an important observation made by the famous nineteenth-century 'Ōiwi (Indigenous Hawaiian) scholar Kepelino: "Ahu kupanaha ia Hawaii imi loa! E noii wale mai no ka Haole-a, aole e pau na hana a Hawaii imi loa . . . Ahu ka hepa ia Hawaii ka moku nui!" 'Ōiwi historian Noelani Arista translates this as, "A heap of amazing things can be learned about Hawai'i 'imi loa! However diligently the foreigner inquires, he cannot fathom all of the doings of far seeking Hawai'i . . . A heap of absurdities is all he has to show from Hawai'i the great land!"[8] Kepelino contrasts the various kinds of ahu/heaps that emerge in relation to a "Hawai'i itself [that is] seeking, searching, and deeply inquiring," suggesting that the land can be a source of alternatively "amazing" and "absurd" insight.[9] With this in mind, the next time you are riding in a plane that approaches its landing on the Reef Runway of the Honolulu International Airport, witness the absurdity that is the transformed land and imagine another, more amazing way of being in this place.

Notes

1   William H. Dorrance, *Fort Kamehameha: The Story of the Harbor Defenses of Pearl Harbor* (Shippensburg, PA: Beidel Printing House, 1993).

2   State of Hawai'i. "HNL 1970S," 2019, accessed August 24, 2017, http://aviation.hawaii .gov/airfields-airports/oahu/honolulu-international-airport/hnl-1970s/.

3   Peter T. Young, "Fort Kamehameha," Ho'okuleana blog, June 6, 2012, accessed August 24, 2017, http://totakeresponsibility.blogspot.com/2012/06/fort-kamehameha .html.

4   Vernadette Vicuña Gonzalez, *Securing Paradise: Tourism and Militarism in Hawai'i and the Philippines* (Durham, NC: Duke University Press, 2013), 74.

5 Dorrance, *Fort Kamehameha*, 4.

6 Mahiʻai Dochin, "I ka ʻōlelo nō ke ola, i ka ʻōlelo nō ka make" (unpublished paper in Hawaiian, May 10, 2017, Word file), 14.

7 Mary Kawena Pukui, Samuel H. Elbert, and Esther T. Mookini, *Place Names of Hawaii*, rev. and exp. ed. (Honolulu: University of Hawaiʻi Press, 1974), 6.

8 Noelani Arista, "Foreword," in *Kepelino's Traditions of Hawaii*, ed. M. W. Beckwith (Honolulu: Bishop Museum Press, 2007), xi.

9 Arista, "Foreword," xii.

Laura E. Lyons

Fantasy Island

From Pineapple Plantation
to Tourist Plantation on Lāna'i

One year after he purchased the Hawaiian island of Lāna'i for an undisclosed price—estimated to be more than $350 million—Oracle's chief executive officer Larry Ellison was the subject of a 2013 profile in the *Wall Street Journal* entitled "Larry Ellison's Fantasy Island." The piece opens with a description of Ellison standing on "the white sand of a deserted beach, bordered by palm trees laden with coconuts. It didn't feel real that he could own the island of Lāna'i, he reflected."[1] The profile further notes that owning the island "had been [Ellison's] far-fetched dream since he was in his 20s, when he first flew over one of the smallest of Hawaii's inhabited islands in a Cessna 172 and was captivated by the thousands of acres of pineapple fields." What Ellison saw as he flew over the island almost fifty years before—vast acreage of pineapple—was actually the last vestiges of James Drummond Dole's own fantasy, what he liked to call "his pineapple island" or "pineapple kingdom."

Ellison purchased the island from David Murdock, who had acquired control over the sixth largest of the Hawaiian Islands in 1986 when he became chief executive officer of Castle and Cooke, which also owned Dole Food Company. Murdock eventually bought up enough stock to privately own both companies. In the late 1980s and early 1990s, he invested millions in his quest to transform the vast pineapple plantation into a profitable, high-end tourist destination. Bill and Melinda Gates were married on the island on New Year's Day 1994, famously buying out all available rooms at the two resorts and the one small bed and breakfast on the island to ensure their privacy. Murdock's quest to make the island profitable, however, was never realized, and he is estimated to have lost between $20 and $40 million annually.[2] In the aftermath of the 2008 financial crisis, he reopened Castle

& Cooke and Dole to public trading and eventually sold his holdings on Lāna'i to Ellison.

It is one thing to own an uninhabited island; it is a different thing altogether to purchase an island, as Ellison has, on which lives a sizable group of permanent residents with far longer connections (including genealogical ones, for many) to the land than the landlord has. For over a century, the lives and livelihoods of the residents of Lāna'i have been tied to the destinies of a succession of white landowners with the resources to change not just the economy but also the geographical terrain of the island in the hope of achieving their singular vision of making the island "profitable." The recent history of Lāna'i tells us something about what happens when those visions fail to bring the imagined prosperity. Not surprisingly, in resistance to having their fates tied to that of the landowner, and in opposition to the kinds of changes Ellison has most recently proposed, some permanent residents on this island, both Native Hawaiians and settlers, are looking to the land itself to redefine what it means to prosper. A discerning visitor to Lāna'i will see not only the obvious evidence of the ways that the island has been made to conform to the man-made fantasies of Dole, Murdock, and Ellison but also how many of its long-time residents honor the land and its history.

What exactly did Ellison's $350 million buy him? He now owns 98 percent of the island, including the two Four Seasons resorts and their championship golf courses, the more modest Hotel Lāna'i, the majority of the luxury homes, and all of the employee cottages. In essence, most of the accommodations on the island are under his control, along with the gas station, the car rental agency, the supermarket, Lāna'i City Grille, a solar farm, and all the buildings that house the small shops and cafes in Lāna'i City. He owns 88,000 acres of former pineapple fields and 50 miles of beaches—but technically, in Hawai'i, no one, with the exception of the U.S. military, is supposed to own beaches or control beach access. Soon after purchasing the island from Murdock, Ellison bought Island Air, one of the two airlines that serviced Lāna'i, and was considering buying the ferry services that shuttle both tourists and workers between Lāna'i and Maui. He never did buy the ferry, and in 2016 he sold controlling interest in the airline, which ended its service to Lānai that year.

This series of sales point to the difficult position that island residents are put in when access to transportation is connected with ownership of the island. While restricting access to the island makes Lāna'i a more exclusive destination, that same control over movement onto and off the island affects its residents' ability to see family on other islands and its high school students' ability to participate in statewide competition. Residents' access to medical care is largely restricted to what they can receive on the island.

Although Murdock sold his land holdings on the island to Ellison, he retained the right to develop a controversial wind farm for the purpose of generating power primarily for Oʻahu and eventually Maui. Murdock's now largely defunct plan has been a point of contention with many Lānaʻi residents because it involves developing sacred land and because the construction of one hundred to two hundred enormous wind turbines over a quarter of Lānaʻi could impact cultural sites, possibly including some of the remaining petroglyphs. Such development would inevitably disrupt and unearth iwi kupuna (ancestral bones), transforming the land and, by extension, people's relationship to it, just as tourism and pineapple cultivation once did, and not necessarily to the benefit of those who now live on the island. The environmental impacts of the turbines themselves, let alone the enormous underwater cables that would connect the wind farm on Lānaʻi to Oʻahu, have stalled the project, perhaps permanently.[3]

Although Ellison bought Lānaʻi over five years ago, the sale continues to leave many in Hawaiʻi wondering how one person could own so completely an inhabited island. Long-time resident Sally Kaye wrote in a tongue-in-cheek open letter to Ellison days after the sale was announced:

> First, don't be intimidated by all the angst over how it could even be possible for a single really, really rich guy to buy an entire island in the state of Hawaii, United States of America, from another rich guy, in this day and age. You have to understand that since the 1850's [sic] and Walter Murray Gibson and all those Mormons, this island has been owned and exploited by one really rich guy or another. There are generations here who don't know any other way to live but under some sort of feudal-serf system. I know this is bizarre, that such a medieval lord-of-the-manor system of control could still be functioning in the Land of the Free, but there you have it.[4]

Kaye is not the only one to describe as feudal the relationship between those who have lived on the island for generations and the landowner. For many Lānaʻians, feudalism best describes how their lives and destinies have been held hostage to the abilities of a succession of white American landowners to realize (or not) their fantasies of transforming the island into their private and profitable (or not) visions, pointing to the enormous and continuously increasing disparities in wealth.

Feudalism entails structures of debt and dependency that are significantly magnified in the context of a small island. Consider rents. While working on the $450 million renovation to the Four Seasons Resort at Manele Bay, construction workers stayed at the other resort, Koele Lodge. With both resorts closed, employment temporarily dropped. Worse yet, when the Manele Bay resort reopened and renovations shifted to transforming Koele Lodge into a $75 million wellness center, the need to house the construction workers elsewhere drove up the rents for those who have lived on the island for generations. It is not uncommon for a two-bedroom home to rent for over $2,000 per month. With an average annual income of $55,000, Lāna'i's residents pay a much greater percentage of their income for housing, much of which is owned by wealthy nonresidents with small holdings or by Ellison himself.[5] For many who live on the island, the paychecks they receive from Ellison are largely returned to him in the form of rents or as payment for goods and services.

Thinking about life on Lāna'i today as neo-feudalism helps us to see not just what happens to the residents and their landlord under such a system, but also the effects on land itself. The idea of buying and selling land didn't really come into being in Hawai'i until the mid-nineteenth century. "The single most critical dismemberment of Hawaiian society," explains Native Hawaiian historian Jonathan Kay Kamakawiwo'ole Osorio, "was the Mahele, or the division of lands and the consequent transformation of the 'āina [land] into private property between 1845 and 1850."[6] Private property rights not only led to the sale of land but also changed the political balance of power in the Kingdom of Hawai'i, as land ownership gave non-Natives greater influence on the politics of the day. Plantations require vast acreage, and U.S. imperialism proved the way to secure that land. By 1893, Queen Lili'uokalani was overthrown by the white oligarchy, many of whom were heavily invested in the sugar industry, with backing from James Dole's older cousin, Sanford Dole, who became the first territorial governor when the U.S. annexed the islands in 1898.

In 1922, James Dole bought the greater part of Lāna'i in a single transaction with the Baldwin family, who had tried large-scale ranching and smaller-scale agricultural development on the island. Dole subsequently acquired more land from owners of smaller holdings, many of them Native Hawaiians. In total, the Hawaiian Pineapple Company spent $1.1 million for the island and invested another $3 million in clear-cutting land for pineapple cultivation, diverting water and providing a new catchment and distribution system for irrigation, and creating a useable harbor for shipping its product.

Dole also built plantation housing for the immigrant fieldworkers, who were mostly from the Philippines. The legacy of that migration is that Lānaʻi's current population of approximately 3,100 people is 45.5 percent Filipino, 14 percent white, 4 percent Japanese, and only 4.4 percent Native Hawaiian.[7] Transforming the island into a plantation caused Dole to leverage himself too heavily, and eventually Castle and Cooke, which had a significant interest in the Hawaiian Pineapple Company, took ownership in the 1960s.

Unlike Dole, Murdock was much more of an absentee landlord and was widely disliked on the island for insisting on his singular vision, punishing residents for his losses, and reportedly referring to the citizens of Lānaʻi as "the children."[8] After the last pineapple harvest on the island in 1993, Murdock set to work building the two large resorts at Manele Bay and Koele Lodge. In contrast to Murdock, Ellison spends significant time on the island overseeing his renovation of the resorts and creating a master development plan for the island as a whole. Not by coincidence, one of Ellison's first acts when he acquired the island was to reopen the public pool, which Murdock had refused to maintain and which had become a health hazard.[9] Such acts, however welcome as they might be, do nothing to change the structure of the relations between he who owns the majority of the island and those settlers who have lived on the island for generations or those Kanaka Maoli for whom Lānaʻi is linked to their ancestral geneologies.

Ellison's plans for Lānaʻi have been slowly revealed since the sale and issued largely through his representative Kurt Matsumoto, who was born and raised on the island and who serves as chief operations officer for Pūlama Lānaʻi, which develops and carries out Ellison's vision for the island. The company's Hawaiian name, according to its website, means "to cherish Lānaʻi." Matsumoto initially held small group discussions with residents to inform them of the plans and to persuade them of the necessity of growth, particularly the need to quickly double the population of the island to provide more workers for Ellison's many sustainable enterprises. Ellison's plans include a second airstrip, a third resort with one hundred beach hales or stand-alone rooms on the beach close to the water, a desalination plant to provide the amount of water required for the resorts and golf courses as well as to reintroduce commercial agriculture. Ellison boasted to the *Wall Street Journal*, "We have the right climate and soil to grow the very best gourmet mangos and pineapples on the planet, and export them year-round to Asia and North America. We can grow and export flowers and make perfume the old-fashioned way—directly from the flowers, like they do in Grasse, France. We have an ideal location for a couple of organic wineries on the island."[10]

Ellison would like to transform Lānaʻi into what he calls a "sustainability laboratory," and he has announced his intent to eventually create a research university dedicated to sustainability on 524 acres south of Lānaʻi City. (By comparison, the University of Hawaiʻi at Mānoa, the state's flagship university, sits on 300 acres.) "It's surreal to think that I own this beautiful island," Ellison has commented. "It doesn't feel like anyone can own Lānaʻi. What it feels like to me is this really cool 21st-century engineering project, where I get to work with the people of Lānaʻi to create a prosperous and sustainable Eden in the Pacific."[11] Whether Larry Ellison feels like he owns Lānaʻi or not, he does, and he is using his considerable personal resources to realize his oxymoronic vision of sustainable tourism and an engineered Eden. If he seems to have more sense of noblesse oblige than his predecessor, Ellison is also known to be fiercely competitive and a man who enjoys beating other billionaires at their own game. For example, he poured millions into winning the America's Cup. Ellison hopes to do for himself and Lānaʻi what Murdock could not: turn a profit on his investment. But should that not happen, or should boredom or frustration set in, Ellison can walk away from his folly with little consequence to his personal fortune: $350 million sounds like a ridiculous amount of money, but *Forbes* estimates that at most Ellison paid only 16 cents per square foot, or $7,000 per acre, much less than the acreage price for most ranches on Maui.[12]

The costs of Ellison's fantasy island for the people living on Lānaʻi are much harder to calculate. Some have been forced off the island because of prices and are replaced by others willing to work for the resorts or on Ellison's other projects. On the one hand, Lānaʻi's permanent residents are repeatedly told that they have very little choice but to participate in whatever projects the billionaire landowner wants to pursue, because that person owns the land, along with most of the businesses, and so controls the majority of jobs on the island. On the other hand, many residents believe that the influx of capitalism over more than one hundred years—the transformation from pineapple plantation to high-end tourism destination, with or without sustainability—has not created enough stability or prosperity that they can afford to be silent and accept whatever plans develop.

While many residents note that the economy on the island since the sale seems to have improved, others are more cautious. Groups like Lānaʻians for Sensible Growth and Friends of Lānaʻi remain vigilant about demanding transparency in all parts of the planning process. Another group, Kupaʻa no Lānaʻi, formed in 2012 as a response to Ellison's plans but also to preserve and protect ancient and historically significant sites on the island. Kupaʻa no

Lāna'i educates the young people of Lāna'i on the ahupua'a system of land division and cultivation in which land was apportioned in sections that went from the mountain to the sea, so that each ahupua'a would contain a lowland mala (cultivated area) and an upland forested region.

Kupa'a no Lāna'i is documenting and trying to preserve and restore the boundary lines of the ahupua'a on the island, and in so doing the group is making a younger generation aware of Native land use as an alternative to the maximally extractive and exploitative practices of development. They believe that the people of Lāna'i must have input on how land is used and preserved in order to keep private landowners such as Ellison accountable. Their focus on ahupua'a education speaks to the ways that Ellison's Pūlama Lāna'i explicitly invokes, or perhaps appropriates, the ahupua'a system in its logo, which incorporates an image of a Cook Island Pine and an ocean wave. Pūlama Lāna'i holds out the promise of a contemporary utopia based on entrepreneurship, workforce education, and a focus on individual and community wellness. Whether that vision can be realized without great expense to the land itself is a question that the many of the residents of Lāna'i see as central to their own well-being and prosperity. Kupa'a no Lāna'i, along with more centrist groups including Friends of Lāna'i and Lāna'ians for Sensible Growth, have worked in coalition with other interests throughout the islands to slow, if not halt, Murdock's "Big Wind" development plan and to keep Ellison's plans in check.

If capitalism is what makes possible the sale of this island and even the wind above it, then there is some irony in noting that rather than feudalism giving way to capitalism, as Karl Marx suggested, the two seem to exist on Lāna'i in a codependent relationship. Capitalism has made it possible for a series of wealthy men to buy the island and to impose and imprint their egos and fantasies on the land. Yet when those visions prove less than profitable or more difficult to realize, these owners turn the island over to the next highest bidder, so that Lāna'i is often on the verge of being abandoned by capitalism. Groups such as Kupa'a no Lāna'i refuse to accept capitalism as the inevitable and only conceivable way to organize their communities economically and politically, and they reject a rhetoric based on the fear of indebtedness to and dependency on landowners such as Murdock and Ellison.

In its work to educate people about the ahupua'a system, Kupa'a no Lāna'i holds the state and Ellison accountable, urging him "to think before you develop," as demanded in a video featuring two teenage girls from the group. They explain, "With every new development the land changes and is destroyed forever. We are too small, and our resources too unique and too significant to our history, to be devalued."[13] Like many other organizations in Hawaiʻi, particularly Native Hawaiian groups engaged in the struggle for sovereignty, Kupaʻa no Lānaʻi is committed to preserving and protecting the ʻāina. Many such organizational and educational efforts will be needed to dispel the fantasies and expose the false promises of the new feudalism. At the same time, such work insists on understanding the realities of the land, both its real vulnerabilities and its real potential to sustain vibrant, prosperous, and self-determining communities.

Notes

1 Julian Gutherie, "Larry Ellison's Fantasy Island," *Wall Street Journal*, June 13, 2013 https://www.wsj.com/articles/SB10001424127887324798904578529682230185530.

2 Morgan Brennan, "At Estimated 16 Cents PSF, Larry Ellison's Hawaiian Island Purchase Is a Steal," *Forbes*, June 21, 2012, http://www.forbes.com/sites/morganbrennan/2012 /06/21/at-estimated-16-cents-psf-larry-ellisons-hawaiian-island-purchase-is-a-steal/.

3 Robin Kaye, "Big Wind Has—Finally—Blown Over," *Honolulu Civil Beat*, August 22, 2017, accessed March 17, 2019, https://www.civilbeat.org/2017/08/big-wind-has -finally-blown-over/.

4 Sally Kaye, "Hi, Larry! From One of Lanai's Two Percent," *Civil Beat*, June 24, 2012, https://www.civilbeat.org/2012/06/16147-hi-larry-from-one-of-lanais-two-percent/.

5 Brittany Lyte, "Leaving Lanai: A Billionaire's Hawaii Could Displace Longtime Residents," *Aljazeera America*, February 14, 2016, http://america.aljazeera.com/articles /2016/2/14/leaving-lanai-larry-ellisons-hawaii.html.

6 Jonathan Kay Kamakawiwoʻole Osorio, *Dismembering Lahui: A History of the Hawaiian Nation to 1887* (Honolulu: University of Hawaiʻi Press, 2002), 44.

7 "Lanai City CDP, Hawaii Statistics and Demographics (US Census 2010)," accessed March 17, 2019, https://factfinder.census.gov/faces/tableservices/jsf/pages /productview.xhtml?src=CF.

8 Jon Mooallem, "Larry Ellison Bought an Island in Hawaiʻi. Now What?" *New York Times*, September 23, 2014, https://www.nytimes.com/2014/09/28/magazine/larry -ellison-island-hawaii.html.

9 Mooallem, "Larry Ellison Bought an Island in Hawaiʻi."

10 Brennan, "At Estimated 16 Cents PSF, Larry Ellison's Hawaiian Island Purchase Is a Steal."

11 Gutherie, "Larry Ellison's Fantasy Island."

12 Brennan, "At Estimated 16 Cents PSF, Larry Ellison's Hawaiian Island Purchase Is a Steal."

13 Hawaii People's Fund Grants Program, "Kupaʻa No Lanai," accessed March 17, 2019, http://changenotcharity.ning.com/video/kupa-a-no-lanai.

Lianne Marie Leda Charlie

Anini

In 2015, I was part of a University of Hawaiʻi class in which I had the privilege of working closely with the longtime families of Kalihikai, Kalihiwai, and (W)anini on the North Shore of the island of Kauaʻi. Throughout the course, we visited the community a number of times and met with some folks who grew up there. I learned that the community has seen a lot of changes over the

past fifty-plus years. With the guidance of our kumu (professor), we helped to record some of the local people's stories of change and resilience.

After one particularly powerful visit to the community, I was moved to create an image that captured the emotion and energy I was feeling after spending time with such vibrant and generous people. The image is a simple collage made of a digital line drawing of the shoreline over photographs of the sky above Kaua'i. But it aims to represent something much more complex. Between the lines, I invite you to see, hear, and feel . . .

A community, whose people demonstrate daily, and in their own special way, what it means to love and care for place.
The sound of the waves crashing on the reef.
Uncle Blue hugging and holding one of his young grandsons in his arms.
The cool silky waters of Kalihikai.
Kau'i's dad holding his baby grandson and singing "You Are My Sunshine" to him.
The view of the shoreline from out in Jerry's channel.
The chill of (W)anini stream.
The roosters.
Aunty Anabelle watching over everyone.
Made with love.

Mehana Blaich Vaughan, William Kinney, Jessica Kauʻi Fu, Aurora Kagawa-Viviani, Francesca Koethe, Cheryl Geslani, Lianne Marie Leda Charlie, Nicholas Kawela Farrant, Emily Cadiz, and Jordan Muratsuchi

---

Kahaleʻala, Haleleʻa
Fragrant, Joyful Home, a Visit to Anini, Kauaʻi

Aloha Anini e waiho nei
ʻOluʻolu i ke ahe a ka makani
Hoʻolono i ka owē mai ā ke kai
Neʻe mālie nei i Kalaehonu
Ka luli mālie lau o ka niu
Hoʻoheno ana me Pōhakukaʻa
Haʻina ʻia mai ana ka puana

Love to Anini laid out before me
Pleasant in the gentle breeze
Listen to the murmur of the sea
That swishes smoothly at Kalaehonu
The lazy swaying of the coconut leaves
Is lovingly serenading Pōhakukaʻa
The story is told
Loved is Anini, a beautiful land

—Mele composed by Aunty Alice Namakelua, October 10, 1959, during a visit to the Goo ʻOhana home at Wanini, Kauaʻi

Anini, a coastal stretch in Haleleʻa, Kauaʻi, encompassed by one of Hawaiʻi's largest fringing reefs, is a popular visitor destination for snorkeling, with a busy beach park and campground. Fewer than twenty full-time residents live along the coast. As recently as the 1960s, however, this coast was home to a thriving multiethnic community of twenty families who lived largely self-sufficient lives growing kalo (taro) and vegetables, fishing and harvesting

Anini, Haleleʻa, Kauaʻi. *Photograph by Mehana Blaich Vaughan.*

from the abundant reef. Today, only two of these twenty ʻohana (families) remain. The sleepy two-lane road, once the main highway, is now lined with luxury vacation rentals and second homes, and is empty much of the year. Local families face the effects of loss of access to coastal lands where they have lived for generations.

This story of Anini is meant to give insight into a place that most visitors only encounter as a pretty beach with snorkeling that falls short of their expectations. Descriptions from guidebooks, travel blogs, and real estate websites are interspersed with stories and place-names from nineteenth-century Hawaiian-language sources and quotes from interviews with thirty-five community members. Most of their families, many of whom lived here for generations, have had to move away, yet they return to hold reunions, care for the resting places of their ancestors, clean up, fish, harvest, camp, and pass on stories and lessons of home to their own children. Although the human and natural communities of this area have changed substantially within just a few decades, layered connections of people and place endure just below the surface of what most visitors see.

I. Beloved and Peaceful Home

Aloha Anini e waiho nei
ʻOluʻolu i ke ahe a ka makani

Love to Anini laid out before me,
Pleasant in the gentle breeze.

"The name used to be Wanini Beach but the W was blasted away with a shotgun by an irate resident who felt it had been misspelled. Other residents assumed the gun-toting spell-checker must have corrected a mistake and the 'new' name stuck. (That's typical Hawaii)."—Andrew Doughty, *The Ultimate Kauai Guidebook: Kauai Revealed*

The two-mile coastal strand known as "Anini," is sheltered by the third largest reef in the main Hawaiian Islands, reaching across three ahupuaʻa—Kalihiwai, Kalihikai, and Hanalei. "Anini," or "Wanini," is actually only a small section of this entire coastline, an ʻili (small land division) of the ahupuaʻa of Hanalei, stretching from the sandy point Ka Lae Honu, named for the turtles that once nested there, to the hill Puʻupehu. This area is also known as Mamalu ("calm" or "sheltered"), perhaps because it is protected from the stiff, prevailing trade winds that dominate the rest of the coast. Families from this place call their home "Wanini," which may come from "Wainini," meaning "poured, spilled, or trickling water," referring to the many springs in the cliffs that feed fresh water to the coast.

"The water was sweet, clear and clean."—Shorty Kaona, Hanapai, 2015

Large sharks troll the channel, Poʻomanaʻeo, near the river mouth, and once came inshore to birth. Snorkeling in this channel is not encouraged as multiple visitors have drowned.

"It was the ambience of the place. The atmosphere. The people, even though they; not family . . . was family. It was like a safe place—safe haven."
—Blondie Woodward, Kalihikai, 2015

II. Abundance of Land, Sea, and Community

Hoʻolono i ka ōwe mai ā ke kai
Neʻe m ā lie nei i Kalaehonu

Listen to the murmur of the sea
That swishes calmly at Kalaehonu

"There are numerous areas along this stretch of sand to swim, snorkel or just frolic. There is a polo field across from the beach; check it out if you're there during summer. Anini Beach is a good place to learn windsurfing. Camping is allowed with county permit . . . ."—Andrew Doughty, *The Ultimate Kauai Guidebook: Kauai Revealed*

"That's just how it was . . . everybody knew everybody. You had a real sense you were a part of a community, part of an extended family."—Jeremy Harris, Anahola, 2015

While most guidebook descriptions of this area describe this coast as a place for recreation, those who grew up here emphasize it as a place of sustenance, feeding, and community. The steady supply of abundant fresh water fed a thriving nearshore ecosystem and one of the healthiest coral reefs around the main Hawaiian Islands. Area elders recall seaweed so thick they could not see the holes in the reef and had to be careful not to fall in them as they walked on the coral to fish and gather.

". . . Before we used to walk and the limu [seaweed] was so long, we couldn't see where the holes [in the reef] were."—Carol Paik Goo, Wanini, 2015

Abundant seaweed meant plentiful food for fish. The name of the wind of this area is Ku'ula, also the name of the Hawaiian god of fishing. The reef's abundance and importance is also captured in a mo'olelo (story) of a pōhaku (stone) in the ocean there, which, when surrounded by fish, signals plentiful fish surrounding the whole island of Kaua'i. In the same story, one of the main characters, a chiefess, craves two famous reef delicacies of the area— he'e (octopus) from Kalihikai and wana (urchin) from Anini.[1]

Elders who grew up here describe abundant populations of over sixty-five different reef species, including fish, seaweed, and invertebrates, which their families ate or used for medicine:[2]

"I used to go with my grandfather, get 'oama, walk in the water and put my hand down and WOOOOSH. Choke. And diving first thing you get in the water you see fish . . ."—Llwelyn "Pake" Woodward, Kalihikai, 2015

One woman who grew up in Wanini remembered her grandmother walking across the road to the beach to catch reef fish for their breakfast:

"We'd wake up early in the morning . . . . She loved manini (convict tang), so she go over there catch manini. Then she go home, she make her breakfast, she always had fish and poi."—Marilyn Aniu Goo, Wanini, 2015

"The reef fed a self-sufficient and sharing lifestyle. Families procured most of what they needed to survive and thrive from the land and sea, only going to the store once a month to buy staples. Though the soil was sandy, families had vegetable gardens. Most also had spring- and stream-fed taro patches, some terraced up the cliffs. Taro also grew in the wetlands across from the present-day beach park, but these were later converted to rice paddies by Chinese families. The area even had a rice mill for a time, located on the site that later became the polo field. Small farms in the area, owned by local Japanese families, grew a variety of vegetables, including 'the biggest cucumbers you ever saw.'"—Gary and Haunani Pacheco, Kīlauea and Wanini, 2015

Families lived simply, and though many who grew up here referred to their ʻohana as "poor," they described lives of abundance and plenty because of their ability to obtain daily meals from the land and sea, and to share as a community:[3]

"Wherever we go, we shared what we had. That's how the Hawaiian custom was you catch, you go through somebody's property, be sure you give them some. My grandfather and grandmother taught us that. You never go through somebody's property and don't give them fish."—Verdelle Lum, Wanini, 2015

III. Changing Resource Health and Harvest

Ka luli mālie lau o ka niu
Hoʻoheno ana me Pōhakukaʻa

The lazy swaying of the coconut leaves
Is lovingly serenading Pōhakukaʻa

"The water can be very shallow, and the snorkeling can be good in many areas when visibility cooperates, though it seems to have been overfished."—Kathy Morey, *Kauaʻi Trails: Walks, Strolls and Treks on the Garden Island*

"We often went at night, and I knew it would be quiet then, so I tried to go back a few years ago. I hadn't been to look for heʻe there for at least ten years since I moved here to Anahola. But there were so many new houses with lights shining on the water, I couldn't see the reef to find the holes. Or the stars. There were always so many stars. I haven't gone back since."—Marilyn Aniu Goo, Wanini, 2015

The reef and coastal resources that once sustained area families with such abundance are now significantly degraded. Overfishing may have played a role in the decline. Elders shared concern that technological advances such as plastic masks, scuba tanks, spear guns, fine mesh nets, and freezers facilitate overharvesting. Other potential threats to resource health include warming ocean temperatures, the leaking cesspools of vacation rentals along the coast, and the introduction of invasive fish. While 50 to 80 percent live coral cover was measured at Anini in 1972, by 2014 over 80 percent of the coral had bleached.[4] Anini is one of the first coral sites in Hawai'i to develop black band disease, which is associated with land-based impacts.

Visitor industry–related developments on the Princeville Resort plateau lands above Anini seem to have affected both the quality and quantity of fresh water entering the coast. A study of Anini stream conducted in 1982 described clear water, 'ōpae (shrimp), and 'o'opu (goby), including at the river mouth where they fed on rocks. In 1989, after grading began for the Prince Golf Course built on the coastal bluffs above Anini, a repeat study found turbid water, sediment covering the bottom of the stream, and few native species.[5] A community member living in nearby Kilauea town has a pile of sixteen thousand golf balls displayed in his yard that he collected near the mouth of Wanini Stream.[6] In one recent storm, the yard nearest the stream was flooded with so many golf balls it appeared to have snowed. Golf balls take one hundred to ten thousand years to decompose and release heavy metals into water, including zinc from their inner core, which can poison surrounding marine life.[7] The area's plentiful rains likely wash fertilizers and herbicides into Wanini Stream and the ocean, along with runoff from condominiums on the bluff. Wanini Stream also runs below the county rubbish transfer station at Princeville. During heavy rains, water from the highway rushes below the trash receptacle, carrying contaminants such as battery fluid and oil into the stream.[8]

The lands across the stream, known as Puahiki, are still owned by the family who lived there over a century and a half ago. Two sisters from this 'ohana recall growing up with taro patches, two springs, and a system of bamboo pipes and chutes their grandfather built to bring water down the cliff behind their home for bathing and washing dishes. After the birth of each child, their father planted a fruit tree: rose apple, orange, and lime. Their grandfather is buried on the ridge above the land, where he used to climb to watch for schools of fish in the channel below.[9]

The graves now sit just off the ninth hole of the Prince Golf Course. The water trickling down the cliff runs through the golf course, some now diverted for ponds and water hazards. Marketing materials for recently proposed hyperluxury "club" developments at Princeville depict a grill, beach club, and stand-up paddling center at Puahiki for exclusive use by "members."[10]

Crossing over the stream and walking west past Puahiki leads you along the coast where area children used to harvest turtles and play in the swimming holes in the reef. The sea here is called Kai olena for the yellowish tinge to the water. Walk past the tents nestled into the roots of the false kamani trees at the base of the hillside. Observant visitors may notice a burnt metal frying pan hung on a nail in one tree, a bed built up on pallets under a tarp among the rocks. These are not camps but houses set up by area homeless and visitors extending their vacation indefinitely. No facilities are available, and those out for a stroll should watch for rusty cans, needles, and human feces among the rocks or buried in the sand. Shoes are highly recommended. Women are not encouraged to linger in this area alone.

IV. Loss of Lands and Access
Haʻina ʻia mai ana ka puana
Aloha Anini he ʻāina nani

The story is told
Loved is Anini, a beautiful land

"If your Hawaiian dreams include peace and tranquility amid unrivalled natural beauty, look no further than Anini Beach House . . . . Throw open your curtains each morning and discover why Kauai is nicknamed the Garden Isle. . . . On one side you'll have access to your own stretch of soft sugar sand, while the remainder of the grounds are enveloped by lush, tropical foliage. The exquisite 5-bedroom villa presents a unique interpretation of a 1950's [sic] tiki-chic home, updated to reflect modern standards of luxury . . . . Practice yoga on the verdant lawn or let your mind wander as the trade winds rock your hammock.—Listing for a 5 bedroom, 5.5 bath home, renting for $2,500–$5,000 per night, www .luxuryretreats.com, Anini Vista Drive Estate-115363

"We can't compete with billionaires. We're just simple people. It's just too much . . . pretty soon we lose our homes and everything we work for. We can't give anything to our grandchildren because we have to sell because . . . we can't afford to pay the taxes. So what little we save, hopefully for our children, it'll be all gone."—Carol Paik Goo, Wanini, 2015

In the shadow of development of Princeville Resort, Anini has transitioned from a peaceful residential community of twenty Hawaiian and plantation families, two churches, and no stores to a strip of transient vacation rentals and second homes. Kūpuna (elders) who grew up in Wanini and Kalihikai recalled playing on the beach all day with no one else in sight and even sleeping on the quiet roadway. Today, hundreds of visitors come to Anini on an average day, most of whom stay along the coast or in Princeville.[11] Use of the beach at the end of road has increased substantially since the Westin Hotel was built on the cliff above, and guests are encouraged to use the old highway trail down to the beach.

Where tourists used to simply visit, over the past twenty-five years many have bought land as a means to stay. Property sales in the neighboring Princeville Resort area, along with the proliferation of second homes and luxury vacation rentals along the coast, have caused property values to increase, raising taxes at Anini beyond what residents can afford. In 1990, actor Sylvester Stallone bought for $401,800 a parcel of land intended for expansion of the area's beach park. He built the first "second home" on the coast, along with a polo field, prompting subsequent sales and ever higher-end construction. The same house, now surrounded by other luxury properties, sold for $11 million in 2017.[12] Today, only 7 of 126 lots in the Anini area are occupied by residents for more than six months each year.[13] Of twenty 'ohana living on the coast in 1940, twelve still owned property in the area in 2015, but only two still lived there. In Wanini, all but two of the parcels awarded to Hawaiian families during land privatization in the 1850s are still held by descendants of the original awardees, making Wanini rare among all Hawai'i. However, all but one family on the coast said they were struggling to hold on to 'ohana lands, with outstanding tax bills ranging from $75,000 to $480,000.[14]

"This is a sad situation. For me, I can see [my 'ohana] there for at least my lifetime. I'm OK. But eventually the parcel will be gone. That's the heartbreak. And it's happening everywhere right now."—Haunani Pacheco, Wanini, 2015

"The last time I came home I went to Anini to say my goodbyes, thinking that would be the last time I could ever go home . . . . I walked off the stairs and walked down the beach. I wanted to cry thinking that the next time I come back I would just be a stranger looking into someone else's home."—Maile Aniu Piena, forty-five-year-old woman who was raised in Wanini but now lives on O'ahu, 2016

V. Beloved and Beautiful Land
Ha'ina 'ia mai ana ka puana
Aloha Anini he 'āina nani

Reprise: The story is told
Loved is Anini, a beautiful land

"Get more genealogical ʻohana to go back and fulfill responsibility. Take their kids there. Their keiki should learn to swim there, fish there . . ."—Kainani Kahaunaele, Kalihiwai, 2015

"We need to protect the area. Keep it from being overused, over-abused."—David Sproat, Kalihiwai, 2015

For relative newcomers, Anini is beautiful. They experience no sense of loss, only gratitude for its present beauty. Many who grew up in Wanini and Kalihikai wish their children and grandchildren could enjoy these places. Although the challenges of the present can seem insurmountable, families who have lost lands in the area still find ways to maintain a presence there. Some take daily walks along the coast; others return to fish. Many families hold all their family celebrations at the beach park, and some make it a point to camp here each year.

Community members are also working to limit further exclusive, high-end development in the area; to acquire lands for community stewardship, gathering, farming, camping, and education programs; to protect burials; to perpetuate place-names and stories; and to find ways to uphold the integrity, self-sufficiency, sharing, and the "simple life" of Wanini and Kalihikai. The essential values and character of this lifestyle live on in area families and in the beauty and resilience of this coast.

"My wish for the future is to have our children grow with a sense of responsibility at the forefront."—Nani Paik Kuehu, Wanini, 2015

"As change continues, at least connection will remain the same."—Kainani Kahaunaele, Kalihiwai, 2015

"For all this encroachment, you still find peace."—Blue Kinney, Hanalei, 2016

Notes

Authors include Haleleʻa community members with ancestral ties to this area and graduate students who participated in a University of Hawaiʻi at Mānoa class, "Kaiaulu Collaborative Care and Governance," focused on compiling knowledge of this area and who conducted the interviews referenced in this piece and coauthored four reports drawn upon extensively in this work. Written with Aloha for all the many community members and Kalihiwai, Hanapai, Kalihikai, and Wanini ʻOhana who contributed their manaʻo about their home: Wendell Goo, Carol Paik Goo, Nani Kuehu, Nadeen Woodward , Blondie Woodward, Jerry Kaialoa, Shorty Kaona, Jim Spencer, Marilyn Inoa Aniu, Linda Akana Sproat, David Sproat, Anabelle Kam, Sterling Chisolm, Sam Meyer, Kuualoha

Marilyn Inoa and family. *Photograph by Erica Taniguchi.*

Hoomanawanui, Verdelle Lum, Kainani Kahaunaele , Jim Maragos, Tom Pickett, Keith Nitta, Haunani Pacheco, Gary Pacheco, Gary Smith, Susan Wilson, Jeremy Harris, Sam Woodward, Llwellyn Woodwar. In loving memory of Uncle Sam Meyer, Aunty Anabelle Pa Kam, Uncle Chauncey Pa, and Aunty Verdelle Constance "Kealaokawaʻa" Peters Lum.

1   Aʻahōaka, published in Hawaiian Language newspaper, *Nupepa Kūokoʻa*, December 1877.

2   Kauʻi Fu, Billy Kinney, Mehana Vaughan, et al. "Aloha Anini e Waiho nei; Stories of Wanini, Kalihikai, and Hanapai, Kauaʻi." Unpublished report, 2015.

3   Emily Cadiz, Aurora Kagawa-Viviani, Noʻeau Peralto. "Anini to Kalihiwai: An ʻOhana-Centered Community." Anini Interviews: Culture and History Team Report. Unpublished report, 2015.

4   A. Russo. "A Preliminary Study of Some Ecological Effects of Sugar Mill Waste Discharge on Water Quality and Marine Life, Kīlauea, Kauaʻi." Technical report No. 31. School of Ocean and Earth Science and Technology, University of Hawaiʻi at Mānoa, 1971; B. Neilson. "Coral Bleaching Rapid Response Surveys: September–October 2, 2014." [PowerPoint slides]. Department of Land and Natural Resources, Division of Aquatic Resources.

5   A. S. Timbol, "Aquatic Macrofauna in Anini Stream, Kauaʻi," prepared for Belt, Collins and Associates, Honolulu: University of Hawaiʻi Sea Grant College Program, 1982; "Kauaʻi Climate Change and Coastal Hazards Assessment," 2014; D. Heacock, "Survey of Anini Stream: The Impact of Shoreline Developments on the Water Quality of the Stream and Nearshore Reef Ecosystems," 1989.

6 Jim Spencer, Kīlauea, 2015.

7 C. Macfarlane, "Golf Balls: Humanity's Signature Litter," CNN, November 10, 2009; J. G. Winter and P.J. Dillon, "Effects of Golf Course Construction and Operation on Water Chemistry of Headwater Streams on the Precambrian Shield," *Environmental Pollution*, 133, no. 2 (2005): 243–53. doi:10.1016/j.envpol.2004.05.037.

8 Ben Kuhaulua, Anahola, 2015.

9 Nani Paik Kuehu and Carol Paik Goo, Wanini, 2015.

10 Duane Shimogawa, "Kaua'i's Princeville Resort May Add Boutique Hotel as Part of $500M Redevelopment," *Pacific Business News*, November 19, 2014.

11 F. Koethe, "Community Perceptions and Priorities for Sustainability in Anini, Kaua'i," MA thesis, University of Hawai'i at Mānoa, 2017.

12 Duane Shimogawa, "Sylvester Stallone's Former Hawaii Estate Sold for $11M," *Pacific Business News*, March 27, 2016.

13 http://files.hawaii.gov/dbedt/op/gis/data/NIParcels.pdf.

14 http://qpublic9.qpublic.net/ga_search_dw.php?county=hi_kauai.

Halena Kapuni-Reynolds and Wendy Mapuana Waipā

Nā Pana Kaulana o Keaukaha

The Storied Places of Keaukaha

Hoʻokūʻonoʻono ka ʻāina i nā pulapula
ʻĀina hoʻopulapula hoʻi o nā kupa, ʻo **Keaukaha**
> The lands bring forth prosperity to the people
> (The) Hawaiian Homelands of the natives
> known as Keaukaha

ʻO Keaukaha ka home o **Puhi**
Kahi e lana ai ka wai, ka home ʻolu o ka ʻohana
> Keaukaha is the home of Puhi
> Where the waters are still
> the pleasant home of the (Nawahī) ʻohana

Kahi e pae mai ai ka nalu
E māewa ai ka wainaku i ke kai piʻi i **Kulapae**
> The place where the waves meet the shore
> Where the wainakū grass
> sways rhythmically in the ocean
> during high tide at Kulapae

Puaʻi ka wai māpuna
A wili ka wai au o waho, ʻo **Auwili**
> The springwater bubbles forth
> Mixing with the waters
> of yonder, (at the place called) Auwili

A ma ka lihi kai, hōʻea aku i **Keōkea**
ʻO ke ōkea i kaulana i ka hala kea, i ka loko iʻa,
    On the seashore, we arrive at Keōkea
    The sandy place that is famed
    for the white hala and the fishpond

I holo aku ka iʻa i kai ʻo **Keonekahakaha**,
Kahakaha maila nā lima o kanaka ma ke one
    The place where the fish
    swim in the sea, Keonekahakaha,
    where hands sketch in the sand

Aloha ʻia nō ka ʻāina o nā Hawaiʻi
Ka ʻāina i pā mau nā mēheu o nā kūpuna
    ʻO Keaukaha, ʻo Keaukaha nō ē!
    Beloved are the lands of our people
    The lands that continue
    to bear the footprints of our ancestors
    (The lands) of Keaukaha
    indeed of Keaukaha!

Hoʻolauna

ʻO Keaukaha ka ʻāina (Keaukaha is the land). ʻO Waiākea ke ahupuaʻa (Waiākea is the ahupuaʻa [a type of land division]). ʻO Hilo ka moku (Hilo is the district). ʻO Hawaiʻi ka mokupuni (Hawaiʻi is the island). This moʻolelo (story) is about Keaukaha on Hawaiʻi Island, and the wahi pana, or storied places, that can be found along its coastline. Like all moʻolelo, what is described here reflects *our* particular understanding and experiences of visiting these wahi pana with friends and family. Note that the wahi pana we describe here are only a few of those in Keaukaha. We chose to focus on six of these wahi pana because they have played a significant role in shaping our community.

Our various genealogical connections to the area are typical of families in Keaukaha. For instance, some ʻohana (family) have roots to this place that predate the establishment of the Hawaiian homestead of Keaukaha in 1924 under the Hawaiian Homes Commission Act of 1920 (Mapuana), and some ʻohana from other parts of Hawaiʻi settled in Keaukaha after receiving a lease to Hawaiian Homelands (Halena). Whether our ties to Keaukaha are recent or rooted in a deeper past, we recognize our kuleana (responsibility) to this ʻāina (land, that which feeds us), to our families, and to the ancestors of this land. Sharing the moʻolelo of our wahi pana is one way that we embrace this kuleana. As kama'āina, born and raised on these littoral lands and brackish waters, we honor our wahi pana through mele wahi pana to ensure that Keaukaha will continue to be cherished and protected for generations to come.

Mele wahi pana are Hawaiian songs that honor the beauty and stories of particular places. The late "Aunty" Edith Kanaka'ole, famed kumu hula (hula expert) and one of Keaukaha's first homesteaders, composed "Nā Pana Kaulana o Keaukaha" (The Famed Places of Keaukaha) in 1979 as a mele wahi pana to recount the storied places found along the Keaukaha coastline. Aunty Edith's mele takes the listener from place to place, starting with Palekai, the area where Hilo's breakwater meets the land, and ending with Leleiwi, a leina (place where spirits jump into the afterlife) near the Hilo/Puna boundary. As a child in the Hawaiian-language immersion program in Keaukaha, one of the authors (Halena) learned this mele and sang it while walking to these various places. In the mele that begins this essay, we build on Aunty Edith's mele by composing new mele wahi pana for Keaukaha.

About the Mele

The mele was written in 2011 by Halena Kapuni-Reynolds and is performed as an oli in the conversational-style of chanting known as kāwele. Wahi pana in Keaukaha are listed sequentially as they appear along the coastline. Beginning in the west (Hilo side) at Puhi Bay and ending in the east (Puna side) at Keonekahakaha, the mele preserves mo'olelo regarding the history and significance of each place within each line. We use the verses of the mele here as points of departure to recall our memories and knowledge of each place. Numerous other wahi pana can be found within and beyond the area covered in this mele. We use this limitation as an invitation for interested readers to learn more about our wahi pana by coming to Keaukaha and learning about our community and coastline through an excursion from one place to another, known as a huaka'i hele.

Keaukaha

Ho'okū'ono'ono ka 'āina i nā pulapula
'Āina ho'opulapula ho'i o nā kupa, 'o **Keaukaha**
> The lands bring forth prosperity to the people
> (The) Hawaiian Homelands of the natives
> known as Keaukaha

It is an early Saturday morning in mid-September. Kānehoalani (the rising sun) has already ascended from the depths of Kanaloa (god of the ocean)

Keaukaha. *Photograph by Lehuanani Waipā Ahnee.*

twenty miles away at *Kumukahi* in the *Puna* moku *(district).* The beauty of the vivid blue sky, populated sparsely by 'ōpua *(cumulus clouds)* floating lei-surely over the sea, is coupled by the calm ocean that beckons passersby to enter its refreshing waters. One by one, we arrive at *Puhi Bay.* We park along the yellow single-wire fence along *Kalaniana'ole Avenue.* Our visitors joining us on a tour today offer a mele komo *(chant requesting permission to enter).* We respond with a mele kāhea *(chant calling out to guests to enter),* welcom-ing them to our community. Together, we proceed to an old *kamani maoli* tree that gazes eternally at the piko *(navel, center)* of Hawai'i, Mauna Kea. Our huaka'i *(journey)* has begun.

Welcome to *Keaukaha,* our home. Today, we are going to take you folks on a walk along the coast to share with you some of the wahi pana, or storied places, that can be found in *Keaukaha.* Teaching others of our wahi pana, their names, and their stories is important because it ensures that the his-tory of our community remains in living memory. We tell these same sto-ries to the next generation of *Keaukaha* homesteaders so that they remain steadfast in their community by instilling within themselves a deep commitment to and love for the ʻāina that has sustained, and will continue to sustain, their ʻohana for generations.

The Hawaiian homestead of Keaukaha was established in 1924, but the name *Keaukaha* is much older. From our oral histories, we know that the old-time families of Keaukaha, such as the Malo ʻohana and the Kahaʻawi ʻohana, translated Keaukaha as the time (ke au) of writing (kaha), perhaps in reference to the development of Hawaiian literacy in the early nineteenth century. Later in our huakaʻi, we will visit Keonekahakaha, a place where, according to our kūpuna (elders), parents and grandparents would take their children to learn how to write, using the sand (one) as their personal writing pad (kahakaha). Other translations of Keaukaha emphasize the name's association with ocean currents (au), which refers to the numerous au that coalesce beyond the Keaukaha shoreline.

Keaukaha is rich in natural and cultural resources. If you ask our elders, many will tell you of the days of their youth gathering limu (seaweed) or catching ʻōhua (baby fish) early in the morning with their parents and grandparents. Some will even speak of the abundance of food that was and continues to be produced here. These moʻolelo are important to share because in the past, outsiders described Keaukaha as a barren and inhospitable place that was not suitable to raise our families. Needless to say, our ancestors proved them wrong. In recognizing the abundance that Keaukaha provided, this area was known as ʻĀina hoʻokūʻonoʻono, or lands that did and still bring forth prosperity for those who live here. Keep this in mind as we visit each wahi pana today.

Puhi

ʻO Keaukaha ka home o **Puhi**
Kahi e lana ai ka wai, ka home ʻolu o ka ʻohana
  Keaukaha is the home of Puhi
  Where the waters are still
  the pleasant home of the (Nawahī) ʻohana

From the kamani maoli tree we walk two hundred feet to the east along cut grass and ʻiliʻili (pebble-sized) stones. There we see a twenty-by-forty-foot tent, a few portable toilets under the shade of an ʻulu (breadfruit) tree, and a flagpole that prominently shows the Hawaiian flag. Cemented rock walls line the natural curve of the shoreline, providing the perfect ledge for children to jump into the crisp and clear waters that lie beyond. The tide is low at this

time of the day, allowing all to see the small springs that bubble forth from
the lava rocks, mixing with the saltwater in a never-ending, life-giving dance.

This is Puhi Bay. Across the street is where the first homestead lots in Keaukaha were created in 1924. Puhi is named for a blowhole that once existed in the area. It was destroyed during the construction of a raw sewage treatment plant that existed nearby for a few decades. A few years ago, the facility was converted into an aquaculture facility that grows fish and pearl oysters.

Because of its location in front of the homestead of Keaukaha, Puhi is a piko of the community. It is a piko because it is where many of our families celebrate the various stages of life, from birth to death. For the local schools in the community, Puhi is an outdoor classroom where we take our haumāna (students) to learn about their natural environment, their culture, and their history.

Although the beach park is officially called the "Keaukaha Beach Park," Puhi is not managed by the state. It is located on Hawaiian homelands and falls under the jurisdiction of the Department of Hawaiian Homelands. For decades, Puhi was overgrown with patches of wainaku grass and filled with trash that littered the coast. All of the improvements that you see here were undertaken by community elders who wanted to develop a safe place to spend time with their mo'opuna (grandchildren) and families.

The small pu'u (hill) in Puhi used to be the location of a beach home that was owned by Emma 'A'ima Nāwahī, an influential political leader during the late nineteenth and early twentieth centuries. Her home was known as Wailana (calm waters), and our ancestors met there during the 1920s to discuss their plans to fundraise and install infrastructure in Keaukaha in order to improve their living conditions.

As you will notice as we continue our walk, numerous springs can be found throughout this portion of the coastline. This is the reason that the waters here are colder than those at other beaches in Hawai'i. Although the waters are cool and the beach is rocky, Puhi is still a favored area for our community.

Kulapae

Kahi e pae mai ai ka nalu
E māewa ai ka wainaku i ke kai pi'i i **Kulapae**
    The place where the waves meet the shore
    Where the wainakū grass
    sways rhythmically in the ocean
    during high tide at Kulapae

Kulapae. *Photograph by Lehuanani Waipā Ahnee.*

Following the natural curve of the grassy coastline, we walk the length of Puhi until we reach a small banyan tree growing along Kalaniana'ole Avenue. Beyond it lies an old one-lane road that we walk on until we reach a small pu'u near a grove of kamani haole *whose far-reaching limbs tower over the coast's edge. We veer from the clearly paved pathway onto the grass, walking straight toward the ocean and past the kamani haole. Numerous* pōhaku *(rocks) line the shore on top of* pāhoehoe *(smooth lava) flats where limu and wainaku grass thrive. As the waves roll in and out, a symphony can be heard crashing gently on each and every pōhaku, producing a natural rhythm that is unique to the area. 'A'ama crabs scuttle along the pōhaku, searching for places to hide from the unexpected visitors.*

Here is Kulapae, an open field (kula) that used to be the location of a paena wa'a (canoe landing). Like Puhi, Kulapae is another area that the Keaukaha community uses heavily for various community and family functions. The English nickname of Kulapae is "Hawaiian Village," which refers to a series of thatched hale (houses) that were constructed here in the 1950s as an attraction and a place for community members to sell their arts and crafts to tourists who arrived in Hilo via cruise ship. You may have seen one of the ships on your way into the community when you passed by Hilo Pier.

Kulapae used to be home to a large pavilion, and like Puhi, it is where Keaukaha families hosted various lūʻau (large family gatherings) for all stages of life, whether a baby's first birthday, a community member's wedding reception, or a hoʻolewa (funeral). Longtime residents of Keaukaha still remember Kulapae as a place for community gatherings and festivities. Although the pavilion is long gone, Kulapae remains as a place where the lives of Keaukaha's people are honored and celebrated; the only difference is that nowadays we have to set up the occasional white canvas tent to house our celebrations.

Today, the thatched houses and pavilion of Hawaiian Village are long gone. All that remain are a paved road and a concrete slab that indicates where the pavilion once stood. Currently, the community plans to build a new pavilion and other related facilities at Kulapae. We hope to revitalize the space as a place where we can greet visiting groups of Kanaka ʻŌiwi and other Indigenous peoples, host community festivities, and provide our residents with a place to pursue their economic and cultural interests.

Auwili

> Puaʻi ka wai māpuna
> A wili ka wai au o waho, ʻo **Auwili**
> > The springwater bubbles forth
> > Mixing with the waters
> > of yonder, (at the place called) Auwili

Leaving Kulapae, we pass by a concrete foundation where the pavilion of Hawaiian Village once stood. A staircase leading down to the ocean can be seen as we make our way east toward Auwili. Descending another set of stairs, we pass a large banyan tree, which gives way to a rocky pond filled with calm, crystal-clear water that is ice-cold to the touch. Hapawai (a type of limpet) cover the pāhoehoe, while ʻōpae swim freely in the pond. Off in the distance, a small puʻu can be seen. We walk along the rocks toward the ocean, stepping carefully onto the wainaku grass that blankets the pāhoehoe beds. The smell of paʻakai (salt) and limu permeate the air.

This place is called Auwili, which means "the twisting currents." It refers to two currents (au) that are known to meet in the waters beyond this area. On a nearby puʻu is a house platform that used to be the home of the Kealohapauʻole ʻohana. We know through our oral histories that Kealohapauʻole are one of a few 'ohana whose lineages predate the establishment of the Keaukaha Homestead. Other 'ohana share these ancestral ties, and many of their descendants live in the homestead today. Below the foundation is a pāhoehoe basin that forms a natural saltwater pool.

Although most of the waters around Keaukaha are frigid because of the fresh water that bubbles from numerous springs along the coast, Auwili's waters are warm because the basin is filled with saltwater from the ocean, making it a favorite and safe place to teach young children how to swim. It is one of Mapuana's favorite wahi pana along the Keaukaha coastline, and it was somewhere she and her family frequented when she was a little girl. The pond we walked past at the base of this pu'u is known locally as "Cold Pond" for the simple fact that its waters are frigid. This was Halena's favorite pond as a child. He remembers jumping into its cool waters and counting the many hapawai and 'ōpae that can be found here. Children often run back and forth between each pond, jumping into the waters to warm up and cool down. Memories of swimming at these two places are shared by many Keaukaha residents.

Keōkea

A ma ka lihi kai, hō'ea aku i **Keōkea**
'O ke ōkea i kaulana i ka hala kea, i ka loko i'a,
> On the seashore, we arrive at Keōkea
> The sandy place that is famed
> for the white hala and the fishpond

Carefully descending down the pu'u at Auwili, we make our way north toward Apapane Road. We walk along the swerving pathway until we reach Lihikai Road, turning left onto a narrower alanui (road) to continue our journey back to the sea. Following the alanui, numerous manicured beach homes are seen on the Hilo side of the road. On the Puna side, we pass by large overgrown kamani haole trees growing in a thicket of grass and overlooking a hau-covered swamp. As we continue walking, the horizon reappears. We descend toward a peculiar white sand beach that is surrounded by beds of pāhoehoe lava, creating a natural barrier between the beach and the open ocean. Looking toward Hilo, one sees a pu'u pāhoehoe (pāhoehoe outcrop) with a small grove of hala growing on its peak.

We have finally reached Keōkea, one of the few places along the Keaukaha coastline that shows up on historical maps because of its strategic location. As the name of the area suggests, Keōkea, which literally refers to white sand (ōkea), is home to one of the few white-sand beaches in Keaukaha. In the

Keōkea. *Photograph by Lehuanani Waipā Ahnee.*

past, the area was also known to produce white hala, though we do not know whether this refers to the kī (fruits) or the lau (leaves). The swampy area that we just passed is also noteworthy, for it is one of the few areas left in Keaukaha where nānaku, the native bulrush, thrives.

In local museums, we find numerous historical photographs of Keōkea from the late nineteenth to early twentieth century. Whether they are scenic shots of its picturesque coastline, pictures of Kanaka ʻŌiwi who lived in the area, or images of malihini (visitors) sitting idly on a waʻapā (short canoe), it was and still remains a favorite place for malihini to visit in Keaukaha. In fact, through these images, we now know that there used to be a rock platform at the top of the puʻu. We are currently doing more research on this wahi pana in order to figure out what that platform was used for so we can better care for it in the future.

During the early twentieth century, Keōkea and the surrounding area underwent drastic changes. Lands that were initially leased by the government as grants to haole and Kanaka ʻŌiwi were eventually converted to fee simple title, resulting in the individual house lots that you see here today. Simultaneously, Keōkea and the surrounding coastline was designated as a state park that was named Lihikai Park. Over time, this designation resulted in the overdevelopment of the eastern portion of the park into a recreational swimming area. Luckily, Keōkea remains relatively untouched.

Keonekahakaha

I holo aku ka iʻa i kai ʻo **Keonekahakaha**,
Kahakaha maila nā lima o kanaka ma ke one
> The place where the fish
> swim in the sea, Keonekahakaha,
> where hands sketch in the sand

From Keōkea, we tread carefully along the uneven coastline, walking through patches of wainaku grass and pāhoehoe lava beds. We reach a point where we take turns entering the ocean, half submerged, to make our way to the other side of the path. Continuing along, the landscape changes. Pāhoehoe beds give way to concrete roads and wooden pavilions filled with numerous cars, trucks, locals, and tourists. The smell of burnt meat mixed with sunscreen fills the air. We walk along the cemented rock wall that follows the natural curve of the coast, stopping at an orange lifeguard shack that looks over a shallow, sandy beach. The beach is filled with children and their families.

This is the last place on our huakaʻi today. This place is known as Keonekahakaha, or Onekahakaha for short. Keonekahakaha is the most developed area that we have visited thus far. It provides us with a glimpse of what the various places that we visited on this huakaʻi might look like if they are designated as state parks and developed for recreational use. Although it is one of our most impacted wahi pana in Keaukaha, we continue to remember its history and try to recover the stories of this area and its significance to our ancestors.

In Aunty Edith Kanakaʻole's mele, "Nā Wahi Pana Kaulana o Keaukaha," she talks about a large kupua honu (supernatural sea turtle) that resided in the area. The honu was cared for by some of the families that used to live here.

A Mormon graveyard is also found here. It is the only physical reminder of the Mormon church that was built in the area in 1906.

The Journey's End

Four hours have passed since we first welcomed our guests. Kānehōʻālani no longer lingers near the horizon. He has reached the zenith, and his radiating heat now warms our salt-dusted bodies. The ʻōpua clouds have given way to clear blue skies. A sea breeze gently caresses our faces, providing cooling relief for the visitors who have treaded Keaukaha's storied coastline.

This concludes our walking tour of the Keaukaha coastline from Puhi to Keonekahakaha. The wahi paha that we visited are significant, for they are places that were and continue to be cherished by the Kanaka 'Ōiwi families that live next door in the Hawaiian homestead of Keaukaha. As suggested by the mele that guided our journey, we do these tours out of adoration and love for Keaukaha, its wahi pana, and its people. Although some of our ancestors are recent migrants to Keaukaha as a result of its designation as a Hawaiian homeland, our upbringing on and connection to the land and ocean in this place have made us familiar with its history, and have given us a kuleana to continually safeguard the wahi pana and treasured resources of this place. We are tasked with learning and retelling the stories of Keaukaha's first inhabitants to the next generation of Keaukaha homesteaders.

Aunty Edith's mele, "Nā Pana Kaulana o Keaukaha," makes references to our link to Keaukaha's ancestors through the line "pā mau i ka mēheu o nā kūpuna" (resounding to the footsteps of our ancestors). This refers to our kūpuna's movement across Keaukaha's landscape and our retracing of their footsteps through mele and huaka'i. It is this same line that the line "Ka 'āina i pā mau nā mēheu o nā kūpuna" in our mele pays tribute to. This line of the mele reminds us of the ways that we follow in the footsteps of our ancestors, whether by passing down ancestral knowledge in the form of wahi pana, or the ways in which we choose to raise our 'ohana. We will continue to tread in the footsteps of our ancestors, teaching the keiki (children) of our wahi pana along the way. And one day, our keiki too will leave their footprints for the future generations.

> Aloha 'ia nō ka 'āina o nā Hawai'i
> Ka 'āina i pā mau nā mēheu o nā kūpuna
> 'O Keaukaha, 'o Keaukaha nō ē!
>> *Beloved are the lands of our people*
>> *The lands that continue*
>> *to bear the footprints of our ancestors*
>> *(The lands) of Keaukaha*
>> *indeed of Keaukaha!*

PART II. **Hana Lima /
Decolonial
Projects and
Representations**

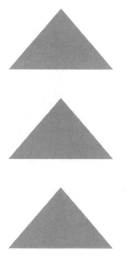

▶▶▶

The contributors to this collection are all committed to material decolonization through the restoration of practices and transformative projects in diverse communities across the pae 'āina (the archipelago). This section is titled "Hana Lima," which means "working with the hands," in order to single out the importance of putting "muscle power" behind the work of creating new visions and kīpuka (oases) of decolonial life. Hana lima is also the labor of restoring, reestablishing, and reaffirming the relationships between people and places through actions based on aloha 'āina. The work of decolonizing must take place in multiple arenas: it requires labor of the mind, the heart, and the hands. The craft, skill, and effort that are marshalled on many fronts in order to generate a new imagination of and future for Hawai'i are highlighted in this section. These essays, art, reflections, and political actions make space for and defend Kanaka 'Ōiwi sovereignty, restore and invigorate cultural practices and knowledge, and mobilize the people of Hawai'i, Native and non-Native alike, in working toward ea.

We begin this section with an image of a painting by Nanea Lum, which expresses a connection to place "beyond the measure of words." It is followed by a poetry-prose essay by No'u Revilla and Jamaica Heolimeleikalani Osorio, who expand our understanding of aloha—its creative and generative power for decolonial work—and thus challenge touristic notions and appropriations of this term. Creating and holding space for cultural protocol through the practice of hula, Maya L. Kawailanaokeawaiki Saffery describes the intentionality that informed her hālau's ceremony welcoming the voyaging canoe *Hōkūle'a*, and how this transformed the community and space in Kailua, O'ahu. Decolonial work demands creative tactics that can contend with the ubiquity of colonialism. Using and perverting the form of the tourist postcard, Karen K. Kosasa and Stan Tomita note the work that Asian settlers in Hawai'i need to enter into as allies to a place that continues to deal with the aftermath of overthrow.

Decolonial work describes the heavy emotional and physical labor of defending and upholding 'Ōiwi cultural practices in the face of various assaults, and the kinds of shifts in thinking and action these efforts have wrought. Malia Akutagawa narrates the process through which people from Moloka'i demanded concessions from visiting cruise ships and their passengers, resulting in a reciprocity agreement on their terms. Noelle M. K. Y. Kahanu pens a love letter to the Bishop Museum, documenting how cultural institutions make space for histories and cultures that are otherwise marginalized, the power they have to validate a people, and the work that Kanaka 'Ōiwi have done to demand accountability from institutions such as these. In fostering new imaginations of Hawai'i, Joy Lehuanani Enomoto asks us to think about the botanical garden and the desires that shaped it, and to imagine what a Native forest did and could look like. Gregory Chun reports how a redefinition of "highest and best" use of Hawaiian land for one of Hawai'i's most powerful landholders transformed land-as-asset back into land-as-'āina.

The act of expressing refusal is critical to decolonization. David Uahikeaikalei'ohu Maile describes the sustained testimony of Native Hawaiians against the federal "gift" of tribal recognition, a tradition that resonates with multiple refusals in Hawaiian history. Iokepa Casumbal-Salazar recounts the stand that Native and non-Native people in Hawai'i have taken and continue to take against the further desecration of Mauna a Wākea in the face of the ongoing struggle being waged around this sacred site.

Finally, in this section we look to examples of building a new vision of Hawai'i that is steeped in the pono practices of tradition as expressions of ea. P. Kalawai'a Moore describes how the skills of building Hawaiian houses and heaiu are being revived in Hāna, Maui, to change the built environment of the island and to restore Kanaka 'Ōiwi pride in the knowledges of our ancestors. Malia Nobrega-Olivera writes a love letter to her child, outlining a promise to uphold their traditional family practice of salt-making against the encroachments of climate change. Finally, Kalaniua Ritte, Hanohano Naehu, Noelani Goodyear-Ka'ōpua, and Julie Warech narrate the story of restoring Keawanui Fishpond on Moloka'i, outlining the physical and emotional demands of this labor of love and the rewards of rediscovering deep connections to the lands and waters of Hawai'i.

The diversity of the projects arrayed in this section reflect the rich creativity and manifold tactics of decolonial work that are needed to bring a vision and reality of ea into being.

Nanea Lum

_____

Ke Kilohana

Ke Kilohana is contemplative of a place, where body and mind behold a space that exists beyond the measure of words. "Kilohana is the highest point of a mountain's reach into the clouds. It is the highest point of elevation on the Ko'olau mountain ridge seen from Kaneohe and from the bay, but never truly seen." The people living in places below this mountain's face are astonished by its impossible heights and mysterious beauty. The Hawaiian word _Kilohana_ means "lookout," "high point," "top," but it also is used to describe excellence beyond measure of words.

No‘u Revilla and Jamaica Heolimeleikalani Osorio

Aloha Is Deoccupied Love

What is Aloha? According to Mary Kawena Pukui and Samuel H. Elbert, aloha denotes a complex set of practices and relationships. In the *Hawaiian Dictionary*, aloha is defined in the following way:

> love, affection, compassion, mercy, sympathy, pity, kindness, sentiment, grace, charity; greeting, salutation, regards; sweetheart, lover, loved one; beloved, loving, kind, compassionate, charitable, lovable; to love, be fond of; to show kindness, mercy, pity, charity, affection; to venerate; to remember with affection; to greet, hail. Greetings! Hello! Good-by! Farewell! Alas![1]

Demonstrably, aloha has mind, body, and spirit. Made alive through generative and honest interactions, aloha is possible when we share things—whether breath, food, shelter, storytelling, information, or desire—with others in sustainable ways. Aloha requires reciprocity and responsibility. While the word is a common expression in Hawai‘i nei, particularly in greetings, it is important to remember that aloha is not tourist-oriented; the practice does not exist for consumption, purchase, or display. Aloha cannot be owned like property, like a souvenir.

What is Occupation? *Occupation* is, in one sense, a legal term that describes extended military invasion of one country by another. By definition, occupation is temporary. Yet in Hawai‘i, occupation by the U.S. military has been ongoing since the end of the nineteenth century. Deoccupation, therefore, requires demilitarization. Deoccupation requires investing in ‘Āina and Kanaka as more than pawns of profit. Deoccupation is the process by which Kanaka Maoli practice historically inspired, life-affirming futures rooted in the ʻāina. In this way, deoccupied love does not possess, does not profit, does not bomb, does not overstay its welcome. Deoccupied love is invited, gives and receives pleasure, and values ongoing, enthusiastic consent. Deoccupied love resists metaphor, is practiced, is informed action. Deoccupied love believes in decolonization and does not surrender sovereignty. Deoccupied love is ea, beginning in our manawa and always, always rising.

Unfortunately, since the arrival of foreigners to Hawaiʻi in 1778, aloha has been seriously fucked with. The sexing and selling of Native bodies, particularly Native women's bodies, continues to define Hawaiʻi to the outside world, and the expectation of "getting leiʻd" upon arrival persists. Although aloha is a living Indigenous practice that ably straddles sexuality, sovereignty, and kinship, it is gratuitously sold as exotic Native love. In the shared labs of colonialism, global corporate tourism, militarization, and heteropatriarchy, aloha has been genetically modified into a diseased host. American colonialism uses aloha as an alibi; tourism uses aloha as a commodity; New Age peddlers of Polynesian sorcery use aloha to gloss over settler identity; and politicians use aloha to define our people as "happy hosts," punishing us when we go off script—when we refuse to perform. Even so-called Christians use aloha to outlaw love even though aloha did not begin in a church and is bound to neither Christianity nor heterosexuality. Aloha is much more than this.

Our aloha is born from the power of creation, as established in our moʻolelo.

Let us be clear: aloha does not carry the limitations of tolerance or economy-driven ploys to attract more visitors; it is not just "hello" and "goodbye." Aloha is a complex set of practices and relationships that keep the integrity of our ʻāina, ʻohana, and lāhui at the center. Born from the power of creation, established in our moʻolelo.

Mele Kumu Honua

ʻO Wākea noho iā Papahānaumoku
Hānau ʻo Hawaiʻi, he moku
Hānau ʻo Maui, he moku
Hoʻi hou ʻo Wākea noho iā Hoʻohōkūkalani
Hānau ʻo Molokaʻi, he moku
Hānau ʻo Lānaʻi, Ka ʻula, he moku
Liliʻōpū punalua ʻo Papa iā Hoʻohōkūkalani
Hoʻi hou ʻo Papa noho iā Wākea
Hānau ʻo Oʻahu, he moku
Hānau ʻo Kauaʻi, he moku

Hānau ʻo Niʻihau, he moku
He ʻula aʻo Kahoʻolawe

This mele koʻihonua, or genealogical chant, provides one story of how our ancestral land was born. In the first three lines of the koʻihonua we learn that Papa, our foundation, our earth-birthing goddess, and Wākea, our wide-open sky, our deity of the heavens, share aloha. From their union, the islands Hawaiʻi and Maui are born as siblings. In lines four through six, Wākea leaves Papa to share aloha with their daughter, Hoʻohōkūkalani, and from their union, Molokaʻi and Lānaʻi are born as siblings. When Papa and Wākea come together again in lines seven through twelve, the islands of Oʻahu, Kauaʻi, Niʻihau, and Kahoʻolawe are born. While this mele koʻihonua features Wākea as the only father, other moʻolelo, or stories, identify multiple parents. Does this make us savages? ʻAʻole. Does this mean we possess no honor or dignity in the ways we love, live, and relate our bodies? ʻAʻole. Our outstretched kinship is a source of strength.

Another mele koʻihonua is the Kumulipo. According to this creation story, Native Hawaiian gods, lands, waters, and people emerged as articulations of Pō and Ao. Its 2,102 lines of world-making are divided into sixteen wā: the first eight wā emerge in Pō, the generative, ancestral blackness from which all life issued; the next eight wā emerge in Ao, or light. Creation time is pono. References to these Hawaiian categories of space and time constitute a political act that reinforces ʻŌiwi conceptions of world-making, genealogy, and belonging. We use our language to return to our bodies. We use our bodies to return to our lands. As ʻŌiwi poets, we recognize that the Pō in our bodies is pili to the Pō in our art and activism. That hot, churning blackness. That blackness that births.

moʻolelo—kino—ʻāina

The word *hōʻao*, for instance, we put in our mouths. Hōʻao means "to stay until daylight," marking the space and time in which lovers bring in the day together. From Pō to Ao. Hōʻao. When we invoke the Kumulipo and call what we do "hōʻao," we are saying we have spent creation together.

stories—bodies—lands

Aloha is deoccupied love.

Whether turning to the Mele Kumu Honua or the Kumulipo, Kanaka ʻŌiwi understand that our islands are siblings, their genealogies and ours an intricate ʻupena, or fish net, of relations. Indeed, Hawaiian culture values who you are and how you are connected, related, accountable. Specifically, our kūpuna valued how we nurtured our connections to ʻāina, lāhui, akua, kuleana, each other. Our moʻolelo remind us that our bodies are extensions of our lands. When we say aloha is deoccupied love, we not only declare our love of ʻāina and lāhui but also, more importantly, that in our love, we will resist and rise.

In the mid-nineteenth century, while missionaries and Kanaka Maoli converts published articles chastising any aloha blossoming beyond the confines of Christianity, and courts punitively legislated the desiring Hawaiian body, Hiʻiaka a wahine and Nānāhuki a wahine shared aloha at the shore of Hāʻena. Sharing hula, names, surfboards, and breath. Born from their union in the Moanianilehua wind was the lehua grove of Hōpoe. Bringing in mornings together, Hiʻiaka and Nānāhuki become more than hōʻao; they become aikāne, intimate companions and lovers.

And we feel this genealogy in our moʻolelo.
We watch as they share a single surfboard and carve the faces of breaking waves.
We hear the pahu bellowing as their bodies ʻoni against each other.
We listen to the rage and mourning in Hiʻiaka's kanikau as Nānāhuki and her lehua grove are set ablaze.
We answer their love memorialized in stone.
We watch as Nānāhuki's lehua is the first to sprout out of Pele's pāhoehoe.

Hiʻiaka and Nānāhuki remind us that after new land is created by fresh lava flow, it is the aloha between them that makes the forest flourish again. The ʻōhiʻa lehua is one of the first plants to grow roots in newly formed lava; it is capable of blossoming from near sea level to over seven thousand feet in wao akua. Like this unsurpassed blossom, aloha is resilient and thrives in many forms. In other words, Hiʻiaka and Nānāhuki remind us that aloha is radical. That radical means roots, and Hiʻiaka and Nānāhuki demonstrate how aloha endures—through destruction, pain, death, and jealousy. Our kūpuna wrote, read, and savored the aloha between these wāhine, who are still waiting for us to meet them in the nāhele.

In 1912, Alice Everett composed the mele "Ua Like no a Like" to celebrate a blossoming relationship between two young lovers in Hilo. Wahi a ke mele, these lovers are called by the playful Kanilehua rain to share aloha in the forest at dusk. The rain is not backdrop but an active lover, and evening after evening the young kāne and wahine are wet with desire and take pleasure together in the forest, only to return before morning. Yet one day, as the Kanilehua mists the lovers' cheeks and lips, they realize they have brought in the morning together. Hōʻao has made them paʻa i ka poli, bound together in love, in the creation of day.

> We trust creation.
> We choose to feel.
> Even when our lehua is set on fire and hardened to stone.
> We plant seeds for tomorrow, for more lehua to follow.

Fundamental to our culture and identity, aloha is an ʻŌiwi ethos of connectivity. In addition to our bloodlines and cultural heritage, we use aloha to navigate our affective networks. What intimacies have we earned? What ways of knowing each other have we cultivated properly? Aloha is judicious and collaborative, and in its intergenerational practice—even if quietly, in order to survive—aloha embraces vulnerability. Of course, that vulnerability is not *come and bomb the kingdom in our chest and commemorate our ruin with a state holiday.* Vulnerability is not *come and poison our waters, divert and privatize our rivers, bottle them industriously, and sell it back to us as waters of life incorporated.* Vulnerability is not *come and desecrate where we are sacred, where worship happens, where gods happen.* Vulnerability is not suffering the violence of settler colonialism, patriarchy, and homophobia and vowing to harden against the world. Aloha is the audacity to feel. Pleasure as well as pain. Play as well as torment. The opposite of violence is creation. We want to create with each other, again and again and again. From Pō to Ao. We spend the night. And when I sleep with you, I sleep with all of your ancestors.

Manu ʻŌʻō

ʻO ka manu ʻōʻō i mālama
A he nani kou hulu ke lei ʻia
Mūkīkī ana ʻoe i ka pua lehua
Kāhea ana ʻoe i ka nui manu

Hui:
Hō mai ʻoni mai
Ko aloha ma nēia
Kīhene lehua

Nō Hilo ē ka ua Kanilehua
Popohe lehua ai Hanakahi

Hoʻokahi aʻu mea nui aia ʻoe
ʻO kou aloha ua hiki mai

Precious honey-eater
Your beautiful and soft feathers are woven into a lei
You sip the lehua blossoms
And are called away by other birds

Chorus:
Come, come to me
To you beloved
Lehua cluster

Your lehua-sounding rain of Hilo
Decorative lehua of Hanakahi
One greatest thing I love is you
Your lover has come
"Manu ʻŌʻō (Black Honey-eater)—Traditional," *Huapala*

Aloha makes good love because in aloha we make good connections. Like in the curve of a woman's arching back, we embody this nectar-seeking as lovers. And in this aloha, the manu wahine penetrates. Over and over and over.

> *the curve of your hips*
> *mūkīkī ana ʻoe*
> *the same curve as an ʻŌʻō bird's beak*

We are satisfied, their backs still arching. In language, satisfaction comes as mūkīkī. What birds do to lehua. Mūkīkī ana ʻoe i ka pua lehua. To sip, suck in the mouth, make sucking noises, to squirt water through teeth, to kiss. Manu ʻŌʻō beautifully reimagines gender roles and norms of pleasure. Who sips and who gets sipped. Mūkīkī ana ʻoe.

> *my worship*
> *my medicine*
> *my nectar-seeking morning*

Aloha is a capacious and generative force of revolution. Papa and Wākea conceived islands, whereas Hiʻiaka and Hōpoe conceived lehua. Today, some kānaka conceive children while others conceive loʻi, mele, schools, and poetry. Some ʻŌiwi identify as heterosexual, homosexual, bisexual, pansexual, asexual, queer, polyamorous, monogamous, slutty, shy, vanilla, kinky, quiet, loud—moe aku, moe mai. Aloha spends the night, wears a strap-on, requires ongoing and enthusiastic consent, cums, ʻōlelo Hawaiʻi, gives keynotes, protects sacred places, grows kalo, carries baby, cooks for grandma, gets dirty lickens, jumps waterfalls, signs antiannexation petitions, weaves baskets, looks you in the eyes, and will not be silenced. Aloha is far too vast, imaginative, and sexy to be reduced to only one man and one woman under one god. Check your sources, check your naʻau. Indeed, we do not offer a singular body of aloha. There is no one body, no one love, no one way to spend creation. Commit this Hilo mele to memory. See where this aloha takes you as it follows a female ʻŌʻō bird as she leaps from lehua blossom to lehua blossom, penetrating the delicate flowers with her long, curved beak.

Note

1   A note on Hawaiian language: In this chapter the authors use Hawaiian language terms without parenthetical citations. To maintain the poetic integrity of this piece, we direct readers to consult the Hawaiian language dictionary online at wehewehe .org to learn denotative and connotative meanings of untranslated terms, or refer to the Glossary of Terms in this volume.

References and Resources

Kanahele, Pualani. "E Ala E," Traditional Chants, *Mauna Kea*. Accessed May 29, 2018. www.mauna-a-wakea.info/maunakea/l2_traditional.html.

The Kumulipo: An Hawaiian Creation Myth. Translated by Liliʻuokalani. Kentfield, CA: Pueo, 1978.

"Manu ʻŌʻō (Black Honey-eater)—Traditional," *Huapala*. Accessed May 29, 2018. www.huapala.org/Man/Manu_Oo.html.

Pukui, Mary Kawena, and Samuel H. Elbert. *Hawaiian Dictionary*, rev. ed. Honolulu: University of Hawaiʻi Press, 1986.

Simpson, Leanne. *Islands of Decolonial Love*. Winnipeg, MB: ARP, 2013.

Maya L. Kawailanaokeawaiki Saffery

Sovereign Spaces

Creating Decolonial Zones through Hula and Mele

A moʻolelo about the greeting of *Hōkūleʻa* by the poʻe hula of Kailua.

On October 16, 2013, the skies over Kailua Beach were clear and the ocean was calm. On such a beautiful day, one would expect to see "America's Best Beach" covered with beach towels and Tommy Bahama lounge chairs; the water full of ABC Store boogie boards ridden awkwardly by sunscreen-soaked foreigners; the outer reefs and small islets cluttered with brightly colored kayaks rented by the hour; and the sky distorted by the kites of surfers speeding through the waves and launching themselves into the air.[1] Unfortunately, when residents and visitors think of Kailua today, these are the images that usually come to mind. People do not typically think of Kailua as a site of Hawaiian decolonization and resurgence, but on that particular afternoon in October 2013, that is exactly what the poʻe hula (hula practitioners) of Kailua created.

Kailua is an ahupuaʻa, or traditional land division, in the district of Koʻolaupoko on the island of Oʻahu. I am a kupa (Native) of this ahupuaʻa and a practitioner of traditional hula. I received my hula training in Kailua and continue to practice my culture and make my home in this ahupuaʻa. In the eyes of many local people (Hawaiian and non-Hawaiian), Kailua has become a playground for malihini (visitors, foreigners)—a place too pricey to live in, too touristy to feel comfortable in, too developed to recognize. In fact, the settler colonial forces that have shaped Kailua are the same ones that box in and distort how hula is practiced, viewed, and experienced across Hawaiʻi today. However, the moʻolelo (story) that I share below describes how the 2013 greeting of the Hawaiian double-hulled voyaging canoe *Hōkūle'a* in Kailua Bay enabled our community to shatter, at least for a few hours, the settler imaginary that has been placed over us. We left lasting cracks in its facade where alternative images of Kailua and its people can shine through.[2] **We used our voices and bodies to fill the sand, sea, and air with words and stories, allowing these cultural expressions to reoccupy a space that has become highly colonized and to create a protected, decolonial zone where we controlled how people witnessed and engaged with us and our 'āina (land).**

Before I describe the ceremonial exchange of hula, mele (songs, chants), and ha'i 'ōlelo (Hawaiian language oratory) that took place between the po'e hula of Kailua and our hoa wa'a (wa'a friends) from *Hōkūle'a* on that beautiful day in 2013, I need to first go back in time. I recount the birth of *Hōkūle'a* over forty years ago and the impact that her very existence had on our lāhui (people, nation). I then jump forward to just over a decade ago, when *Hōkūle'a* first sailed into Kailua Bay in 2005, and describe the impact that her first landing had on our hula community of Kailua. Both of these events were foundational in shaping and influencing the ceremonial exchange that occurred on that calm, sunny afternoon in 2013 on ke one o Kūali'i (the sands of Kūali'i).

Hānau Hōkūle'a, he wa'a kaulua

[Born was Hōkūle'a, a double-hulled voyaging canoe]

In 1975, *Hōkūle'a* was born from the sands of Hakipu'u, Ko'olaupoko, O'ahu, and launched into the waters of Kāne'ohe Bay. She became a symbol of Hawaiian excellence and hope for the future of our lāhui upon the success of her first voyage from Hawai'i to Tahiti in 1976, using only the ocean swells, stars, sun, moon, clouds, and birds to guide her way. At that time, more people in Hawai'i thought *Hōkūle'a* and her crew would fail than thought they would accomplish their goal of reviving Polynesian voyaging. In the eyes of the majority of people who lived in Hawai'i at the time, including

▶ **Kūali'i**

Kūali'i (or Kua-ali'i Kūnuiākea Kuikealaikauaokalani) was an ali'i nui (high-ranking chief) born in Kala-pawai, Kailua, O'ahu, and who reigned during the seventeenth and early eighteenth centuries. Just like his great-great-grandfather Kākuhihewa, Kūali'i ruled the island of O'ahu from Kailua during much of his reign. Kūali'i is forever tied to Kailua after his piko (umbilical cord)–cutting ceremony was performed at the heiau (shrine/altar) of Alāla to the voices of the sacred pahu (drums) 'Ōpuku and Hāwea. When we greeted *Hōkūle'a* and her crew after they landed in our ahupua'a, we did so literally in the shadow of Alāla, which is located on the ridge just above the Kailua boat ramp. Therefore, I honor an ali'i nui of O'ahu and kupa of Kailua when I poetically refer to the spot on Kailua beach where our arrival ceremony occured as "ke one o Kūali'i."

Kānaka (Native Hawaiians), anything Hawaiian was just not good enough to succeed.

Occupation and colonization by American missionaries and their descendants for more than 150 years had planted seeds of self-loathing and doubt in the naʻau (gut) of many Kānaka who came to believe that our traditions, culture, language, and knowledge systems were inferior to those of our colonizers and that the only way to survive would be to shed our ʻŌiwi (Native Hawaiian) identities and assimilate into American society. Before Hōkūleʻa, no waʻa kaulua (double-hulled voyaging canoe) had been built or navigated in the way of our ancestors for a few hundred years. People began to forget the stories of how our kūpuna (ancestors) traveled ka Moananuiākea (the vast, deep ocean) on large sailing canoes, navigating back and forth between some of the most remote islands in the world using only the natural elements to guide them. Instead, people accepted dominant theories of the time, which suggested that our ancestors were not skilled enough to purposefully discover and populate every livable land mass in the Pacific but rather made their way by accident, drifting at the mercy of ocean currents and winds.

A small group of individuals led by Herb Kawainui Kane, Ben Finney, and Tommy Holmes (the founders of the Polynesian Voyaging Society) refused to believe these demeaning, yet popular, theories. Instead they returned to our own moʻolelo about our great voyaging chiefs and chose to believe that, as descendants of these aliʻi holo moana (voyaging chiefs), Kānaka could sail in the wake of our ancestors once again. Their courage and radical imagination paid off. In 1976, Hōkūleʻa and her crew successfully sailed from Hawaiʻi to Tahiti in thirty-four days and were greeted by over seventeen thousand Tahitians—more than half of the island's population. Since that first voyage, Hōkūleʻa has successfully traveled over 150,000 nautical miles throughout the Pacific and now around the world using noninstrument navigation. These traditional methods of navigation went unpracticed in Hawaiʻi until Pwo Navigator Pius Mau Piailug from the island of Satawal in Micronesia agreed to teach Hawaiians to sail like our kūpuna once again. Now, Kānaka will always know that we could—and still do—navigate our canoes using the stars and swells in order to, like Māui, "pull small islands from the sea."

After Hōkūleʻa's first voyage along our ancestral route to Tahiti, a fire that had laid dormant within our people for decades was reignited. Kānaka were proud to be Kanaka again, and things Hawaiian were no longer associated with shame and failure but instead were evidence of our people's bravery, intelligence, ingenuity, and resilience. This renewed pride inspired Kānaka and our allies to fight to protect our sacred sites from development and military expansion; to organize against forced evictions of farmers and other communities; to struggle for the return of wai (water) to our many waterways; to revitalize ʻōlelo Hawaiʻi through the opening of Hawaiian-language immersion schools and university programs; and to perpetuate hula and other cultural and spiritual practices in the contexts for which they were originally intended.

Ua hiti ē ʻo Hōkūleʻa ē
[Hōkūleʻa has arrived]

This is a reference to a line from a mele from the repertoire of Ka ʻOhana Waʻa, written by Pua Case, and is used to celebrate the arrival of Hōkūleʻa.

Hōkūleʻa arrives in Kailua. After three decades of voyaging throughout Hawaiʻi and Polynesia, Hōkūleʻa made her first landing in my ahupuaʻa of Kailua on May 1, 2005. Her arrival was a part of the Mālama Kailua Festival that recognized the achievements of students from four Kailua schools in increasing public awareness of issues affecting Kailua's ocean ecosystems. The work of more than six hundred students to learn about and share with our community how to better care for the shorelines and seascapes of our ahupuaʻa resonated with the Polynesian Voyaging Society, which led them to acceptance an invitation to help open the festival by bringing Hōkūleʻa to Kailua.

This arrival was a historic event for many reasons. It marked the first time in Hōkūleʻa's thirty years that she would sail into Kailua. This is significant because Kailua is an ahupuaʻa that was not only the birthplace and seat of power of ruling chiefs of Oʻahu for centuries but also an ʻāina that is tied to some of our most celebrated navigators and voyaging chiefs, such as Paumakua and Kauluakalana. Sailing into Kailua Bay allowed the navigators and crew of Hōkūleʻa to connect themselves to the larger voyaging genealogies of our kūpuna while at the same time expanding those genealogies to include Hawaiʻi's latest generation of waʻa kaulua and holo moana. My kumu hula (hula teacher), Māpuana de Silva, recalls that Hōkūleʻa's arrival was also a significant moment for the hula community of Kailua because it was the first

> ▶ **Paumakua and Kauluakalana**

Paumakua and Kauluakalana were voyaging chiefs from Kailua. Their legacy of sailing to nā kūkulu o Kahiki, the pillars of Kahiki, the farthest reaches of the ocean, are documented in mele probably composed during the tenth or eleventh centuries. Paumakua's voyages to Kahiki and back are said by some, such as Poepoe, to predate the migration of Pele and her family to Hawaiʻi, and Paumakua is reported to have returned from one voyage with two haole from whom a line of Oʻahu priests traces its descent. Kauluakalana is credited with bringing the lepo ʻai (edible mud) to Kawainui (Kailua's largest fishpond), which we know later fed aliʻi such as Kamehameha, Likelike, and Pauahi.

time that the majority of Kailua's hālau hula (hula schools) came together to plan and participate in a single event where we could collectively represent the rich cultural traditions that we continue to perpetuate in our community.

Our presence and practices as po'e hula, especially the offering of hula in ceremonial contexts at popular sites like Kailua Beach, had been absent from the view of most of Kailua's residents and visitors for years. Our wahi pana (sacred places) were being overrun, making kupa of Kailua feel like it was almost impossible to engage with our wahi pana in a cultural or spiritual way without being gawked at or made to feel like strangers in our own lands. However, the arrival of *Hōkūle'a* and the mana of the canoe brought the po'e hula of Kailua together in 2005 with a shared goal to host our hoa wa'a in an arrival ceremony on the sands of Kailua. This was our chance to take back our sacred places and remind everyone that the po'e hula of Kailua are united, holding fast to our traditions in order to honor our akua, ali'i, 'āina, and mo'olelo (deities, chiefs, lands, and histories). This opportunity to work together ultimately inspired the kumu hula of Kailua to create their own organization called Kini Kailua, which to this day plans events for the purposes of sustaining relationships and keeping the hula traditions of our ahupua'a alive and visible in our community.

As an 'ōlapa (dancer) for Hālau Mōhala 'Ilima based in Ka'ōhao, Kailua, I was lucky to be a part of this arrival ceremony in 2005 alongside my kumu, hula sisters, and extended hula family. We were successful in fulfilling our kuleana (responsibility) to welcome our hoa wa'a of *Hōkūle'a* to our ahupua'a of Kailua with gifts of hula and mele. The lasting relationship between hālau hula and other Hawaiian organizations in Kailua resulting from this exchange is another positive consequence of this first landing of *Hōkūle'a* in Kailua. Finally, this historic event allowed me to grow as a hula practitioner and prepared me to help plan the next welcoming of *Hōkūle'a* in Kailua eight years later. Some instances during this beautiful event in 2005 reminded us all about the widespread existence of consumerist perceptions of hula and Hawaiian culture that still permeate our community. Just like I cannot forget how it felt to offer hula and mele to *Hōkūle'a* and her crew on the same sands that once embraced the wa'a of Kūali'i and Paumakua, I also cannot forget what it felt like to be bombarded by curious onlookers attempting to invade the protected zone we created between us as kama'āina (children of the land) and our invited hoa kipa (guests).

Collisions between our traditions and our very bodies, with manifestations of the colonial/capitalist state, happened almost immediately. Even before *Hōkūle'a* was able to moor off shore, she was surrounded by kayaks, one-man canoes, motorboats, and surfboards, delaying and impeding the crew's ability to safely anchor and disembark. As we waited on shore in quiet reflection, preparing for our ceremonial exchange and taking in the sight of Hōkūleʻa entering our waters for the first time, the growing crowds unnervingly stared at us, photographed us without consent. We were intrusively questioned by pushy reporters and blocked by spectators standing in front of and between us trying to get the best view. Once the crew made it to shore, our two groups—the kamaʻāina of Kailua and our hoa kipa from Hōkūleʻa—stood facing each other at the water's edge, intentionally creating a sacred space on the sand between us to exchange mele, hula, and haʻi ʻōlelo. But to the curious onlookers, our sacred space was simply an empty area on the sand waiting to be filled. Almost as soon as it was created, it was swarmed by people and photographers who were not aware that something special was about to happen in that space and that they should stand to the side to bear witness instead of trying to be right in the middle of it.

The purpose of the ceremony that day was for the community of Kailua to greet and welcome our guests, and the initial interaction was reserved for the Kanaka, the First Peoples of this place, to culturally and ceremonially call out to our hoa waʻa and introduce them to our kulāiwi (homeland, community; literally, "the plain where the bones of one's ancestors are buried"), as our ancestors have done for generations. But this purpose was completely unfamiliar to many onlookers who gathered that day; the pervasive imagery of hula as a commodity free to be consumed by all influenced the way that some portions of the crowd viewed and interacted with us. But, in spite of all this, the crew still stood firmly at the water's edge with their beloved Hōkūleʻa behind them, understanding their role as guests to ask permission to land and wait for their hosts to respond before fully coming ashore. And we as poʻe hula stood proudly on the beach with our beloved Koʻolau mountains behind us, doing our best to block out all the noise and focus on our kuleana as hula practitioners and kupa of Kailua. In spite of all the distractions, we succeeded in creating a sacred space on the sand between our two groups, where we exchanged mele and hula. Although some spectators tried to come between us and get themselves a front row seat, **we were clear who our words were for, who our stories were for, who our dances were for, and I believe those entities received them and appreciated them.**

While we had hoped that our actions that day would push up against colonial frames that distort the image of hula and hula people into objects to be consumed whenever and however the audience desires, in many ways this experience just reconfirmed how relentless those forces can be. At the same time, however, it also strengthened our resolve as poʻe hula of Kailua to continue to practice our culture on our terms and hold our ground no matter what other forces try to push and pull us (literally and figuratively). We learned much that day about how to create safe, decolonial zones through our traditions, and we were lucky to have a chance to implement our ʻŌiwi rules of engagement in the same context eight years later when *Hōkūleʻa* returned to Kailua as part of her sail around Hawaiʻi before leaving on her Mālama Honua Worldwide Voyage. We were able to draw on relationships with Hawaiian cultural organizations and practitioners in Kailua that were first developed in 2005 and sustained over the years through Kini Kailua to successfully conduct a ceremony in 2013, where we were positioned not as objects disrupted by the settler imaginary but as agents of ea (life, breath, sovereignty), acting to disrupt settler colonialism itself.

I kamaʻāina ka waʻa iā Kailua
[May the canoe become familiar to Kailua] [3]
This phrase acknowledges *Hōkūleʻa*'s return to Kailua, this time not as a malihini but as a kamaʻāina, a reference to the ʻōlelo noʻeau, "Hoʻokahi nō lā o ka malihini, "a stranger only for a day" (Mary Kawena Pukui, *ʻŌlelo noʻeau: Hawaiian Proverbs and Poetical Sayings* [Honolulu: Bishop Museum, 1983], 115). *Hōkūleʻa* was no longer a stranger to Kailua; this was her second landing in our ahupuaʻa.

Hōkūleʻa **returns to Kailua.** I now return to the scene with which I opened this moʻolelo: the clear, sunny day of October 16, 2013, when *Hōkūleʻa* returned to Kailua and the shores of our ahupuaʻa were transformed from "America's Best Beach" to a site of visible Hawaiian decolonization and resurgence. Drawing on my experiences from 2005, I helped to plan this second landing and hosting of *Hōkūleʻa* and her crew for several days by our Kailua community. The schedule of events began with an arrival ceremony on Kailua Beach at the same site of the 2005 welcoming. There the poʻe hula of Kailua and our hoa waʻa of *Hōkūleʻa* once again came together to create a sovereign space through the sharing of mele and hula chosen for this specific context.

With just enough wind to fill her sails, *Hōkūleʻa* sailed proudly into Kailua under her own power, around Mōkapu, past Mōkōlea, through a natural channel in the reef, and close to shore, where our group of cultural practitioners, community leaders, and school groups were waiting for them. We were flanked on either side by treasured koa canoes, cared for and still paddled by canoe clubs deeply rooted in Kailua. These kūpuna were our kiaʻi (guardians), both protecting the people, places, and practices that converged during the ceremony and signifying to spectators that this area, the people within it, and the protocols conducted therein were to be respected and given their space. They were welcome to observe and witness from the side but not to insert themselves into the ceremony. They were asked to wait until after the kapu (taboo) of the ceremony was lifted to engage directly with the crew and po'e hula. The usual dynamic in highly colonized places across Hawai'i like Kailua Beach, where outsiders tend to be advantaged and catered to while the kupa are largely ignored or invisible, was flipped. We made sure to consider the physical area of the beach as an integral participant that shaped our ceremony before any words were spoken or dances were offered. **As a result, the kama'āina (Native-born Kānaka) of Kailua were lifted up and given a privileged space in which to be recognized as the children of the land, the ones with the kuleana to greet and grant *Hōkūle'a* and her crew permission to enter our ahupua'a.**

After setting anchor, the crew was ferrried to the beach aboard wa'a paddled by members of various Kailua canoe clubs and greeted with chant and lei by seven of Kailua's kumu hula. The first voices that were heard were those of the po'e hula of Kailua raised in chant. The first interactions were the giving of lei and exchanging of hā (breath) between guest and host. Offering mele for Kailua as we placed lei on the shoulders of the crew, who remained ankle deep in the water, infused the space and our very bodies with pride and aloha, thus continuing to transform us all, 'āina and kānaka. The site of our ceremony—an indistinguishable "no-name" section of Kailua Beach across from Buzz's Steakhouse—was being re-membered into its ancestral name, Kanukuoka'elepulu ("the mouth of Ka'elepulu"), which honors one of the two fishponds of Kailua (the other being Kawainui) that traditionally fed the communities of Kailua and neighboring ahupua'a. Filling this space with aloha for one another and aloha for our 'āina led to an extraordinary exchange the likes of which had not been enacted or seen in Kailua for generations.

Before our guests emerged completely from the water, *Hōkūle'a* crewmember Kaleomanuiwa (Kaleo) Wong responded to these initial gestures of aloha by calling out to the kama'āina of Kailua and asking our permission to come ashore.

E ke kama'āina, eia lā he wa'a, he kaulua
i pae mai nei
He nonoi kēia e pae ka wa'a
E kama'āina ka wa'a iā Kailua

Kaleomanuiwa Wong, crewmember of *Hōkūle'a*, delivering his oratory in 2013 upon the arrival of *Hōkūle'a* in Kailua. *Photograph by Kīhei de Silva.*

E kama'āina 'o Kailua i ka wa'a
He welina, he leo aloha wale nō kēia.

To the children of this land/the native borns of
Kailua/our hosts, here is a canoe, a double-
hulled voyaging canoe that has just landed
This is a request to come ashore
The canoe shall become familiar to Kailua
And Kailua shall become familiar to the wa'a
This is a greeting, a voice of aloha.[4]

On behalf of his hoa wa'a, Kaleo addressed the kama'āina of Kailua, including those Kānaka physically on the beach, who have dedicated their lives to
learning, teaching, and practicing Hawaiian language and culture, as well as
the kūpuna of Kailua, seen and unseen, who were also there to bear witness
to this historic event. He recognized their presence and depth of knowledge
by delivering his words directly to them, speaking only 'ōlelo Hawai'i and
recounting the genealogies of both the wa'a kaulua who brought them there
and the land who now welcomed them. He had no doubt that his hosts would
be able to understand every poetic saying he referenced, recognize every

ancestral name he honored, and appreciate the intention behind every word he spoke. And he was right. After listing the islands that *Hōkūleʻa* had visited just before arriving in Kailua, he proclaimed, "Noke i ka holo a pae mai i ke one o Kākuhihewa, ka heke o nā moku" (*Hōkūleʻa* continued to sail until landing on the sands of Kākuhihewa [Oʻahu], the best of all islands), generating exclamations of pride from the crowd. When he recounted the names of Kailua's sacred places and ancestors, such as Alāla and Kūaliʻi, Maunawili and Kahinihiniʻula, Kawainui and Hauwahine, Pāmoa and Kākuhihewa, shouts of "eō" erupted all around. While reaffirming for some, this listing of names helped many other people change how they see our places in Kailua. **Disconnected stops on a tour printed in a visitor guidebook once again became wahi pana with storied histories, ʻāina with genealogies that feed us physically and spiritually.** It was as if he was calling out to these kūpuna and inviting them to participate in the ceremony, their presence thus demanding excellence and accountability from us all as we moved forward.

Upon the conclusion of Kaleo's eloquent address, one of the kamaʻāina and poʻe hula of Kailua, Kahikina de Silva, responded with a speech of her own, welcoming Kaleo and the others to our kulāiwi and inviting them to come ashore.

This was not a preplanned performance that she choreographed with Kaleo beforehand. It was a spontaneous interaction between two Kānaka who were reviving in that moment the cultural practice of Hawaiian oratory. In fact, this was probably the first time that this kind of exchange of aloha ʻāina (love for the land) between guest and host in only the Hawaiian language had been heard in public in Kailua for more than a century. Ua pā i ka leo (To be struck by the voice)—Kahikina was struck by Kaleo's speech and was inspired to respond on behalf of the other kamaʻāina of Kailua. The result was an intertwining of words, names, genealogies, and histories that created a lei around us all, a lei that celebrated our presence as kupa of Kailua, as ʻŌiwi of Hawaiʻi. Their call and response lasted only about ten minutes, but the power of this spontaneous act continued to echo and reverberate long after their initial words were spoken.

Any time we use ʻōlelo Hawaiʻi, whether it be through mele, hula, or oratory, it is an act of resurgence because we are consciously choosing to give ea to the words of our kūpuna in our contemporary time. These words are intimately tied to our land- and water-based practices as well as to the contexts in which these practices were developed. When expressed aloud, our Native languages have the ability to animate our environment, shape our surroundings, and yield real responses from our places that, in turn, define and shape us. They are a reflection of who we are, what we value, and how we

Kahikina de Silva responding to Kaleo's oratory at the arrival ceremony for the *Hōkūleʻa* in Kailua alongside Kumu Hula Māpuana de Silva and hula sister, Maya Saffery. *Photograph by Kīhei de Silva.*

understand and engage with the world; thus their survival is intimately tied to the survival of our people.[5] The ability of the two orators to speak exclusively in ʻōlelo Hawaiʻi and the ability of most participants in the ceremony to understand their words with no English translation was also a powerful testament to the wealth of knowledge still held in Kailua and our steadfast commitment to putting this knowledge into practice. The wonderful connection between this celebration of ʻōlelo Hawaiʻi in our community and the revitalization of Hawaiian language as part of the Hawaiian renaissance in the 1970s, a movement sparked in part by *Hōkūleʻa*, was not lost on us. Even those present at the ceremony who did not understand Hawaiian sensed the significance of what they were witnessing, appreciated the power of Hawaiians engaging in Hawaiian language on Hawaiian lands, and left that day forever changed. **Ua pā i ka leo—in that moment, we were all reminded of the power of our Native voices in our Native language to breath ea into our songs, chants, and spoken words in order to enact and inspire Indigenous resurgence for the decolonization, re-culturation, and regeneration of ourselves and our communities.**

'Ōlapa (dancers) and kumu hula of Hālau Mōhala 'Ilima offering mele and hula to the crew of *Hōkūle'a* during the 2013 arrival ceremony in Kailua. *Photograph by Kīhei de Silva.*

Immediately following Kaleo and Kahikina's oratory, as we all stood in the sand and surf, my hula sisters and I presented a hula to the crew of *Hōkūle'a.* The space on Kailua beach initially carved out by chants and oratory was about to be further animated by mele in motion, words and stories delivered not only through the chanting of my kumu but also through the movement of 'ōlapa to the beat of her pahu. The hula we offered was 'Ūlei Pahu i ka Moku, a mele poignantly relevant not only to our wa'a-related context but also to the current state of our ahupua'a. It was originally chanted by a priest at a heiau in Waimea, Kaua'i, who foresaw the arrival of foreigners before the arrival of Captain Cooke. This prophecy of loss warns Hawaiians that if we do not hold fast to the steering paddle of our canoe (E ku i ta hoe uli), others will take it from us and the result will be A he mea/A he mea 'oe, translated by Mary Kawena Pukui as, "You are nothing/You Hawaiians will be as nothing." However, Patience Namaka Bacon gave us hope when she told my kumu that these final lines can also be interpreted as a question instead of a statement—Who are you? Will you let someone else define who you are and the direction your "wa'a" (canoe, community, etc.) will take you or will you take hold of the hoe

'Ōlapa from Hālau Mōhala 'Ilima offering the hula pahu (drum dance), 'Ūlei Pahu i ka Motu, to the crew of *Hōkūle'a* during the arrival ceremony. *Photograph by Bert Kaleomanuiwa Wong.*

uli (steering paddle) and navigate your own paths to ea (life, sovereignty, self-determination)? It is our choice.

As we danced with the sand between our toes and the ocean spray crystalizing on our faces, we were conscious of this highly consequential choice posed to us by our kūpuna in this mele. We did our best to try and answer the question "Who are you?" in every movement, every gesture, and every facial expression. We worked to communicate through our hula the message from our kūpuna that we must be daring enough to "kū i ka hoe uli," to literally and metaphorically take hold of the steering paddle in all aspects of our lives and navigate our own way along our course to our destination just beyond the horizon, lest someone else assume control of our wa'a and lead us astray. In that moment, as the words and motions of 'Ūlei Pahu coursed through me, who I am as a hula practitioner from Kailua as well as what po'e hula individually and collectively are capable of contributing to our communities became clear. **Offering mele and hula in appropriate contexts on the** land can not only create safe, sovereign spaces that we can return to over and over again, these decolonial acts can also help us to envision alternative futures for our community.

The exchange between guests and hosts, Kānaka from the sea and Kānaka from the land, created a piko, or convergence of ea, that required everyone there to ask themselves, **"What is my relationship to this piko and how does my positionality define my kuleana to it?"** The coming together of people and place through mele, hula, and haʻi ʻōlelo created "a space of storied presencing, alternative imaginings, transformation, reclamation—resurgence."[6] It was a celebration that, in spite of all the changes to our lands and waters by foreign influences, we are still here. But we are not just present but thriving, ready to steward our lands and lead our community in envisioning a healthy and prosperous future for Kailua. Our collective actions that day and those they inspired in the weeks and months that followed directly challenge the settler narratives that discredit the current leadership, capacity, and integrity of the Kailua Hawaiian community. As exemplified by the arrival ceremony planned and executed by the poʻe hula of Kailua, there is no doubt that we have our hoe uli firmly in our hands and are navigating our waʻa toward a distant yet visible shoreline where our presence in Kailua is real, recognized, and resurgent.

Notes

1 Kailua Beach Park was named "America's Best Beach" in 1998 by the self-proclaimed "Dr. Beach" (Dr. Stephen P. Leatherman). He has shared his winners every year online, in travel magazines, and on TV shows, triggering an increase in tourist activity in Kailua.

2 The settler imaginary is made up of beliefs and images that settlers use to imagine away the colonization and marginalization of Indigenous peoples in order to make the ʻŌiwi presence and cultural practices palatable and nonthreatening to the status quo that validates their dominance. Blinders they place on themselves and others who buy into this false narrative serve to perpetuate these erasures by disguising them as how things have always been.

3 This phrase acknowledges *Hōkūleʻa*'s return to Kailua, this time not as a malihini but as a kamaʻāina, a reference to the ʻōlelo noʻeau, "Hoʻokahi nō lā o ka malihini, "a stranger only for a day" (Mary Kawena Pukui, *ʻŌlelo noʻeau: Hawaiian Proverbs and Poetical Sayings* [Honolulu: Bishop Museum, 1983], 115).

4 Translation by author. This is only an excerpt of the entire haʻi ʻōlelo.

5 A reference to (1) the wise saying, "I ka ʻōlelo nō ke ola. I ka ʻōlelo nō ka make" ("In language there is life. In language there is death" [Pukui, *ʻŌlelo noʻeau*, 129]), and

(2) a newspaper article in the Hawaiian-language newspaper *Puuhona o Na Hawaii* (January 26, 1917) entitled "Olelo Hawai'i," about the link between language and national identity.

6   Leanne Simpson, *Dancing on Our Turtle's Back: Stories of Nishnaabeg Re-creation, Resurgence, and a New Emergence* (Winnipeg, MB, Canada: Arbeiter Ring, 2011), 96.

Resources

Polynesian Voyaging Society, www.hokulea.com. Founded on a legacy of Pacific Ocean exploration, the Polynesian Voyaging Society seeks to perpetuate the art and science of traditional Polynesian voyaging and the spirit of exploration through experiential educational programs that inspire students and their communities to respect and care for themselves, each other, and their natural and cultural environments.

Karen K. Kosasa and Stan Tomita

_____

Settler Colonial Postcards

Stan and I are third-generation Japanese American settlers. In 2001 we created a postcard project for an art exhibition on tourism at CEPA Gallery, Buffalo, New York. We titled the work "whose paradise? a DIDACTIC (de) TOUR
project" and produced three postcards for it.

We wanted the postcards to complement our other artwork and art installations on the invisibility of settler colonialism in Hawai'i. We also created
"whose paradise?" to counter the ubiquitous "wish you were here" sentiment
of postcards. And unlike our usual work, we wanted to be straightforwardly
direct and didactic. Our images were linked to specific interpretations, leaving little room for speculation.

In the art world, didactic art is considered "bad" art because it dictates
the meaning(s) of an image and limits the viewer's participation in the
meaning-making process. It is frequently associated with communist propaganda art, and most artists are trained to avoid it. For our postcard project,
however, proscribing the meanings of our images was essential. Being didactic was necessarily strategic and our contribution to "responsible tourism."

Our project in this _Detours_ anthology continues the work Stan and I
began in 2001, but with a set of four new and improved postcards. One is
entirely new, whereas three are significantly "improved" versions of previous
ones. In our signature postcard we recognize the growing discussions of occupation alongside conversations about settler colonialism. We include references to both situations in an image of clouds above hotels along Waikīkī
Beach to underscore the complexity of the political context(s) in Hawai'i. The
other postcards refer to the difficulty of finding a reference to the site of the
1893 overthrow, an excerpt from the 1993 Apology Bill, and the construction

☒ settler colonialism

OCCUPATION

WARNING

Settler Colonialism/Occupation:
Over a Century of Conquest in Hawai'i
Did you know that in 1893 the constitutional monarchy in Hawai'i was
overthrown by U.S. diplomatic, military, and business personnel? In
1898 Hawai'i was illegally annexed by the U.S. as a territory, and in
1959 it became the 50th state of the U.S. through an illegal plebiscite.

Some scholars describe the historic and contemporary situations as
examples of *settler colonialism*. Others explain that under international
law Hawai'i is under *occupation*, similar to what occurred when the
U.S. invaded Iraq in 2003. Shouldn't all visitors to Hawai'i be aware of
the tumultuous political background of this place?

[Images on front: Warning flag and hotels along Waikīkī Beach.]

whose paradise? a **DIDACTIC (de) Tour project**

Settler Colonialism/Occupation: Over a Century of Conquest in Hawai'i.

See exhibit panel in back hallway

NOTICE

HOOLAHA!

SCENE OF A CRIME: 1893 OVERTHROW OF HAWAIIAN MONARCHY

Aliʻiōlani Hale: Scene of a Crime – 1893 Overthrow
The world-famous statue of King Kamehameha I stands in front of a building widely recognized for housing the fictive police/detective unit in the popular Hawaiʻi Five-0 television series (2010-2018). It was the scene of a real crime and violation of international law. On January 17, 1893, the government of the Kingdom of Hawaiʻi was overthrown by U.S. diplomatic, military, and business personnel. Queen Liliʻuokalani was deposed and a proclamation announcing the creation of a provisional government occurred at the makai (ocean) entrance to the building. Later, in 1898, Hawaiʻi was illegally annexed by the U.S., and still later, in 1959, it became the 50th state of the U.S. through an illegal plebiscite.

Aliʻiōlani Hale currently houses the Hawaiʻi State Supreme Court. Can an American judicial system ethically function within a colonized or occupied country? How is this possible? Whose paradise is this?

[Images on front: Aliʻiōlani Hale, statue of King Kamehameha I, and elements of an exhibit panel found in the back hallway of the historic building. Panel depicts the overthrow: U.S. marines mobilized to "protect American lives and property," portraits of the men who planned the overthrow, bulletin declaring Martial Law by provisional government in January 1893. Because of its location, visitors rarely see this panel.]

whose paradise? a **DIDACTIC (de) Tour project**

Aliʻiōlani Hale: Scene of a Crime—1893 Overthrow.

Whereas, in pursuance of the conspiracy to overthrow the government of Hawaii, the United States Minister and the naval representatives of the United States caused armed naval forces of the United States to invade the sovereign Hawaiian nation on January 16, 1893, and to position themselves near the Hawaiian Government buildings and the Iolani Palace to intimidate Queen Liliuokalani and her Government.

Public Law 103-150, 103d Congress, November 23, 1993, Joint Resolution

"ACT OF WAR" SINCE 1893

When is an apology not enough?
On November 23, 1993, the U.S. Congress passed Public Law 103-150 by a joint resolution acknowledging the active participation of the U.S. in the overthrow of the Hawaiian Kingdom in 1893. It further acknowledges that the Native Hawaiian people never relinquished claims to their inherent sovereignty. Known as the "Apology Resolution," it was signed by President William Clinton. In the final section it warns that "Nothing in this Joint Resolution is intended to serve as settlement of any claims against the United States." What does this say about the integrity of the U.S. – to admit to a crime but provide no legal restitution for those who were wronged?

[Images on front: Statue of Queen Lili'uokalani, last reigning monarch of the Kingdom of Hawai'i with flower lei and gifts honoring her person and legacy. Text excerpt from the Apology Resolution. Photographs in lower right from a Hawaiian sovereignty/independence rally: 1) Kingdom of Hawai'i flags flying upside down to signal political "distress," 2) banner depicting the words of U.S. President Grover Cleveland in December 1893 denouncing the invasion of Hawai'i as an "act of war" by the U.S. on a friendly nation.]

whose paradise? a DIDACTIC (de) Tour project

When is an apology not enough?

CURRENT THREATS: miconia

feral pigs

apple snails

banana poka

fountain grass

rapid 'Ōhi'a
death

settlers & tourists

POTENTIAL THREATS: brown tree snakes

Potential/Actual Harm: TMT
predators
competition
habitat alteration
cultural practice impacts
other telescopes

Under Siege in Hawai'i

Government and private agencies in Hawai'i are currently battling a
"silent" invasion of alien plant and animal species threatening the
fragile island ecosystem. Measures have been established to combat
the arrival of these "pests." No agency exists, however, to assess the
historic and contemporary damage done by the invasion of another
alien species -- non-Hawaiian settlers -- nor to make recommendations
for remediation. In 1991, Native Hawaiian scholar Haunani-Kay Trask
wrote a damning critique of tourism and the relentless
commodification of the Indigenous culture. She famously asked
tourists to stop coming to the islands. More recently, many Native
Hawaiians and their allies have protested the construction of an
18-story-high Thirty Meter Telescope (TMT) on the sacred mountain of
Mauna Kea, where over a dozen multinational telescopes already
exist. As far back as 1998, a state audit chastised the manager of the
telescope complex, the University of Hawai'i, for failing to protect the
mountain and its natural and cultural resources. Today, protests
continue against the proposed intrusion of TMT. Should the desire to
see ancient galaxies in the sky prevent us from recognizing the
cumulative effect of assaults on the land and violations of traditional
Hawaiian practices on earth? Whose paradise is this?

[Images on front: Details of Waikīkī Beach and proposed Thirty Meter
Telescope on Mauna Kea.]

whose paradise? a DIDACTIC (de) Tour project

Under Siege in Hawai'i.

of a thirty-meter telescope on Hawai'i Island. In two instances our explanations are so lengthy they leave little space for the visitor/sender to write a personal message. This is regrettable but of secondary concern. What is more significant is showing that the image on the front may not be immediately understood by everyone. Its meanings must be decoded on the back. Even then, what we offer is not adequate but a start.

Our postcards function well in classes. Teachers use them to encourage classroom conversations about the content of our postcards and related issues, and to show a simple format for speaking back to the world. Stan and I are pleased to be a part of a respected tradition of using this ubiquitous and innocuous tourist object to counter expected, hegemonic messages. Furthermore, we are grateful to be included in an anthology committed to pedagogy, to providing readers and viewers with insights and perspectives about Hawai'i that are not always available, accessible, or visible unless you are trained to look for them.

Malia Akutagawa

An Island Negotiating a Pathway for Responsible Tourism

Tourism Is a Dirty Word

As a Native Hawaiian born and raised on Molokaʻi, I have always considered *tourism* a dirty word. I'm not alone in this perception. Ask any Molokaʻian walking down the street and at least seven in ten will tell you the same thing. Tourism. It feels like cultural prostitution—the canned Hawaiian lūʻau experiences, the wide plastic smiles of hula dancers wearing cellophane skirts and false eyelashes, the automatic expectation of visitors that a lei greeter and limo should be waiting for them as they get off the plane.

It means being on display and looked upon with fascination. I remember making an excursion to Pōhakumāuliuli, a beach on the west side of Molokaʻi. It is usually a quiet cove of white sand just off a neglected piece of golf course at an old, shuttered resort at Kaluakoʻi. The old condominium apartments are now owned primarily by snowbirds who rent out their units as transient vacation rentals. Many times I am the only person on the beach, or one of a handful. It is a peaceful refuge that renews my spirit.

I love this place for its tide pools. Here the pua (baby fish) are sheltered and feed on limu (seaweed) clinging to the rocks. Tiny crustaceans and sand crabs crawl and burrow there too. Loli (sea cucumbers) lie placidly among the rocks. I often sit quietly in these little ponds and let the pua nibble at my arms and legs. As a fisher, I am happy to know the pua are thriving and will replenish the sea. From here I gauge the power of the ocean surge. I hear the long, deep breaths of Papahānaumoku (Earth Mother) from these western shores, which are known for their impressive surf. The waves strike the shore, climb over the rocks, and refresh the tide pools with seawater. The pull of the waves as they ebb back to sea tells me how strong the ocean currents are and helps me discern the general mood of Kanaloa (the ocean god). I use this quiet time to count the sets and determine when lulls occur—the best time to enter the sea.

It was during one of these excursions at Pōhakumāuliuli that loud whispers interrupted my peaceful reverie: "Is that a real Hawaiian?!" A group of American tourists openly gawked at me. My long hair and brown skin probably epitomized for them that Hawaiian mystique, a kind of Polynesian goddess rising out of the sea. It would have been OK if they had greeted me and struck up a friendly conversation. But it seemed that they preferred to objectify me as an exotic curiosity than to see the soul inside me. I can't stand tourism because it isn't about any kind of personal exchange, talking story, getting to know those who visit. Often, it's about people who have no clue about our culture and no desire to learn.

Moving away from earshot and the tourists' line of sight, I found a peaceful patch of sand on which to rest. The faint outline of O'ahu Island nestled on the horizon. I could see the reverse view of Waikīkī's iconic Diamond Head Crater. I thought of what that place meant to me and how I can no longer access the real waiwai (wealth) that Waikīkī had offered in the past. Today it is a place defiled for the sake of delivering a fantasy for strangers from thousands of miles away.

Tourism, to me, is a slow but insidious grip around my neck, choking and suffocating me, pushing me out of my favorite places, smearing my memories of Waikīkī beaches with a slick of suntan oil. Those special waters I swam in and the sand castles my O'ahu cousins and I built exist only in memory. Those sands I used to sink my feet in with happy contentment are now riddled with cigarette butts and too many footprints of strangers who are all too eager to make postcard pictures of themselves.

I wuz there too. But it was as if I never was.

It is this fear of being erased, an afterthought in one's own homeland, the 'āina (land) being so disfigured and unrecognizable, a place abandoned by the kūpuna (ancestors), that evokes these lamentations in my soul.

Moloka'i Nui A Hina
Moloka'i Great Child of Hina
Moloka'i 'Āina Momona
Moloka'i the Fat Land
Moloka'i Pule O'o
Moloka'i, Powerful in Prayer
Moloka'i, Rooted in Aloha 'Āina

The one solace in my heart is that Moloka'i is still very much a place where the living and the ancestors walk side by side. I feel the spirit of the kūpuna and the enduring strength and wisdom of my dear island Moloka'i Nui A Hina (Moloka'i Great Child of Goddess Hina). In ancient times it guided our powerful kahuna (priests, sorcerers) to stand in prayer in order to defeat enemies who sought to conquer the land and people, and it continues to guide us today in aloha 'āina (Hawaiian activism representing the people's love of the land). Listening to the land here is easy. There is no dissonance; no loud sounds of traffic to confuse our thoughts; no skyscrapers to block us from the gentle touch of our island's soft breezes; no endless roads and sidewalks of asphalt and concrete covering the soil and barring the flow of the island's mana (spiritual power), which permeates the soles of our feet and the soul of our being as we seek to touch and commune with this sacred earth. Our piko (umbilical cord) to our 'āina hānau (birthplace) is strongly rooted and therefore our nā'au (gut) as the seat of our nā'auao (wisdom) remains vibrant, guiding us as outspoken and vigilant protectors of Moloka'i Pule O'o (Moloka'i, Potent in Prayer).

Moloka'i tests all who call this place home. To earn the privilege of living here, we are obliged to abide by a simple lifestyle that honors Moloka'i as a living being and our living kupuna. It is through this way of life that our island reveals and shares its gifts as Moloka'i Āina Momona (the fat, abundant land). For me it has meant that I can always rely on my island to feed and shelter me. It has done so for many generations of my family, since time immemorial. The land is pregnant with food—fish and limu from our reefs and fishponds; venison, goat, and wild pig in the mountains; lo'i kalo (wetland taro patches) and mala (dryland) gardens; and ripened mango, citrus, papaya, coconut, and 'ulu (breadfruit) trees. Wherever I traverse, the land gives and gives. All that is expected is that we mālama (care for) Moloka'i when she is threatened.

Here at Pōhakumāuliuli, I reflect on the visible reminders of the battles we undertook to protect Moloka'i over the past four decades. On either side of me are Kaiaka Rock and Kawakiu Bay, places that were slated for resort development. They remain untouched because my mākua (parent genera-tion) fought and defeated those prospectors seeking to profit from the land.

In the 1970s the movement to Aloha 'Āina blossomed on Moloka'i with the organizing of Hawaiian activists under the banner of Hui Alaloa, a group with the goal of reopening the ancient trails that were fenced off with "No Trespass" signs. Moloka'i, like the other islands, did not escape the effects of American colonialism. Ownership of vast swaths of land—more than one-third of the island—has become concentrated among a handful of private landowners with large holdings. This has translated into the criminalization of Native Hawaiians who must climb barbed wire fences to gather plants for medicine and food, to fish, to hunt, and to conduct customary and religious practices.

The fiercest activist among us, Uncle Walter Ritte, recalls hearing a story from an elder who remembered so many fish along the shore that she could sit in one place and gather the skirts of her muʻumuʻu in her lap to harvest them. Uncle Walter asked her where she fished. She said, "Oh, it is blocked off now. In my day, there were no fences." It did not occur to Uncle Walter that there was any life before fences. Hui Alaloa organized its first act of resistance by walking the ancient Kealapūpū Trail, lined with seashells, to shine a path in light and even dark times. Passing over many fences, they walked the trail from the northwest coastline at Moʻomomi Bay to west-facing Kaluakoʻi. Ultimately, Hui Alaloa defeated developers in court and were successful in keeping Kawakiu Bay and Kaiaka Rock undeveloped.

The only resort that was able to gain a foothold in the west was the resort at Kaluakoʻi. In the 1990s, however, operations at Kaluakoʻi began to phase out. The landowner, Molokaʻi Ranch, had initially attempted to "bank" water by wasting it in dry gulches, so that in better economic times it could proceed with more grandiose resort development plans. Apart from being wasteful, increased water usage at Kaluakoʻi would mean taking substantially more water from an irrigation system built to support Native Hawaiian Homestead farmers. These Kanaka farmers challenged Molokaʻi Ranch's water use permit application at the agency level and then in court. The homesteaders prevailed before the Hawaiʻi Supreme Court. The case expanded Hawaiʻi's unique jurisprudence, which emphasizes water as a constitutionally protected public trust. Included in this public trust is the protection of Hawaiian Homesteader rights and maintaining the health and vitality of natural and cultural resources that are important for perpetuating Native Hawaiian subsistence rights and traditions.

We Have Been Tested Before

But for the intervention of Aloha ʻĀina activists on Molokaʻi, we would have been denied the sustenance and spiritual renewal that this place gives us. Wary of outside pressures to alter our traditional lifestyle, and knowing that most major land use decisions were being made in a vacuum, without our input, by government agencies located on Oʻahu and Maui Islands, we know that we have to take control of our own destiny. This means that we have had to push back at government and insist that we have our own island planning commission. It means that we have had to learn about planning and zoning and to use these tools in order to determine appropriate land uses in different parts of our island. It means volunteering on various boards, commissions, and working groups. It means testifying at endless meetings on weeknights and afternoons, even if we have to take off from work and sacrifice family time. It means protesting and even occupying lands slated for construction. It means making friends with "fish and poi" lawyers—those public interest Hawaiian and environmental attorneys who are willing to do pro bono work for us. We exercised every legal guerrilla warfare tactic in the book in order to delay development and wear down the confidence of investors.

We are best known for our obstinacy. We are the only Hawaiian island that does not rely on a tourist-based economy. At first glance, many dismiss us as backward. In a sense, that is true. There is a Hawaiian saying: "I ka wā ma mua, ka wā ma hope." It means that we look backward to history and heritage in order to move forward. From this vantage point, we have been guided to restore ancient fishponds so they produce food again. We push for food sovereignty and sustainability by training the next generation of farmers and establishing a food hub that transports produce farmed locally to stores, restaurants, and homes. We have various cooperatives to provide seed, tools, and equipment for farmers and a livestock cooperative to process and sell organic, grass-fed Moloka'i beef, venison, and pork at a small, humanely operated slaughterhouse. We are creative social entrepreneurs, small-business owners running mom-and-pop enterprises rather than fast food franchises and popular box store outlets. We are traditional crafters, artists, inventors, farmers, teachers, conservationists, and leaders. We write our own destiny.

'Aha Kiole: The People's Councils

Moloka'i has fully embraced a more traditional model of local governance based on the ancient 'Aha Kiole (people's councils) founded over a thousand years ago by our Hawaiian ancestors. In 2008, the people renewed the 'Aha Kiole model as a vehicle to convey community input to government agencies and lawmakers regarding land use issues and matters affecting natural and cultural resource management. Moku (regional) leaders were chosen to work collectively with residents in their district on issues unique to their place.

The first real test of the 'Aha Kiole came in the fall of 2011 with the unannounced arrival of a small cruise ship at Kaunakakai Harbor. This incident took residents by surprise and rapidly escalated into a maelstrom of public outrage and a heavy-handed government response that involved gunboats enforcing a harbor security zone. In the last week of October, a 36-passenger, 145-foot-long, boutique luxury American Safari Cruises cruise ship arrived in Kaunakakai Harbor. The thirty-some *malihini* disembarked and were greeted by local tour vans. They drove eastward to hike Hālawa Falls, then snorkeled and kayaked along uncrowded beaches.

By the end of the day, the island was buzzing with commentary about the cruise ship. Most people viewed its arrival negatively.

"Eh! Why they so mahaʻoi (nosey)? They think they can come here and no ask permission!"

"Tscha! They no respect nothing! We the hosts, but they no care about our traditions. I like see these guys eyeball to eyeball, talk story with them before they just go holoholo (cruising, adventuring) all over the place."

I didn't know how to feel about it. The voice of my father rang in my ears: "No let them even stick their big toe in the door, or else they will kick the door wide open!"

At the time I was also the director of the Molokaʻi Rural Development Project (RDP), and I was tasked with helping to strengthen Molokaʻi's economy and provide workforce training to unemployed and underemployed residents. I took on this role to challenge myself and take on the kuleana of helping to create a strong Molokaʻi economy. I was keenly aware of the criticisms lodged at me and my family as aloha ʻāina activists. Some hold Molokaʻi's activists responsible for a depressed cash economy. Yet on a deeper and likely unexpressed level, they are also grateful to the activists in our role as defenders of this Hawaiian island and the slow-paced lifestyle Molokaʻi affords. I had something to prove: a healthy economy need not sacrifice the ʻāina. We could keep mālama ʻāina as our foundation by embracing sustainable industries.

One of the projects we sponsored at RDP was the creation of a Molokaʻi Responsible Tourism Plan, which revealed a community vision of a tourism industry that

- is local, traditional, and Indigenous-based;
- enhances the community's quality of life;
- protects and restores environment and culture;
- yields a fair exchange of value between the host and the hosted;
- preserves the community's sense of place and brings dignity and pride to the host;
- cultivates friendship and mutual understanding in the host-guest relationship;

- offers culturally authentic activities and shares real culture by the people who practice it; and
- limits visitor numbers to preserve a sense of place.

In conversation with friends who wanted a community-centered approach to tourism on Moloka'i, it became clear that we needed to adhere to a traditional process of making decisions and caring for our 'āina. The 'Aha Kiole should have at least been consulted.

Uncle Merv, our Kawela moku representative and respected elder, hosted an emergency 'Aha Kiole meeting and invited Dan Blanchard, CEO of American Safari Tours, to explain his intentions. He asked Blanchard to delay visits to Moloka'i until the community could be polled and have a chance to decide whether certain conditions should be imposed on the cruise ship visits. Mr. Blanchard stated he had already met with the "community" five years earlier; that "community" comprised a handful of local tour operators and vendors.

One community member, Patricia, spoke up: "This is not what our kūpuna are used to . . . we have a protocol that our island historically goes through. . . . This was a sneak attack, another overthrow. Queen Lili'uokalani was taken down by seven or eight business members. The same thing is happening here. Seven or eight business members took it upon themselves to make a plan for Moloka'i, which very well could end up with bigger boats coming in."

Blanchard asserted that American laws guaranteed his ship safe harbor at Kaunakakai. He was a legitimate business owner and was not breaking any laws of doing business on the island. He was flabbergasted that we would insist he participate in what seemed to him an archaic, Indigenous process based on an old and conquered sovereign—one foreign to the American rule of law.

Next, Lawrence, a Hawaiian tour operator, stood up and stated his refusal to recognize the legitimacy of the 'Aha Kiole. He said this "illegal" body had no authority to make decisions for Moloka'i. His words hit me the most, as I knew he was one of the people who considered himself the "konohiki" (traditional steward) of Hālawa Valley, and his exclusive, paid tours to the waterfall were making it difficult for locals to access the traditional trail. His disregard for Hawaiian traditional protocols while insisting that locals and Hawaiians living outside Hālawa respect his wishes as konohiki galvanized my kāne (male partner) and I to join protestors two days later. Blanchard proclaimed Lawrence as his guide and cultural leader. Blanchard ultimately decided to continue his planned cruise ship visits to Molokaʻi without input from the ʻAha Kiole.

We gathered at Kaunakakai Wharf at sunrise with the rest of the protestors. Uncle Walter Ritte spoke with the police officers who came to keep the peace. He then gathered us together to lay out the ground rules that would ensure our safety. While he explained the strategy, I saw a handful of our community elders being escorted onto a boat and welcomed aboard by the captain and a friendly crew. They met with the passengers and were apprised by the crew that the ship had been branded as an "UnCruise" cruise ship. It was thus named for its commitment to maintaining a minimal, low-impact footprint with its boutique services and eco-friendly practices.

I did not begrudge the kūpuna who were taken in by the sales pitch. I had seen this before. It was like a courtship dance that the hospitality industry uses to curry favor with the locals or the Natives. This is one of the oldest plays in the playbook. These kūpuna were expected to go out into the community and provide glowing praises of their experience on the ship, to reassure us of the company's benign intentions. I knew these kūpuna were being used for their kindness and graciousness, for they embodied aloha, a trait well known in our culture. Aloha requires us to generously welcome visitors. The aloha we were all raised with is our finest characteristic as a people, but also our greatest vulnerability.

We held our signs and picketed as the vans loaded the cruise ship passengers. Bullhorn in hand, Uncle Walter started the chant: "NO CRUISE SHIP! NO CRUISE SHIP!" As the vans headed our way through a chain-link fence, the drivers paused and the police allowed us to picket in a circle for a few minutes and then signaled us to break the line and allow the vans passage. Through tinted windows the tourists gazed at us silently. Curiously. I felt at that moment like an animal in a wildlife park. No wonder the cruise line was called "American Safari Tours." I imagined their thoughts: "Oh, look at those restless natives."

Our peaceful protests went unheeded by Mr. Blanchard. We knew we had to increase the pressure in ways that risked government ire. On November 26, the cruise ship headed once more to our shores after touring Maui and Hawaiʻi islands. Several protestors on surfboards and in fishing boats lined up to block the entrance to the harbor. After a tense thirty-minute stand-off, the cruise ship finally turned around and headed back out to sea.

The next day, Uncle Walter Ritte and I met with Blanchard and his cultural guide Lawrence. Blanchard reasoned, "Look, we run a small operation. It's a small boat. In fact, we call ourselves the 'UnCruise' ship because we visit remote areas and we do things sustainably. We are the antithesis of the kind of cruise ships you should be worried about."

I asked him, "Do you think Moloka'i remains beautiful and unspoiled by accident? No, you have us activists to thank for your 'UnCruise' experience."

Frustrated, he asked, "Well, what is it going to take to make this go away?"

Uncle Walter replied, "Submit to our 'Aha Kiole process."

"But what assurances do I have that I will benefit from this process?"

Giving him a hard look, I said, "If you don't utilize the 'Aha Kiole, I can definitely assure you that you will join the pile of carcasses of all those who failed in their plans and underestimated the commitment we have to protecting our 'āina."

Uncle Walter added, "Look, we are giving up something too. We will end our protests and honor whatever decision comes out of this community process."

Noncommittal, Blanchard told us he would defer to Lawrence, who would be hosting a community meeting that evening. He was quite confident that he would get community buy-in. In his mind, we were an outspoken minority.

Over a hundred people showed up to the meeting, most of them testifying angrily. They didn't want this maha'oi cruise ship and curious tourists visiting prime fishing spots and walking the traditional trails to access subsistence gathering areas. White-faced and resigned, Blanchard spoke into the mic, "It's clear you need time to think about this as a community, so I'll respect your wishes and follow your process." Blanchard promised he would postpone the next round of visits in order to provide a cooling-off period and allow the 'Aha Kiole to convene community meetings.

Incensed by the activists for imperiling Hawai'i's multimillion-dollar tourism industry, then-Governor Neil Abercrombie sent a SWAT team and gunboats to enforce harbor security and the cruise ship's safe entry. These Big Brother scare tactics fueled greater resentment and brought larger protests at the harbor.

'Aha Kiole Achieves Historic Agreement

Despite these setbacks, the 'Aha Kiole moved forward and conducted a community survey. Results showed that the majority were opposed to the cruise ship operations, unless certain conditions were imposed. The 'Aha Kiole hosted four community meetings, one in each moku. Seventy-five to one hundred fifty people participated in each moku gathering. The 'Aha Kiole reviewed the minutes from all the meetings and compiled a list of proposed conditions and recommendations that reflected the community mana'o (feedback). Additional moku meetings were arranged to allow residents to weigh in on the draft recommendations. Heads from the Hawai'i Department of Land and Natural Resources and the Department of Transportation, Harbors Division, also reviewed the recommendations. In instances where the government could not enforce certain conditions, the 'Aha Kiole asked Blanchard if he would agree to make concessions on those issues.

In a matter of a few months we were able to reach a mutually beneficial agreement that culminated in a signing ceremony between Blanchard, the protestors, the 'Aha Kiole representatives, and several government leaders. The agreement included the following terms:

1   All American Safari guests must view a community-produced orientation video on Moloka'i so that they are made aware of the specialness of our island and our cultural protocols.
2   Cruise passengers must avoid visiting certain named subsistence areas and sacred cultural sites.
3   The number of annual visits is capped, and no more than thirty individuals are allowed per visit in order to keep numbers sustainable and acceptable to the community.
4   Visitors commit to patronize local vendors.
5   Moloka'i must be selected as the first and/or last port of call so that tourists may fly into the island and elect to use Moloka'i hotel lodgings for a few extra days before or after their cruise.
6   Trash cannot be discarded from the cruise ship on Moloka'i, so as to avoid potentially introducing invasive species (e.g., coqui frogs, fire ants, papaya ring spot virus, banana bunchy top virus).
7   A percentage of the revenues accrued by American Safari Cruises shall be donated to the Hawai'i Community Foundation and earmarked for a special Moloka'i fund to support cultural and environmental conservation projects.

Moloka'i, The "Friendly" Isle

In the beginning, I characterized *tourism* as a dirty word. I concede it can be a good word too. I have made amazing connections and lifelong friendships with visitors. I have shared with them the very best of Moloka'i—not because I had to, but because I wanted to.

Believe it or not, Moloka'i has been coined the "Friendly" Isle. The late celebrity chef Anthony Bourdain found it incredulous after outsiders warned him about coming here, "[Moloka'i] is famously *not* the Friendly Island. It's supposed to be the most unfriendly island."[1]

Uncle Walter Naki, a highly skilled fisherman who gave Bourdain a tour of the reef, explained it this way: "Depends which way you look at it. Traditionally we're very, very friendly. Now, 'unfriendly' is when you're going to try and 'fix it,' make it 'better,' or try to take something. That's when we become unfriendly."

Uncle Walter Naki then took Bourdain in the water to spear his first he'e (octopus). The celebrity chef sampled the cooked he'e he had caught as well as pulehu (barbecued) venison, laulau (steamed pork enclosed in taro leaves), poi, and other traditional foods with a number of Hawaiian activists.

Bourdain asked the group, "So, who gets to be Hawaiian?"

Hanohano Naehu, a kia'i loko (fishpond caretaker), aloha 'āina warrior, and slam poet, responded, "Hawaiian is a nationality, brah! You can be Hawaiian."

"Really? Come on! Don't shit me."

Hanohano elaborated further:

Our blood is Kanaka. You cannot be Kanaka. Hawaiian is our nationality. . . . You see this what we standing on? This is 'āina and it matters so much that if you love this place and you don't wanna develop it, destroy it, [or] abuse it, then we on the same team. If you eyeing this place and its resources as a money-making vehicle for yourself, we enemies. Right? And it doesn't matter what race, religion, what sex you [are]. If you love this place and you can mālama our 'āina the way we love it and our ancestors loved it, then brah, we can be more than friends, we can be family.

Note

1   *Anthony Bourdain: Parts Unknown*, season 5, episode 7, "Hawaii," directed by Erik Osterholm, featuring Anthony Bourdain, aired June 14, 2015, on CNN.

Noelle M. K. Y. Kahanu

Ka Hale Hōʻikeʻike a Pihopa
A Bishop Museum Love Story

Ola ka inoa o nā kūpuna
E hoʻomau ia i ke kahua hoʻomanaʻo
Kūkulu ia e Konia me Paki
Ka Hale Hōʻikeʻike a Pihopa

Ancestral names live on
Perpetuated at this commemorative foundation
Buildings named for Konia and Paki
At the Bishop Museum[1]

This is a story of what remains and what endures. It is a story of a storied place where mountains turn red at sunset, framing the plains of Kaiwiʻula. It is a story of a land that passed through the hands of five aliʻi (one born of royal heritage) until it finally became the home of a museum to celebrate those whose voices had begun to fade. This is a story of my fifteen-year love affair with Ka Hale Hōʻikeʻike a Pihopa, also known as Bishop Museum, and how it continues to stir the passions of those who make it their destination, their point of grounding and departure, the lens through which they encounter Hawaiʻi's complexities, pains and losses, joys and celebrations.

They say that love should never be easy. Such is the case with Bishop Museum, beginning with how you even find out about it. Although it is Hawaiʻi's largest museum and "the premier natural and cultural history institution in the Pacific, recognized throughout the world for its cultural collections, research projects, consulting services and public educational programs," it is the equivalent of a tourism wallflower.[2] Neither popular nor hip, it doesn't make anyone's top ten list of "things to do on Oʻahu," ranking only twentieth on TripAdvisor, behind the Battleship *Missouri* Memorial (number four), surfing (number nine), and hiking at Makapuʻu Lighthouse (number eighteen). Nor can you stumble upon Bishop Museum serendipitously. It is not within easy walking distance of Waikīkī. You cannot climb onto a red double-decker bus or an express bus and hop off onto its parking lot. Getting there means an hour-long ride through Waikīkī, Ala Moana, and downtown Honolulu, maybe even transferring buses before walking the final three blocks. If you are renting a car, it means meandering through the streets of dusty Kalihi. You have to *want* to find this place.

And once you *have* found Bishop Museum, you have to commit. You cannot "dash in and out" just to kill an hour of time on your way to the airport. It is a daylong date in which you choose to get to know one another; where you bring comfortable shoes, an open mind, and a willingness to suspend all that you thought you knew of the Hawaiian people, our history, and culture. It is a place of welcome where you are invited to experience a maoli worldview; a safe place to learn, explore, and ask questions of a docent. Indeed, going to Bishop Museum will transform how you experience Hawaiʻi. In a video on the second floor of Hawaiian Hall, orator, artist, and historian Sam Kaʻai tells of the smallest of fishhooks made for women "so they can laugh and giggle like birds on the reef as they hook fish. That's the makau liʻi liʻi [small fishhooks]—the small kisses that you always remember." My relationship with Bishop Museum has been like that: a decade and a half filled with innumerable loving, tender, heartbreaking, unforgettable kisses.

To be honest, I didn't know that I would fall in love. I barely knew of Bishop Museum, even as a lifelong Oʻahu resident whose obligatory fourth-grade Hawaiian history field trip sent generations of students to the museum's fabled three-story Hawaiian Hall. I stood in awe beneath the shadow of the great suspended palaoa, or sperm whale, while simultaneously wary of musty smells, darkened corners, and strange dioramas of stuffed dogs and frozen-in-time Native Hawaiians pounding kapa (bark cloth). When I finally returned twenty-five years later it was as a new employee, oblivious to the fact that I was walking in the footsteps of my great-great-aunt Martha Hohu, a Hawaiian docent who in the 1950s stood at the entrance, the portal to Hawaiian Hall, greeting visitors and shushing aberrant youthful voices. Even before that, my grandfather, as a student of Kamehameha Schools in the 1930s, lived on the very grounds of Kaiwiʻula, his ROTC boot–clad feet running laps upon the grounds fronting Hawaiian Hall. Thus my love affair was born of generations, one lost to time but renewed in the late 1990s when a grant enabled me to work in the museum's collections.

Through my work in the museum, I met its namesake, Princess Bernice Pauahi Bishop. She was the great-granddaughter of King Kamehameha, who unified the Hawaiian Kingdom in 1810. When the princess was born in 1831, the Native population numbered about 124,000, but by the time of her death in 1884, only 44,000 Hawaiians remained. Within her brief fifty-two-year life span, she witnessed a 65 percent decline in the population of her people. Wave upon wave of Hawaiians perished from diseases that devastated both the young and the old, the maka'āinana (people of the land) and the chiefly class. Indeed, the very grounds of Bishop Museum, known as Kaiwi'ula (literally the "red bone"), tell this repeated story of depopulation and loss. The ahupua'a (land division) of Kapālama, within which Kaiwi'ula is situated, was awarded to Prince Moses Kekuaiwa in the Māhele land division of 1848. In November of that same year he died from measles at the age of nineteen, and the lands passed to his sister, Victoria Kamāmalu. Because she had no issue, the lands passed to her brother, King Kamehameha IV, Lot Kapuāiwa. Because the king died at age forty-two without children, the lands were inherited by his half-sister, Princess Ruth Ke'elikōlani. She died at age fifty-six without surviving children, and thus her estate passed to her beloved cousin, Princess Bernice Pauahi Bishop. Finally, when Pauahi died without children, her lands were dedicated in trust for the establishment of a school for Hawaiian children. Thus, within a single generation, the land had passed laterally through five relations because none had lineal heirs. For a people who so loved their children, who celebrated procreation and multiple relations, and the flourishment of the lāhui (nation), such repeated losses were devastating. Although we cannot imagine the grief our chiefs endured during their lifetimes, that is, in many respects, the task of Bishop Museum—to keep the names, the struggles, the successes, and the stories of our ali'i's lives.

Although promised in marriage to Prince Lot Kapuāiwa, who would eventually become King Kamehameha V, Princess Pauahi met and wed Charles Reed Bishop, a New York merchant ten years her senior. The marriage, which had been orchestrated by the Cookes, a Protestant missionary family charged with educating the young chiefs, was opposed by the traditional Hawaiian ruling class, including her parents, Konia and Pākī, but it was eventually accepted. The young couple established themselves within the Hawaiian and developing business community, and Charles rose to hold prominent leadership positions within the Hawaiian monarchy. The couple also enjoyed traveling abroad and visited numerous museums across Europe, returning with a shared desire to create a museum that would preserve a Hawaiian heritage that was disappearing before their very eyes. Five years after his wife's death, Charles Reed Bishop brought this dream to life and established a museum whose original mission was to "preserve and display the cultural and historic relics of the Kamehameha family that Princess Pauahi had acquired." But the museum's founding collections also would come to include those of two other high-ranking ali'i wahine: Princess Pauahi's cousin, Princess Ruth Ke'elikōlani; and Queen Emma Rooke. All contemporaries, these three high-ranking chiefesses passed away without surviving children, their treasured heirlooms forming the founding collections of the museum. Bishop Museum's very existence is thus owed to our chiefs; its founding collections represent what our ali'i treasured and loved yet could no longer pass on to their lineal descendants.

Hō'ike'ike i na mea i hana 'ia
Me ka no'eau a nā kāhiko
Na mea hana lima i ho'iho'i ia mai
I ke one hānau o Hawai'i Nei

Exhibited are unusual objects
Skillfully manufactured by our forebearers
Whose ancient artifacts from distant lands
will return to Hawai'i

Over time, the museum's collections expanded, leading to a need for additional buildings and exhibition space. As Hawaiian Hall was being constructed in 1894, the Hawaiian newspaper *Ka Leo o ka Lahui* observed that "[t]his thing being built is a great treasure [*kekahi mea waiwai nui*]" that "will show our progressive state [*ke kulana holomua*]" and "become a place much visited by visitors and locals." In the face of tremendous upheaval—indeed, a mere year after the illegal overthrow of the Hawaiian Kingdom—the mana of generations of Hawai'i's monarchs could still be preserved and protected within the basalt structures of Kaiwi'ula.

As predicted, the grand, three-story Hawaiian Hall quickly became the jewel of the campus, housing the vast majority of the Hawaiian collection. In 1903, the year it opened, 1,467 Hawaiians visited the museum, representing 27 percent of the total visitors. But over the past century, this jewel has shown its age—peeling lead-based paint, termite-ravaged koa cases, rotting wood, and outdated electrical wiring. And just as its physical condition diminished, so too did the museum show the effects of time. Among the oldest of entities in Hawai'i, it has a storied past: purchasing skulls and tattooed limbs, excavating thousands of human remains, and denying the community access to its collections. Despite its Indigenous foundation, the museum was nonetheless at its core a fundamentally Western institution. But the museum has also done good things: collecting, preserving, and translating the chants, stories, and oral histories of Native Hawaiians; publishing some of the most important Hawaiian-language and cultural resources; and caring for the treasures of our ali'i. As with any institution with such a long history, Bishop Museum has many things to make up for, lessons to learn, relationships to mend, and wounds to heal.

When I began working at the museum in 1998, I was struck by the hostile attitude many Hawaiians had toward the museum, ranging from views about its irrelevance to feelings of multigenerational resentment. It was not seen as a welcoming place. Even for tourists and other residents, the exhibits were tired and dated. One college professor had been bringing his exchange students through Hawaiian Hall every year for over a decade, and he always used the same worksheets because nothing ever changed.

But in the mid-2000s, a shift happened. Temporary exhibitions started to address Hawaiian content such as the seasonal gods and their responsibilities, or the art of kapa making, and included Hawaiian cultural practitioners and visual artists. Beginning in 2006, Bishop Museum helped launch Maoli Arts Month with an annual Native Hawaiian arts market and contemporary exhibition in downtown Chinatown. And perhaps most importantly, Bishop Museum embarked on a long overdue project to renovate Hawaiian Hall, which by then was over a century old. As one of the five members of the internal content development team, I can attest to our recognition of the importance of not just looking at the process as a physical renovation, but as a restoration.

And what does one restore? One restores health, one restores trust, one restores faith, one restores a foundation, one restores a nation. This was an opportunity to forge reconnections with communities long since estranged from the museum and to create more meaningful, relevant, and responsive permanent exhibitions. We accomplished this in part through a commitment to a new style of engagement, ending practices such as speaking *about* Hawaiians rather than *with* them. We no longer described "lost" arts, and we steered away from the objectification of Hawaiian artifacts. We grounded the project upon Hawaiian values and perspectives instead of perpetuating romantic distortions of history through Western lenses.

Interior view of renovated Hawaiian Hall. *Photograph courtesy of Bishop Museum.*

Through consultation with Hawaiian community leaders, scholars, artists, and practitioners, the museum strove to create a hall that reflected a Hawaiian world view. A decade later, I now recognize the extent of our decolonial engagement, which fundamentally altered a history of institutional practice by moving beyond mere community consultation and toward shared authority and decision-making.

Today, a tour of Hawaiian Hall reveals three floors that have been overlaid with the physical and spiritual realms of the Hawaiian people: from the first floor of Kai Ākea (the wide expanse of the sea); to the second floor, Wao Kanaka (the realm of humans); to the third floor, Wao Lani (the heavenly realm). The exhibition reflects upon the gods—their different bodily forms, their areas of responsibility, and their seasonal changes. It illuminates the lunar cycle, which determined how Hawaiians fished, planted, and worshiped. The hall is filled with Hawaiian voice through chants, proverbs, and moʻolelo (stories) shared through audio and video, labels, and interactive media displays. Each floor contains works by contemporary Hawaiian artists alongside those created by our ancestors, emphasizing the continuity of the Hawaiian people through time. On the third floor is the world of our chiefs—not only who they were, but how they were related, for these are the threads of mana, of power, that formed the living tapestry upon which our kingdom was founded. But this is not merely an honorific treatment of our ali'i; it is a recognition of both their blessings and their burdens as they carried the weight of a nation upon their shoulders.

Importantly, the exhibition also addresses the illegal overthrow of Queen Lili'uokalani in 1893, what lead to it, what transpired, and how the Hawaiian community responded—whether through a thwarted armed insurrection, the writing of a song, or the fine stitching of a protest quilt. An interactive kiosk enables users to search tens of thousands of names of those who signed the anti-annexation petitions in 1897–98 to protest the annexation of Hawai'i by the United States. The final display in Wao Lani is a mural created by over a dozen Native Hawaiian high school students who were asked to reflect upon the prophecy of Kapihe, who lived during the time of Kamehameha the Great. He predicted an overturning that came to pass with the overthrow of the Hawaiian kapu, or religious system, and the coming of Christianity.

E iho ana o luna
E pi'i ana o lalo
E hui ana nā moku
E kū ana ka paia

that which was above would come down
that which was below would rise up
the islands shall unite
the walls shall stand firm

This chant represents a change in the social and political order and is as relevant today as when it was first uttered. It enables us to look not only at the overthrow of the kapu system, or that of Queen Lili'uokalani, but also at the Hawaiian renaissance movement of the 1970s through today. This chant acknowledges difficulty and sorrow, heartache and turmoil, warfare and destruction. It acknowledges that despite these profound changes, we are still here. It is a prophecy that we will stand together in the face of adversity and that we are a stronger and more united community, not in spite of our past, but because of it.

The opening of Hawaiian Hall in 2009 was a major community event marked by hula (dance), pounding pahu (drums), waiving kāhili (feathered standards), and oli (chant) lifted by the 'olauniu breeze that blew through the grounds. It was a moment of pride that transcended Bishop Museum itself, and perhaps most importantly, the museum was able to restore its relationship with the Hawaiian community. In the words of artist Imaikalani Kalahele, "For the first time, Hawaiian Hall feels Hawaiian."

I would be remiss if I did not point out the newly renovated J. Watumull Planetarium, with its daily shows; the Science Adventure Center, which explores the science of the stars and the seas; Castle Memorial Building, which houses special traveling exhibitions; and the newest restored permanent exhibition space, Pacific Hall. Indeed, the planetarium played a key role in revitalizing long-distance Polynesian wayfinding; present-day master navigator Nainoa Thompson used the site in the late 1990s to study the movement and positions of celestial bodies, laying the foundation for the development of a Hawaiian star compass in use to this day. Bishop Museum has much more to it than the three-storied Hawaiian Hall, and yet that is where I believe its piko, or center, resides, in all its multilayered complexity. Are the exhibitions perfect? No, far from it. Do they adequately address the enduring challenges of military occupation, commercial exploitation of Hawaiian culture, and the lack of recognition of our sovereign status? Indeed not. Nonetheless, Hawaiian Hall represents a fundamental step forward from the museum's dated, colonial past, as it is filled now with the living presence of Native Hawaiians as embodied in and animated by our works, our stories, and our voices.

And if you plan your visit right, on Wednesdays at mid-day you can find a dozen Hawaiian artists and practitioners set up under a tent on Bishop Museum's central lawn. This weekly event is not an official scheduled program; you won't find it on the website. Rather, it has unfolded organically throughout this past decade, beginning with just a few people coming together to hone their skills communally in the presence of their ancestral works. The group has now doubled in size, and you can almost always find at work wood carvers and lauhala (pandanus) weavers who relish the opportunity to share their love of the arts with fellow practitioners, students, and visitors.

In the end I left Bishop Museum, and it was one of the hardest decisions I ever made. But she endures as my wahi pana, a sacred place where I breathed in our history, agency, activism, and our enduring ea, our self-determination. And still, I return, because every moment, every intimacy, every label, every artist statement, every art piece, every ancestral work continues to resonate as brightly as Kaiwi'ula's red-framed mountains at sunset. Over the past two decades I have come to love Bishop Museum, just as I imagine those first visitors did over a century ago. There is heartbreak and loss in the stories she holds, but so too is there brilliance and resilience. Museums, when they are at their very best, are places of transformation, capable of changing us fundamentally, intellectually, emotionally, and spiritually. That is the gift that Bishop Museum offers if you have the will to accept her embrace.

Ka ʻāina kahua nani o Kaiwiʻula
Nā mea makamae a kāhiko
Hoʻomaikaʻi mākou i ka poʻe i alu like mai
No laila ko mākou aloha
E kou lokomaikaʻi he nui
E ka Wahine-hele-la o Kaiona
E ola o Pauahi Lani
A kau i ka puaneane

The beautiful land, Kaiwiʻula
Where all may observe these ancient treasures
We thank those who made it possible
Therefore, our love
For your great goodness
The lady Kaiona
Long live the Chiefess Pauahi
To the extreme end of life

Notes

1   This oli was written for Bishop Museum by Mary Kawena Pukui. It is distributed
    throughout this essay but usually is presented as a whole.
2   Bishop Museum (website), accessed July 6, 2017. www.bishopmuseum.org/about-us/.

Resources

Kamakawiwoʻole Osorio, Jonathan Kay. *Dismembering Lāhui: A History of the Hawaiian
    Nation to 1887*. Honolulu: University of Hawaiʻi Press, 2002.
Restoring Bishop Museum's Hawaiian Hall: Hoʻi Hou Ka Wena I Kaiwiʻula. Honolulu:
    Bishop Museum Press, 2009.
Rose, Roger. *A Museum to Instruct and Delight: William T. Bingham and the Founding of
    Bernice Pauahi Bishop Museum.* Honolulu: Bishop Museum Press, 1980.

Joy Lehuanani Enomoto

Reclaiming the 'Ili of Haukulu
and 'Aihulama

I began thinking seriously about the role of botanic gardens and arboretums as tools of empire while working with the rare book collection at the University of Hawai'i at Mānoa. The sheer volume of eighteenth- and nineteenth-century texts devoted to botanical collections gathered during scientific expeditions revealed that controlling nature was a definite aspect of colonization. "Scientific imperialism and exotic botany came together in the creation of the colonial botanic gardens."[1]

I was working as a reference librarian in the Hawaiian Pacific collection when I came across books that discussed the ways that the Hawaii Sugar Planters' Association planted fast-growing economic trees in an effort to save the watershed. They wanted to protect the watershed in order to grow sugar propagated in experiment stations, one of which was where Lyon Arboretum now stands. Harold Lyon, for whom the arboretum is named, was convinced that those recommending the use of native species for reforesting the watershed were wrong. He was fully convinced that Hawai'i's native forests were doomed and so recommended the introduction of over eight thousand plants, shrubs, and economic plants between 1918 and 1936.[2]

It pushed me to learn which plants and trees existed before the Lyon Arboretum and the sugar planter experiment stations. What plants were known to Native Hawaiians in the areas named 'Aihualama and Haukulu in Mānoa Valley? The meaning of place-names provides a complex *map* for Hawaiians. 'Aihualama (to eat of the fruit of the lama) implies healing and enlightenment and also informs us that lama trees grew in the area. Wood from the endemic lama tree was used for medicine and placed on hula altars because its name, which means "torch," suggested enlightenment. A sick person was

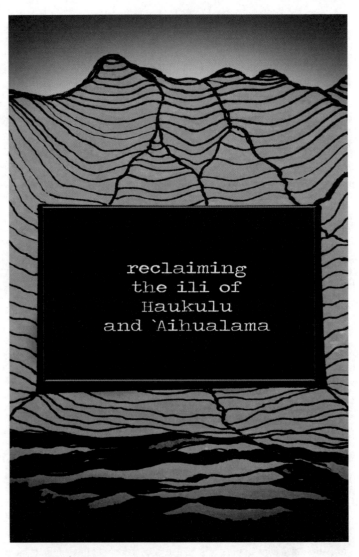

reclaiming
the ili of
Haukulu
and `Aihualama

Richard Harry Drayton, *Nature's Government: Science, Imperial Britain, and the "Improvement" of the World.*

Native plants: hoi kuahiwi, 'iliahi, lola, ohe kukuluaeo.

Native plants: ʻohia ʻai, kī, hāhā, p̄ia, maiʻa.

Native plants: nānu, awa, kukui, māmaki, kalo.

Native plants: lama, lehua, hame, ʻolena.

Non-native plants: strawberry guava, poha berry, lantana, passion flower.

Non-native plants: blackberry, sow thistle, blackjack, dogtail, Japanese hawkweed,
Barbados cherry.

placed inside structures made of lama wood that were constructed in a single day during daylight.

Haukulu, on the other hand, means "dripping dew" and refers to the dew that drips from the hau trees in the area. The hau tree is considered to be one of the kinolau (plant forms) of Kahaukani, whose wife was Kuahine and their daughter was Kahalaopuna. Kahalaopuna was killed by her husband, who believed she had been unfaithful. Out of grief, her mother became the rain known as ua Kuahine of Mānoa and her father became the wind called makani Kahaukani and a hau tree. The tree moaned in grief whenever royalty died.[3] It is also said that Queen Kaʻahumanu kept a home near this area and grew hau trees.

Hawaiians also introduced plants from other parts of the Pacific—plants for food, for medicine, for ceremony, and for better understanding their world. Europeans who arrived in the eighteenth through early twentieth centuries altered the landscape with the intention of taming nature and exploiting it for economic gain. Botanic gardens became exotic displays of their triumph over nature.

Of course, much has been learned since the days of Harold Lyon. Many current ongoing efforts aim to restore Native plants to the arboretum. But it is important to understand that botanic gardens have complicated and oppressive histories. Scenic hikes through nature with conveniently carved out trails came at a high cost to Native Hawaiians, who relied on the streams and plants of the valley for survival. Tourists should not take botanic gardens and arboretums at face value, as natural, but instead as an attempt to escape history.

Notes

1   Richard Aitken, *Botanical Riches: Stories of Botanical Exploration* (Aldershot, UK: Lund Humphries, 2007).

2   Robert V. Osgood and Robert D. Weimer, "Plant Introduction Needs of the Hawaiian Sugar Industry," in *Alien Plant Invasions in Native Ecosystems of Hawaiʻi: Management and Research*, ed. Charles P. Stone, Clifford W. Smith, J. Timothy Tunison, 726–31 (Honolulu: University of Hawaiʻi, Cooperative National Park Resources Studies Unit, 1992).

3   Mary Kawena Pukui and Dietrich Varez, "'Ōlelo Noʻeau 1574," in *'Ōlelo Noʻeau: Hawaiian Proverbs and Poetical Sayings*, Bernice P. Bishop Museum Special Publication 71 (Honolulu: Bishop Museum Press, 1983).

Gregory Chun

_____

Keauhou Resort

Rethinking Highest and Best Use

The Keauhou Resort ("Resort") comprises approximately 2,200 acres situated five miles south of Kailua-Kona Village on Hawai'i Island. The region of Kona has a strong tradition of leadership, both before and after Western contact, that profoundly shaped the course of Hawaiian history—something that has been ignored in the marketing of Kona as a visitor destination. The 'āina (land) upon which the resort was established is owned by Kamehameha Schools ("KS"). These lands were deeded by Princess Bernice Pauahi Bishop, granddaughter of Kamehameha 'Ekahi, to the Bishop Estate Trust ("Trust"), which is charged in perpetuity with supporting the education of Native Hawaiian children.

The Keauhou Resort was envisioned in the 1960s to address the land-rich, cash-poor position of the trust. Actual development began later in the decade, and at its peak the resort consisted of three hotels offering over a thousand visitor rooms, a retail shopping center, thirty-six holes of golf, and single- and multi-family residential developments targeting second-home buyers. Over time, however, the resort did not keep pace with its competitors. The Keauhou Master Plan was adopted in 2001 to rebrand the resort as a cultural and educational destination targeting an eco-culture-savvy visitor and includes a commitment to the restoration of wahi pana (legendary places) and development of place-based curricula for students and visitors.

As the process unfolded, there emerged a profound shift in awareness of the highest and best use for the 'āina. Today, after over a decade of significant investment, the Keauhou Master Plan, which revolved around an economic concept of "highest and best use," has been shelved in favor of remaking the resort lands with education as a priority. This is the story of how this happened and what it means for development in Hawai'i. It is written as a reflection of someone who led this process. The result, it is hoped, is that developers seeking to share the story of place see with fresh eyes how to honor the Indigenous people of those lands.

Travelogue, August 2004: Keauhou, A New Era

I am privileged to be gifted leadership of the Keauhou Resort and steward of 2,200 acres of historically significant legacy 'āina owned by the largest private landowner in Hawai'i. The kuleana (responsibility) I have stepped into includes overseeing the implementation of the Keauhou Master Plan ("Plan").

The primary purpose of the Plan is to exercise the Trust's fiduciary responsibility to ensure its assets are made productive for the support of Kamehameha Schools' educational mission. It was adopted in 2001 after a protracted review of Trust holdings, coming on the heels of years of political and legal turmoil threatening the Trust's very existence, in which the Resort came to be viewed as an "underperforming asset." The vision seeks to reposition the Resort as a cultural and education destination, integrating the rich and significant history of this 'āina with place-based educational programming targeting an eco-culture-savvy visitor *and* Native Hawaiian learners while retaining many traditional resort elements. At full build-out it includes 1,200 new homes and time-shares, a golf course, and a revitalized shopping center. This vision is intended to leverage the considerable educational, cultural, and land stewardship expertise the institution has developed as an Ali'i Trust and a leading Native Hawaiian–serving organization in the state. Preliminary estimates suggest returns on our investment could run in the mid–six figures. It is a bold vision and one that has never been attempted at this scale in the history of resort development in Hawai'i. Keauhou, literally translated as "a new era," is born once more from its 1960s origins, and it is both an honor and a humbling experience to be asked to navigate this journey.

Travelogue, September 2005:
Keauhou, The Returning Current

As is the case in all significant development projects in Hawai'i, it is best to begin by immersing yourself in the history of the place. *Development* and *being a developer* are loaded terms in today's world, especially if you are Native Hawaiian like myself. Through becoming kama'āina (a person of the land), you open yourself to allowing the people, environment, and history of the place to shape your worldview and your understanding of the relationship between nature and humans. Through that process you gain valuable insight on how to shape your vision to be compatible with the physical and social elements defining the context in which you are operating.

Compatibility with place and people are critical components not just of successful development in Hawaiʻi but also of our aspirations for sustainability and social justice. They also happen to be critical elements for creating rich visitor experiences. The voyage begins with an immersion into the history and legacy of these lands, (re)connecting to voices of the land, past and present, that bestir a returning current, yet another translation of Keauhou.

The Natural Landscape

To understand traditional life and custom as it must have been lived on Kona, one must first understand the natural elements that characterize this region. In the Hawaiian worldview, life and custom start with a close understanding of and intimate relationship with ʻāina, typically translated as meaning "land." But ʻāina is far more complex than that; it literally means "that which feeds." Thus, Hawaiian life and custom were based on an intimately spiritual relationship to all elements and resources that sustained life, inclusive of land, sky, and sea. In the traditional Hawaiian creation story called the Kumulipo, humans' relationship to ʻāina is familial in that we share a common genealogical ancestry.

The Resort spans the makai (seaward) portions of three ahupuaʻa (traditional land divisions)—Kahaluʻu, Keauhou I, and Keauhou II. Ahupuaʻa represent more than a means of defining land units. They represent separate resource management units derived from the intimate relationship Hawaiians held with ʻāina and from ecosystem knowledge developed through keen observational skills. Typically, though not always, they span stretches of ʻāina that run mauka to makai (from the mountain to sea) through which traditional governance were exercised and agriculture and commerce managed. Thus, ahupuaʻa served as the physical infrastructure within which sociopolitical and economic activity was practiced. While similar systems are found elsewhere in Polynesia, it seems to have been developed to a higher degree of complexity in Hawaiʻi, and on Hawaiʻi Island in particular, reflecting the complex system of rule that defined culture, politics, and daily life in traditional Hawaiian society.

Hawaiians also organized their activity across elevation changes within ahupuaʻa. The lands of the Resort cover what Hawaiians referred to as the kahakai (the area near the sea often referred to as the strand or beach area), kula (arid coastal lands upland from the sea), apaʻa (dryland forest and

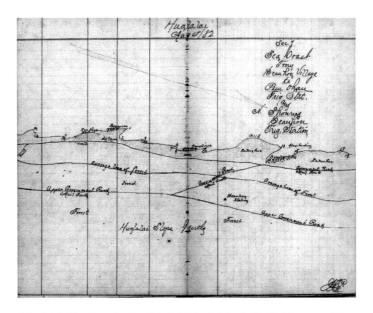

Early sketch of lands south of Keauhou, indicating kula lands. *Map by J. Perryman, 1883.*

grassland ecosystems), and the amaʻu (fern belt). These ecosystems have been greatly impacted by ranching and plantation agriculture over the years, not just in Keauhou but also across the Hawaiian Islands in general. So much of the present-day ecosystems do not match the environmental conditions Hawaiians once knew and relied upon. In general, in traditional times the kahakai, kula, apaʻa, and amaʻu zones were actively "managed" for habitation, gathering of various resources, ceremonial uses, and agriculture.

Keauhou is a semiarid region whose climate and soil conditions are defined and dominated by the convergence of Hualālai and Mauna Loa, massive shield volcanoes upon whose slopes the project was developed. Climbing steadily eastward from the Pacific shore, this geography creates a rain shadow effect whereby precipitation in West Hawaiʻi is mostly due to the effects of evapotranspiration, the daily accumulation of condensation mauka fueled by marine evaporation, heating of the land, and the blocking of the dominant northeast trade winds by Mauna Loa. A great disparity exists between the precipitation rate in the uplands above the Resort and that in the coastal zone. The relatively young age of Hualālai (300–500 million years old) and Mauna Loa (700,000 to 1 million years old), and the basaltic nature of their geologic composition, results in rocky, shallow, and porous soil.

Kona is and has always been known for its rich marine environment and the bounty of its nearshore and pelagic fisheries. Together, rainfall patterns, soil conditions, and the ocean characterized early life in the region; agricultural activities occurred mostly at higher elevations and habitation at lower levels, leading to an almost daily mauka-to-makai rhythm and pattern of subsistence and commerce.

Settlement Patterns and Land Use

Characteristics of the natural landscape shaped settlement patterns across all of Polynesia. Consistent with other Polynesian island nations, the initial settlement of the Hawaiian Islands is believed to have occurred along the wetter and more fertile windward coasts, where conditions were optimal for farming and where ample marine resources existed. Less hospitable leeward environments, such as at Keauhou, were also occupied, but typically only intermittently, perhaps seasonally. Permanent leeward expansion inland is believed to have occurred only with the development or improvement of dry land cultivation methods and, here in Hawai'i, possibly with the introduction of sweet potato (between AD 1100 and 1400, about six hundred to nine hundred years after the initial settlement of Hawai'i). Archaeological studies and radiocarbon dating from data recovery excavations in the Resort over the years suggest four chronological phases of settlement consistent with the projected timetable for leeward expansion: phase 1 (AD 1250–1450), phase 2 (AD 1450–1650), phase 3 (AD 1650–1820), and phase 4 (AD 1820–1955).

Between AD 1250 and 1450, permanent habitation occurred primarily in the coastal areas, whereas inland sites were more likely temporary habitation sites associated with agricultural features. Initial settlers used higher, wetter elevations for agriculture in order to ensure the success of their crops. The coastal settlements were located relatively close to the upland fields, which were at an elevation of 900–1,100 feet—probably no more than an hour's walk. The relatively easy distances involved did not necessitate the establishment of permanent or even temporary heavy-use habitation sites in the upland areas. The drier, less optimal conditions of leeward Hawai'i suggest that inhabitants were heavily dependent on marine resources for subsistence before agricultural activities further mauka were intensified.

Phase 2 generally parallels what some archaeologists have interpreted as the "expansion" or "intensification" period (AD 1450–1650). Archaeological evidence from the phase 2 period indicates a dramatic increase of inland habitation and the number of agricultural sites, as well as the earliest evidence for sweet potato in the ahupua'a. A common interpretation of the move inland and the increase in agricultural activity is that a growing population required more food to be produced. Supporting this interpretation is that one also sees during this phase an increase in the development of other infrastructure to support a growing society, such as large, monumental heiau.

Heiau, roughly equivalent to a temple or place of worship, come in many sizes and varieties, but the larger ones took on a more pronounced role in society. These structures were labor intensive to construct, requiring more "management" and direction by the Ali'i (the leadership class). They were also places where more complex ritual and protocol were practiced, suggesting an evolving religious system. The construction of new monumental heiau was a possible response to a growing community and an indication of a maturing social structure. The Resort—indeed the Kona area in general—is home to the remains of significant heiau and development, indicating the prominence of this region in the governance of the island during this early period and eventually of the Hawaiian nation.

The pattern of increasing development inland and mauka continues and intensifies in phase 3 (AD 1650–1820), particularly in areas above the Resort where agricultural consolidation starts to occur. One of the unique agricultural technologies developed by early residents is known as the Kona Field System, a complex network of stone structures built in a variety of designs intended to capture and direct moisture, between and upon which a range of crops were grown. Accounts of the Kona Field System by Captains Cook and Vancouver, and missionaries such as Ellis, indicate that the system extended from the uplands of Kealakekua south of the Resort to the uplands of Keahole (above the current day airport), a distance of more than twenty miles. The system was mostly developed between elevations of one thousand and two thousand feet (the typical rain belt), although remnants of the system can be found in some areas at lower and higher elevations. Recent research indicates that the system was designed to maximize production in the microclimate conditions at specific locations. Together, this information suggests that early Hawaiians had developed a high degree of knowledge and skill that allowed them to optimize production in dry land agriculture.

Between AD 1820 and 1955, land use and development on the lands of Keauhou were defined by the growth of ranching and, to a lesser extent, plantation-style agriculture (primarily sugar), the result of Western contact. This period in Hawaiian history is also when we begin to see the dislocation of people from land as a result of the imposition of Western forms of land ownership. In economic and social terms, the changing settlement patterns between the early historic period and the twentieth century reflects the gradual shift from subsistence agriculture and the harvesting of marine resources to a market economy in the latter part of the nineteenth century. The focus of habitation and commerce shifts from the coast to the uplands, farther west and inland, and most of the productive economic activities become associated with ranching inclusive of pipi (cattle), kao (goats), and hipa (sheep).

These animals were originally allowed to roam freely, although kapu (restrictions, in this case associated with the capture and eating of pipi) were set by Kamehameha I at the request of Captain Vancouver in 1794. By the early 1800s these wandering animals caused enough damage to warrant the construction of walls and walled enclosures to keep them from further destroying crops, homes, and forests. Remnants of one such significant walled structure, the Kuakini Wall (named after John Adams Ki'iapalaoku Kuakini, who served as governor of Hawai'i Island from 1820 to 1844), remain throughout the Resort.

Travelogue, April 2007 to June 2009: Five Men, Five Heiau

It is clear that this is no ordinary asset and that the Plan requires a different approach if we are to achieve this balance of educational and economic interests with integrity. Consistent with most communities created from master plans, development proceeds first with the community-building elements of the project. In our case, implementation of the master plan begins with a significant commitment by the Trust to restoring the significant heiau in the Resort and developing place-based curricula to support their interpretation in ways that serve the Trust's educational and economic goals.

Contrary to what might be assumed from a Hawaiian organization dedicated to education, cultural preservation, and land stewardship, this commitment does not come naturally. As an organization founded on Christian values, the restoration of wahi pana such as these, which were once home to the practice of "pagan religion," raises significant questions from both internal and external stakeholders as to the purposes of this work. The issue is resolved only when we successfully persuade the trustees and the Native Hawaiian community that physically restoring a site does not mean reestablishing all the practices once associated with it, and people are able to see the value these sites can serve as educational platforms not just for telling the history of our people, but for honoring the science, technology, and the arts of our ancestors as well. A compromise is reached.

Restoration begins with the sites at Kahalu'u makai. This complex is unusual in the sense that in very few places across the islands does one find a collection of this many religious structures co-located in one area. Historical evidence indicates that Kahaluʻu makai was home to many Hawaiʻi Island aliʻi between AD 1400 and 1800, and its physical development supports the notion that Kahaluʻu was a seat of governance for those in rule at a given time. Kahaluʻu makai was where our leaders were born and trained, and it is where they convened and governed from, making many significant decisions affecting the course of Hawaiian history.

The work of restoration begins with lifting the kapu associated with the complex of five heiau located there. This is important protocol because we need permission from the ancestors to do this work, as we will be physically manipulating the tangible remains of their vision, intentions, practices, and efforts. The men who will work on this need to be protected from any hewa (curse) that lingers with these sites. We can only work on one site at a time, and the decision is to begin with Hapaialiʻi, a large platform heiau whose purposes are not well documented. In the amber of sunset the ceremony concludes, and our men hear voices calling out from the nearby heiau: "Don't forget us, don't forget us, please don't forget us." We take this as a hōʻailona (sign) that the work we embark on is deemed acceptable by the ancestors and that after years of neglect and development, the aliʻi have returned. It is a special moment in history because KS has never embarked on such a monumental endeavor. No one has. This *is* a big deal.

Over the course of the next two years we complete the restoration of five heiau through the efforts of five men and a Bobcat. Impressive, but also not without controversy. Some question our use of modern equipment in completing the work—we are told that "it's not how our ancestors would build a heiau." We seek guidance from one of our kupuna (elder) advisors, a retired heavy equipment operator, on his estimate for completing this work using nothing more than physical labor and hand tools. He thinks the work will require two hundred to three hundred men working over a five-year period. We ask for volunteers; few step forward. So, even if we wanted to remain true to the practice of our ancestors, we determine it is unrealistic. Thus the work continues and is completed.

Restoration of a cultural site is never complete unless it is interpreted and its story told. In our case, the restoration was also not complete until the sites were repurposed as educational venues for the teaching of culture, history, science, and the arts. Before commencing restoration activities, numerous place-based educational and visitor activities were developed and those programs now enjoy the added benefit of these restored sites serving as the classroom. These programs touch hundreds of learners annually.

Kahaluʻu Manowai with hotel. *Photograph by Kamehameha Investment Corporation.*

Travelogue, 2008–2011: Ancient Ways, New Beginnings

However, something unforeseen begins to occur as the cultural foundations of the Resort are reawakened. As the heiau rise from the ocean, and as the light is ignited in the eyes of those learning about this place—young and old, kamaʻāina and malihini (visitors)—we begin to see the project anew and to ask different questions about our institutional purposes and values as they relate to the master plan. Can 1,200 homes, and the people who occupy them, coexist amid such historical and cultural significance? Can history and culture be preserved, and can education be delivered, all with integrity in a project of this scale? When the remnants of our past are brought to life in the way they have been here, our naʻau (intuition) raises doubts.

The clarity of this discord is evident when considering the physical elements of what we wanted to do on the land with the evidence of what was already there. We overlaid the results of years of archaeological and historical studies on the proposed master plan. The resulting images proved disconcerting. The consolidated map of the archeological sites—which number in the thousands—overlapped heavily with the planned development areas for the Resort.

The culmination of this emerging dissonance comes at two separate junctures. First, standing atop the Keauhou Beach Resort (KBR) upon completion of the heiau restoration, one of the trustees turns and says to me in utter innocence and awe, "How can we develop time-shares on these lands as called for in the master plan? I can't see it. This place is screaming to be preserved as an educational asset." This was more than significant, it was monumental, for it introduced the idea that the highest and best use of an asset may not be economic. To consider this goes against the grain of every developer, including KS. It also contradicts the very definition of this core real estate concept. But it was and is consistent with the multiple objectives we were trying to achieve, so the idea had space to incubate in our cognitive universe.

The second moment came during our search for a development partner to assist us with implementing the master plan. Our vision of building a resort community around a theme of lifelong learning and cultural stewardship was unique and unlike what successful resort developments were doing at the time. The tensions between optimizing economic returns over the values of culture, education, and community defined every negotiation we entered. It was proving more and more difficult to find a partner who valued the same things, in the same proportions, as we did. Finally, a friend and competitor framed the conflict we were feeling as such: "You folks are in a position to do something game-changing but you first need to get clear on one thing. Are you a resort that happens to have this huge collection of historically and culturally important wahi pana throughout your property deserving of preservation, or are you a wahi pana that happens to have resort zoning? Once you decide that, you'll know which way to go."

Travelogue, 2011–2013: Redefining Highest and Best Use

Institutional change is always difficult and can be costly and have negative results. But change can also have profound positive outcomes, especially when guided by values that are true to the mission of the organization. KS is a unique organization in its mission (education, culture, community, and land stewardship) and in its assets ($10.6 billion in 2015–16). Few could make the change they have decided on here in Keauhou. After years of investment, planning, replanning, and reflection, in 2013 it was decided that the Keauhou Master Plan would be abandoned in its entirety. A new plan for Kahalu'u makai was adopted.

Kahaluʻu Manowai's highest and best use. *Photograph by Kamehameha Investment Corporation.*

Named Kahaluʻu Manowai in reference to the system of underground freshwater circulation that Kahaluʻu was known for, this new plan serves as a metaphor for the renewal of these special lands. The new plan calls for the demolition of KBR and the redevelopment of the heiau complex and adjoining twenty-one acres into an educational center focused on developing ʻāina-based, hands-on programs that teach culture, history, science, and the arts. This vision is bold, dedicating the last remaining oceanfront property in KS' portfolio of developable lands and repurposing it strictly for education and cultural preservation. In this case, "highest and best use" means that education prevailed over economics. This is a gutsy call and, for the future of the Hawaiian Lāhui, a huge investment in the future.

David Uahikeaikalei'ohu Maile

'A'ole Is Our Refusal

'A'OLE

No, not, never; to be none, to have none.

'A'ole loa! Certainly not! Not at all! I should say not! Never!—*Mary Kawena Pukui and Samuel H. Elbert*

In the summer of 2014 the U.S. Department of the Interior (DOI) held public meetings throughout Hawai'i and on the North American continent in Indian Country to garner feedback on reestablishing a government-to-government relationship between Kanaka Maoli and the United States. The meetings, mandated by the Advance Notice for Proposed Rulemaking (ANPRM), solicited input on whether and how an administrative rule should be implemented to provide a procedure, or legal pathway, for U.S. federal recognition of a reorganized Kanaka 'Ōiwi governing entity. It was a busy summer for the DOI, but also for Kānaka Maoli, who, with incredibly short notice, came out in full force to attend the public meetings and refuse what the DOI was selling.

When the DOI arrived in Hawai'i, Kānaka Maoli unapologetically rejected the offer of federal recognition. During the first public meeting on June 23 held in Honolulu, O'ahu, Juanita Kawamoto testified to representatives from the DOI, "I'd just like to say **no thank you**. Also, I'd like to be clear, all the things that you're doing here today are completely inappropriate, and I'm speaking in clear English so that all of you can understand, this is very inappropriate, to the point of [being] absolutely disrespectful to our people here." The refusals called out the DOI's push to federally recognize a new

Native Hawaiian governing entity as well as the executive department's presence in Hawai'i, tying this historical moment to an earlier moment of protest. "Oh, honest Americans," Lākea Trask exclaimed at the July 2 meeting in Keaukaha, Hawai'i, "I stand before you today empowered by the nearly 40,000 who signed the Kū'ē Petitions and said no to annexation, the hundreds who testified already on their behalf. I stand here, humbled, ha'aha'a, that you folks have come all this way to meet us face-to-face, alo i alo. And I stand before you, angered and outraged at your motives for being here, for trying once again to steal our identity." Kānaka Maoli opposed and challenged the proposal by drawing upon a historical tradition of resistance not simply to U.S. annexation but to American imperialism, empire, and settler colonialism in Hawai'i. As Trask's testimony illustrates, the invocation of the Kū'ē Petitions represents one example, among many others, in a mo'okū'auhau (genealogy) of 'Ōiwi refusals to U.S. control of our nation.

The Kū'ē Petitions, also known as the Palapala Hoopii Kue Hoohuiaina (petition protesting annexation), were signed by more than 38,000 Kānaka Maoli in protest against U.S. annexation of Hawai'i. Delivered to the Senate in 1897, the petitions persuaded senators to vote down a treaty of annexation and ultimately demonstrate that Kānaka Maoli have actively resisted U.S. colonialism. In her book *Aloha Betrayed*, which uncovers the petitions, Noenoe Silva discusses another document, the Palapala Hoopii (memorial), that was sent to President William L. McKinley and Congress in the same year. It was a memorial that "served as a moral challenge to the United States" to "live up to their own democratic principles and body of law."[1] A line from the Palapala Hoopii states, "The project of Annexation . . . would be subversive of the personal and political rights . . . of the Hawaiian people and Nation."[2] Silva writes that the Palapala Hoopii was crafted by Kānaka 'Ōiwi from the Komite o ka Lehulehu (Citizens' Committee).

One member of the committee and endorser of the memorial was C. B. Maile, my kupunakāne kualua (great-great-grandfather). I'll never forget the moment when I saw his name in the text *Aloha Betrayed*. I felt as if I was shaken from a hazy slumber. A feeling of immense pride came over me. Later, I would find out from my 'ohana that C. B. Maile also signed the Kū'ē Petitions. This discovery forced me to confront and accept my genealogical kuleana (responsibility). These moments were indeed liberating—they changed what I desired and how I lived—not just by recuperating the mo'olelo (stories and histories) and working to understand my mo'okū'auhau in relation to them, but because it compelled me to act, to do as my great-great-grandfather had done, and to be steadfast in protecting our lāhui, our people, our nation.

During the summer of 2014, I was pursuing my doctoral studies in Albuquerque, New Mexico, within the territory of the Pueblo of Sandia, and I was unfortunately unable to attend the DOI's public meetings in Hawai'i. After fifteen meetings in Hawai'i, the representatives of the DOI, accompanied by representatives from the Department of Justice and the Office of Hawaiian Affairs, traveled to Indian Country to solicit input on the ANPRM. I drove approximately seven hours from Albuquerque to Scottsdale, Arizona, to testify. I shook with nerves. But I wanted to make my kupunakāne kualua and 'ohana proud. I wanted to stand up for the lāhui. I wanted to communicate our unyielding refusal to be regulated, to be subordinated, and to be marginalized. On the territory of the Salt River Pima-Maricopa Indian Community, I felt C. B. Maile with me, guiding my voice, as I testified against U.S. federal recognition by saying, "With mahalo for the people Indigenous to these lands, and with great emphasis, I must say 'A'OLE to the Department of Interior." It is our collective story of Kanaka Maoli refusals that I humbly tell here.

From the DOI's perspective, extending federal recognition to Kanaka Maoli makes sense for several reasons. First, congressional statutes recognize an existing relationship with Native Hawaiians. This relationship, however, is not formally recognized as a government-to-government relationship. Second, the statutes created programs and services for Kānaka Maoli, such as the Hawaiian Homes Commission, which have produced more problems than they have solved despite the ANPRM claiming that "Congress has consistently enacted programs and services expressly and specifically for the Native Hawaiian community that are, in many respects, analogous to, but separate from, the programs and services that Congress has enacted for federally recognized tribes in the continental United States."[3] Third, federal recognition of Native American tribes implies a government-to-government relationship, allegedly bestowing sovereignty, granting self-determination, and providing benefits, but "the benefits of the government-to-government relationship have long been denied to one place in our Nation, even though it is home to one of the world's largest indigenous communities: Hawaii."[4] This rationale forged a rhetoric through which the DOI markets, sneakily indeed, the so-called gifts of federal recognition.

To me, the DOI's attempt to federally recognize a reorganized Native Hawaiian governing entity is an attempt to settle legal claims against the U.S. and settle Hawai'i once and for all. This is another hollow gesture, the latest scheme to dispossess and displace Kānaka Maoli. For instance, the DOI admits that the U.S. perpetrated the overthrow of the Hawaiian Kingdom. Yet, its admission has been warped and manipulated to provide evidence that "there has been no formal, organized Native Hawaiian government since 1893," when Queen Liliʻuokalani's government was illegally overthrown, and to suggest that reestablishing a government-to-government relationship is reconciliation.[5] One of the statutes deployed for this legal ruse is Public Law 103-150, the 1993 Apology Resolution, which confesses and acknowledges that ʻŌiwi sovereignty was never surrendered. The Apology Resolution contends that "the indigenous Hawaiian people never directly relinquished their claims to their inherent sovereignty as a people or over their national lands to the United States, either through their monarchy or through a plebiscite or referendum."[6] However, it absolves the U.S. from any culpability. J. Kēhaulani Kauanui argues that the Resolution is a no-fault apology: "It is clear that this particular apology is nothing but an empty gesture that served a limited political goal to recognize the one hundredth anniversary of the U.S.-backed unlawful overthrow of the Hawaiian Kingdom."[7] The ANPRM confirmed this empty gesture by asserting that federal recognition would not actually transform the existing relationship between the U.S. and the Native Hawaiian community in a way that would meaningfully address past wrongs. The apologetic state, it seems, wants to cure, vis-à-vis reconciliation, the harms it perpetrated. Testimony from the DOI meetings suggested, however, that Kānaka Maoli clearly see this legal trick as an attempt to coerce us into submitting to Congress's plenary power and acquiescing to U.S. settler sovereignty. Commenting on the settlement process enacted through federal recognition, Julian Aguon refers to this as "the red carpet the assassin lays out before the murder takes place."[8]

Therefore, when the DOI hosted public meetings to solicit feedback regarding whether and how the U.S. should federally recognize a reorganized Native Hawaiian government, Kānaka Maoli unequivocally responded: ʻaʻole. According to Protest Naʻi Aupuni, an organization formed on the ʻāina in response to federal and state initiatives for recognition, approximately 90 to 95 percent of Kānaka Maoli who testified opposed the proposed rulemaking. At the meeting in Waimānalo, Oʻahu, on June 23, Shane Pale succinctly addressed each threshold question by opining, "The short answer, again **no, no, no, no and no.**"

Despite explicit opposition, the DOI dismissed our testimonies and issued the Notice for Proposed Rulemaking (NPRM), which shored up the rhetoric from the ANPRM. The NPRM mandated that "nothing in this proposed rule would alter the sovereign immunity of the United States or the sovereign immunity of the state of Hawaii."[9] It further suggested that "reestablishment of the formal government-to-government relationship will not affect title, jurisdiction, or status of Federal lands and property in Hawaii. This provision does not affect lands owned by the state of Hawaii or provisions of State law."[10] What this means is that federal recognition would undeniably strengthen U.S. sovereignty to exercise territorial rule over Hawai'i. But, "to accept these conditions," according to Audra Simpson, "is an impossible project for some Indigenous people, not because it is impossible to achieve, but because it is politically untenable and thus normatively should be refused."[11]

Despite gross attempts to settle legal claims against the U.S. and settle Hawai'i overall, I believe it is crucial to map out how Kānaka Maoli refused the gifts of federal recognition with 'a'ole. At the meeting in Kahului, Maui, on July 8, Tisha-Marie Beattie responded to the threshhold questions by saying, "Your answer from me is **no**. You cannot give me back something I never gave up . . . take your thing you wanna give us, throw 'em in the trash. **We don't want it. We sovereign.**" During the same meeting, Kaleikoa Ka'eo proclaimed:

> **No consent, never.**
> No, Department of the Interior.
> **No treaty, never.**
> No, Department of the Interior.
> **No cession of our citizenship.**
> No, Department of the Interior.
> **No justice for our people for 120 years.**
> No to the Department of the Interior.
> **No lawful authority to sit upon our people and step upon our necks.**
> No to the Department of the Interior.

In Kapa'a, Kaua'i, on July 1, James Alalan Durest testified, "For you guys' answers for the questions, **hell no**." The refusal was resounding, and much more than just an answer of no. It was an answer of 'a'ole rooted to and articulating our historical tradition of resistance. At the same meeting in Kapa'a, Puanani Rogers posited, "I protest and oppose the advance notice [for] proposed rulemaking . . . and say **'a'ole**, which means **no** in English." Likewise, Mitchell Alapa noted, "All I got to say to you folks is 'a'ole. **All these things is 'a'ole.**" At Waimea, Hawai'i, Gale Ku'ulei Baker Miyamura Perez said, "I'm here to say **'a'ole, or no, to all of your questions.**" The 'a'ole also suggested that the DOI must leave, or, as Heali'i Kauhane phrased it in Keaukaha, "**go away.**" In Kaunakakai, Moloka'i, on June 28, Lawrence Aki demanded, "**You need to go home.**" At that same meeting, Walter Ritte concluded, "These hearings represent an honest reaction from the Hawaiian community. The majority is in no mood to continue our subservient relationship with the United States."

'A'ole, as a Kanaka Maoli enunciation of refusal, is a practice and politics for decolonization. In other words, 'a'ole is an 'Ōiwi refusal that offers a way to actualize decolonization. For Kānaka Maoli rejecting the unwanted offer of federal recognition, 'a'ole is our refusal to the ongoing colonization of Hawai'i. Settler colonialism is a system of power that seeks to dispossess, eliminate, and replace our lāhui, but it fails with every 'a'ole uttered. It fails with each 'a'ole performed in protest, protection, or blockade. Our 'a'ole exposes the failure of settler colonization. This is how 'a'ole maintains a decolonizing function. 'A'ole refuses the settlement of our 'āina. It refuses to forget our mo'olelo and mo'okū'auhau. It refuses legal subordination and asserts our own sovereign independence—our ea—within and beyond law. Like not giving an oli komo (welcome chant) when asked for permission to enter through an oli kāhea (entrance chant), we deny consent. Our swelling and firm 'a'ole to federal recognition is consent's revenge.[12] 'A'ole to DOI federal recognition of our lāhui. 'A'ole to that and much more. We must continue to assert 'a'ole, honoring the histories and stories of past refusals, in order to refuse, both in the present and future, *state*-determination in place for genuine *self*-determination.

It is time those being told **'A'OLE** actually listen.

Notes

Epigraph: Mary Kawena Pukui and Samuel H. Elbert, *Hawaiian Dictionary: Hawaiian-English, English-Hawaiian* (Honolulu: University of Hawai'i Press, 1986), 27.

1   Noenoe K. Silva, *Aloha Betrayed: Native Hawaiian Resistance to American Colonialism* (Durham, NC: Duke University Press, 2004), 154.

2   Silva, *Aloha Betrayed*, 153.

3   Office of the Secretary, Department of the Interior, Advanced Notice for Proposed Rulemaking, "Procedures for Reestablishing a Government-to-Government Relationship with the Native Hawaiian Community, 1090-AB05," *Federal Register* 79, no. 119 (June 20, 2014): 35299, https://www.gpo.gov/fdsys/pkg/FR-2014-06-20/pdf/2014 -14430.pdf.

4   Office of the Secretary, Department of the Interior, "Procedures for Reestablishing," 35298.

5   Office of the Secretary, Department of the Interior, "Procedures for Reestablishing," 35298.

6   Joint Resolution to Acknowledge the 100th Anniversary of the January 17, 1893, Overthrow of the Kingdom of Hawaii and to Offer Apology to Native Hawaiians on Behalf of the United States for the Overthrow of the Kingdom of Hawaii, Pub. L. No. 103-150, 107 Stat. 1510 (1993), 1513.

7 J. Kēhaulani Kauanui, "A Sorry State: Apology Politics and Legal Fictions in the Court of the Conqueror," in *Formations of United States Colonialism*, ed. Alyosha Goldstein (Durham, NC: Duke University Press, 2014), 113.

8 Julian Aguon, "The Commerce of Recognition (Buy One Ethos, Get One Free): Toward Curing the Harm of the United States' International Wrongful Acts in the Hawaiian Islands," *'Ohia: A Periodic Publication of Ka Huli Ao Center for Excellence in Native Hawaiian Law* 1, no. 1 (2012): 64.

9 Office of the Secretary, Department of the Interior, Notice for Proposed Rulemaking, "Procedures for Reestablishing a Government-to-Government Relationship with the Native Hawaiian Community, 1090-AB05," *Federal Register* 80, no. 190 (October 1, 2015): 59126.

10 Office of the Secretary, Department of the Interior, "Procedures for Reestablishing a Government-to-Government Relationship with the Native Hawaiian Community," 59126.

11 Audra Simpson, *Mohawk Interruptus: Political Life across the Borders of Settler States* (Durham, NC: Duke University Press, 2014), 22.

12 Audra Simpson, "Consent's Revenge," *Cultural Anthropology* 31, no. 3 (2016): 326–33.

Resources

"'AHA ALOHA 'ĀINA." *'Aha Aloha 'Āina* blog. Accessed July 26, 2018. http://www.ahaalohaaina.com.

Goodyear-Ka'ōpua, Noelani. "'Now we know': Resurgences of Hawaiian Independence." *Politics, Groups, and Identities* 6, no. 3 (2018): 453–65. https://doi.org/10.1080/21565503.2018.1472021.

Goodyear-Ka'ōpua, Noelani, and Bryan Kamaoli Kuwada. "Making 'Aha: Independent Hawaiian Futures." *Dædalus, the Journal of the American Academy of Arts and Sciences* 147, no. 2 (2018): 49–59.

"PROTEST NA'I AUPUNI." *Protest Na'i Aupuni*. Last modified March 3, 2017. http://www.protestnaiaupuni.wordpress.com.

Teves, Lani, and Maile Arvin. "Recognizing the Aloha in 'No.'" *Hawaii Independent*, July 7, 2014. http://www.hawaiiindependent.net/story/recognizing-the-aloha-in-no.

Iokepa Casumbal-Salazar

"Where Are Your Sacred Temples?"
Notes on the Struggle for Mauna a Wākea

Every day on Hawai'i Island, somewhere between 240 and 300 people drive 13,796 feet above sea level to visit the summit of Mauna Kea for recreational and scientific tourism. Close to a dozen commercial tour companies service the mountain, where visitors enjoy spectacular sunrises and sunsets, amateur stargazing at Hale Pōhaku (the midlevel visitor's center at 9,300 feet), and tours of the thirteen observatories on the summit. During winter months, when snow falls, many people go to sled, snowboard, and play. Others picnic, hike, or photograph the endlessly breathtaking views from this, the tallest peak in all of Oceania.

Since the first 12.5-inch telescope and state-funded six-mile road were built in 1964, Mauna Kea has become a world-class astronomical observatory, hosting some of the largest instruments of science in the world. It has also become a site of conflict between Kānaka 'Ōiwi and people who want more telescopes. The battle over development on Mauna a Wākea is like the broader struggle over Hawai'i. Indeed, the protests against astronomy expansion on Mauna a Wākea are a symptom of 125 years of military occupation of Hawai'i by the United States. Hawaiians have, for just as long, fought against a settler state dependent on the excesses of tourism and a distortion of history. Today, Western astronomy's cultural imperative to explore the universe and discover new worlds provides new justification for further land grabs. As an advocate for the protection of our ancestral homelands and our people's future, I write about Mauna a Wākea as a symbol of our collective struggle for life, land, and independence to contribute to raising a critical consciousness about settler colonization under U.S. occupation.

More Than a Telescope

For many, when thinking of Mauna Kea astronomy, people don't think, "Telescopes? Oh right: *structural violence!*" Generally, the assumption is, "Telescopes? Oh, yes: *progress* and *science*. How wonderful!" Yet, I argue we should be asking, "Who gets to decide what the future of Hawaiʻi should be?" Kānaka ʻŌiwi have a different conception of progress. For many, land is not a "resource" to be exploited for capitalist gains. Nor is it a "gift" to the world, as many would like to suggest. Our ʻike kupuna (ancestral knowledge) teaches that land is a relation, a perspective carried in the idea of aloha ʻāina. Often translated as "love of the land," this concept encompasses a deeper relationality than that found in Western notions of environmentalism. Indeed, ʻāina is the word for "land," but it translates to "that which feeds." ʻĀina is also a source of knowledge: it nourishes and teaches. A land-based orientation to the natural world, aloha ʻāina reflects the ways Kānaka form identities and values concerning future generations. When Kānaka fight to protect ʻāina—be it in the courts or by obstructing bulldozers—we, like other Native peoples the world over, are also fighting for freedom and the human right to determine the future of ancestral places, our ways of being, and our communities.

The telescope controversy signals a new stage in the Hawaiian movement. Argued to be the next "world's biggest telescope," the so-called Thirty Meter Telescope (TMT) would be astronomers' latest monument to Western scientific achievement. As the state talks of "progress" in its support for the TMT, it is borrowing from science its cultural authority as a voice of reason. The value of science to the state is the ideological substance it provides in justifying schemes to profit from land *as a resource*—one to be packaged, sold, and developed. In this sense, the struggle is about more than a telescope. It is about settler legitimacy, possession, and absolution from the guilt derived from accepting the spoils of U.S. imperialism in the Pacific. This struggle is about how we relate to land and water and to each other. It is about power and control.

Why Astronomers Love Mauna Kea

To astronomers, Mauna Kea is an unparalleled site for ground-based observations. The dormant shield volcano, located in the northern half of the Big Island of Hawaiʻi, is ideal for looking into space. The island's remote location means airstreams travel undisturbed for thousands of miles before reaching its shores, creating "smooth laminar flows" that help reduce atmospheric

View from Mauna Kea Observatory Road looking northwest toward Maui, with Haleakalā in the distance. From left to right, Subaru Telescope, W. M. Keck Observatory I and II, and NASA's Infrared Telescope Facility. *Photograph by Iokepa Casumbal-Salazar.*

turbulence and light distortion. Rising above nearly 40 percent of Earth's atmosphere, the summit is extremely dry and cold. It receives little light interference because it sits above the general cloud layer. Capturing views of the northern sky that telescopes south of the equator cannot, the "seeing" capabilities of telescopes on Mauna Kea are unsurpassed.

Since 1968, the University of Hawai'i (UH) has rented Mauna Kea's summit for a dollar per year through a sixty-five-year lease from the state of Hawai'i. Initial approval was to build one observatory, but within two decades seven telescopes had been erected and the giant twin Keck Observatory was under construction. In what is known as the Astronomy Precinct of the Mauna Kea Science Reserve, twenty-one telescopes are somehow counted as thirteen "observatories." The site is world-renowned for its innovations in telescope design and research, including findings that demoted Pluto to a dwarf planet, detected the supermassive black hole in the center of the Milky Way, and provided evidence of the accelerating expansion of the universe (for which astronomers won a Nobel Prize in 2011).

Today, however, these thirteen telescopes are not enough. Talk of a next generation of ELTS, or extremely large telescopes, began after a Keck expansion project was shot down in a legal challenge by Kānaka and allies. The Mauna Kea Science Reserve is in the "resource subzone" of the conservation district. According to conservation district laws, "astronomy facilities" are one of eight "identified land uses of the resource subzone." However, the category "resource subzone" was only added in 1994—thirty-three years *after* the laws creating the conservation district were written in 1961. This means that a new category of land use was created retroactively to legalize what would otherwise be prohibited: industrial development on protected lands. In 2010, the UH applied for a conservation district use permit to build the TMT—a $1.4 billion project that would stand eighteen stories tall, excavate eight acres of earth, and drill two stories down. In 2011, the permit was awarded and a contested case was initiated to hear public testimony.

Astronomers say that to understand the evolution of the universe and the very origins of humankind, they must study the oldest, most distant light. Astronomy is competitive, and the infinite expanse of space is rivaled only by astronomers' ambitions to know more. Designed to be the most powerful telescope in the world, the TMT promises a clear view to the ends of the universe: the ability to witness the formation and death of stars, to look further back in time than was ever before possible. During my interviews with astronomers, one argued that astronomy offers a "basic human knowledge that everyone should know," like "human anatomy." I argue, however, this framing presumes what constitutes "humanity" can only be measured according to Western knowledge systems. The implication of such models of humanity is that Indigenous knowledges do not count as "basic human knowledge."

A 2005 follow-up to a 1998 legislative audit found that, for thirty years, management by UH was "inadequate to ensure the protection of natural resources," controls were "late and weakly implemented," historic preservation was "neglected," and the "cultural value of Mauna Kea was largely unrecognized." UH was in danger of losing allies and sought to remake itself as a reformed caretaker. Acknowledging but yet downplaying a series of well-documented failures, UH assumed a mantle of "cultural sensitivity." It "recommitted to inclusivity" and promised "to do the TMT the right way." UH and astronomers now suggested they were honoring Native Hawaiian traditions of ocean voyaging, star-based navigation, exploration, and discovery. Like "ancient Hawaiians," they suggest, "modern astronomers" also share feelings of wonder and skill in studying the heavens—like "brothers and sisters." Not only was there an assumption that Native land should remain accessible to Western science, but even Native culture, history, and language were theirs for the taking. One thing TMT advocates fail to acknowledge, however, is the debt they owe to imperialism. Seldom do they account for the legacies of settler colonialism that rendered Native lands available to scientific tourism in the first place. Rather than turning over a new leaf, this seeming transformation is a move to settler innocence where astronomers, administrators, and TMT advocates imagine themselves as inheritors of Native traditions or heirs to Indigenous lands at the same time they cry victimhood. In the case of Mauna a Wākea, the idealized image of a Hawaiian as hospitable or compliant is welcome, but actual Hawaiians, those who think and protest, are not.

Kū Kiaʻi Mauna

The people leading the charge to defend Mauna a Wākea call themselves "kiaʻi," or "protectors," not protesters. While some TMT advocates criticize Hawaiians for inventing traditions and using religion as a political tactic to stop the project, it was actually settler colonialism that made being Hawaiian a political act—not the other way around. Contrary to such beliefs, Kānaka are not opposed to science or development. We are not ignorant of the value of science, nor are we backward-looking, unreasonable, and naive in our demands. As kumu hula and cultural practitioner Pua Case contends, "We are not anti-science. We are anti-another telescope." The problem is not that Kānaka are just opposed to everything for the sake of opposition, as many will argue. Our demands are actually quite practical. We are opposed to the legal structures that silence us and discredit our claims to land and self-determination. We are opposed to structures that diminish our knowledge systems to justify the continued exploitation of Hawaiʻi. This is the broader context in which the kiaʻi are challenging the TMT.

The controversy exploded on October 7, 2014, when a dozens of kiaʻi marched to the summit to disrupt a "traditional Hawaiian groundbreaking and blessing ceremony." The goal of the televised event was to somehow authenticate the TMT as if Hawaiians now approved the project. Speeches by "dignitaries" representing the science community, UH, and the five partner countries (Canada, India, Japan, China, and the U.S.) had been scheduled in a gratuitous display of self-congratulation. How could TMT break ground while the 2011 permit was still under appeal in Hawaiʻi's Supreme Court? To many Kānaka ʻŌiwi, this was an extreme insult.

Days before the action, the Office of Mauna Kea Management had caught wind of a planned demonstration aimed at stopping the ceremony. Kiaʻi were denied access to the summit while a caravan of shuttles carrying invited guests had been allowed entry. Video footage shows one kiaʻi, Joshua

Joshua Lanakila Mangauil confronts the audience and Kahu Danny Akaka at the TMT groundbreaking ceremony, October 7, 2014. *Screen capture from video filmed by Dave Corrigan of* Big Island Video News.

Lanakila Mangauil, who, in traditional regalia, had run barefoot past police blockades to the site and held off the ceremony for twenty minutes until the others arrived. In a riveting speech of justified resentment and clarity, Mangauil condemned the assembly. "Like snakes, you are! . . . We were full of aloha . . . but what do [you] do? . . . Slither in like slimy snakes to come up and desecrate our sacred lands!" He exclaims, "Where are *your* sacred temples?" The organizers attempted to proceed with the ceremony, but more kiaʻi arrived chanting and carrying drums, cameras, and signs. A confrontation ensued before a growing audience. Mangauil admonished the guests, "This is not continuing. E kala mai, iaʻu [excuse me]. Pack it up! You are going home!" He turned and addressed Kahu Danny Akaka, the priest hired to conduct the blessing. "Uncle Danny, I have followed you for many years. We have done many things together, but for this, I cannot stand and support you. You are about to try and make sacred the act that would desecrate our most sacred temple." The dignitaries were eventually overwhelmed by the kiaʻi. So, they decided to pack up and go home.

About five months later, when construction crews attempted to haul heavy equipment to the summit—and while decisions on two appeals were still pending—workers were met by dozens of kiaʻi who had had enough. This time, however, the kiaʻi had fashioned their own roadblocks and checkpoints, shifting the discourse from "angry Hawaiians" to the question of authority over stewardship. On April 2, Hawaiians blocked construction crews. Hundreds more Hawaiians showed up, and by the end of the day, thirty-one kiaʻi had been arrested.

Four kiaʻi draped in Hawaiian flags ready to block construction crews from reaching the TMT project site on the summit of Mauna Kea in early April 2015. *Photograph by Cory Lum of Honolulu Civil Beat.*

A hui (group) of committed young Kānaka ʻŌiwi decided to set up an encampment near the visitor's center to block returning construction crews. A series of highly televised police crackdowns revealed how Governor David Ige, the Department of Land and Natural Resources, and UH coordinated to suppress the peaceful demonstrations by using scare tactics and force. This only sent the occupation of the mountain viral. On June 24, twelve more arrests were made when 750 highly organized kiaʻi again managed to prevent police-escorted work crews from reaching the summit. By summer's end, thousands from around the world would visit Mauna a Wākea to stand in solidarity with the kiaʻi, mobilizing under the hashtags #KūKiaʻiMauna, #ProtectMaunaKea, #WeAreMaunaKea, and #AoleTMT. The critical consciousness of the kiaʻi motivated Kānaka across islands and oceans to hold their own demonstrations in a display of resistance and unity that mirrored the struggle to stop U.S. naval bombing of Kahoʻolawe in the 1970s and the 1992 centennial observation of the U.S. invasion of the Hawaiian Kingdom, when over twenty thousand marched in Honolulu. Despite routine harassment and mass arrests, the kiaʻi grounded their actions in what became known as kapu aloha.

A rule of accountability, the kapu aloha was a restriction on language and behavior in the commitment to nonviolent direct action. It was implemented to remind the kiaʻi of the reason for these demonstrations: to protect the mauna from irreparable harm. The kapu aloha encouraged compassion and respect while engaged in politicized expressions of outrage and disobedience, even while being arrested by police (many of whom were Kanaka). It was not about casting particular in-group behaviors as deviant and others as respectable in order to win over a mainstream audience. Instead, it was about tactical, culturally grounded, and unapologetic resistance. Even as police ambushed them in the night, made arrests during prayer circles, and violently handled those taken into custody, the kiaʻi remained nonviolent. Some claimed, without evidence, the kiaʻi were aggressive. The state imposed excessive charges against those arrested, passed new laws to criminalize them, and even removed the portable toilets to force them out; but the kapu held. The struggle tested the kiaʻi, but the kapu aloha proved to be an effective strategy of refusal that would unsettle the state's business-as-usual attitude and rubber-stamp approach to industrial development on ecologically fragile lands and sacred places.

By December 2015, the spectacle of an Indigenous uprising culminated with the Hawaiʻi Supreme Court revoking the original permit issued in 2011. The victory, however, was bittersweet, as the decision to rescind the permit was justified not because of the project's legal, ethical, cultural, or environmental transgressions, but instead because the permit was granted *before* a contested case was held. A failure of due process in granting the permit before hearing public testimony, the Board of Land and Natural Resources had "put the cart before the horse." It was a precarious triumph, as the court's ruling was less a turn toward justice and more a reinscription of state authority. In September 2017, after a second lengthy contested case proceeding, the Board of Land and Natural Resources approved another permit. On October 30, 2018, the Supreme Court ruled in favor of the Board's decision to issue the permit.

It should be noted, however, that if not for the land protectors' direct political action, ethic of nonviolence, and centering of ʻike kupuna, the Hawaiʻi Supreme Court may not have reviewed the permitting process at all. For years, people have opposed the seemingly endless approval of telescopes by the state, its agencies, and the media, but to no avail. The grounded refusal of these kiaʻi who put their bodies on the line for months on end also raised the critical consciousness of land and water protectors around the world. Today, these kiaʻi and accomplices are organizing under the banner #SeeYouOnTheMauna.

How Is Mauna Kea Sacred?

In many ways, the term *sacred* fails to capture what Kānaka ʻŌiwi experience when relating to their ancestral homeland, but it is about the closest thing in the English language. Writing in the 1950s about an isolated community of "country Hawaiians" in the southern district of Kaʻū, Hawaiʻi Island, the esteemed historian, ethnographer, composer, and archivist Mary Kawena Pukui articulated a perspective on why non-Hawaiians have difficulty understanding the sort of relationship Kanaka ʻŌiwi have with the natural world. She wrote:

> It is hard for the modern intellectually regid [*sic*] and extroverted mind to sense the subjective relationship of genuine Hawaiians to Nature, visible and invisible. But without in some degree sensing the feeling that underlies this quality of consciousness in those who live intimately in a condition of primary awareness and sensitivity on the plane of subjective identification with Nature, coupled with perceptions and concepts arising therefrom—without some comprehension of this quality of spontaneous being-one-with-natural-phenomena which are persons, not things, it is impossible for [the foreigner] . . . to understand a true country-Hawaiian's sense of dependence and obligation, his "values," his discrimination of the real, the good, the beautiful and the true, his feeling of organic and spiritual identification with the ʻaina (homeland) and ʻohana (kin).

This "plane of subjective identification with Nature" is a compelling idea. Pukui is arguing that—at least for Kānaka ʻŌiwi—a people's collective understanding of their very being is inextricably linked to the places they and their ancestors inhabit, the activities they practice, the ceremonies they conduct, and the intimacies they develop thereon. This is not a novel idea but is shared among many Indigenous peoples the world over. Again, the very term for the earth we walk on—ʻāina—reminds us that it also nourishes our bodies. This recognition of the importance of the land—as food, as kin, as a relation—instills in Kānaka ʻŌiwi a sense of humility, responsibility, and respect for the natural world. This relationality is at the heart of Kanaka identity and their commitment to defend the land as a kuleana: one's *responsibility* and *privilege* to care for, tend to, love, and identify with something. As a land-based ethic, the kuleana that underpins aloha ʻāina is a commitment to the well-being of future generations.

Mauna a Wākea, like all lands in the archipelago, is sacred also because of how it fits into Kanaka genealogies. While the stories of Kānaka ʻŌiwi origins are diverse and varied, the epic cosmogonic genealogy or mo'okū'auhau (genealogical succession), known as Kumulipo (beginning in intense darkness), is among the most beloved. This mo'okū'auhau begins with the birth of the universe, recounts the emergence of all beings from out of darkness, and documents virtually every physical entity, big and small, known to Kānaka.

Originally passed through generations within the mo'olelo ha'i waha (oral traditions) in the form of ko'ihonua (cosmogonical chants), the Kumulipo served at least two purposes: First, it mapped the evolution of all things in the observable worlds of Kanaka 'Ōiwi. Second, it gave meaning to the idea that everything is related in a concrete, material sense. Far from religious belief, it was acute scientific observation. These meanings were imbued with greater value through descriptions of the interrelatedness of all things as existing within *familial relations*. Humans are not mere occupants, owners, or masters, but *descendants* of the land. This is a powerful metaphor, but it is also grounded in knowledge of matter and physics. Both figuratively and materially, all things share a common fate in that our bodies are *of the earth* and return to the earth in the passage of time. The language of genealogy was a way to understand our place in the cosmos, in the natural world, and in time and space.

In the Kumulipo, there are two original ancestors—Papahānaumoku (Papa who gives birth to islands) and Wākea (the expanse of the sky), also known as Earth Mother and Sky Father. The cultural importance of lessons gleaned from stories about their deeds has elevated them to the status of akua (gods). Papa and their daughter, Ho'ohōkūkalani ("to bestud the heavens with stars") are said to have "birthed" the islands and the first humans. The eldest is Hawai'i Island, and of the five mountain summits on Hawai'i, Mauna Kea is the makahiapo (firstborn). As it reaches higher than the rest, piercing through the clouds, the mountain has also come to be known as Mauna a Wākea, the mountain belonging to or in the realm of Wākea.

These are the elder siblings to Hāloanakalaukapalili (or Hāloanaka) and Hāloa, two children of Wākea and Ho'ohōkūkalani. The elder Hāloanaka was stillborn, then buried, and from that place emerged the first kalo (taro), the staple food for centuries of Kanaka 'Ōiwi. The younger brother, Hāloa, would become the first mō'ī (ruler); he taught his family and descendants to cultivate the kalo. Thus, Hāloanaka, in the form of kalo, embodies 'āina and Hāloa represents the Lāhui, the people or nation. Like Hāloa, the Lāhui cultivates 'āina to provide sustenance for living and future generations—a practice that carries a distinct kuleana that Kanaka 'Ōiwi know as mālama 'āina (to care for the land). When the phrase aloha 'āina is used today, it may be understood as invoking this genealogical, temporal, and spatial relationship of the people to the land. In the face of settler colonialism's structures of dominance, many Kānaka draw strength from their aloha ʻāina as sacred relations to sacred places.

The Value of Mauna a Wākea

Colonialism is not a thing of the past, and the struggle over Mauna a Wākea is evidence that it continues to impact the lives of Kānaka ʻŌiwi today. I ask that you consider how, for many people, telescope expansion on the summit does not represent a universal human necessity, an unequivocal economic benefit to all, or a symbol of modern achievement and progress. Consider also how the proposed TMT reflects and perpetuates the structured violence of U.S. militarism, American tourism, and settler governance in Hawaiʻi. For the kiaʻi mauna who stand for its protection, the value of Mauna a Wākea is intrinsic. It is valuable without world-class telescopes, high-tech industry, or the dubious promise of jobs. Kānaka ʻŌiwi will continue to defend Mauna a Wākea into the future, just as we will continue to defend all of our ancestral homelands. We do this not for profit or prestige, not because we are irrational or antiscience, but because we refuse to surrender our lands to the insatiable desires of settler colonial society. We stand for Mauna a Wākea—mindful, patient, deliberate, and justified.

Resources

Big Island Video News. Accessed July 31, 2018. http://www.bigislandvideonews.com/?s=tmt.
KĀHEA: The Hawaiian-Environmental Alliance. Accessed July 31, 2018. http://kahea.org/.
Kauakipuupuu. "Sacred Mauna Kea: Ka Makahiapo Kapu Na Wākea" blog. Accessed July 31, 2018. https://sacredmaunakea.wordpress.com/.
Mauna Kea ʻOhana. "Mauna a Wākea" blog. Accessed July 31, 2018. https://maunaawakea.com/.
Mauna Kea: Temple Under Siege. Nāʻālehu, Hawaiʻi: Nā Maka o ka ʻĀina, 2006. DVD.
Nā Maka o ka ʻĀina. "Mauna Kea." Accessed July 31, 2018. http://www.mauna-a-wakea.info/.
ʻŌiwi TV. *Mauna Kea—Temple Under Siege*. Posted October 3, 2011, accessed July 31, 2018. https://oiwi.tv/oiwitv/mauna-kea-temple-under-siege/.

P. Kalawai'a Moore

Kūkulu Hale in Hāna, East Maui
Reviving Traditional Hawaiian House and Heiau Building

A people's architecture holds ideas about community, what they value and how they relate to the natural world around them. The traditional Hawaiian house, or hale, and the rock-built religious structures called heiau, have diminished in and disappeared from the landscape in Hawai'i. In Hāna, Maui, the revitalization of traditional hale and heiau building practices are opportunities for community gathering, and the restored structures have become places for teaching. While these structures are not used according to their historical function, the work of thatching, stacking, and securing each stone, log, frond, and grass bundle serves to revive and restore these building practices and instills pride that comes from living traditional Hawaiian values.

Since the early 1990s, the East Maui communities in the Hāna area have been at the heart of the revival of Hawaiian hale and heiau restoration. Revived hale and restored heiau are the major cultural landmarks of the Hāna and East Maui area. If one were visiting Hāna, Maui, a mandatory stop would be Kahanu Gardens, a U.S. National Tropical Botanical Garden that is home to Pi'ilanihale Heiau. Pi'ilanihale is the largest heiau in the Pacific; it is constructed of stone, with a front face wall fifty feet in height, and covers an area equivalent to two football fields.

At Pi'ilanihale are two examples of traditional Hawaiian wooden house structures, a hale kipa (visitor house) and a hālau wa'a (canoe house), both built in a customary design from materials that were harvested in the local vicinity. Hāna town boasts a cultural center with a kauhale (housing compound) consisting of hale in five different styles that one would see if visiting a chief's compound. Across the street from the cultural center is the Akule Hale, a hale built on a bluff overlooking Hāna Bay, where residents still gather today and watch for the seasonal run of akule fish and engage in a traditional style of communal fishing and dividing of the catch among the townspeople. Five smaller hale dot the roadside along the one-lane highway winding through the East Maui communities; another twenty-by-forty foot hale stands at the pathway to the Seven Sacred Pools, part of the Haleakalā National Park in Kīpahulu. Just outside Hāna town in Hōlani stands a thirty-by-one-hundred-foot hale, the biggest hale in the Hawaiian Islands today, where many local celebrations and meetings take place.

These projects were driven by the community and built and headed by Francis Palani Sinenci, born in Kīpahulu and resident of Hāna; Sinenci is the only recognized traditional Kuhikuhi Puʻuone (master architect and engineer) in Hawaiʻi. Kumu Palani, as he is known, has been recognized as one of the key people who have helped bring back the customs and techniques of traditional Hawaiian hale building. He is also a recognized master dry stack mason who has been involved in restoring some of the most prominent heiau in Hawaiʻi. Starting in the early 1990s, Kumu Palani began to reconnect with the knowledge of hale building and heiau restoration. He began his hale-building journey in 1992 at the request of Helemano Elementary School, where he taught Hawaiian studies as part of the Department of Education Kupuna Program. He was asked by teachers and students to build a Hawaiian hale; at that time he responded, "Oh, you mean a grass shack." He started by meeting with Uncle Rudy Mitchell, a kupuna (elder, ancestor) who worked at Waimea Falls Park on Oʻahu. Uncle Rudy guided Kumu Palani to research how to build Hawaiian hale. He studied ethnographic accounts written by nineteenth-century Hawaiians, as well as descriptions by non-Hawaiian explorers and missionaries. Palani examined the models still preserved at the Bishop Museum; he studied designs and techniques he observed while working with different archaeologists, and he studied the detailed construction practices documented through Russ Apple's 1967 work restoring Hale-o-Keawe (a chiefly burial house) at Hōnaunau on Hawaiʻi Island.

Kumu Palani's hale-building work also involved work on rock foundations and rock walls. His work with rock building for hale led him to work restoring ancient rock walls and platforms. He credits working on those old rock structures as his greatest teacher. The traditional method for working with rock is known as uhau humu pōhaku (dry stack rock masonry), a form of masonry in which rocks are fitted together to make structures without the use of a binding medium such as cement. Kumu Palani developed expertise in traditional styled rock work, which led to his work restoring the Piʻilanihale heiau and other rock-built religious structures of note.

Francis Palani Sinenci shows us the fifty-foot front face of Pi'ilani Hale, which he helped restore with the Hāna community. *Photograph by P. Kalawai'a Moore.*

Hālau Wa'a, a sixty-by-thirty-foot canoe house at Kahanu Gardens in Hāna. *Photograph by Joel Bradshaw.*

In piecing together traditional building designs and techniques, Kumu Palani recognized that the revival of traditional Hawaiian hale and heiau building would work only if it coincided with a revival and strengthening of Hawaiian protocols and values, including a desire for and pride in the revival of cultural knowledge that would come with reestablishing hale and heiau. He also recognized that some prejudices and misconceptions existed about the strength of traditional structures and building techniques that needed to be overcome.

One of the fallacies that Kumu Palani confronted are misconceptions of Hawaiian hale as inferior types of "grass shacks" or "grass huts," and the idea of Hawaiian heiau as places of pagan worship that should be destroyed and dismantled. The first Christian missionaries to Hawaiʻi played a key role in these conceptions and saw the "grass house" as an embodied form of heathen ideology and morality. The grass house was cast as inferior in a conversion effort wherein a change in Hawaiians' religious beliefs was thought to necessitate a change in the manner of house in which they lived.[1] As one noted missionary, Hiram Bingham, stated, "Such a habitation whose leafy and grassy covering[s] . . . are ill adapted to promote health of body, vigor of intellect, neatness of person, food, clothing and lodging and, much less, longevity . . . cannot be washed, scoured, polished and painted to good purpose, nor be made suitable for good furniture . . . nothing would be more natural than that a heathen people occupying such habitation . . . [would be predisposed to] listlessness and lethargy from which only the stimulus of tobacco, rum or awa gives a temporary relief."[2]

Upon arrival, the missionaries themselves had to live in Hawaiian grass houses, which they quickly rearranged to conform to some of their more important beliefs; hanging mats and curtains to "introduce concepts of domestic privacy," and enlarging doors and adding locks, in contrast with Hawaiian household ideas of "freedom of access." Converted Hawaiians "were made to eat at tables, sit in chairs, and replace their sleeping mats with a proper Western bed." Hawaiians were instructed to live in single-family houses instead of kauhale (household clusters of extended family); these houses were set in grid formations that imposed a Western order on the land instead of built in Hawaiian ways "in which the landscape imposed order on the [location] of dwellings and the people . . . it was the missionaries' transformation of the grass house . . . that made it virtually impossible for the old ways [of living and worshipping] to reassert themselves."[3] Conversion to Christianity went hand in hand with a devaluation of both the Hawaiian hale and a rejection of the old religious heiau sites.

Hawaiian heiau began declining and being outright destroyed after Li-holiho (Kamehameha II) and Queen Kaʻahumanu declared in 1819 the end of the traditional religion and ordered that the old heiau be destroyed. As Kaʻahumanu converted to Christianity, missionary opinions of heiau added to the decline of their upkeep and in many cases the destruction of traditional Hawaiian religious structures. Hiram Bingham, an early missionary and advisor to Kaʻahumanu, spoke about heiau as "monument(s) of folly, superstition and madness, which the idolatrous conqueror and his murderous priests had consecrated with human blood," "fortification(s) of Satan's kingdom," and "altars of heathen abomination."[4]

As Christianity took hold, Western-inspired architecture came to dominate life in Hawaiʻi, especially in the newly developed concept of the town. By the end of the nineteenth century, the hale, the embodied form of heathen ideology and morality, was supplanted in the towns and was disappearing, albeit more slowly, from the countryside. Heiau were dismantled in the town areas and the rock was used for other projects. Over the next century, Hawaiian hale were marginalized through recasting the "little grass shack" as an iconic symbol of paradise, a form of kitsch that was used for decades in promoting tourism. Alongside the grass skirt and the tiki, Hawaiian hale became associated with fakeness and plasticity. Kumu Palani notes the impact of kitsch on hale: "I still run into it all the time. The idea that Hawaiian hale are grass huts, and that they can't be strong enough to be used as homes. People don't know how advanced the technology is, and their only knowledge about hale is from tourist ads and movies."

As he confronted some of the preconceived notions about Hawaiian hale and heiau, Kumu Palani began to think about the practices and values he would bring back. He chose to focus on values that were culturally grounded and would resurrect the idea of community working together, foster our traditional connections to land, and show the ingenuity of our traditional structures. He wanted to combat preconceived ideas about hale and heiau as culturally inferior and structurally unreliable. Among many of the values that stood out, Kumu Palani has highlighted three in particular that help bring everyone together: Laulima, Mālama ʻĀina, and Maiau.

Kumu Palani developed hale building and heiau restoration around the Hawaiian concepts of community cooperation through what is known as **Laulima**, which means "many hands," "cooperation," and "to work together." When Kumu Palani is asked to lead projects to build hale or restore heiau, he involves the community in all aspects of the build. He works with alakaʻi (leaders under him) to teach them all the traditional knowledge and any

Laulima, meaning "many hands," is a part of every aspect of a build, as is Mālama ʻĀina, meaning "to care for the land" that provides all of the material for shelter. *Photograph by P. Kalawaiʻa Moore.*

newly adapted techniques associated with the work. All volunteers become haumana (students) and learn traditional prayers, traditional knowledge on how to choose a location on the basis of the land and elements, and how to gather and prepare the building materials from the land. They learn wood cutting, lashing techniques, how to thatch roof materials, and then the final preparation for blessing the hale or heiau.

Each day in the process is called a "Laulima day," and Kumu Palani asks the community to help with not only the build and the protocols but also in providing the food and water necessary for all who come, and shelter for those who might need to stay to continue the work. In this way, everyone who wants to be involved in the building process can find a role to play, and all are asked to contribute to help build a hale or restore a heiau. Communities across the island rally to the call and volunteer by the dozens on each Laulima day, filling in roles as needed as they learn the process of traditional Hawaiian structure building. As Kumu Palani puts it, "people not only feel pride in building our kupuna's hale, they feel connected, to the hale, and to each other. Everyone is involved. If there is no laulima, there's no hale."

Mālama ʻĀina means to care for and relate to the land. It is a Hawaiian concept rooted in one of the creation stories of the Hawaiian people from the time of Papahānaumoku (Earth Mother) and Wākea (Sky Father). In this creation story, the Hawaiian Islands and the staple food crop, kalo (taro), are birthed before the Hawaiian chiefs and are considered the elder siblings of the Hawaiian people. In Hawaiian and Polynesian family relationship systems, the elder sibling has a duty to feed and protect the younger sibling. In return, the younger sibling must honor, respect, and also care for the elder sibling. Mālama ʻĀina speaks to the Hawaiian people's familial relationship to the land and our obligation to protect and honor it, as it in turn feeds and protects us.

A hale is a manifestation of how plants and trees from a well-honored and cared for land lend themselves to the actual physical protection of the people. Heiau are constructed from the earthly rock itself, connected to the energy of the ʻāina. Hale building materializes our familial relation to the ʻāina. Timbers are cut from local community forests, thatching for the roof is gathered from locally grown trees or grasses, and traditional cordage is made from various plant materials that grow on our islands. Rock for heiau, wall, and foundation building are gathered from the land and have a life force that comes from Papahānaumoku. Kumu Palani teaches about traditional endemic and indigenous plants and trees and how to use them in building hale. Haumana learn how to incoporate nonnative plants and trees for hale building, repurposing trees that are otherwise seen as invasive and harmful to our native ecosystem. Kumu Palani teaches how to build hale in harmony with the layout of the land and the movement of the elements. Hale foundations and doorways are placed using traditional religious and societal ideas. The knowledge of what to use when building hale and heiau reinforces mālama ʻāina and our understanding of our connection to natural forces and our responsibility to care for and protect the land as its younger siblings.

The last main value Kumu Palani incorporates is **Maiau**. Maiau means neat and careful in work, skillfull, ingenious, expert, thorough, meticulous. Kumu Palani explains that we must take pride in the ingenuity of our kupuna, work diligently to learn what they have left for us, and then seek to execute what we have learned with an eye toward deliberate excellence. He explains that "building hale and restoring the heiau of our ancestors is how we show both ourselves and the world the genius of our traditional cultural building practices, contrary to the way they have been painted as inferior." Kumu Palani has brought back the ʻike (knowledge) of hale and heiau building design and techniques, and in reviving these practices, Hawaiians and non-Hawaiians

Maiau, meaning "excellence," in an example of cut and fitted wooden joints held together by specific lashings. Hawaiian hale were held together without the use of metal. *Photograph by P. Kalawai'a Moore.*

have found that strong and beautiful structures are built through the use of these methods. The timber cuts and the wood pieces that fit together, the lashing that holds tight the wooden joints, and the ingenious method of literally sewing rocks together are innovations unlike any in the world, and these methods were perfected without the use of metal. Each time one of these projects is undertaken and finished, the concept of Maiau, excellence in our traditional structures, is seen and more clearly understood.

The revival of hale building and heiau restoration has integrated some of our best traditional values with materials from the land to produce a unique form of architecture and engineering. The revival and adaptation of these practices by Kumu Francis Palani Sinenci and the East Maui community allows those of us who participate in the work an opportunity to live out the values of Laulima, Mālama 'Āina, and Maiau, and to feel pride in taking part in reviving the ingenuity of traditional Hawaiian technologies. If you are traveling through East Maui, take a moment to appreciate the opportunity to see and feel the the strength and beauty of hale and heiau, restored and remembered with pride and aloha.

Notes

1   Kaori O'Connor, "Kitsch, Tourist Art, and the Little Grass Shack in Hawaii," *Home Cultures: The Journal of Architecture, Design and Domestic Space* 3, no. 3 (2006): 260.

2   Hiram Bingham, *A Residence of Twenty-One Years in the Sandwich Islands*. (Hartford, CT: H. Huntington, 1848), 116.

3   O'Conner, "Kitsch, Tourist Art, and the Little Grass Shack in Hawaii," 261.

4   Bingham, *A Residence of Twenty-One Years in the Sandwich Islands*, 84, 85.

Resources

For more information on hale building and the East Maui Community where hale and heiau are prominent, please visit the following websites:

http://holanihana.org/—Holani Hana, a cultural organization dedicated to building and teaching about Hawaiian hale and culture

https://www.hanaculturalcenter.org/—Hāna Cultural Center and Museum, dedicated to preserving Hāna history and culture

https://ntbg.org/gardens/kahanu/—Kahanu Gardens, a National Tropical Botanical Garden built around Piʻilanihale heiau and several traditional hale

Malia Nobrega-Olivera

—————————————

Pū'olo Pa'akai

A Bundle of Salt from Pū'olo, Hanapēpē, Kaua'i

This pū'olo, or bundle of words, is tied together in the form of a letter I wrote to my daughter Ka'ai'ōhelo, born in 2015, to share with her the story of our family that genealogically connects us to our 'āina and our resources.

Iā 'oe e Ka'ai'ōhelo, He lei poina 'ole ke keiki na ka makua
[To you Ka'ai'ōhelo, A beloved child is a lei never forgotten by the parents]

> Iā 'oe e Ka'ai'ōhelo
> ku'u kama aloha
> ku'u lei aloha
> ku'u keiki alualu aloha ē
> kanu 'ia me ke aloha
> ma ka 'āina aloha
> 'O Kaauwaikahi
> ke aloha, ke aloha nō ē

> To you Ka'ai'ōhelo
> My beloved child
> My beloved garland
> My beloved stillborn
> Buried with love
> In our beloved land
> Kaauwaikahi
> With love, with love indeed.

Kaʻaiʻōhelo, mom has a moʻolelo, a story, for you
A moʻolelo about community engagement, kaiāulu
A moʻolelo about ancestral knowledge, ʻike kupuna
A moʻolelo about family, ʻohana
A moʻolelo about torches, lamakū
A moʻolelo about the lunar calendar, kaulana mahina

On your birthday, kuʻu pē (my child), your mākua (parents) made a lamakū to honor you, to honor your name, to honor our deep love for you, a child who will never be forgotten.

This lamakū kukui (a candlenut torch) was made using kukui nuts (candle nuts) that were gathered from Hanapēpē, the ahupuaʻa (land division) that our ʻohana have lived in for generations.

We crack the kukui nut very carefully, if we're lucky and the nut remains whole, we then string them on niʻau, the midribs of the coconut leaf, and when we have about seven niʻau we are ready to hōʻā i ka lama, to light the torch.

Say it with me,
hōʻā i ka lama
ʻōlelo hou (say it again),
hōʻā i ka lama

We lit the torch, we sang together, and we were so amazed at the beauty of this fire, the colors, the growth of the fire as it passed from one nut to another.

The lighting of this torch, lamakū
is like the work mom does in the community, the kaiāulu
we are lighting one lamakū at a time
we are sharing our story, our moʻolelo

Kaʻaiʻōhelo, this is our ancestral knowledge, the ʻike kupuna,
the knowledge that is passed from one generation to another and each of us has the kuleana (responsibility) to continue to teach the next generation

Kaʻaiʻōhelo, our ʻohana, our family, has many traditions
One of them is the tradition of making paʻakai Hawaiʻi, or Hawaiian salt
Paʻakai (salt) traditions continue at ka lae ʻo Pūʻolo (Pūʻolo Point), Kauaʻi
Paʻakai, kuʻu pē (my child), is Hawaiian salt
say it with me: paʻakai
ʻōlelo hou, paʻakai

A lamakū kukui (a candlenut torch) made with love by Malia and Victor Nobrega-Olivera, parents of Kaʻaiʻōhelo, to honor her life lived within her mom's honua and the love they have for her. *Photograph by Malia Nobrega-Olivera.*

Maikaʻi Kauaʻi, Hemolele i ka mālie
[Beautiful Kauaʻi, Perfect in the calm]

The paʻakai of Kauaʻi is very special. It is the only place in all of Hawaiʻi that continues this cultural practice.

Kauaʻi Island is found at the western end of our pae ʻāina o Hawaiʻi (Hawaiian archipelago). There are five moku (districts) on Kauaʻi: Haleleʻa, Koʻolau, Puna, Kona, and Nā Pali.

Paʻakai is made in the moku of Kona, in the ahupuaʻa of Hanapēpē, in the ʻili (land section) of ʻUkulā, at ka lae ʻo Pūʻolo.

Kaʻaiʻōhelo, it's important for us as Kanaka Maoli (Native people of Hawaiʻi) to honor the ancestral names of our family, and this includes our ʻāina, our land. Growing up in Hanapēpē we would always call the salt-making area "Salt Pond." But as we learn more about our 'āina through conversations with kūpuna (elders), maps, Hawaiian newspaper articles, and mele (songs) and oli (chants), we learn the traditional place names and we give life to them as we compose new songs and use them in our daily life. Here's a mele I wrote that gives life to some of the traditional place names of Pūʻolo:

E Ola Mau ʻO Pūʻolo

Aloha Kauaʻi Moku ʻo Kona
'Āina Kupuna
Kaulana ʻo Hanapēpē mai uka a i kai
Aloha ʻĀina
Ola ka lae ʻo Pūʻolo, pūʻolo paʻakai
'Āina Kupuna
Paʻakahi, Kuunakaʻiole, ʻUkulā, Kunakaiawe
Aloha ʻĀina
E ola mau ʻo Pūʻolo, e ola nō ē
E ola!

Pūʻolo Continues to Live

Beloved Kauaʻi, Kona District
Ancestral Land
Famous is Hanapēpē, from the uplands to the ocean
Love for the land
Pūʻolo Point lives, salt bundles
Ancestral Land
Paʻakahi, Kuunakaʻiole, ʻUkulā, Kunakaiawe
Love for the land
Pūʻolo continues to live, lives on indeed
Life!

Line seven in the mele teaches us four traditional place-names that are not heard very often today but that we can all bring life to: Paʻakahi, Kuunakaʻiole, ʻUkulā, Kunakaiawe.

Paʻakahi is found on the eastern side of Pūʻolo, near Hanapēpē Bay, looking out toward ʻEleʻele and Port Allen Boat Harbor.

Kuunakaʻiole is on the opposite end of Pūʻolo, near Salt Pond Beach Park, looking out toward the island of Niʻihau.

'Ukulā is the name of the land section within the ahupuaʻa of Hanapēpē.

Cleaning the puna allows new saltwater to seep through the salt shelf before it is transferred to the waikū. *Photograph by Malia Nobrega-Olivera.*

Kunakaiawe is specifically the area where pa'akai is made today.[1] Mahalo nui to kupuna Christina Kali for sharing this traditional name with all of us, and now we carry it on and continue to give life to it.

How Is Pa'akai Made at Kunakaiawe, Pū'olo, Hanapēpē, Kaua'i?

The salt making process includes three main parts—the puna (well), the waikū (secondary well), and the lo'i (salt bed).

As taught to us by Tūtū nui (great-grandpa), the puna is the well that provides the main source of salt water that comes from the ocean, travels up through the earth and through a salt shelf. The puna is cleaned as needed by removing any debris that may have entered the puna during the wet season when the area is flooded. The cleaning is done by our kāne, or men, and is not something that can be done easily by just one person. Our kupuna teach us the importance of laulima and that with many hands working together, the workload becomes easier.

The waikū is the secondary well. Water is transferred above land from the puna to the waikū using a one-gallon scooper. Today we also use a water pump to transfer the saltwater. Preparation of the waikū also requires a lot of hard work by experienced family members and friends. This process includes getting on your hands and knees to first scrape the top layer of soil using a U-shaped metal scraper to reveal the clay layer of earth. This is a key component of making paʻakai. This clay layer is then skillfully rubbed with a smooth river rock gathered from Hanapēpē river that fits perfectly to the hands of the salt maker. In addition to sealing the floor of the waikū, ʻohana members mix the soil and clay together to form clay balls to build the wall to contain the saltwater. The design of the waikū follows the traditional design that the generations before have always used.

The loʻi is the third part of the salt-making process. The loʻi are prepared in the same way as the waikū. The saltwater that fills the multiple loʻi comes from the waikū and is transferred in the same way. Through the process of evaporation, salt crystals form and the salt builds up in the loʻi day by day.

After a number of weeks, the paʻakai is ready to harvest. The paʻakai is raked into mounds, washed, and prepared to be taken home for further drying in puʻu paʻakai, or salt mounds.

We make paʻakai during kauwela (summer). These are the traditional names of the summer months according to our Hawaiian lunar calendar:

Ikiiki
Kaʻaona
Hinaiaʻeleʻele
Hilinaehu
Hilinamā
ʻIkuā

In my lifetime, Kaʻaiʻōhelo, our family has not been able to make paʻakai for five consecutive years. One of those years was 2015. Under the Hoku moon (one of the full moon phases), in the month of Kaʻaona (traditional name of a month around June/July), the ocean tide was high, the waves crashed over the sand dunes, the ocean water flowed over into the salt-making area. It flooded the area. I had never seen this before. Tutu (grandma) said she never saw this before. We are asking the community to stop driving on the sand because it is causing the sand dunes to get lower and lower, and the only way to mitigate this and to protect the salt-making area from additional flooding is to not drive on the sand. It's easy enough to park in the parking lot and walk for two minutes and enjoy the beach area with your family.

Besides the ocean washing over this area, we are also experiencing an increase in the amount of rain during the summer months, and the puna are

The waikū and loʻi are prepared similarly. This includes building up the walls with clay balls and using your hands and smooth river rocks to seal the earth. *Photograph by Malia Nobrega-Olivera.*

The harvesting process begins with skilled salt makers raking the paʻakai in the early morning in preparation for family and friends who will come to help rinse the paʻakai before they are put into large puʻu paʻakai, or salt mounds. *Photograph by Malia Nobrega-Olivera.*

also rising higher than usual. All of this adds to the flooding of the area, and we were always taught by Tutu nui that when the area is flooded we don't enter; we wait until it is dry.

Ka'ai'ōhelo, climate change for some is an issue of life or death.

It's having an impact on our human rights, our cultural rights, our rights as Indigenous peoples, as Kanaka Maoli.

Ka'ai'ōhelo, e ho'opili mai (repeat after me): 'Aimalama

'Aimalama is a collective movement of Pacific practitioners to revitalize lunar calendar knowledge.

It's a solution.

It's a tool.

It's a methodology that teaches us to be better observers, kilo.

To be active observers, kilo.

To be environmental forecasters or kilo in our kaiāulu (community).

Ka'ai'ōhelo, mom is working with her friends to create tools that we can take to our kaiāulu.

> We are publishing moon phase planners
> that include the Hawaiian months, Malama,
> the Hawaiian moons, Mahina,
> and are laid out in a traditional time period of ten days, anahulu
> We are using the moon phase journal
> to document our observations,
> to gather our data
> We are sharing lunar calendars that are created for specific locations
> We are strengthening our lāhui Hawai'i (Hawaiian Nation)
> We are sharing solutions
> Solutions that can restore the balance for Mother Earth
> Solutions that are based on our 'ike kupuna, ancestral knowledge
> Solutions that our kaiāulu, our community, can use
> Solutions that your generation, Ka'ai'ōhelo, will share with the generations to come
> We also Hō'ā i ka lama—on the night of the full moons
> We "get off the grid" and we "plug in" to our inner selves
> We gather as 'ohana
> We enjoy the beauty of the evening
> We learn about the stars
> We make lei

We cook together

We kani ka pila

We do things that don't require us to be dependent on "the grid"

It's a small action

but if we all do it together collectively

on every full moon, then we make a bigger impact

How do we become more intuitive like our ancestors? We strive to be mau-liauhonua. Mauliauhonua have personal collective experiences from their surroundings that inform their methods of survival. Mauliauhonua communities have learned about the winds, rains, characteristics, seasons, flora and fauna resource behaviors, and social and political changes to a point where they are able to adapt and survive efficiently in their own environments. Collectively, they have become specialized experts of their own geographical locations.

As salt makers, we continue to learn to be more mauliauhonua as our climate changes so that we can successfully and collectively adapt to and survive the changes that are coming.

We use pa'akai for food—hū ka 'ono o ka 'ai (oh how delicious it makes the food).

Some of our favorite food uses is as an additive to our fresh poke (raw fish cut into cubes), to salt our meats before cooking them on the grill, and as a preservative for drying fish.

We use it for medicine—ke ola kino—ua ola (health—we live on).

Common medicinal uses include mixing it with water and gargling to heal a sore throat, soaking a sprained limb to lessen the swelling, mixing it with 'alaea and drinking it to replenish a lack of iron.

We use it for blessings—palekana (to ward off).

Many practitioners add pa'akai to fresh water and use it in ceremony to ward off bad energy and purify the area. It's used in blessings of homes, boats, gatherings, and so on. Many of us carry it with us wherever we go in order to provide that kind of protection in our daily lives.

In 1964, the Hui Hana Pa'akai o Hanapēpē (Salt Makers Organization of Hanapēpē) was created as a community-based organization to become a collective voice for the twenty-two families who practice the making of pa'akai, as recognized stewards of the land. The salt produced in Hanapēpē is not sold in the stores. It is not sold at all. All of the salt-making families are committed to continuing the practice of sharing the salt with others as a makana (gift), and we also barter it in exchange for other items such as fish, meat, 'opihi (limpets), and other delicacies that one can share.

Kaʻaiʻōhelo, this is a moʻolelo that our family will continue to share with others so that the names of our ʻāina, the cultural practices of our people, the relationship we have with our ʻāina, the caring for our kupuna (including the land) can live on forever and ever. This is aloha ʻāina (love for the land).

kuʻu kama aloha
kuʻu lei aloha
kuʻu keiki alualu aloha ē
ke aloha, ke aloha nō ē

My beloved child
My beloved garland
My beloved stillborn
With love, with love indeed.

Note

1   *Salt Making at Hanapepe, Hawaii* (Hanapepe: Kauai Community College for Kauai Historical Society, 1974), video.

Kalaniua Ritte, Hanohano Naehu,
Noelani Goodyear-Kaʻōpua, and Julie Warech

_____

"Welcome to the Future"

Restoring Keawanui Fishpond

Welcome to Keawanui, a fifty-five-acre marvel of Hawaiian ancestral aquaculture technology over eight hundred years old. Welcome to the future. We invite you to envision futures differently with us. We invite you to a future that makes Indigenous people and our cultural food systems central to the survival of all people, particularly in these times of rising temperatures and seas. If you come as a respectful visitor to Keawanui and to Molokaʻi, you need to think about what you can give to this vision and to this island, not just what you want to see or do or take. Visitors to any part of Hawaiʻi cannot truly know our lands and waters without developing relationships with the kānaka (people) who reside upon and work these ʻāina, these places that feed us.

Located in the ahupuaʻa (district) of Kaʻamola, Keawanui is the largest loko iʻa (fishpond) on the island of Molokaʻi, and the only one that has been restored to functionality. Molokaʻi traditions tell us that centuries ago, thousands of people—probably a third of all the residents on the island—came together to pass stones hand-to-hand over the steep mountainous terrain separating the north and south shores of Molokaʻi. Like a lei adorning the island, they stood shoulder to shoulder, transporting the basalt rocks that would become the kuapā (walls) of the sixty-eight loko iʻa that once existed on the south-facing side of the island (the northern seas and shoreline were too rough for such structures). From a bird's-eye view, the fishponds themselves became like a lei gracing and adorning Molokaʻi, the island child of Hina. Long before the loko iʻa were built, Hina herself walked along the southern coast, creating freshwater springs by plunging her ʻōʻō (digging stick) into the soft earth. A few of these springs still feed Keawanui fishpond.

For centuries loko iʻa have provided Kanaka Maoli with regular supplies of herbivorous fish, which are both more sustainable and more reliable than hunting for deep-water carnivorous fish such as the tuna or swordfish that are more frequently consumed today. It is estimated that in 1901, over one million pounds of fish were still being raised in fishponds on the islands. By the 1970s, this figure had dropped to only about twenty thousand pounds per year. On Oʻahu, fishponds were filled in for suburban development or destroyed during the construction of military bases. On Molokaʻi, loko iʻa became neglected as a capitalist plantation economy rose, challenging the subsistence economy.

The restoration of Keawanui fishpond is a product of one of the first Hawaiian community-driven efforts, dating back to the 1980s, to restore loko iʻa in the contemporary era as part of a vision for food self-sufficiency through the use of Indigenous cultural traditions and innovations. The kiaʻi loko (fishpond caretakers/guardians), Kalaniua Ritte, and Hanohano Naehu, who co-wrote this piece, acknowledge that even though they have been working to revitalize Keawanui since 2001, we have only begun to scratch the surface of what this cultural, historic treasure left by our ancestors can do for us in these present days. As modern Kānaka, we see Keawanui as an ancient answer brought into contemporary context. As a new generation of kiaʻi, we improvise without compromise. The value of aloha ʻāina (love of land and country) continues to drive us, just as it guided our mentor, Walter Ritte, and the kūpuna (ancestors) who came before. While we make slight adaptations and modifications to the fishpond, we hold fast to the cultural practice of aloha ʻāina because we know it is the only way to secure a sustainable and just future for generations to come.

ʻĀina is kanaka is ʻāina is kanaka. The format of this essay illustrates the ways ʻāina and kanaka are intimately connected and co-constitutive. If you were to visit Keawanui in person, Hanohano would point out the three elements necessary for a structurally restored loko iʻa: the kuapā (wall), the mākāhā (gate), and the pūnawai (freshwater source). In this piece, we guide the reader through these three different parts of the loko iʻa; a narrative tour of what a fully functioning fishpond looks like. As scholars who have visited and supported Keawanui, Noelani Goodyear-Kaʻōpua and Julie Warech have noted the ways the kiaʻi themselves are a fourth necessary aspect of the loko iʻa. Throughout the piece, we juxtapose the structural elements and show how they act as metaphors for the three kānaka who have brought the fishpond back to life: Walter Ritte, Kalaniua Ritte, and Hanohano Naehu. The layout of this essay is meant to mimic the ways the kiaʻi carefully choose and lay stones one on top of another to build the various elements of the pond. Here, photos and blocks of text are consciously arranged to emulate that stacking, which builds a strong and lasting wall, protecting the waters and beings within the loko kuapā.

The Kuapā/Uncle Walter

Loko iʻa are an aquacultural innovation unique to Hawaiʻi, and they took several different forms depending on the resources of the area. Keawanui is a premier example of the loko kuapā style, which uses a seawall built from stones to protect an area of relatively shallow water. Loko kuapā cannot be found anywhere else in the world outside of Hawaiʻi, and the islands of Molokaʻi and Oʻahu were known for this technological advancement. Their invention resulted from intimate observation of environmental processes specific to particular places and from the deep relationships that Kanaka Maoli had (and some still have) with our ʻāina and kai (seas).

Walter Ritte Jr. has been a leader of aloha ʻāina movements for most of his adult life. A native of Molokaʻi, he became involved in the Hui Alaloa's fight to maintain Hawaiian access rights for subsistence and cultural practices in the 1970s. Because of his hunting prowess, he was asked in 1976 to join a group resisting the U.S. Navy's bombing of the neighboring island of Kahoʻolawe. Walter and eight others made the first landing in January of that year. He returned to Kahoʻolawe less than two weeks later with his wife, Loretta, and sister, Scarlet. The following year, he and Richard Sawyer made the longest of the 1970s protest landings on the island. And that was only the beginning.

Walter's strategic view of Hawaiian politics only grew over the next decades. He served in the 1978 Hawaii State Constitutional Convention and was one of the first trustees elected to the Office of Hawaiian Affairs. He has fought numerous battles to protect his home island from foreign-driven, corporate-controlled change, including cruise ships and biotech giants, such as Monsanto. He is the founder of Hui o Kuapā, an organization that works to restore ancestral fishponds. Hui o Kuapā was started in 1989, and the collective began restoring fishponds across Molokaʻi, starting with Honouliwai and Kahinapōhaku. For Walter and the other founding members, engaging Molokaʻi youth in this process was critical; they integrated the physical labor of rebuilding kuapā with leadership training to fortify communities.

The formal restoration process at Keawanui began in 2001. When Hui o Kuapā first arrived, the pond was in disrepair, not having been used since the 1940s. The place was like a swampy jungle, overgrown with mangrove and buffalo grass. If you walked into the pond from shore, you would be up to your hips in mud from the sediment runoff. And there was a massive opening in the wall. The kuapā was therefore the first element to be restored at Keawanui. It is the most visibly recognizable feature that defines and sets the scope of this loko iʻa. The wall stands higher than the highest tide, and it protects the pond, to a certain extent, from predators and poachers.

The vision for Keawanui emerged a few decades before restoration began, in the late 1970s, when Walter visited Keawanui "with the kūpuna, and they said this place has to be kept for the Hawaiians . . . so we started to figure out whose place is this and it became known to us that it was Kamehameha Schools." Kamehameha was planning to develop the area, "to have dredging done out on the reef, put hotels out there, and then they also talked about having a landing strip." Walter emphasizes, "we stopped it." This is what a kuapā does: it protects a bounded area from encroachment and provides a sanctuary in which young ones can grow.

At more than fifty acres, Keawanui is the largest loko iʻa on Molokaʻi. Here it is pictured in the context of its location within the ahupuaʻa of Kaʻamola, a land division that stretches from mountain to reef. Hui o Kuapā's long-term vision is to work with the landowner, the Kamehameha Schools, to restore the whole ahupuaʻa to allow sustainable food production. *Photograph by Noelani Goodyear-Kaʻōpua.*

Since Hui o Kuapā began its work at Keawanui, the hui has taken responsibility to manage a total land and water area of nearly seventy-five acres. Of this area, the kuapā bounds about fifty-five acres within the loko iʻa itself. Much of the early work was in rebuilding the kuapā. Following a traditional style, rocks are strategically placed so that each interlocks with the others around it. In order to ensure stability, rocks of various sizes are used to minimize gaps. Yet, the wall is both sturdy and porous. In a way, it breathes with the tides, allowing a certain amount of flow and exchange between the waters within and the waters outside. Furthermore, the outer side edge of the wall that faces the ocean is designed with a slight slope, not a ninety-degree angle. This slope allows wave energy to dissipate as it hits the wall. Such pulses then roll off and create less of an impact.

By 2004, under the leadership of Uncle Walter, whom we sometimes call "the general," the team had fully repaired the wall and closed in the pond. Over the next five years, we moved into improving the surrounding infrastructure, building small hale kiaʻi (guardian outposts), which also serve as places for community visitors to sit and observe the rhythms of the pond. Around this same time, Uncle Walter and the other kiaʻi became deeply involved in the struggle against the patenting and genetic modification of Hāloa, the kalo (taro) plant and the elder sibling of Kanaka. One of their biggest concerns was the potential privatization and corporate control of kalo, as well as the way this was tied to the growing presence of biotech corporations on their island. For the kiaʻi of Keawanui, the loko iʻa provides a living alternative to unsustainable, mono-crop, capitalist approaches to agriculture and food production that have implanted themselves in Hawaiʻi. These approaches deplete rather than enhance the natural resources of the islands.

One of the main purposes of a loko kuapā is to cultivate pua, or baby fish, to maturity. The kuapā protects an area of rich resources and keeps predator attacks to a minimum. At Keawanui, the kiaʻi see the pond as a way to support restocking the fishing grounds along the entire coast, not just as a way to trap fish for their own consumption. It is about creating a safe space for growth and for replenishing the abundance of the island.

Unfortunately, in 2010 a tsunami generated by an earthquake in Chile blew a huge hole in the kuapā near one of the gates. Before the kiaʻi could finish repairing the wall, another tsunami hit in March 2011, this time originating from a Japan earthquake. The kiaʻi remember it flattening the entire wall, except for a few small areas in which mangrove roots held it together. Only one hale was left standing. This was a huge blow to the fishpond physically and to all of the work the kiaʻi had done at the pond over the years. But the kiaʻi whom Uncle Walter had trained stayed strong. After a few tears and a few beers, the rebuilding work began, and today, once again, the wall stands tall.

Uncle Walter Ritte stands alongside a life-size model of the kuapā (fishpond wall) and ʻauwai, or passageway through which ocean water flows into and out of the loko iʻa. The kiaʻi greet visitors at this spot on the land-based side of their ʻāina ("that which feeds"). *Photograph by Noelani Goodyear-Kaʻōpua.*

The Mākāhā/Hanohano

In a loko kuapā–style Hawaiian fishpond, channels are constructed in the wall so as to maintain a balanced flow of water into and out of the enclosed section. These channels are called ʻauwai o ka mākāhā, or simply ʻauwai. The kiaʻi chose where to locate the ʻauwai with respect to prevailing currents in the area, and their function is critical to the health and life of the loko iʻa. The kiaʻi then constructed mākāhā (sluice gates) across the ʻauwai to regulate what fish come into the pond and to make catching fish in or near the ʻauwai easier. In the old days, Kānaka used a single gate, but the kiaʻi at Keawanui use a double-gate system. As expert lawaiʻa (fisherpeople), our ancestors knew that fish gather in areas of current, swimming against it. When the tide is dropping and the gate is open, fish swim into the loko iʻa, smelling the rich waters that are pouring out. And when the tide is rising, fish in the loko iʻa swim back toward the ocean. Going with the ebb and flow of the fishpond's waters, the kiaʻi can lure fish near the mākāhā to catch them or simply to monitor the health of their loko iʻa.

One of the four ʻauwai (channels) built into the kuapā at Keawanui. At either side of the opening, one can see the mākāhā (sluice gates) that regulate what fish come into and go from the loko iʻa. The kiaʻi at Keawanui use a variety of materials, both traditional and nontraditional, to construct gates. The rebar and metal fencing show that their concern is to use repurposed materials that are functional, rather than to insist on using what looks iconically Hawaiian. *Photograph by Noelani Goodyear-Kaʻōpua.*

Hanohano Naehu leads an anti-GMO rally on Maui. The kiaʻi of Keawanui see their activism as complementary to their daily acts of aloha ʻāina. Their involvement in the anti-GMO movement in Hawaiʻi has focused on opposing pesticide drift that poisons communities and corporate influence in the political system. *Photograph by Justin Zern.*

Hanohano Naehu was born and raised on Moloka'i on lands his 'ohana (extended family system) has stewarded for countless generations. Coincidentally, he lives in the valley upland from the first fishpond that Hui o Kuapā worked on in Honouliwai, at the east end of Moloka'i. However, when his best friend, Kalaniua, went to work at Honouliwai fishpond, the waters were not yet rich enough to draw Hano into the pond. He was pulled other directions and always viewed fishponds as a last resort, swimming up to the sluice gate only to turn away.

Hano was born in the 1970s, a decade defined by cultural resurgence and Native Hawaiian activism. However, this emergent collective consciousness still required individuals to untangle themselves from the icy grip of settler colonial logics that have devalued Hawaiian knowledges for so long. When Hano first graduated high school, he viewed the fishpond through a narrow lens of hard work for little pay. He felt a lot of pressure to "make it," which meant leaving his community to seek material wealth and "overcome" his small-town background, a common narrative embedded in a colonial capitalist valuation system of "success." Being "somebody" meant going away and being more like the haole (foreigners). So, Hano went to the U.S. mainland to attend college and play football, and when he returned to Moloka'i, he sought well-paying jobs at Moloka'i Ranch and in Mycogen Seed's corn fields.

At Keawanui, there are four 'auwai. The kia'i keep them all closed, except for the one farthest out toward the ocean, where the flow is strongest and the most action happens. Even when the water appears calm on the surface, the pull of current in to or out of this channel can topple a strong person off their feet. The kia'i regulate these 'auwai with a double sluice gate system, a modification that draws on an innovation introduced by Chinese immigrants to the Hawaiian Kingdom in the mid-1800s. At Keawanui, a twenty-foot "raceway" is bounded by two parallel gates that can trap fish on either side.

Hano's journey back to the loko i'a began on a journey far from home. He traveled to Holland to hear the Lance Larsen v. Hawaiian Kingdom case at the Permanent Court of Arbitration at the Hague. This was a pivotal moment for him, as he heard Keanu Sai retell the history of the ongoing U.S. occupation of Hawai'i. During that trip, he began to rethink the dominant narratives he had learned and to revalue what our kūpuna have left us. He saw the need to choose to be Kanaka, to choose to give energy to the Hawaiian things—such as fishponds—that dominant American society says *doesn't matter. Choosing to be Kanaka meant embracing the "hard work for little pay" at fishponds and developing a relationship to an ancestral food system his kūpuna left behind.*

The kiaʻi constructed a funnel into the oceanside gate. When the fish run in with the current, they hit the gate then swim toward the funnel's large opening and into the raceway. If the kiaʻi want the fish to keep running right into the loko iʻa, they keep the inside gate open, or they place a second funnel facing the same direction. The system keeps the fish moving in one direction not only because they are moving against the current, but because they rarely find the funnel's smaller hole suspended in the middle of the water column. When the tide is coming up, the kiaʻi reverse the second funnel on the inner gate so that it points inward, toward the raceway. The fish swim in but cannot get out, making them easy to catch.

Now, over fifteen years since Hano started working at Keawanui, he has become the voice, the "talking chief," of Keawanui. A gifted orator, poet, and rapper, Hano combines the traditional stories of the place with contemporary beats and language as a means to draw youth and other visitors into the vision and work of restoring ʻāina. He is the kiaʻi who typically greets visiting groups and welcomes them through educational tours at the loko iʻa. In a sense, he is the figurative mākāhā, catching those who come in and out. Hano's enamoring personality, witty humor, and infectious laugh immediately draw in the younger generations and get them excited to connect to their ancestors, history, and ʻāina.

The mākāhā at Keawanui is not built to be pretty or to look "traditional." It's built to be functional and to stand the test of time against elements that push on it day in and day out. Before our forests were denuded to make way for ranches and plantations, mākāhā were made of ʻōhiʻa or other hardwoods. Long pieces are lashed together to leave vertical spaces small enough that baby fish can swim through but larger fish cannot. The kiaʻi at Keawanui used the materials available to them—stones, thick steel rebar (often used inside concrete structures), and plastic-coated metal mesh fencing—to re-create a system inspired by ancestral technologies but that looks quite different. The mākāhā is a blend, a remix, of teachings from Hawaiian elders such as Uncle Graydon "Buddy" Keala, from Chinese immigrants, and even from a book about masonry in Middle Age European monasteries. But most of all, the mākāhā is bound together by the ingenuity and creativity of the kiaʻi loko of Keawanui.

*A self-titled "aloha ʻāina warrior," Hano has used his knowledge as kiaʻi
loko to lobby in Washington, D.C., for Marine Monument expansion and
in various parts of Oceania, such as Rapanui and Tahiti, in order to help
Pacific Islanders in their own environmental efforts and struggles to weave
together scientific technology and traditional knowledge. As he likes to say,
we should "modernize without compromise," keeping aloha ʻāina as our
guiding principle.*

The Pūnāwai / Kalaniua Ritte

If loko kuapā are the largest and most productive types of Hawaiian fishponds, what makes them abundant is the mix of fresh and saltwater, wai kai. This brackish environment within the loko iʻa is what nurtures the growth of the limu (seaweed) and algae that fish find so ʻono (delicious). Each fishpond has its own unique freshwater sources, some fed by streams and others by springs. In any case, the freshwater source is essential to the health and productivity of the loko kuapā.

Keawanui is fed by springs, or pūnāwai, which are known to have been originally discovered by Hina in ancestral times long past. In particular, this loko iʻa benefits from one large pūnāwai that was rediscovered and restored through Kalaniua's vision. Today, the pūnāwai provides an ice-cold swimming hole for kids and a sovereign water source for irrigating a permaculture garden on the land side. The kiaʻi describe it as the heart of the pond because it continuously pumps fresh water into the loko iʻa, attracting and feeding small fish.

*Kalaniua's journey as a kiaʻi loko began immediately after high school at
Honouliwai fishpond. He was inspired by the potential of fishponds to provide solutions to food security issues on Molokaʻi, at a time when resources
were visibly starting to dwindle. At Honouliwai, Ua learned how to operate
and build fishponds through an "intensive aquaculture" framework that
relies on external inputs, such as fertilizer, to maximize production. Seeing
the fundamental unsustainability of such an approach, Ua felt in his gut
that this could not be the way. The project was straying too far from the
value of aloha ʻāina.*

*When Hui o Kuapā came to Keawanui in 2001, Kalaniua was able to
break free of the intensive aquaculture framework and the need for profit
within commercial aquacultural enterprises. Instead, he turned his focus
toward the specific environment of Keawanui. Going back to one simple
belief—if we allow ourselves to be in the environment, we learn by spending
time in it and observing—he trusted the learning that would emerge.*

When the Hui first came to Keawanui, no sources of water were visible because the invasive grasses were too thick. As overgrowth was cut back, Kalaniua noticed a consistent bubbling from one particular area near the shoreline. After watching it for two months, he and a group of students he was leading began to dig out the top layer, revealing a spring filled with a thick, soft mud. For years, the spring was left like this, partially revealed and ever-flowing, the mud being too heavy to be removed any further.

Kalaniua Ritte stands on lands in Kaʻamola, looking over the fishpond at Keawanui. His rifle is not a weapon for use to ward off poachers or unwelcome visitors. Rather, it is a tool that he and many other Molokaʻi families use for hunting deer. The axis deer provide a major source of protein for Molokaʻi folks, and in turn, subsistence hunters keep the deer population at a level that is less harmful to upland ecosystems. *Photograph by Noelani Goodyear-Kaʻōpua.*

Ten years later, after becoming much more familiar with the loko iʻa system as a whole, Ua borrowed a friend's pump to determine if the spring could be expanded. Slowly, over the course of a month, he carefully pumped out the soft mud and began to line the sides of the revealed underground chamber with stones.

You have to understand: If you grow up on Molokaʻi, you don't swim in fresh water unless you have connections to a boat driver who can take you to the north side of the island. Everything is saltwater and mud flats. Molokaʻi is not known for fresh water. So, uncovering such an abundant freshwater source is truly unique, and it allows a kind of self-sufficiency

The pūnāwai is the heart of the Keawanui loko iʻa. Any loko iʻa is only as healthy as its freshwater source. This spring feeds the fishpond and provides water for the organic gardens kiaʻi have planted on the land side of the loko iʻa. *Photograph by Noelani Goodyear-Kaʻōpua.*

that is not possible if you have to rely on the county water utility. Thus, the waters of Hina feed the pua within the loko iʻa and provide a respite and a gathering area for the people. The kiaʻi call it a **sovereign** water source.

At Keawanui, Hui o Kuapā restored the fishpond in a way that puts education, rather than commercial profit, at the center. And that process has been an educational and research enterprise for Kalaniua, whom Hanohano calls the "mind's eye" of the kiaʻi team. Hano reflects that it was Ua who taught him how to see the ʻāina: what used to be and what has to be put back; what will be and how to reach that future; what has to be left alone to keep the ʻāina and kai healthy. For example, Kalaniua learned how to incorporate mangrove—a nonnative

species written off by aquaculture literature and other fishponds as invasive and merely destructive—as a beneficial piece of their fishpond, if it is managed correctly. As tides rise and storms grow more frequent as the climate changes, controlled mangrove cultivation may help solidify the kuapā, and the kiaʻi are experimenting with leaving stands of mangrove growing within the wall. Additionally, Ua has used the mangrove wood to build hale kiaʻi where the kiaʻi, community members, and their guests can lounge in the shade next to the pool.

But by far, Ua's proudest accomplishment at the loko iʻa has been uncovering and restoring the pūnāwai. Like him, it is calm on its surface but continuously draws from a deep source to pump fresh energy into the life of the fishpond and its people day after day, year after year.

Conclusion

Through all of the ups and downs, from watching years of hard work leveled by natural disasters, to rationing the organization's limited funds in order to continue fulfilling their kuleana (responsibilities and authority), the kiaʻi continue to stand by Keawanui because this place is a part of their families. Maintaining a healthy ʻohana requires intergenerational transmission of knowledge and kuleana. This is one reason why the Hui o Kuapā has been so committed to stewarding Keawanui as an educational site. In fact, one of the first students, Kahekili Pā-Kalā, who went through their program in middle school, returned as an adult a couple of years ago, and he continues to work as a new generation of kiaʻi-in-training. For Keawanui to thrive for another eight hundred years into our future, many more kiaʻi will need to be raised up.

For the current kiaʻi, Keawanui is the ʻāina we lean on: an ancestor, a lover, a provider, a healer. As Hanohano told Anthony Bourdain when he featured Keawanui on *Parts Unknown* a few years ago, "if you can love

Uncle Walter Ritte stands in one of the hale kiaʻi (guardian outposts), pointing across the loko iʻa to the wall on the other side. He and the other kiaʻi also point us toward more sustainable Hawaiian futures. *Photograph by Noelani Goodyear-Kaʻōpua.*

this place without developing, destroying, or abusing it, we are on the same team. But if you are eyeing this place as a money-making vehicle for yourself, we are enemies." People of all backgrounds can and should aloha ʻāina, and in that process, you won't become Kanaka Maoli, but you can become family. Family means you have obligations to respect this place and other ʻāina in Hawaiʻi, obligations to understand its history and genealogy, to mālama or care for it, to share its story, and most importantly, to help Keawanui and its community thrive. When you give to the ʻāina, the ʻāina reciprocates and feeds you in ways that nourish your whole existence. Eventually, in the futures the kiaʻi of Keawanui offer, we will all understand ourselves as inseparable from ʻāina.

PART III. Huakaʻi / Tours for Transformation

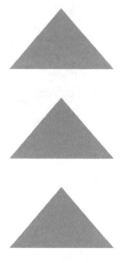

▶▶▶

A huaka'i is not an empty itinerary or a list of must-dos, but rather a journey defined by intention. A huaka'i is not meant to be an easy walk in the park or a leisurely stroll along the beach. It is demanding. It demands that your journey be deliberate and purposeful, and that you remain open to what you might learn about a place and yourself. It will place you in relationship to people and to the land in ways that you might not expect and that will demand something of you—a shift in perspective, an injunction to take action, a challenge to get involved, a request to step back or stand aside. The huaka'i offered in this section have precise aims for moving people through a place and providing new and old ways of looking at and interacting with some of the histories, struggles, and relationships that shape Hawai'i.

Some of the contributors/guides who offer their tours here in the form of narratives and maps make a regular practice of taking people through specific places and narrating them in ways that tranform the participants' understanding of and relationship to those places. Aunty Terrilee Keko'olani and Kyle Kajihiro's DeTour project remaps O'ahu through the lens of U.S. militarization, which has come to dominate land usage on the island. Their tour provides a narrative map of U.S. military occupation that travels from 'Iolani Palace to Ke Awalau o Pu'uloa (Pearl Harbor), as well as sites where deoccupation is taking place. The DeTour ends at Hanakehau Learning Farm, where the work of Andre Perez provides a place where Hawaiian hands can be returned to Hawaiian lands, and where the goal is to grow food and to grow Kānaka.

Similarly, Davianna Pōmaika'i McGregor narrates the experience of visiting Kanaloa and reclaiming Kaho'olawe as a place of cultural and historical significance to Kanaka 'Ōiwi, its place as a fulcrum of aloha 'āina struggles to reclaim it from a history of U.S. military bombing, and its tranformation into an island where Indigenous sovereignty is manifested. Continuing the theme of militarization and demilitarization, Laurel Mei-Singh and Summer Kaimalia Mullins-Ibrahim document the struggles and tensions between the state's approach to conservation and that of the local fishers and community members who practice mālama 'āina in Ka'ena and Mākua on the western shore of O'ahu. Community-led tours became a key strategy for exposing how conservation and environmental protection actually worked against people who were preserving traditional practices in these places.

The image of Hawai'i as multicultural paradise often obscures the collusions and coalitions that are wrought with the migration of people from other U.S. colonized spaces. Ellen-Rae Cachola takes us through Waikīkī, the iconographic symbol of mass tourism in Hawai'i, on a tour that highlights migrant settler labor in hotels built on occupied land. The tour models how settlers can both work in and against empire. Visually, N. Trisha Lagaso Goldberg considers the intertwined fates of Filipino workers transported for plantation labor from another U.S. colony in the Pacific, conveying the resonances among colonized people by drawing on the Hawaiian quilting tradition.

In this section, we also have itineraries and tours that foreground the forgotten or suppressed histories of particular neighborhoods. Craig Howes's tour of downtown Honolulu is a script of the layered histories written on the land at parks, intersections, and architectual design. This walking tour begins at an intersection of roads and history where ali'i, haole power brokers, enterprising merchants, Native Hawaiians, and settlers alike jockeyed for power. The tour ends at the statue of Queen Liliʻuokalani, who gazes upon the seal of the state of Hawaiʻi at the capitol. Tina Grandinetti writes and Adele Balderston maps the history of Kakaʻako, a neighborhood in Honolulu, revealing a land- and waterscape that existed before the current high-rise development boom. The walking tour of the neighborhood around Pūowaina (Punchbowl) Noenoe K. Silva created with her students uncovers and reveals a complex, layered history hidden in plain sight. This tour teaches us how to read signs in a new way, animating different relationships and events that haunt her neighborhood.

Finally, huakaʻi have transformed the guides themselves: the work they do with and for ʻāina and community is guided by an ethic of giving back rather than of taking. Candace Fujikane's work with the Concerned Elders of Waiʻanae began with her involvement as a concerned but uninformed community member on a bus tour of Oʻahu's leeward side. That huakaʻi established an ongoing partnership with the kūpuna of Waiʻanae. Her essay describes how the kūpuna continue to offer the bus tours in order to raise awareness of how environmental pollution and urban development projects are at odds with what residents want, while simultaneously foregrounding an ʻŌiwi understanding of wahi pana.

Kyle Kajihiro and Terrilee Keko'olani

The Hawai'i DeTour Project
Demilitarizing Sites and Sights on O'ahu

It is impossible to understand Hawai'i today without knowing the processes of U.S. imperial formation and militarization in the islands. It is also impossible to understand how the United States became an empire without knowing Hawai'i's pivotal role in that process. As some scholars have noted, the military is everywhere in Hawai'i, and yet it is hidden in plain sight. We began the Hawai'i DeTour Project with a simple yet daunting wager that if we could make visible some of the hidden aspects of militarization in Hawai'i, we might be able to have conversations about the costs and consequences of this militarization and begin imagining other possible futures for Hawai'i and the Pacific.

Under the auspices of the American Friends Service Committee Hawai'i Area Program and its successor, Hawai'i Peace and Justice, the Hawai'i De-Tours Project set out to reclaim the mo'olelo 'āina (histories of the land) and question patriotic U.S. narratives that portray the military as protector and provider. What began as a mostly informal practice to introduce visiting friends to social justice issues that have been glossed over by touristic depictions of Hawai'i as "paradise" has grown into a more organized program of educational tours aimed at various social justice–minded constituencies. Since 2004, we have engaged more than 1,400 participants in our DeTours and helped start other similar projects in Wai'anae and Waikīkī. While our DeTours have included a variety of military sites on O'ahu, including Mōkapu, Waimānalo, Waikāne, Līhu'e, Kunia, Lualualei, Mākua, and Keawa'ula, the centerpiece of the tour is Ke Awalau o Pu'uloa (a.k.a. Pearl Harbor). Each DeTour is a unique experience tailored to the particular interests and knowledge of the participants and drawing on current social and political events. Here we take you through some of the main sites and topics commonly discussed on our DeTours.

Situating the Hawaiian Kingdom Geopolitically

Our first stop is downtown Honolulu, where the statue of Kamehameha I and ʻIolani Palace, the historic center of the Hawaiian Kingdom and a living symbol of the contemporary Hawaiian sovereignty movement, stand opposite each other. In 1810, through wars of conquest and political alliances, Kamehameha I consolidated his rule over the archipelago to establish the Hawaiian Kingdom. However, we point out that because of the violence of this unification, some present-day descendants of the conquered kingdoms may still regard Kamehameha as an invader rather than a unifier. The subsequent rulers of the Hawaiian Kingdom strove to maintain fundamental aspects of the Indigenous culture while rapidly developing a modern, cosmopolitan nation-state. On November 28, 1843, Great Britain and France recognized Hawaiʻi as independent and sovereign; the United States did so in 1844. Hawaiʻi became one of the first nonwhite countries to be recognized as an independent nation-state within the emerging international system. The Hawaiian Kingdom soon had treaties with at least seventeen other states and maintained more than ninety legations throughout the world. Through reforms implemented by Kamehameha III, the Hawaiian Kingdom became a liberal constitutional monarchy and adopted a hybrid Hawaiian-Western land-tenure system.

ʻIolani Palace: A Living Symbol of Hawaiian Sovereignty and the "Scene of the Crime"

ʻIolani means "heavenly hawk." Built between 1879 and 1882, King Kalākaua commissioned the construction of ʻIolani Palace during a time when his authority was being challenged and his country's sovereignty threatened. The palace conveyed the modernity and sophistication of the Hawaiian Kingdom as worthy of recognition by other states. The decoration on the Coronation Pavilion, located on the southwest lawn, includes the coats of arms of the countries with which the Hawaiian Kingdom had treaties. It was also designed to convey Kalākaua's chiefly mana (spiritual and political power) to be mōʻī (supreme ruler). Although the architecture is borrowed from different European styles, the foundation of the building and the sacred symbols incorporated into its construction followed Indigenous religious ceremony, such as that of a traditional heiau (temple). As geographer Donovan Preza says, the palace is Hawaiian at its core, wrapped in a Western skin.

Despite its serene and majestic appearances, ʻIolani Palace is also the scene of the crime, where in 1893 U.S. troops intervened to support the white settler coup d'état against Queen Liliʻuokalani. Standing at the front gate to the palace grounds, one can imagine Marines lined up across King Street with their Gatling guns aimed at the palace, the queen, and her supporters.

The DeTour briefly recounts events leading up to the overthrow, including the Treaty of Reciprocity and the Bayonet Constitution, events that centered around the American military interest in acquiring control of Ke Awalau o Puʻuloa.

As we discuss the 1897 anti-annexation campaigns by Hawaiian nationals, Terri Kekoʻolani shows the DeTour participants a copy of the Kūʻē Petitions, with the signatures of Solomon Peleiohōlani, her great-great-grandfather, and several other ancestors highlighted. Like most Hawaiians, she was unaware that her own ancestors opposed annexation until the petitions were publicly displayed on the ʻIolani Palace grounds in 1998, one hundred years after the purported annexation.

Hawaiian anti-annexation efforts were successful in helping to defeat the proposed treaty of annexation in the U.S. Senate in 1897. Constitutionally and under international law, the United States could not legally annex a sovereign country without such a treaty. The Hawaiian independence movement argues that without such a lawful transaction of sovereignty, the United States is illegally occupying the Hawaiian Kingdom. However, the outbreak of

▶ **Ke Awalau o Puʻuloa**

Kanaka ʻŌiwi had several names for what is now called Pearl Harbor. One of the original names was Ke Awalau o Puʻuloa—the many bays of Puʻuloa. Another name was Waimomi, the pearl waters, which referred to the abundance of pipi (Hawaiian pearl oysters) and other fish and shellfish. Fed by streams and springs from the Waiʻanae and Koʻolau mountain ranges, the estuary was a fertile and highly productive agricultural and aquacultural resource. It is estimated that Ke Awalau o Puʻuloa had more than thirty fishponds and was considered to be ʻāina momona (fat or abundant land), a food basket

for central Oʻahu. These resources also made the ʻEwa district an important center of political power for the ancient Oʻahu chiefs.

Ke Awalau o Puʻuloa is a sacred geography to Kanaka ʻŌiwi. Many legends exist about deities and ancestral spirits who dwell there. Kānekuaʻana is the powerful female lizard/water spirit who brought an abundance of sea life to the area and was the guardian of the fishponds of Puʻuloa. These stories are not just fanciful folk tales. They are poetic narratives, political commentaries, and lessons about ethical conduct. In an account published in a Hawaiian-language newspaper in the 1880s, Kānekuaʻana took

the abundance of fish away from Puʻuloa because of the greedy and abusive actions of a konohiki (land manager). It mentions that the oysters were replaced by pahikaua (sharp serrated objects, swords, and a type of shellfish), possibly a poetic commentary on the sails of foreign ships that began to invade the harbor.

Another important guardian of Ke Awalau o Puʻuloa was Kaʻahupāhau, the great shark goddess who protected the people of ʻEwa from "man-eaters." Kaʻahupāhau issued the kapu (ban) on human sacrifice in repentance for killing a young woman who had stolen flower offerings from one of Kaʻahupāhau's human relatives.

the Spanish-American War in 1898 became the excuse for the U.S. to seize control of Hawai'i as a matter of military necessity.

The palace grounds were once an ancient burial site for ali'i (chiefs). In the eastern corner of the grounds is Pohukaina, a subterranean burial mound containing the remains of deceased ali'i. Near this site is a contemporary *ahu* (stone altar), which was built in 1993 on the centennial observance of the overthrow, when more than ten thousand Hawaiian sovereignty supporters marched and rallied on the palace grounds. The pōhaku (stones) making up the ahu were brought by people from their homelands across all parts of Hawai'i. This ahu and the entire palace grounds have become a contemporary sacred space for Hawaiians as living symbols of Hawaiian sovereignty.

Chinatown, 'A'ala Park, Kapālama, Kalihi

From 'Iolani Palace, the DeTour passes through old sections of Honolulu where new immigrants historically settled in Hawai'i. In the early twentieth century, parts of Chinatown, nicknamed "Hell's Half-Acre," housed tough neighborhoods of slums, bars, brothels, tattoo parlors, and strip clubs. Although prostitution has never been legal in Hawai'i, the police tolerated prostitution as long as it remained within the confines of Chinatown. The tour also passes two sites relevant to the Massie-Kahahawai Incident.

Beginning in the early 1960s, urban redevelopment displaced many residents of the area surrounding 'A'ala Park, many of whom were recent immigrants from the Philippines. In the 1970s, as another wave of development threatened to displace Chinatown residents and radically transform the character of the community, People Against Chinatown Evictions organized resistance and saved some of the residences. This was part of a larger wave of antieviction struggles throughout the islands. Today, displacement

---

▶ **The Massie-Kahahawai Incident**

In 1931, Thalia Massie, the wife of a naval officer, claimed she has been kidnapped, beaten, and raped by a group of "Hawaiian" men near Waikīkī. Five local teens of Japanese, Hawaiian, and Hawaiian-Chinese ancestry were arrested as suspects after they had been involved in a traffic altercation at the intersection of Liliha and North King Streets (one of the points of interest on the DeTour). The story of brown men attacking a white woman struck a racist nerve in the United States and made the Massie case one of the most sensational news stories in America in 1932. Admiral Yates Stirling, commandant of Pearl Harbor said, "Our first inclination is to seize the brutes and string them up on trees." Military leaders even planned to institute a military commission government in order to control what they considered to be Hawai'i's racially dangerous population; this threat materialized ten years later, when martial law was imposed for three years in the wake of the Pearl Harbor bombing.

After the jury in the rape trial failed to reach a verdict, vigilantes led by Thalia's husband, Thomas Massie, and her mother, Grace Fortescue, kidnapped and murdered Joseph Kahahawai, one of the teenagers who had been on trial. Police caught the killers

of people and criminalization of the poor continue. Many homeless who still congregate in ʻAʻala Park have faced increasingly draconian policies to remove them and take their belongings.

Fort Shafter, Moanalua, Kapūkākī (Red Hill), and Hālawa

Heading west on the Moanalua Freeway, we pass Fort Shafter in the ahupuaʻa (traditional land division) of Kahauiki. Built in 1907, it is the headquarters of the U.S. Army in the Pacific. Later we drive past Moanalua Valley, a site where environmentalists and Native Hawaiians stopped and rerouted the proposed H-3 freeway, a defense-related freeway that threatened endangered species and cultural sites. At Kapūkākī (a.k.a. Red Hill), we pass the Navy's massive underground fuel tank complex that was secretly built during World War II. Each of the twenty tanks measures 100 feet in diameter by 250 feet in height and has a capacity that holds 12.5 million gallons. All of these tanks have leaked, the most recent of which was the release of 27,000 gallons of jet fuel, discovered in January 2014. Although environmental groups and the Board of Water Supply have demanded that the tanks either be retrofitted to meet current environmental safety standards or be decommissioned, the Navy and the Environmental Protection Agency have resisted. The tanks sit one hundred feet above the Hālawa aquifer, which supplies 25 percent of Honolulu's fresh drinking water, from Moanalua Valley to Hawaiʻi Kai. As we descend toward the ʻEwa plains we pass the H-3 freeway, which was moved to Hālawa Valley after being blocked in Moanalua. Despite a months-long Kanaka ʻŌiwi (Native Hawaiian) protest encampment led by women at the Hale o Papa heiau, a temple honoring Papahānaumoku, a goddess of the earth and creation, the freeway was pushed through after politicians exempted the freeway construction from key environmental and cultural protection laws.

attempting to dump Kahahawai's body and charged them with murder. The famous attorney Clarence Darrow, representing the accused killers, argued that it was an "honor killing." Despite enormous political pressure to exonerate Kahahawai's killers, the jury found them guilty of manslaughter. However, the territorial governor commuted their sentences to one hour in his office, after which they were free to leave the islands.

In Kalihi, the tour passes the Puea Cemetery, where nearly two thousand people attended Kahahawai's funeral. Kahahawai's headstone is inscribed with his date of birth and the date he was killed (as opposed to the date he died); the epitaph reads "Hoomanao" ("remember").

The Massie-Kahahawai incident stills haunts race relations in Hawaiʻi. In November 2011, Christopher Deedy, a haole U.S. State Department agent who was in Honolulu to provide security for foreign leaders at the Asia Pacific Economic Cooperation Summit, fatally shot Kollin Elderts, a Hawaiian man, during a drunken altercation in Waikīkī. Deedy initially tried to claim immunity as an agent in the diplomatic corps. Coinciding with #BlackLivesMatter protests across the United States, the Elderts murder trial brought to the surface long-simmering tensions over racism and police abuse.

Camp Smith, the Head of the Heʻe (Octopus)

Arriving at the top of Halawa Heights Drive outside the fence surrounding Camp Smith, headquarters of the U.S. Indo-Pacific Command, we gaze down on the waters of Ke Awalau o Puʻuloa. In 1872, Major General John Schofield may have had a similar view when he masqueraded as a tourist and led a secret military survey of the Hawaiian Islands. Schofield reported that "Pearl Lagoon is the key to the central Pacific Ocean. It is the gem of these islands."

Citing a metaphor coined by Kaleikoa Kaeo, a respected Kanaka ʻŌiwi scholar and activist, we describe how the U.S. military in the Pacific is a monstrous heʻe, with Hawaiʻi as its head and Camp Smith, the very place where we are standing, bristling with supercomputers and communication networks, its brain and nervous system. The radars, telescopes, satellite tracking systems, and surveillance centers are its eyes and ears. At Camp Smith, we point out the surveillance camera on the telephone pole; the camera turns to watch our group. Sometimes the military police question and try to intimidate us. The excrement of this octopus is symbolized by the hundreds of contaminated sites within the Pearl Harbor Naval Complex. And its tentacles are the web of military bases that occupy other lands within the region, including Okinawa, Guam, Korea, the Philippines, Australia, New Zealand, and the Marshall Islands.

On the island of Oʻahu, the military controls 24.6 percent of the land. The U.S. Indo-Pacific Command is the oldest and largest of the unified commands, encompassing more than half the surface of the earth and a majority of its population. Today, the U.S. military occupies 118 sites in Hawaiʻi on more than 230,000 acres of land across the islands. In 2011, President Obama announced a military "pivot" toward Asia and the Pacific, which is causing further destructive military expansion in Hawaiʻi and other places across the region. For the Pacific, however, this pivot began more than a century ago, and Hawaiʻi is its fulcrum.

Military Landscapes

We next make our way through Navy housing and shopping areas, where we see the contrast between the design of military communities and that of neighboring civilian areas. Military housing areas emulate the uniformity and sprawl of suburban America, whereas the surrounding working-class neighborhood is a menagerie of colors and architectural styles geared toward multifamily utility. The privatization of military housing, along with the voucher-like housing allowance system for military families, has created

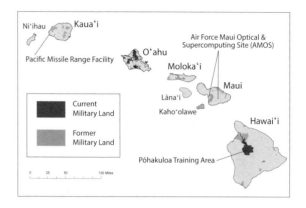

Map of military occupied lands in the Hawaiian Islands. *Map by Kyle Kajihiro.*

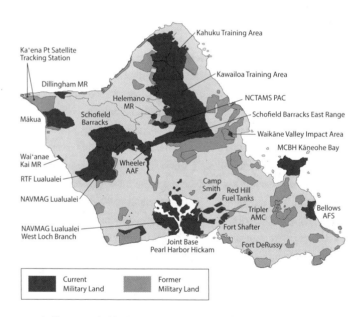

Map of military occupied lands on Oʻahu. *Map by Kyle Kajihiro.*

an inflationary housing market in Hawaiʻi; civilian residents are increasingly outcompeted by subsidized military buyers and renters.

We follow the fence line of the Navy Marine Golf Course, one of nine military golf courses in Hawaiʻi. Besides using lots of land, water, and chemicals, golf courses signify the elite status of the military in Hawaiʻi.

"The Mall at Pearl Harbor" is the largest Navy Exchange in the world. It includes a commissary and a department store. Only active duty and retired military personnel have access to the commissary. All military and veterans have access to the department store. While these commercial centers provide affordable goods to military families and some employment and purchasing opportunities for local vendors, they are shielded from the state's general excise tax and alcohol and tobacco taxes, meaning that the subsidized goods at these military retail outlets are a relatively weak stimulus for the local economy.

Reading "Pearl Harbor" across the Grain

Our DeTour's next stop is Ke Awalau o Puʻuloa, where the World War II–centric site of the Pearl Harbor memorial is located in the midst of an active military base.

Moananuiākea or American Lake? A large map of the Pacific Ocean is on the ground at the entrance to the Pearl Harbor memorial. Polynesians called the Pacific Ocean "Moananuiākea" (the deep, vast ocean)—an oceanic continent, a sea of islands teeming with connections and flows. But colonizers saw the ocean as an emptiness with small, remote islands that could be easily partitioned into colonial possessions. In the late nineteenth century, U.S. politicians and military leaders viewed the Pacific as an opportunity for America to expand its western frontier toward the new prize of China and Asia. They coveted Hawaiʻi as a stepping stone in traversing the Pacific and defending the Americas. Thus, even before President Obama declared it as such over a century later, Hawaiʻi had become the fulcrum for the first U.S. "pivot" into an overseas empire, enabling the United States to win the Spanish-American War and acquire former Spanish colonies from Puerto Rico to the Philippines. Hawaiʻi became both a casualty of U.S. empire and an accessory to the actions of that empire.

At the "Remembrance Circle," where the bronze relief of Oʻahu is located, we discuss the topography of Oʻahu, which makes Ke Awalau o Puʻuloa a particularly important resource for Kanaka ʻŌiwi but also a prime location for naval planners. Across the channel is Mokuʻumeʻume, the original name of what the Navy calls Ford Island, a site associated with many legends and

At the Remembrance Circle, *Arizona* Memorial. *Photograph by Kyle Kajihiro.*

sacred places. It is also the location of the USS *Arizona* Memorial and the USS *Missouri*, the two "bookends" of World War II. It is a good place to reflect on how the Pearl Harbor memorial reproduces particular narratives about the U.S. military and its role in the world. Would it be different if the site was designed as a peace memorial instead of a war memorial?

In the Road to War Gallery, the newly renovated museums that narrate the history of Pearl Harbor, we reflect on the role of imperialism in World War II. Oʻahu is portrayed as a fortress and "citadel" during the build-up to the war, and the Japanese saw the U.S. military in Hawaiʻi as a threat. It is fair to ask whether the massive U.S. military presence in the islands made Hawaiʻi safer. We observe how weapons, machines, and technologies of war are displayed with great reverence and in some cases are even humanized. Yet the "enemy" is typically dehumanized.

At the outdoor "Oʻahu Court," sandwiched between the two main galleries of the museum, Hawaiʻi's story is related on placards that line the walkway, easily ignored by passing or resting visitors. One of the placards contains a crucial but subtle sentence: "The Hawaiian Kingdom was overthrown in 1893." Despite its sanitized, passive-voice construction, this was one of the most controversial lines in the whole exhibit because it acknowledges the

U.S.-backed overthrow of Queen Liliʻuokalani, which unsettles the United States' claims to Hawaiʻi.

In the Attack Gallery, visitors are immersed in the visuals and sounds of the attack. Graphic photos of American casualties from December 7, 1941, are displayed. And yet, because of a controversy over the inclusion of a photo of the devastation of Hiroshima caused by the atomic bomb, the museum displays only a single photo of the ruined city seen from a distance, devoid of any people or signs of human suffering. A wall-sized photograph of the celebrated all-Japanese 442nd Battalion dwarfs the small photo of the Honoʻuliʻuli internment camp. We consider how the historic conflation of Japanese American military service with citizenship in the World War II narrative relates to contemporary debates about civil rights and immigration. The exhibit is muted on the oppressive nature of martial law or its implications for civil liberties. Approximately 1,942 persons of Japanese ethnicity were interned in concentration camps. Hawaiʻi's economy would have collapsed if the entire Japanese population were to have been interned. Instead, martial law turned all of Hawaiʻi into a de facto military-controlled concentration camp.

Hanakehau Farm, Waiawa Makai

The last stop on our tour is Hanakehau Learning Farm, nestled in the wetlands of Waiawa Makai near Leeward Community College. Currently owned by the Kamehameha Schools, these spring-fed lands once sustained a large community of Kanaka ʻŌiwi who cultivated wetland kalo (taro) and fish.

As the bus pulls through the gate the sun reflects brightly off the dry grass and kiawe trees. After lining up, Terri chants an oli kahea to request permission to enter. Our host, Andre Perez, welcomes us. Huddled under a gray tarp canopy, we eat and talk. Andre explains the ordeal they went through to remove tons of illegally dumped construction debris left behind by the previous tenant. Three hundred feet away, an earthen berm and chain-link fence mark the navy-controlled parcel where hazardous materials were once buried and burned and used to fill ancient fishponds. A short distance down the path is the "boneyard," an area where the navy parks its decommissioned ships until they can be used as targets during naval exercises.

Delving into old land records and maps, Andre discovered that these lands had been highly productive. He gestures upland. The springs still flow and the water is clean. He intends to restore the loʻi kalo (wetland taro fields). But Andre makes clear that his vision is not to make this into a full-blown agricultural venture. Rather, he sees his primary mission as "growing con-sciousness." By engaging in traditional cultural practices and political organ-izing skills, and teaching these to others, he wants Hanakehau to be a kīpuka (oasis of forest in the lava flow; an opening into a different state of being) in the "belly of the beast," one that preserves and spreads traditional knowl-edge and develops activists.

"Remember that slogan and song: 'Keep Hawaiian Lands in Hawaiian Hands'?" Andre asks the group, most of whom are too young to remember. "We need to flip it over: 'Keep Hawaiian Hands in Hawaiian Lands'! As my mentor, Kaleikoa Kaeo says, 'The land will not be returned to Hawaiians until Hawaiians return to the land.'"

Resources: Community Groups

Hawai'i Peace and Justice works to counter the impacts of militarization in Hawai'i and builds solidarity with peace movements around the world. It is the sponsor of the Hawai'i DeTours Project: www.wp.hawaiipeaceandjustice.org.

DMZ Hawai'i/Aloha 'Āina is a clearinghouse and network of groups confronting militari-zation impacts in Hawai'i: www.dmzhawaii.org.

Women's Voices Women Speak is a group of multiethnic women in Hawai'i who chal-lenge militarism and promote genuine security as part of the International Women's Network Against Militarism: http://wvws808.blogspot.com/.

Protect Kaho'olawe 'Ohana (PKO) is the group that stopped the bombing of Kaho'olawe and now leads cultural access to Kaho'olawe every month: www.protectkahoolaweohana.org.

Mālama Mākua is a group leading efforts to stop military training at Mākua and to re-store the land and Native Hawaiian cultural practices in the valley. They lead cultural access activities in Mākua twice a month: www.malamamakua.org.

Malu 'Āina Center for Non-violent Education and Action works on peace and social justice issues on Hawai'i Island, including opposition to the military bombing of Pōhakuloa: malu-aina.org.

KAHEA: The Hawaiian-Environmental Alliance works on a number of Native Hawaiian and environmental issues, including protecting Mauna Kea and supporting environmental justice in Wai'anae: kahea.org.

Additional Readings

Ferguson, Kathy E., and Phyllis Turnbull. *Oh, Say, Can You See? The Semiotics of the Military in Hawai'i*. Minneapolis: University of Minnesota Press, 1999.

Gonzalez, Vernadette Vicuña. *Securing Paradise: Tourism and Militarism in Hawai'i and the Philippines*. Durham, NC: Duke University Press, 2013.

Kajihiro, Kyle. "Resisting Militarization in Hawai'i." In *The Bases of Empire the Global Struggle against U.S. Military Posts*, ed. Catherine Lutz, 299–332. London: Pluto, 2009.

Kajihiro, Kyle. "Moananuiākea or 'American Lake'? Contested Histories of the U.S. 'Pacific Pivot.'" In *Under Occupation: Resistance and Struggle in a Militarised Asia-Pacific*, ed. Daniel Broudy, Peter Simpson, and Makoto Arakaki, 126–60. Newcastle upon Tyne, UK: Cambridge Scholars, 2013.

Rosa, John P. Rosa. *Local Story: The Massie-Kahahawai Case and the Culture of History*. Honolulu: University of Hawai'i Press, 2014.

Stannard, David E. *Honor Killing: How the Infamous "Massie Affair" Transformed Hawai'i*. New York: Viking, 2005.

Davianna Pōmaika'i McGregor

Kanaloa Kaho'olawe
He Wahi Akua/A Sacred Place

Alert!

"The kūpuna warn that Kaho'olawe is not for everyone. It is a rugged and challenging place!"[1] This warning opens the Protect Kaho'olawe 'Ohana ('Ohana) safety video at the orientation that all visitors to the island are required to attend. It continues: "Kaho'olawe is a wahi pana or a sacred place to be treated with reverence and respect. . . . Commercial activity within the reserve is strictly prohibited." Indeed, Kanaloa Kaho'olawe is not for commercial tourism. It is a sacred island where one goes to learn and practice Kanaka 'Ōiwi culture.

Permission

To enter the island, one must learn a chant that asks the spirits of the island for permission to safely land. Once a response chant of welcome is called out, participants may disembark from the boat that carried them from Maui; they enter the ocean and swim ashore. This protocol helps participants on the huaka'i (cultural field service trip) make the transition from the secular world in which we live and work into the sacred realm of Kanaloa Kaho'olawe. While on the island, participants engage in activities that begin a process of initiation into becoming Hawaiian cultural practitioners. No one is an observer or tourist. Everyone is a participant, taking on the responsibility of a contributing member of an 'ohana (extended family) while on the island—picking up rubbish on the beach, cooking meals, cleaning dishes, opening and maintaining trails, bathing in the ocean, and sharing experiences and insights. Without running water, electricity, or facilities, participants are immersed in the natural elements. Everyone engages in observations of nature in relation to the

Having chanted and received permission to land, a group transfers from ship to shore on an inflatable zodiac, enters the ocean, and forms a line to unload food and supplies for a four-day visit to the island in April 2011. *Photograph by Noa Emmett Aluli.*

moon phase and seasonal rise of the sun. Most importantly, participants work to heal the land by getting rid of invasive species, planting native plants, or both. When participants leave, they also chant to ask permission to safely leave and to prepare themselves to reenter their regular lives.

A Sacred Island

Every island has sacred places. However, the entire island of Kanaloa Kahoʻolawe (Kanaloa) is sacred. Kanaloa is the only island in the Pacific originally named for a god, Kanaloa (god of the ocean). The realm of Kanaloa is both vast and deep, and the island is the only part of the realm that rises above the ocean's surface and is available to kānaka (humans) to live on. Historically, the island was a center for the training of wayfinders who navigated epic voyages across the broad expanse of the Pacific Ocean. For our ancestors, the island itself served as a portal into the spiritual realms of Kanaloa and of Kāne, the god of fresh water and sunlight, and Haumea, the Earth Mother (also known as Papa). It was a point of departure and arrival for transpacific voyaging, connecting Hawaiʻi with the island peoples of the Pacific. In the contemporary era, the island reconnected Kanaka ʻŌiwi (Native

Before stopping the bombing on October 22, 1990, the U.S. Navy had two huge targets made of tires painted white on the landscape for ship-to-shore shelling of the island. The targets were removed during a cleanup of unexploded ordnance from 1993 to 2003. *Photograph by Noa Emmett Aluli.*

Hawaiians) of the twenty-first century with ancestral wisdom and the natural life forces that were honored as deities by ancestors. Through Kanaloa Kahoʻolawe, these deities were called back into the daily lives of Kānaka ʻŌiwi.

Desecrated

Kanaloa was desecrated and abused by the U.S. Navy for nearly fifty years, from 1941 through 1990, when it was used for live-fire ordnance training delivered by ship-to-shore shelling, bombing, mortar shelling, and amphibious landings. Through the efforts of the ʻOhana, with the spiritual guidance of the Edith Kanakaʻole Foundation, the island has been reborn in our contemporary consciousness as a sacred place.

Protect Kahoʻolawe ʻOhana

Protect Kahoʻolawe ʻOhana (Extended Family for Kahoʻolawe) was founded in 1976 to stop the bombing and all military use of the island of Kanaloa Kahoʻolawe. The organization's founders were advised by kūpuna (elders) to organize in a Hawaiian way—to embrace the island as a family member and work together as an extended family to heal the island. Throughout the first year, occupations of the island drew national attention and led to arrests, imprisonments, and letters barring those arrested from returning to the island. Unexpectedly, the 'Ohana's slogan, "Aloha 'Āina" (Love the Land; Love the Hawaiian Nation) awakened a consciousness among Kānaka 'Ōiwi throughout the Hawaiian Islands. It sparked a grassroots, islands-wide resistance to the uncontrolled development of tourist resorts and expensive subdivisions that began to change a way of life established in Hawai'i since statehood in 1959. In March 1977, leader George Helm Jr. and Kimo Mitchell were lost in the ocean near Kanaloa Kaho'olawe during one of the landings. Their martyrdom galvanized the movement to mature, expand, and persevere. The occupations took a serious toll on the lives of 'ohana members. The strategy turned toward building a base of support in order to make a political impact in the courts and the legislature. Finally, on October 22, 1990, the bombing of the island was halted. With the transfer of ownership of the island from the U.S. Navy to the state of Hawai'i in May 1994, all military use of the island ended and the painstaking work to heal the island began.

Continuing Threat

From November 10, 1993, through November 11, 2003, the U.S. Navy conducted an omnibus cleanup of ordnance on the island. After fifty years of use as a military weapons range, the island's 28,800 acres were contaminated with shrapnel, target vehicles, and unexploded ordnance. The U.S. Navy signed an agreement with the state of Hawai'i to clean up the ordnance across 30 percent of the island's subsurface. In 1993, the U.S. Congress appropriated $460 million for the U.S. Navy to fulfill this obligation, and the Navy coordinated what is acknowledged to be the largest unexploded ordnance remediation project in the history of the United States. Over 10 million pounds of metal, 370 vehicles, and 14,000 tires were removed from the island and recycled. Rather than clearing 30 percent of the island to a depth of four feet, however, the Navy contractor cleared only 2,650 acres, or 9 percent, of the island's subsurface. Another 19,464 acres, or 68 percent of the surface of the island's landscape, was cleared of ordnance, but 6,686 acres—23 percent of the island—has not been cleared at all.

A disturbing fact is that the U.S. Navy can only guarantee (with 90 percent confidence) that 85 percent of the ordnance within the 2,650 acres was cleared down to a depth of four feet. Given that only 9 percent of the island has been cleared beyond the surface, someone with knowledge of the cleared areas and who has been trained in identifying and avoiding ordnance must accompany anyone visiting the island.

First Lands

In 1993, in anticipation of the return of the island of Kanaloa Kahoʻolawe to the state of Hawaiʻi, the legislature passed a law, Hawaiʻi Revised Statutes Chapter 6K, that provided for the eventual transfer of the island to a sovereign Hawaiian entity. The law states that "the resources and waters of Kahoʻolawe shall be held in trust as part of the public land trust; provided that the State shall transfer management and control of the island and its waters to the sovereign native Hawaiian entity upon its recognition by the United States and the State of Hawaiʻi."[2]

According to John Waiheʻe III, who was governor at the time of the transfer,

> this State has always taken the position that with respect to Hawaiian issues that certain groups have, because of their involvement in the issues, become trustees for that particular responsibility . . . In the instance of Kahoʻolawe, that was the Protect Kahoʻolawe ʻOhana. They became the trustees because of what they did to ensure the return of Kahoʻolawe: people went to jail, people died, people gave up their children so that we can have this island. It is not something that simply ought to be dismissed as a natural current of events, as another piece of state real estate.

The governor also explained that Kanaloa "was not placed back into the DLNR [Department of Land and Natural Resources] inventory, it was set aside with a special commission to say that it actually belonged to the Hawaiian Nation. You can talk about it coming back to the state of Hawaiʻi, but it was specifically set aside by the people of this state, by their elected representatives, *as the first piece of sovereign soil.*"[3]

Vision

The state of Hawaiʻi established the Kahoʻolawe Island Reserve Commission, an entity administered by the Hawaiʻi Department of Land and Natural Resources, to manage the island until a sovereign Kanaka ʻŌiwi governing entity was established that would be recognized by the Hawaiian state and U.S. federal governments. The Commission has seven members appointed by the governor, a member of the ʻOhana, two members nominated by the ʻOhana, the chairperson of the Board of Land and Natural Resources, a representative of the Office of Hawaiian Affairs, and a member of a Native Hawaiian organization.

The vision adopted by the Commission for the island acknowledges the importance of the island as a sacred place for Kanaka ʻŌiwi, where the land and the culture are nurtured. It states: "The *kino* (physical manifestation) of Kanaloa is restored. Forests and shrublands of native plants and other biota clothe its slopes and valleys. *Nā Poʻe Hawaiʻi* (the People of Hawaiʻi) care for the land in a manner, which recognizes the island and the ocean of Kanaloa as a living spiritual entity. Kanaloa is a *puʻuhonua* and a *wahi pana* (a place of refuge, a sacred place) where native Hawaiian cultural practices flourish. The piko of. Kanaloa (the navel, the center) is the crossroads of past and future generations from which the native Hawaiian lifestyle spread throughout the islands."[4]

▸ **The Edith Kanakaʻole Foundation**

The Edith Kanakaʻole Foundation is a culture-based organization founded by the ʻOhana of Luka and Edith Kanakaʻole. Founded on the traditions and rich cultural heritage of the Kanakaʻole family, it is the foundation's mission to heighten Indigenous Hawaiian cultural awareness, knowledge, and participation through its educational programs and scholarships. The Edith Kanakaʻole Foundation focuses on maintaining and perpetuating the teachings, beliefs, practices, philosophies, and traditions of Edith and Luka Kanakaʻole. Edith Kanakaʻole was a Hawaiian practitioner, kumu hula (master hula teacher), chanter, composer, Nā Hōkū Hanohano award–winning recording artist, and instructor of Hawaiian studies at the Hawaiʻi Community College and the University of Hawaiʻi-Hilo.

Forty Years of Aloha ʻĀina

In January 2016, the Protect Kahoʻolawe ʻOhana celebrated its fortieth anniversary. The mission of the ʻOhana is to perpetuate Aloha ʻĀina (love and respect of land and nature) throughout the Hawaiian Islands by engaging Kanaka ʻŌiwi and the general public in cultural, educational, and spiritual activities that heal and revitalize the cultural and natural resources of Kanaloa. In the work to heal Kahoʻolawe, the ʻOhana strengthens the relationship with the land and pays respect to our spirits of the land. On their home islands, the ʻOhana protects the natural and cultural resources of ancestral lands.

Learning Center

Kanaloa Kahoʻolawe is a unique and singularly important venue for learning and practicing Kanaka ʻŌiwi culture. Without electricity, paved roads, or running water, one is fully immersed in the natural life forces on this island. The remote and raw landscape enhances the cultural experience and enables ceremonies and protocols to be conducted without distractions or becoming a spectacle for tourists. Numerous and diverse cultural sites are accessible and can be appreciated within the context of their

At Moaʻulaiki, the second highest peak on Kanaloa Kahoʻolawe, a panoramic view of all of the islands and a 360-degree view of the horizon makes it an ideal location for training navigators. Protect Kahoʻolawe ʻOhana has built a wooden lele for placing offerings for Lono, the Hawaiian god of agricultural productivity, during the annual Makahiki rainy season from October through February. *Photograph by Noa Emmett Aluli.*

original cultural landscape. Participants can experience the ʻāina and the environment as our ancestors experienced it, and can reconnect with the spiritual life forces of nature in the same manner as our ancestors, who honored these forces as gods. Kanaloa is a cultural puʻuhonua (refuge) and the best place to learn and master cultural and spiritual Native Hawaiian practices. It is important for the island to continue to be managed as a reserve for Native Hawaiian cultural and spiritual beliefs, customs, and practices outside of commercial tourist routes.

Kūkulu Ke Ea A Kanaloa

In 2009, the Edith Kanakaʻole Foundation provided a cultural plan for the island as a learning center for the training of cultural practitioners. The Kūkulu Ke Ea A Kanaloa Culture Plan for Kahoʻolawe outlines three elements of this training: lololo, or observation, documentation, analysis, and new insights; hana kaulike, or justified work; and aha hoʻohanohano, or ceremony and protocol. The plan serves as both a source and a guide for the cultural learning experience program for participants on a huakaʻi.

The lololo involves group observations of the natural elements and wild-life from before dawn to sunrise. It includes conscious observation of the natural marine and terrestrial resources throughout one's journey on the island. Over time, as observations are documented and analyzed, new insights regarding the seasonal changes in the condition of the resources are chronicled through ʻōlelo noʻeau, or wise sayings. For example, "Pua ke akiaki, hiki mai ke koholā" (When the akiaki grass blooms, the humpback whales arrive). Those on huakaʻi scheduled for the spring and autumn equinoxes and the summer and winter solstices make careful observations of the alignments of features in ancestral cultural structures with these seasonal astronomical events and surrounding landscape features.

The hana kaulike involves the development of the around-the-island Ala Loa or Long Trail. On some huakaʻi, new sections of the trail are opened, grubbed, and lined with stones. On other huakaʻi the work involves trail maintenance. The Ala Loa will eventually be used for the procession of the Akua Loa image of Lono around the island during the annual Makahiki ceremony.

Ala Loa

Participation in a huakaʻi is a life-transforming experience that awakens the spiritual consciousness through pilina ʻāina, immersion in the natural life forces of Kanaloa and the practice of aloha ʻāina. Most of those who have been on a huakaʻi with the ʻOhana share how the huakaʻi helped reconnect them to their soul as a Hawaiian and to their ancestors, and how it inspired them to practice their culture in their day-to-day lives. Many have changed their livelihoods to include the practice of aloha ʻāina in their everyday lives.

▶ **Makahiki and Lono**

Lono is the Hawaiian god of agricultural productivity. He is associated with the wet season's weather system that brings the annual rains to Hawaiʻi from October through February. His body forms are the dark clouds, heavy rains, and partial rainbows that are observed during this season. Hawaiians honored Lono with ceremonies called Makahiki that involved offerings of harvested plants. The image of Lono was taken in a procession around each island. Hoʻokupu (offerings) were placed at the boundary points between each land division.

Aha Hoʻohanohano involves the learning of several chants: Mele Komo, asking permission to land; Ke Noi ʻAʻama, seeking a safe departure; E Ala E, greeting the sunrise; and Pule Hoʻomana (E Ho Mai), a chant to bring focus for the group. Participants are also provided the Pule Nā ʻAumakua, a chant acknowledging the presence of our ancestors and asking for their inspiration, strength, wisdom, and vision. Upon arrival, all huakaʻi participants engage in a Kapu Kai. This is a cleansing ceremony conducted in the ocean to enable them to release worries, concerns, and issues they bring with them so that they can focus on the purpose and activities of the huakaʻi. In the evenings, participants engage in the cultural practice of kukākukā—the sharing of observations and insights gained while on the island.

While on the island, groups do predawn observations and then chant "E Ala E" as the sun rises out of the ocean and over Haleakalā on Maui, May 2014. *Photograph by Noa Emmett Aluli.*

Those who work on the Ala Loa have a sense of fulfillment in that they are giving of their sweat and labor and aloha to the island. They are inspired with the understanding that their work is laying the foundation for the hundreds and thousands of Hawaiians and non-Hawaiians who will journey to Kanaloa in the future. They can tell their children and grandchildren that they helped to build the Ala Loa. In the process, the experience provides insights into their personal Ala Loa—their pathway of life.

Aloha Mai, Aloha Aku

The ʻOhana and those who visit the island with them have learned that the more one gives to the island, the more one receives in return. Throughout the four decades that the ʻOhana has served as kahu (stewards of the island), Kanaloa Kahoʻolawe has responded by revealing extraordinary sites and insights into ancestral wisdom. We have learned lessons that can serve as a general guide for entering cultural places. Cultural places in Hawaiʻi are connected to generations of Native Hawaiians. When one enters such a place, one should acknowledge the ʻuhana, or spirits of the ancestors of the land, and ask their permission to enter. One should enter for a specific purpose and visit with respect for both the land and the people of that land. One should visit to give aloha to that place—a very different approach from that of commercial tourism, which commodifies cultural lands and places money at the nexus of the relationship between the visitor and the place and its people. Kanaloa Kahoʻolawe can serve as a model of how to revitalize relationships of aloha with Hawaiʻi's cultural places and its ancestors.

Notes

1   Photos for this essay were provided by Noa Emmett Aluli, MD, who was among those who made the first landing in January 1976 and who founded and continues to be a leader of Protect Kahoʻolawe ʻOhana.
2   Hawaiʻi Revised Statutes, § 6K-9 (2012).
3   From the testimony of Governor John Waihee III before the Senate committees on Hawaiian affairs and on water, land, and Hawaiian affairs, February 12, 2011; emphasis added.
4   "I OLA KANALOA! A Plan for Kanaloa Kahoʻolawe through 2026," Kanaoloa 2026 Working Group, 2014 (last accessed July 22, 2018), http://www.kahoolawe.hawaii.gov/plans /I%20OLA%20KANALOA.pdf.

Resources

Edith Kanakaʻole Foundation, https://www.edithkanakaolefoundation.org.

Laurel Mei-Singh and Summer Kaimalia Mullins-Ibrahim

Fences and Fishing Nets

Conflicting Visions of Stewardship for
Kaʻena and Mākua

Fences and fishing nets shape the landscape of the ahupuaʻa (land division) of Kaʻena, located at the northwestern tip of the island of Oʻahu and bordering the moku (districts) of Waialua and Waiʻanae. As a traditional fishing ground for as long as Kanaka ʻOiwi have treaded the shores of the islands, Kaʻena continues to be a place rich with fish, turtles, shellfish, and monk seals. It is a wahi pana (storied place) of the leina a ka ʻuhane, from which souls leap after death. Signs of colonial modernity are also present. From 2008 to 2011, the state of Hawaiʻi's Department of Land and Natural Resources (DLNR) built a 630-meter-long fence from shoreline to shoreline at Kaʻena Point with the stated purpose of keeping out predators in order to protect seabirds and Indigenous plants. During both the planning and construction phases of the predator fence, the DLNR issued numerous fines to fishers for having "camping paraphernalia" in state parks after sunset. Because lawaiʻa (fishers) often fish overnight, many feel that the fence was part of a strategy of displacement and criminalization meant to secure the space for tourism.

The ways of life practiced by lawaiʻa, which are based on daily interactive relations with ʻāina (earth, "that which feeds"), threaten a particular vision for Kaʻena espoused by the DLNR, advocates of the tourist economy, and environmentalists aligned with both: as wilderness meant to be visited and left untouched. For the latter groups, acceptable behavior in the area includes walking in, observing and taking pictures, then leaving without actively interacting with the land and sea. In fact, public officials and local environmental groups behind the fence blamed lawaiʻa for harming

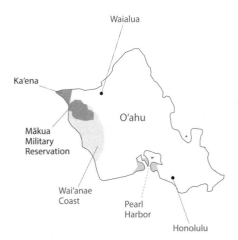

Map of Oʻahu with Kaʻena and Mākua highlighted. *Map by Manu Mei-Singh.*

Kaʻena's environment. Yet lawaiʻa understand that it is in their interest to protect and care for the resources that have supported their families for generations. Fences and fishing nets promote two contrasting ways of life: the first relying on enclosure and displacement, the latter on ancestral relations between humans and the environment as the basis of collective abundance.

Confronting the dispossession of ways of life premised on subsistence, community, and ancestral relations to land, in 2008 Kaʻena lawaiʻa formed two organizations, the Lawaiʻa Action Network and the Kaʻena Cultural Practice Project. That year, these groups organized the fishing community to show up in full force to a meeting at Camp Erdman in Waialua, where lawaiʻa expressed disappointment in the DLNR's vision of fencing and criminalization as the basis of conservation. As an alternative to this enclosure-driven conservation strategy, the Kaʻena Cultural Practice Project now organizes huakaʻi (tours), community cleanups, and plantings to nurture a sense of kuleana—collective responsibility—for generations to come. This model of stewardship empowers community members and visitors by highlighting the importance of relationships between land and people. In addition, the Lawaiʻa Action Network facilitated opportunities for lawaiʻa to connect with each other in order to confront the growing harassment of fishers and hunters, particularly by supporting fellow lawaiʻa contesting citations in the courts. These efforts challenge the notion of nature as a pristine wilderness that exists solely for the purposes of recreation and leisure while remaking human-environment relations as premised on mutual care as a daily practice.

Lawaiʻa Al Sabagala throwing net off the coast of Kaʻena, December 2010. *Photograph by Summer Kaimalia Mullins-Ibrahim.*

Hiʻiaka Tours and the Moʻolelo of Kaʻena

While tourism has generated many of the problems confronting Kaʻena fishers, the lawaiʻa also recognize the power of tours to teach people about the importance of a place from the perspective of those vested in protecting it. The Kaʻena Cultural Practice Project's Hiʻiaka Tours began in partnership with lawaiʻa and kumu (teachers) from Kamehameha Schools and impart the web of relationships between humans, deities, and the natural world; in other words, the genealogies that inform ethical interaction when traveling through a place. The huakaʻi share the moʻolelo (stories, history) of Hiʻiakaikapoliopele (also known as Hiʻiaka), the Hawaiian deity who is the patron of healing and hula, and the favorite younger sister of Pele, the famed deity of volcanoes and fire.

On a typical tour, lawaiʻa guide visitors around Kaʻena while sharing moʻolelo of Hiʻiakaikapoliopele. The tour begins with the story of Hiʻiaka's arrival to Kaʻena and her oli kāhea (chant asking permission to enter) directed to her relatives named Kaʻena and Pohakuokauaʻi (also a place in Kaʻena).

Summer Kaimalia on a Hiʻiaka Tour with the kupua Pōhakuloa, 2012. *Photograph by Kyle Kajihiro.*

Along the way, the tour stops at Manini Gulch, which lies hidden along a cliffside. The tour continues along the main access road to a large boulder named Pōhakuloa, the kupua (shapeshifter), who now rests at Kaʻena after a bout with Hiʻiaka herself. Today, recreational off-road vehicles threaten Pōhakuloa by regularly driving on top of it. The tour also visits the unnamed sandy cove where Hiʻiaka landed her waʻa (canoe) and continued to travel along the point on foot. While visiting each of the places mentioned in Hiʻiaka's huakaʻi (journey), participants learn the ʻŌiwi names of the peaks and gulches, ponds, and rocks that surround them while also encountering remnants of Kaʻena's more recent past: the Oahu Railroad, fences from ranches, and concrete rubble from gun emplacements built during World War II. By sharing significant place-names, the tours enable people to understand that Kaʻena is not just an empty, wild space. The moʻolelo give meaning to its storied landscape and propose worldmaking systems as alternatives to those promoted by fences.

Moʻolelo of Hiʻiakaikapoliopele span the island chain. One version ran as a daily series in the Hawaiian-language newspaper *Ka Naʻi Aupuni* from 1905 to 1906, describing Hiʻiaka's adventures at Kaʻena and neighboring Mākua on her journey to the island of Kauaʻi. Published just over a decade after the overthrow, the story challenged the new colonial authority and reminded people of Hawaiʻi's storied history and Kanaka ʻŌiwi relations with the land, even while the territorial government controlled the islands. The Hiʻiaka Tours draw from this legacy to raise awareness about the continuing need for mālama ʻāina (caring for the land) through protecting resources by educating participants about Kaʻena's cultural and historic significance.

The Kaʻena Point Ecosystem Restoration Project:
A Moʻolelo of Dispossession

While the Kaʻena Cultural Practice Project breathes life into Hawaiian moʻolelo and place-names, the fence promotes an entirely different model of land management, dispossessing lawaiʻa and others who hold genealogical ties to the place. Plans for the fence at Kaʻena Point surfaced at the end of 2007, when the Hawaiʻi DLNR sent out a preconsultation letter regarding fence construction to "interested agencies, organizations and individuals"—excluding fishing groups and individual lawaiʻa. The DLNR's failure to contact lawaiʻa during this phase is significant: the fishing community, who has always been one of the dominant users of Kaʻena, hold generational and experiential knowledge of the place. Summer and her father had not been contacted as interested individuals despite being actively involved in the state of Hawaiʻi's previous efforts to garner community advisement and input for land stewardship and management starting in the 1990s.[1]

Yet in December 2008, Laura Thielen, the chair of the DLNR, clearly stated her target demographic in a message to state legislators: "We believe that the department can, with partners like Camp Erdman and Friends of Kaʻena Point, provide enhanced and safe recreational opportunities for residents in this beautiful area." These partners center around wealthy landowners from the North Shore, an area adjacent to Kaʻena that is frequented by visitors, casting these segments of the population as ideal stewards of what is now a state of Hawaiʻi park reserve.

Not only had the state of Hawaiʻi excluded the fishing community from resource management decisions, Division of Conservation and Resource Enforcement officers employed by the DLNR increasingly harassed and criminalized lawaiʻa and houseless people. In 1999, the Board of Land and Natural Resources (the governing body of the DLNR) had put in place a camping rule that criminalized houselessness and the use of camping paraphernalia in state parks. Under this rule, starting in 2008, officers increasingly harassed fishers and hunters who spent time in Ka'ena (and other state parks) after sunset as they always had. According to Thielen, the camping rule serves to protect wildlife and tourists from the invasion of "tent cities" comprised of houseless people.[2] It is important to note that this rule leaves what constitutes "paraphernalia" to the interpretation and discretion of individual enforcement officers. Far too often, officers targeted lawai'a for carrying coolers, having a cot for a sleeping child, and using tents to shelter children and kūpuna (elders) while fishing at night. The policing and criminalization of lawai'a and houseless people escalated as prime features of DLNR policy amid its efforts to build a fence.

Because of grassroots community organizing, the fishing community finally achieved representation in the Ka'ena Point Advisory Group in 2009. Lawai'a were able to voice their concerns and share their mana'o (thinking) with the rest of the group. Yet, at those meetings, other members of the Ka'ena Point Advisory Group singled them out and acted as though the fishing community was a problem and not capable of becoming part of the solution to protect Ka'ena's resources. The first two fishing representatives in this group, both founding members of the Lawai'a Action Network, resigned in April 2010 as a result of this mistreatment.

Here, we see dispossession enacted not only through the harassment and attempted displacement of lawai'a from places where they have generational ties, but also through their exclusion from political power and decision-making processes that affect their daily lives. At its core, dispossession entails the rupturing of communities and their connections to particular places, a process that encompasses the transformation of economic systems, familial ties, and ways of life. Yet displacement is not complete. Sustaining generational practices, lawai'a continue to fish at Ka'ena, generating waiwai (wealth, abundance) for their neighbors and extended families.

Fences, Displacement, and Resistance at Mākua

Winding northward along the Farrington Highway on O'ahu's west side, a traveler passes Mākua Military Reservation five miles southeast of Ka'ena, also a contested and politically important locale marked by both displacement and grassroots efforts to reclaim connections to the place. The U.S. Army began to acquire land for training in 1929, and it evicted all residents of Mākua in December 1941, after the Pearl Harbor bombing, to use the entire valley for target practice. After the war, the Army officially seized more than four thousand acres. A 1964 executive order signed by Lyndon B. Johnson renamed the valley Mākua Military Reservation and leased the valley for sixty-five years

Sparky Rodrigues, Leandra Wai, and 'ohana in front of their Mākua home, May 20, 1996. *Photograph by Ed Greevy.*

for one dollar. For decades, the U.S. military used the valley for live-fire training, causing massive deforestation and imperiling the endangered species, heiau, and other culturally significant sites in the valley.

Despite the military occupation of the valley, people returned to Mākua to live on the beach, near where deities named Papa and Wākea (Earth Mother and Sky Father) gave birth to the Hawaiian people, according to Oʻahu moʻolelo. In 1996, 282 people—83 percent of whom were Hawaiian—lived at Mākua Beach, sharing fish from the ocean, produce from the sandy soil, and other types of food. While life at Mākua was never perfect, the ocean and surrounding environment animated a healing process; many living on Mākua Beach were confronting poverty and illness while yearning to reconnect with Hawaiian culture.

This community no longer lives at Mākua. On June 18, 1996, a convoy of vehicles arrived at Mākua at dawn. More than one hundred law enforcement officials evicted sixteen people who stayed at Mākua in an act of civil disobedience. Former resident Sparky Rodrigues describes that morning: "They ran their bulldozers over everything, destroyed everything, and for them it was a shock and awe kind of thing. . . . So you couldn't survive, you would have to start from scratch. And at that point they blocked off the whole area. Put up the fences . . ."

This story is typical in Hawaiʻi and has been repeated throughout its history: when Hawaiians and others form self-sufficient communities that rely on subsistence, local agriculture, and cooperative governance, the state of Hawaiʻi and the U.S. military wield the power at their disposal to enclose and evict them.

And communities have always fought back. This eviction spurred the formation of Mālama Mākua, a community organization dedicated to protecting Mākua. Sparky Rodrigues and other community members initiated a lawsuit in the late 1990s, and a 2001 settlement required at least twice-monthly huakaʻi in the form of community accesses. This advocacy eventually prevented the military from bombing the place for live-fire training and mandated conservation programs to protect over forty endangered and threatened species in Mākua's valleys and the surrounding mountain range. In mid-December 2001, community members held a Makahiki celebration at Mākua. Over fifty people stayed overnight to celebrate the beginning of what the Hawaiian calendar marks as a period of peace and well-being. Despite ongoing negotiations with the military to continue cultural accesses, Mālama Mākua opens the gates of the military base to celebrate the opening and closing of Makahiki every year.

Similar to the Hiʻiaka Tours at Kaʻena, huakaʻi at Mākua reconnect people to places. On a typical huakaʻi, visitors begin with an oli kāhea then give hoʻokupu (offerings) at an ʻahu (altar). They see pōhaku kiʻi (petroglyphs) engraved in upright rocks, a well under a mango tree, and the Ukanipō heiau (place of worship) surrounded by stone walls. These visits, led by Mālama Mākua, expose the military's continuing destruction of wahi pana and offer a new vision for a demilitarized Mākua beyond the fences upholding the military occupation of this land.

The fences at Mākua and Kaʻena differ in obvious ways: At Mākua, the U.S. military encloses its valleys for war purposes while contradictorily touting their commitment to stewardship through their conservation programs. At Kaʻena, the state of Hawaiʻi constructed the fence for a wildlife reserve, encouraging tourism and securing conditions for capitalism while displacing lawaiʻa who have treaded its shores for generations. Amid this, both places

A vision of stewardship based on kuleana. Sign created by Kamehameha seniors from the class of 2014 for the Ka'ena Cultural Practice Project. *Photograph by Summer Kaimalia Mullins-Ibrahim.*

remain historic fishing grounds. Just as fences are seemingly fixed, enclosing land purportedly for "protection" while facilitating touristic consumption and war, the fluidity of fishing nets reflect the flexibility of Hawaiian ways of life that have sustained families and communities for generations.

Partitioning living space while criminalizing and displacing lawai'a and houseless people, fences regulate and control grassroots efforts for self-determination predicated on daily interaction with the natural world. Yet huaka'i led by Mālama Mākua and the Ka'ena Cultural Practice Project show the potential for guided tours to transform colonial methods of resource management and land abuses and for promoting the stewardship of intimate relations with 'āina. As the 'ōlelo no'eau (Hawaiian proverb) goes: Inā mālama 'oe i ke kai, mālama no ke kai iā 'oe. Inā mālama 'oe i ka 'āina, mālama no ka 'āina iā 'oe. (If you care for the ocean, the ocean will care for you. If you care for the land, the land will care for you.)[3]

Profile 1: Al Sabagala's Mo'olelo of 'Uhane (Spirits)
Old Man Aku taught Al Sabagala's great uncles to fish the traditional Hawaiian way—throwing net and observing kapu. To this day, Al regularly fishes at Ka'ena. Al's kūpuna were plantation workers, and while he does not know of

any Hawaiians in his family line, he identifies with and supports movements for Hawaiian self-determination. In fact, non-Hawaiian lawaiʻa play a critical role at Kaʻena: by continuing fishing traditions in a place where knowledge of ancestral practices is increasingly limited, they ensure that the knowledge will continue through the next generation.

While sleeping at Kaʻena one night in 2008, Al heard a deep rumbling like thunder. The next morning, he saw a large pōhaku (rock) resting at the bottom of an incline. This was during an early stage of fence construction, and the worker who was posted to watch fence materials overnight explained to Al in the morning that the boulder had materialized seemingly out of nowhere, rolled down the mountain, and landed near his station. This story affirmed that the surrounding environment will eventually destroy the fence, and lawaiʻa have observed that the saltwater spray—the subject of countless Hiʻiaka chants—and strong winds of Kaʻena have taken down and decayed portions of the fence that the DLNR claimed would stand for at least a decade. If policymakers had consulted lawaiʻa for place-based knowledge before building the fence, both its construction and deterioration could have been avoided.

On another occasion, Al captured a photograph of the ghost of a fisherman wearing a malo (loincloth) at Kaʻena one night. Because of the location of the leina a ka ʻuhane, moʻolelo about ʻuhane in areas like Kaʻena are common; in fact, some believe that Kaʻena is a place where the spirit world and our present world inhabit the same space. Stories of wandering spirits, events such as the rumbling pōhaku, and environmental forces destroying human-made structures frequently surround unpopular developments. Such stories express the pain associated with the loss of land and life and articulate Hawaiian knowledge rooted in interconnectedness between the living, the ʻāina, and ancestors.

Profile 2: Summer Kaimalia Mullins-Ibrahim, Lawaiʻa and Caretaker of Kaʻena

Summer is a Kanaka Maoli cultural practitioner and community organizer with generational ties to Kaʻena and Mākua. Summer's great-great-grandmother came from the Waialua side of Kaʻena, married into a family living at Mākua, and stayed for generations. Her family was part of the church choir and they worked in the area, some with the railroad and others as paniolo (cowboys) for the McCandless Ranch at Mākua. Her grandmother was born in 1920 and lived nearby in Wahiawa, next to Schofield Barracks on the other side of the

Waiʻanae range, because Summer's great-grandfather worked for the railroad. The train connected Mākua to the rest of the island, including Wahiawa, Honolulu, and Ewa. Summer's grandmother, during her childhood, frequently visited family at Mākua.

Summer's family remains connected to the ʻāina of Mākua and Kaʻena. They know that members of their family are buried at Mākua. Summer's own experiences at Kaʻena began in utero, and she visited frequently with her father and grandmother as she grew up. She spent weekends and holidays with extended family at Kaʻena, learning to fish and gather limu (seaweed), shellfish, sea urchins, and crab. It was during these times with family that Summer developed a sense of kuleana for the place, recognizing that Kaʻena had provided for her family for generations, and that this mutual responsibility to care for the land and sea both created and sustained life. And yet the fences at Mākua and Kaʻena provoke a sense of dislocation. Summer describes the suffering that results from displacement: "We've been plucked out of the ground, taken out."

In a cove at Kaʻena Point, between two large coral rocks dotted with circular shell-shaped patterns (the remains of prehistoric shellfish that once graced the oceans of Kaʻena), Summer explains, "The fish are our ancestors. We come from the darkness, we come from all of these little organisms, the coral polyps." She refers to the Kumulipo, a creation chant that chronicles the origins of the earth, its plants and animals, humans, and deities. Summer stresses that there's "a sense of identity that's developed through the smallest parts of this environment, the ecosystem. These parts of the environment have become a part of us, and are what we come from." Such cosmologies challenge the separation of "environment" from "human," recognizing that social organization depends fundamentally on relationships with land. People do not operate independently of the universe and natural world; rather, they are connected to all parts of it.

Summer regards the fences at Kaʻena and Mākua as disruptors of ways of life predicated on a relational way of knowing and being in the world. She asks, "When keiki are separated from the ʻāina of their ancestors, when they are unable to nurture their relationships to the land and the kuleana that comes with them, kuleana once passed on for generations—what happens to the ways in which we once perceived the value of this land and the resources it provides? Will the next generation be as impassioned as those who came before to stand up for land that they are unable to step foot on?"

Notes

1   A 1990s formation called the Kaʻena Point Stewardship Group consisted of staff from various state agencies under the DLNR. Despite lawaiʻa participation in initiatives and meetings related to this group, the state of Hawaiʻi neglected to include fishers in later processes that led to fence construction. This seems to indicate that the state knew that fishers would block fence construction and intentionally excluded them from the process.

2   For more on the legal and settler colonial implications of the fence, see Bianca Isaki, "State Conservation as Settler Colonial Governance at Kaʻena Point, Hawaiʻi," *Environmental and Earth Law Journal* 3, no. 1 (2013): article 3, https://lawpublications.barry.edu/ejejj/vol3/iss1/3/.

3   Kāwika Kapahulehua in Maly, Kepa, "Ka Hana Lawaiʻa: Volume II–Oral History Interviews," Kumu Pono Associates, 2003, 1148, http://www.ulukau.org/elib/collect/maly2/index/assoc/Do.dir/doc1358.pdf.

Resources

Kaʻena Cultural Practice Project, http://kaenapractitioners.blogspot.com/.

Kaʻena Cultural Practice Project Facebook page: https://www.facebook.com/Kaena-Cultural-Practice-Project-114231678616195/.

Kaʻena Defenders Facebook page, https://www.facebook.com/kaena.defenders/videos?lst=504867288%3A100001881686304%3A1532369606.

Mālama Mākua, https://www.malamamakua.org/.

Mālama Mākua Facebook page, https://www.facebook.com/MalamaMakua.

Ellen-Rae Cachola

Beneath the Touristic Sheen of Waikīkī

For tourists, Waikīkī is an iconic place of sun, sand, and hotels. They are welcomed into a "Hawaiian paradise" by the manicured gardens and paved streets leading to the hotels, boutiques, and restaurants of Kalākaua Avenue, the main thoroughfare between two natural markers. Lēʻahi (Diamond Head) stands grandly at the eastern part of the southern coastline, and Kālia (Fort DeRussy) is a western coastal corner that bends into Ala Moana.

But beneath the façade of paradise are histories of upheaval, war, and displacement. Two Hawaiʻi-based demilitarization organizers, Kanaka ʻŌiwi woman Aunty Terri Kekoʻolani and Ilocana plantation labor descendant Ellen-Rae Cachola, designed a DeTour from Lēʻahi to Kālia to point out how military and tourist infrastructures keep Indigenous and immigrant peoples enmeshed in the transnational structures of empire, hidden in plain sight. The history of modern Hawaiʻi has been about the theft and occupation of lands of the Hawaiian Kingdom in order to make way for plantations, hotels, and military bases. Wealthy businessmen orchestrated Kānaka ʻŌiwi displacement from their traditional lands and livelihoods and organized immigrant labor to work for their corporate enterprises. According to the Department of Business, Economic Development and Tourism, a large portion of the workers in the visitor industry are from the Philippines, China, and Micronesia. Yet since the turn of the twentieth century, Kanaka ʻŌiwi and immigrant laborers have raised their consciousness regarding the restoration of Hawaiian self-determination and the return of their lands for peaceful societal needs. This vision is complicated by the majority of Hawaiʻi's population being dependent on these industries for their livelihoods.

Keko'olani and Cachola's DeTour through the military-tourism infrastructures of Waikīkī recalls the violence of imperialism in this place and how its occupation was part of the violence wrought on places across the sea. The DeTour's weaving of stories about Waikīkī also aims to educate people about its heritage of resistance.

DeTour through Dispossession

Kānaka 'Ōiwi harnessed the spouting fresh waters of Waikīkī by weaving the stream flows from Makīkī, Mānoa, and Pālolo at Kālia, the western shoreline of Waikīkī, into an alchemy of living abundance. There, loko i'a (fishponds) and lo'i kalo (wetland taro patches) were cultivated as sources of food and livelihood for the Hawaiian Kingdom. But the overthrow of the Hawaiian monarchy in 1893 by Euro-American businessmen, backed by the U.S. Marines, ushered in a transformation of land by war economies. In 1898, Camp McKinley was set up at the foot of Lē'ahi, in what is now Kapi'olani Park, as a temporary barracks for U.S. soldiers who arrived from San Francisco on their way to the Philippine war zones during the Spanish-American War.[1] The iconic volcanic cone of Lē'ahi (Diamond Head)—once used by Kānaka 'Ōiwi as a vista point to light fires in order to communicate to canoes out at sea— was turned into a military installation. During World War I, the U.S. military appropriated the high coastal position of Lē'ahi to carve a multilevel lookout and artillery installation camouflaged in the walls of the dormant volcano. The neighboring peak of Tantalus served as a surveillance point, collecting data on the locations of ships and planes from afar. The coordinates would be sent to those stationed at Fort DeRussy's massive automatic rifles situated in batteries Randolph and Dudley, on the west side of Waikīkī, to an 'ili (land division) known as Kālia.

In the 1920s, the streams flowing mauka (mountainward) to makai (seaward) were severed by the construction of the Ala Wai Canal. The stoppage of water dredged and dried up the loko i'a and lo'i kalo, which were then used as real estate for the hotels, roads, and other infrastructure we see today. Sewage, debris, and urban runoff darken the waters of the Ala Wai Canal. The Ala Wai demarcates Waikīkī as a territory where tourist desire is paramount, Indigenous lifeways are erased by a patchwork of hotels, and where workers shuttle in from elsewhere on the island to serve a new kind of plantation economy.

Fort DeRussy's Randolph and Dudley batteries have been out of commission since World War I. But these installations have been transformed to house the U.S. Army Museum, which glorifies the military use of Waikīkī, and

Lēʻahi (Diamond Head). In the distance, the U.S. military installation carved into the walls of Lēʻahi is camouflaged from ground view, rendering the image of the dormant volcanic cone a classic symbol of touristic Waikīkī. *Photograph by Jesse Stephen.*

the whole island of Oʻahu, as part of the touristic narrative of Americanized Hawaiʻi. Next door is the Hale Koa Hotel, built on property owned by the U.S. federal government. This hotel is a site of rest and recreation for U.S. military personnel who enforce U.S. jurisdiction over the state of Hawaiʻi. Over 20 percent of the military installations in Hawaiʻi are currently concentrated on Oʻahu Island, such as at Pearl Harbor, Schofield Barracks, Kāneʻohe Marine Corps Base, and Mākua Valley. The U.S. military occupation of various sacred sites throughout Oʻahu inaugurated the islands' new role as launching pads for U.S. occupation throughout the Pacific and Asia.

War and nuclear testing caused displacement and devastation, propelling people from their homelands to Hawaiʻi in search of livelihoods in the tourist economy that accompanies and romanticizes the militarized presence in the islands. The transformation of the Pacific from a Spanish lake to an American lake was about the U.S. increasing the number of military bases in the region in order to tap markets. After the Spanish-American War, the U.S. sought to control the Philippines, instigating the Philippine-American War. Since then, the Philippine economy and political system have been configured to meet national and international corporate interests—not those of a self-sufficient domestic economy. This led to the mass emigration of its own people to work abroad. Filipinos are the largest workforce in the Waikīkī hotels; they send earned monies back to their families in their homelands.

The rise of China is one reason for the Obama administration's "Pivot to Asia," or the increase in military construction and investment in Asia and the Pacific. Immigrant Chinese are a rising labor demographic in Waikīkī hotels today. China's economic growth is causing much rural-urban inequality, pulling many rural Chinese to migrate to urbanized areas in China and abroad as maids, janitors, and migrant teachers.[2] The U.S. has developed a "strong" image as a global power through its nuclear weapons research and development. U.S. nuclear weapons testing occurred in Micronesian islands such as Bikini, Rongelap, and Ebeye in the 1950s. Since then, Micronesians have been migrating to Hawai'i because of the bombing and radioactive devastation of their lands.[3] In Hawai'i, they struggle to find housing and health care, and they work in service, sales, production, and laborer positions.[4]

Aloha 'Āina in the Labor Struggle?

U.S. imperialism has transformed lands into military bases protecting the capitalist economy as if it were the only way to be. But the people have not been conquered. The history of interracial labor movements between immigrant and Indigenous peoples demonstrate how collective action can dramatically transform the culture and political economy of Hawai'i. Aloha 'āina (love of land, patriotism) is a Kanaka 'Ōiwi value of feeling ancestral connections to their lands, even so far as to go against the prevailing order to protect their homeland from further destruction and corporatization. For many immigrants working in the hotels, this feeling of connection to land is obscured by a material need to survive the dominant settler economy, as relations to ancestral lands had been severed by war, economic displacement, and migration. The attention to militarism and tourism in Waikīkī during the Waikīkī DeTour reveals how the interlocking settler economies of agricultural plantations, tourism, and militarism can bridge labor organizing in Waikīkī to Kanaka 'Ōiwi–led movements seeking freedom from imperial control.

Since 1893, the Indigenous people of Hawai'i have been opposing the theft of their lands by corporate capitalists who consolidated into the "Big Five" (Alexander and Baldwin, American Factors, Castle and Cooke, Theo H. Davis, and C. Brewer and Co.), and were all owned by haole (Euro-American) elites who acquired a great deal of land and monetary wealth on the islands before and after the overthrow of the Hawaiian monarchy. A characteristic of this Euro-American settlement was the establishment of military bases as collateral for the U.S. military, which assisted the businessmen during the overthrow. Thus, Diamond Head and Fort DeRussy were developed and used for southern coast defense purposes in 1911, before World War I broke out.

Around this time, agricultural plantations were strengthening throughout the islands, diverting water from the traditional ahupuaʻa at the windward sides of the islands to arid areas for cultivating sugarcane and pineapple cash crops.[5] More workers were imported and segregated into Chinese, Japanese, Korean, Filipino, Puerto Rican, and Portuguese plantation camps all over the islands. Newer immigrants who came to Hawaiʻi were eager to earn wages, as they had been disenfranchised in their own homelands. Established workers noticed the racial and income inequalities in the plantations and organized strikes against the exploitative conditions of the plantations. Filipinos received the lowest pay, whereas earlier waves of Chinese, Japanese, Korean, and Portuguese migrants received incrementally higher wages, respectively, based on race.[6] Blood unionism was the initial strategy for plantation workers to organize those with shared ethnicity, dialect, or "blood" because they were in close proximity to each other in the same camps and spoke the same languages. But workers of other ethnic groups would break picket lines, or even sabotage union-building efforts; thus workers began to learn the importance of interethnic organizing to resist the ways that working people were often divided and pitted against each other. Some of the first Japanese-Filipino strikes occurred in plantation camps in Waipahu and Ewa, Oʻahu.[7]

A major leader of interracial union organizing was Harry Kamoku, a Kanaka ʻŌiwi–Chinese labor organizer with the Hilo chapter of the International Longshore and Worker's Union (ILWU). Kamoku recruited people from all over the islands using a message of unity: regardless of the color of their skin, everyone had the same red blood in their veins. This unity was the major force behind the Indigenous and immigrant workers resisting corporate exploitation through the Great Sugar Strike of 1946, which brought the Big Five to their knees.

But when the agricultural corporations saw they could cut costs through automation and by shifting operations to other countries, the agricultural industry began to lay off workers. In its place, the tourism economy emerged as another opportunity for workers to gain wages. To protect themselves from this new kind of industrial exploitation, workers of the Royal Hawaiian and Moana hotels, the first hotels in Waikīkī, won contracts during the 1940s. But during World War II, from 1941 to 1945, the hotels were closed because Waikīkī became a site of rest and recreation for the U.S. military. The Moana and Royal Hawaiian hotels were encircled with barbed wire, meant to protect Oʻahu's southern coast from a potential Japanese attack on the shoreline. Hawaiian girls would dance hula for the USO mess halls in Waikīkī.

Navy sailors would stand in long lines outside of brothels along Hotel Street, Chinatown, to buy sex from Indigenous and immigrant women caught in the prostitution industry.[8]

The Cold War of the 1950s brought the Red Scare, and many of Hawai'i's labor organizers were profiled, blacklisted, detained, or killed as "communist threats" against the U.S. During the 1960s to the 1990s, Hawai'i's economy accelerated its shift from agricultural plantations to tourism.[9] It was a dangerous time to organize, as fear of being labeled "un-American" was high. Harriet Bouslog was the attorney of the ILWU, and Helen Kanahele was a Kanaka 'Ōiwi woman organizer who joined the Women's Auxiliary of the ILWU and was secretary treasurer of the United Public Workers union. They organized women in the professional ranks of the Hawaii State Teachers Association, Hawaii Nurses Association, Hawaii Government Employees Association, and Local 5, creating racially diverse unions across the state and empowering workers to navigate and assert their rights in the service economy.[10] The strength of their organizing to unite a broad base was founded on traditional Hawaiian values of mutual responsibility to one another and a sense of 'ohana, or family. There were tensions, however. Kanahele resented Bouslog's co-optation of the Native Hawaiian lei and terms such as aloha and 'ohana, and labor organizers were selective in their historical and cultural understanding of Indigenous Hawai'i. The majority of the labor movement supported U.S. statehood in 1959, bypassing the desires of Indigenous Hawaiians who wanted their national sovereignty restored.[11] In the end, the plebiscite for statehood was voted on by a majority of the non-Indigenous residents of Hawai'i. As a result, U.S. occupation of Hawai'i continues to this day.

The story to unite the labor movement with struggles of the broader community is waiting to be told, though there have been moments of solidarity. In the 1970s, during the Vietnam War, the Hale Koa Hotel opened for U.S. military personnel in Kālia, next door to batteries Randolph and Dudley, so that their families could stay on vacation in Hawai'i and visit the U.S. Army Museum. Between 2004 and 2005, complaints of sexual harassment arose between a military veteran–turned–parking manager John "Jack" Lloyd and one of his female staff, Ernestine Gonda. Gonda reported unwelcomed touching and sexually explicit gifts from Lloyd, her boss. When she tried to report to the Equal Employment Opportunity (EEO) Office at U.S. Army Fort Shafter, following human resources policy, she was ignored. Lloyd served as the EEO counselor for the Hale Koa Hotel, which made Gonda suspect that her reports were being intercepted. She then approached the Army Morale, Welfare and Recreation Command, but no one responded to her complaints. Gonda was facing a long history of normalized sexism in military ranks, whereby sexual violence committed by officials against lower-ranked personnel occurs without investigation in order to silence victims and avoid upsetting the military hierarchy. Lloyd's harassment continued, driving Gonda to leave the hotel altogether. This case brought forward more women of Vietnamese and Filipina descent to share that they too had experienced sexual harassment by Lloyd. The labor union representing the Hale Koa workers created a movement to file a class-action complaint against Jack Lloyd for alleged sex and race discrimination.[12] The settlement resulted in Hale Koa removing Lloyd from the hotel, agreeing to hold sexual harassment workshops, and making other human resource changes at the management level.[13] This historical moment set a precedent through which immigrant hotel workers began to challenge and change the sexualized, militarized structure of Waikīkī. This herstory shows how the global network of military bases that militarizes Hawai'i and local people's homelands is the cause for racist and sexist violence against those peoples. It also reveals that if immigrant workers from the Pacific and Asia bring an understanding of militarism to their opposition against exploitative working conditions, points of solidarity with Kānaka 'Ōiwi can be found in resistance against U.S. occupation that displaces them in their own homeland.

What Will Be the Story That Unifies?

Unions and antiwar organizations across the United States have organized coalitions toward a common vision to demilitarize U.S. foreign policy and to support workers' rights.[14] One technique for use in working toward this vision is to engage in dialogue with different movements and sectors of society. The Aikea Movement, spearheaded by the Local 5 union, has facilitated dialogues between labor organizers and Indigenous-led movement organizers to communicate, share information, and build skills and relationships in order to work together for a common cause.

This DeTour was created by Kanaka 'Ōiwi woman Aunty Terri and an Ilocano woman, Ellen-Rae, to engage in dialogue with Local 5 organizers and the children of hotel workers in order to find a common context and explore how we can work together as a unified movement. These dialogues have invoked memories of the labor movement throughout Hawai'i in order to assess the layers of settler economies that occupy this place and attempt to divide people. But also in these stories are the struggles and will of island peoples to weave their stories together in an effort to strengthen

Gun emplacement on Diamond Head. This retired, northeast-facing gun emplacement at Battery 407 on Diamond Head is one node within a network of military installations that integrate Lēʻahi into the militarized infrastructures of Waikīkī. *Photograph by Ellen-Rae Cachola.*

homegrown social movements driven by a collective belief in the sacredness of these lands and of our collective labor, beyond corporate and military ownership. But most importantly, this lens of history reminds us that if we do not like how we are being used by corporate owners, how can we be the ones to see and treat each other as allies in order to create a different economy and future for this place? The responsibility is not just local but requires those who come from afar to see that their arrival can either add to the oppression or help dismantle it. To the tourists from afar, or who arrive here: you too are included in this work, as it is your money and physical presence that are inevitable factors in this dynamic. Whoever you are—will you contribute to this settler colonialism, or are you willing to help use your position to dismantle this oppression?

Notes

1   M. J. Stenzel, "A Brief Overview of NY in the Spanish American War April 25, 1898-August 12, 1898," New York State Military Museum and Veterans Research Center, NYS Division of Military and Naval Affairs, March 19, 2008, https://dmna.ny.gov/historic/articles /spanamer.htm/.

2   Arianne M. Gaetano, *Out to Work: Migration, Gender, and the Changing Lives of Rural Women in Contemporary China* (Honolulu: University of Hawai'i Press, 2015).

3   Joseph H. Genz, Noelani Goodyear-Ka'ōpua, Monica C. La Briola, Alexander Mawyer, Elicita N. Morei, John P. Rosa, "Indigenous Responses, Resistance and Revitalization," in *Militarism and Nuclear Testing in the Pacific*, Teaching Oceania Series, vol. 1, ed. Monica C. LaBriola (Honolulu: Center for Pacific Islands Studies, University of Hawai'i-Mānoa, 2018), http://hdl.handle.net/10125/42430/.

4   Ann M. Pobutsky, Lee Buenconsejo-Lum, Catherine Chow, Neal Palafox, and Gregory G. Maskarinec, "Micronesian Migrants in Hawaii: Health Issues and Culturally Appropriate, Community-Based Solutions," *Californian Journal of Health Promotion* 3, no. 4 (2005): 59–72.

5   Pauahi Ho'okano, "Aia i Hea ka Wai a Kāne (Where Indeed Is the Water of Kāne?)," in *A Nation Rising: Hawaiian Movements for Life, Land and Sovereignty*, ed. Noelani Goodyear-Ka'ōpua, Ikaika Hussey, and Erin Kahunawaikla'ala Wright, 222–23 (Durham, NC: Duke University Press, 2014).

6   Moon-Kie Jung, "Race and Labor in Prewar Hawai'i," in *Reworking Race: The Making of Hawaii's Interracial Labor Movement* (New York: Columbia University Press, 2006), 66–68.

7   Dean Alegado, "Blood in the Fields: The Hanapepe Massacre and the 1924 Filipino Strike," *Filipinas Magazine*, October 1997. Reprinted in Hawaii and International Workers Day Handout, 2012, 17–32.

8   Ted Chernin, "My Experiences in the Honolulu Chinatown Red-Light District," *The Hawaiian Journal of History* 34 (2000): 212–13.

9   Noel Kent, *Hawaii: Islands under the Influence* (Honolulu: University of Hawai'i Press, 1983).

10 Megan Elizabeth Diskin Monahan, "Introduction," in *Hawai'i's Twentieth Century Working Women: Labor Feminists in Their Own Right* (PhD diss., Fordham University, 2015), 7–9.

11 Diskin Monahan, "Introduction," 19.

12 Kari Lydersen, "Harassment Unchecked at Army Hotel," *In These Times*, October 15, 2007 (accessed August 15, 2014), http://inthesetimes.com/article/3370/harassment_unchecked_at_army_hotel/.

13 Nina Wu, "Hale Koa Harassment Case Settled," *Star Bulletin*, November 30, 2007 (accessed August 15, 2014), http://archives.starbulletin.com/2007/11/30/business/story03.html/.

14 "Mission Statement," adopted by the National Labor Assembly for Peace in Chicago, October 25, 2003 (revised February 12, 2012; revised January 13, 2014), https://uslaboragainstwar.org/AboutUSLAW/MISSION%20STATEMENT.htm/.

Resources

Genz, Joseph H., Noelani Goodyear-Ka'ōpua, Monica C. LaBriola, Alexander Mawyer, Elicita N. Morei, John P. Rosa. "Indigenous Responses, Resistance and Revitalization." In *Militarism and Nuclear Testing in the Pacific*. Teaching Oceania Series, vol. 1, edited by Monica C. LaBriola. Honolulu: Center for Pacific Islands Studies, University of Hawai'i-Mānoa, 2018. http://hdl.handle.net/10125/42430/.

Trask, Haunani-Kay. "Settlers of Color and 'Immigrant' Hegemony: 'Locals' in Hawai'i." *Amerasia Journal* 26, no. 2 (2000): 1–24.

N. Trisha Lagaso Goldberg

_____

Sakada

Sakada represents one of three Hawaiian quilt squares designed in honor of my grandfathers, Florencio Lagaso and Primitivo Cortes Torres, who were *sakada*, or first-generation Filipino immigrants who came to Hawai'i to work on the sugarcane plantations. Sakada used three tools to harvest cane: the machete, pick axe, and hoe. Often these implements were made by the workers themselves. My maternal grandfather, Primitivo Cortes Torres, was a gardener after his days on the plantation, so these signs are meant to honor both labor practices.

Conventionally, with Hawaiian quilt squares, the subject is taken from the plant world in order to depict and honor local foliage such as the ulu (breadfruit), 'ilima flower, or kalo (taro). When studying under a trained and long-time Hawaiian quilt maker, students learn that rules exist around what a practitioner should and should not do, and it is considered radical contemporary practice to illustrate subjects outside the natural world. Because the custom is to honor, for instance, plant life, but *never* the people who actually tend to our local plants, agricultural fields, or their related economies, this project is meant to credit these historically invisible workers—to take inspiration from one tradition in order to create another.

Queen's Quilts
The Hawaiian quilt square depicting 'ulu is often the first pattern quilters learn. In these iterations of the Hawaiian quilt, the words *cleanse* and *forgive* are cut out and taken from the song, "Queen's Prayer":

Sakada (Machete), 2006. Laser-cut black acrylic Plexiglas (48 × 48 × 1¼ inches).

Sakada (Pick Axe), 2006. Laser-cut white acrylic Plexiglas (48 × 48 × 1¼ inches).

Sakada (Hoe), 2006. Laser-cut white acrylic Plexiglas (48 × 48 × 1¼ inches).

Behold Not With Malevolence (Forgive and Cleanse), 2006. Laser-cut bronze mirrored Plexiglas (36 × 36 × 2 inches).

Curse of the Gilded Cage (I live in sorrow imprisoned), 2006. Laser-cut bronze mirrored Plexiglas (36 × 36 × 2 inches).

Your loving mercy
Is as high as Heaven
And your truth
So perfect

I live in sorrow
Imprisoned
You are my light
Your glory, my support

Behold not with malevolence
The sins of man
But forgive
And cleanse

And so, o Lord
Protect us beneath your wings
And let peace be our portion
Now and forever more

Amen

The "Queen's Prayer" was composed by Queen Lili'uokalani on March 22, 1895, while she was under house arrest at 'Iolani Palace. This hymn was dedicated to Victoria Ka'iulani, heir apparent to the throne.

Craig Howes

A Downtown Honolulu and
Capitol District Decolonial Tour

If tourists actually leave Waikīkī and don't go to Ala Moana Center, Pearl Harbor, or the Polynesian Cultural Center, downtown Honolulu and the Capitol District are their destinations. Most of Hawai'i's iconic tourist sites are there, and this tour includes them, but it also takes note of other places both present and disappeared. These lie in the area between Honolulu Harbor and Beretania Street, and from just past Punchbowl Street on the Diamond Head side to Nu'uanu Avenue, the boundary between the historic downtown, where some of the earliest buildings are still intact, and Chinatown, which was obliterated by fires in 1886 and 1900. Our stops should not be thought of as discrete sites but as points in a matrix of relations that make up Honolulu's, and Hawai'i's, conflicted histories. We therefore go from place to place, but also from time to time, often in the same place.

Kou, the Harbor, and Merchant Street
Many Hawaiian mo'olelo—stories and histories—tell of events at Kou, where a stream entered Honolulu Harbor. We start here and immediately confront the results of the rapid transformation of this spot into Honolulu beginning early in the nineteenth century. This was the harbor most suited for the Western ships arriving more and more frequently to the islands, and it soon became the primary contact zone for visitors and the most powerful ali'i, or chiefs. This spot is why O'ahu, the third largest island, is home today to 70 percent of Hawai'i's population.

We are standing in a green area that no one knows is called Walker Park (marked **1** on the map), looking across six busy lanes of Nimitz Highway at Aloha Tower Marketplace. This development surrounds the iconic 1926 tower itself and includes the terminal at Pier 10, just to our right. Built the same year, this is where tourists disembarked on Boat Days, before air travel to Hawai'i became routine in the 1950s.

Under the highway asphalt farther to the right was the site of a canoe wharf and heiau, or stone platform for worship, known as Pākākā. In the early 1800s, Kamehameha I, his powerful consort Ka'ahumanu, and a cluster of high-ranking ali'i lived here. Late in life, John Papa 'Ī'ī, an ali'i who served Kamehameha in 1810, wrote a vivid account of the maritime activity, the work and leisure, and the court politics of that time. Kamehameha did not stay long. By 1813 he had returned to the island of Hawai'i, and although his sons Liholiho and Kauikeaouli (Kamehameha II and III, respectively) would have residences here in the 1820s and 1830s, it would never again boast the same concentration of ali'i. But this spot had its own momentum, as the warehouses, provision stores, bars, brothels, churches, eateries, and customs offices accompanying any maritime trade center multiplied.

A decolonial tour must be stratigraphic—layered—because one place often serves many ends as power relations shift. For instance, Nimitz Highway now covers the area where a fishing village, a religious site, a compound for the highest-ranking ali'i, a busy maritime port, and several roads used to be. And where we are standing now has also seen six or seven states of development and hosts their mingled fragments.

John Papa 'Ī'ī tells us that the Kamehameha's warriors used this as an exercise ground. In 1816, after the court left, a Western-style block house was built here. This was the origin of the Honolulu Fort, the reason why the pedestrian mall heading toward the mountains behind us, once the busiest road in Honolulu, was called Fort Street. For almost forty years the fort was repeatedly expanded and was the Hawaiian Kingdom's official presence here in the economic hub. A few coral blocks and one of its cannons remain here as reminders.

The fort was the point of encounter between Hawaiians and the British, French, American, and other nationals who arrived; it also served as a jail for residents and foreigners who violated the laws of the kingdom. But its proximity to the piers also made it an obvious target when foreigners bristled at not getting their way. It was here that Kamehameha III declared his frustration as he transferred his authority to Admiral Paulet, who briefly and illegally laid claim to Hawai'i for Great Britain in 1843. Then in 1849, a French naval crew occupied and trashed the fort. It was, in short, a magnet for trouble, and in 1857 it was demolished. Most of its coral blocks were used as fill for a new shoreline esplanade that made moving between the ships and

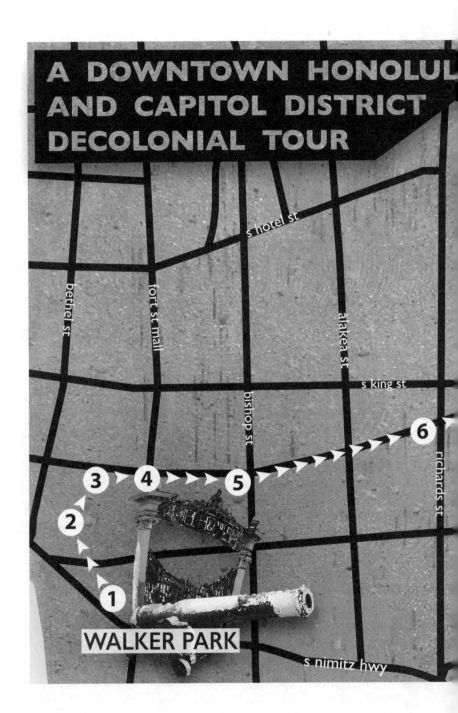

A DOWNTOWN HONOLUL
AND CAPITOL DISTRICT
DECOLONIAL TOUR

s hotel st

bethel st

fort st mall

alakea st

s king st

bishop st

richards st

6

3 **4** **5**

2

1

WALKER PARK

s nimitz hwy

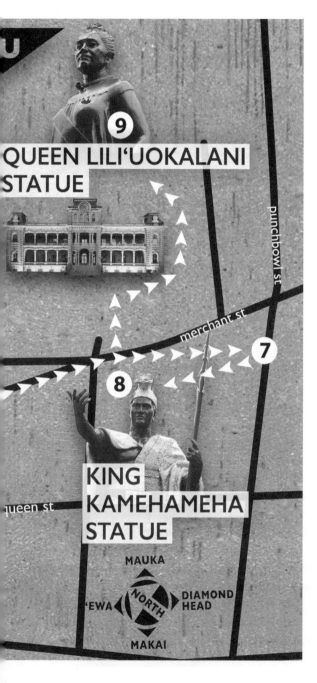

9

QUEEN LILI'UOKALANI
STATUE

punchbowl st

merchant st

7

8

queen st

KING
KAMEHAMEHA
STATUE

MAUKA

NORTH

'EWA DIAMOND HEAD

MAKAI

Map of down-
town Honolulu.
*Map by Adele
Balderston.*

shore easier. If we were to cross Nimitz Highway, head right until we reached the interpretive sign for Pier 12, and look into the water farther down, we would see some of those blocks. Formerly Brewer's Wharf, Pier 12 is where the sailors disembarked from USS *Boston* on January 17, 1893, on their way to assist with the overthrow of the Hawaiian Kingdom.

But even after the fort was demolished, kingdom law enforcement and government were still present where we are standing. In 1857, a courthouse was erected that also served as the kingdom legislature. It too would be trashed in 1874, when Hawaiians objecting to the selection of David Kalākaua over Queen Emma as the new mōʻī, or monarch, rioted, attacking the Hawaiian legislators who had supported Kalākaua and gutting the building. (Yes, some Hawaiian mōʻī were chosen democratically.)

Fortunately, Aliʻiōlani Hale, the new court and legislature under construction, was almost completed, and the kingdom's institutions were relocated to the Capitol District. The battered courthouse then became part of the economic engine when Heinrich Hackfeld, a German commercial agent operating on Fort Street, turned it into his business premises. H. Hackfeld and Co. prospered, eventually building a distinctive domed corporate headquarters here. The Hackfeld green iron gates are still standing, but the buildings came down in 1968, replaced by the multistory tower at the mountain end of the park. Renamed "American Factors" because of anti-German sentiment during World War I, Hackfeld and Co. was one of the "Big Five" corporations that together controlled Hawaiʻi's territorial economy.

This park is one of many sites that hide and expose Honolulu's history. Only a few traces and a modern concrete tower remain, and the reason for any of it lies under the asphalt of a nondescript thoroughfare. Recalling what has disappeared can, however, expose the dynamics that drove the changes, and as we will see, in downtown Honolulu, the places where the former occupants and institutions relocated often lie close by.

Let's turn toward the mountains and cross Queen Street at the crosswalk. Look to your right. Built in 1930, that low-slung building was formerly the corporate headquarters of C. Brewer and Company, the smallest of the Big Five and the reason why there was a Brewer's Wharf. Now turn left, and walk until you are standing in front of the breezeway that passes through Harbor Court, a forty-one-story condominium and parking lot completed in 1994 (number 2 on the map).

As harbor trade increased, warehouses, stores, and other offices multiplied here. Kaʻahumanu Street ran between them, and as we walk through Harbor Court, we are tracing its path. In the twentieth century, a multistory municipal parking lot was plunked down here. Eventually demolished to make way for Harbor Court, it was the reason why the developers had to include several stories of public parking. The iwi (bones) of Hawaiians uncovered during construction were placed under a small stone platform in the alleyway behind the older buildings on our right. A locked metal door keeps people out.

We have arrived at Merchant Street, and we'll stop at the curb (3). Directly to our left is the two-story coral block and stuccoed Melchers Building, the oldest Western structure in downtown Honolulu, built in 1854 as a storehouse. You can see on the sides of the upper windows where the hinges for large wooden shutters used to be. Workers pushed cargo unloaded from the ships up ramps into the second floor. Boxlike and utterly nondescript, this building suggests how purely functional most of the structures here initially were.

The beautifully restored building on our right embodies later and higher aspirations. Built in 1877, this was the new home of the Bank of Bishop, which started in 1858 in offices at Queen and Ka'ahamanu, back behind us. Many years later, it would become First Hawaiian Bank. The founder was Charles Reed Bishop, the husband of the high-ranking ali'i Bernice Pauahi, a descendent of Kamehameha I. When she died in 1884, he was the chief executor of her will, which established a trust to administer her huge landholdings for the benefit of what came to be known as the Kamehameha Schools. The endowment today runs into the billions of dollars, but it was impressive even then, and this bank became its administrative center, leading to the erection in 1896 of a darker stone building next door to house the offices of the Bishop Estate and the Bishop Museum.

The building across the street to our left also testifies to this location's economic centrality in the nineteenth century. As Kamehameha I and his court had sixty years earlier, the Customs House examined the contents of arriving ships and levied the appropriate duties. It was built in 1870 and later became the post office; state offices now occupy its upper floor. Before 1870, this was the site of Honolulu Hale, which among other things housed the printing presses for several publications. The first offices of the *Pacific Commercial Advertiser*—founded in 1856 and, after several changes of ownership, still publishing today as the *Honolulu Star-Advertiser*—were located in the little park right in front of us. As the paper's original name suggests, it advocated for the economic activity swirling around it. Since 1994, the ground floor of the customs house–turned–post office has been the home of Kumu Kahua Theatre, dedicated to producing plays by, for, and about Hawai'i's people.

An earlier complex addressing other harbor needs stood farther left on that side of Merchant Street. In the 1830s, the Seamen's Bethel Chapel and Reading Room offered spiritual and educational support to visiting sailors and foreign residents, and in 1843 it started publishing *The Friend*, an English-language paper containing devotional and temperance materials, missionary reports from the Pacific, community notices, and, above all, news about the comings and goings of ships in the Pacific. It ran for over one hundred years.

Honolulu's continuing importance as commercial hub during the territorial period (1900–59) accounts for the building now standing on the far corner of Merchant and Bethel, to our left. Built in 1909 primarily for Hawai'i's Japanese residents, the Yokohama Specie Bank was seized and turned into a police holding cell during World War II. Years later it became the home of *Honolulu Magazine*. First published in the 1880s as *Paradise of the Pacific*, and still appearing today, it is another of the many Merchant Street publications. A preschool now occupies the building.

If we were to turn left and walk past the Melchers Building on this side of the street, we would see why turning the bank into a jail made sense. A police station has been on the opposite corner since 1885, but the current building, now a city and county office named after Walter Murray Gibson (a controversial publisher, monarchist, and cabinet minister for David Kalākaua during the 1870s and 1880s), was formerly the main Honolulu police station. Opened in 1931, its stucco and tile Spanish Mission and Mediterranean architecture is common to many territorial buildings. From this station, the police fanned out on foot into Chinatown, or headed over to the piers, the flashpoint of contact between sailors, tourists, and residents, and between businesses and laborers. When police arrested striking dockworkers and their leaders, they brought them here.

In fact, after World War II, the Bank of Bishop building we are standing next to became the offices of Harriet Bouslog and Meyer Symonds, lawyers for the International Longshore and Warehouse Union and legal advocates for labor and the poor from the 1940s to the 1980s. Bouslog was often accused of being a Communist. Red paint was splattered all over a wall where the wooden doors are now.

Let's turn right and head Diamond Head on Merchant Street. We are walking where the first sidewalk in Honolulu ran, beside the bank and the Bishop Estate building, then past the U.S. consulate, which occupied the space next door. Arriving at the corner of Merchant Street and the pedestrian mall, once Fort Street (4), we now stand where foreigners and the children of foreigners labored to gain political and economic control over nineteenth-century Hawai'i. Attorneys, executives, and editors, including many of those who plotted the 1893 overthrow of the kingdom, had their offices here, but professions and politics had mingled at this intersection for quite some time. The Judd Building, an 1898 structure on the harbor-side corner, stands where the early missionary and later government minister and diplomat Gerrit P. Judd had his medical offices. From 1900 until 1930, this building was the home of Alexander and Baldwin, the third Big Five company we have encountered. Retail commerce has flourished here as well. During the territorial period, McInerny's, one of the first big department stores, operated on the mauka (mountain) side of Merchant Street.

Continuing Diamond Head and passing the Stangenwald Building, another very early twentieth-century structure, we approach a smallish square building, now hosting a copying center. Built in 1905, it housed the offices of the *Hawaii Star*, one more Merchant Street newspaper. Look down the alley to the right. That much larger building behind the offices is where the *Star* was printed. Making our way to the corner of Merchant and Bishop Streets (5), we now stand next to the current headquarters of Alexander and Baldwin. The water buffalo heads featured on the wall beside us, and the Chinese characters and mosaics of underwater scenes at the main entrance down Bishop Street to the right, all declare Alexander and Baldwin's international reach.

This monument to financial success is echoed by a 1929 structure across Bishop Street and farther down to the right. Although this even larger Italianate building did not house one of the Big Five corporations, it was home to Dillingham Transportation, a major developer of territorial infrastructure. But just to our right across Bishop stands a twenty-two-story tower with a huge representation of a whaling adventure on its side. Built in the 1960s, this is the Davies Pacific Center, the fourth monument to a Big Five corporation. Originally a British-owned business with offices at the harbor, it became Theo. H. Davies and Company, a major player in the sugar industry.

But where is Castle and Cooke, the only member of the Big Five we haven't encountered? Although it too started in this area, its offices, not surprisingly, are in what was once the Dole Pineapple Cannery, which Castle and Cooke owned and operated in Iwilei, at the 'Ewa end of the harbor.

As we cross Bishop and continue along Merchant Street, a glance to the left takes in the skyscrapers of post-statehood Hawai'i, containing the most powerful banks, corporate offices, and legal firms. Many started back at the harbor, including the huge skyscraper that fills the entire block right across the street. This is the current headquarters of First Hawaiian Bank; we've already walked by its first and second homes.

Two more blocks and Merchant Street ends. We have arrived at Richards Street, on the edge of the Capitol District (6).

The Capitol District: Palaces, Churches, Homes, Statues, and Seals

To get the best sense of this second center of Honolulu, let's cross and turn left on Richards, then turn right on King Street and walk to Punchbowl Street. We are walking past the most famous buildings and statue in Hawaiʻi, but we'll be back. Kawaiahaʻo Church, the coral-block building across Punchbowl, is a key location (7). Completed by the congregation in 1842, it occupies the site of the first Congregational Mission Church on Oʻahu. The residences of the missionaries, who first began arriving here in 1820, still stand behind the church. As centers for Christian worship and education, Kawaiahaʻo and the New England–style wooden homes presented themselves as examples of what "real" buildings should be like.

First metaphorically, and then literally, Kawaiahaʻo loomed over this area for fifty years. When many aliʻi returned to Honolulu after Kamehameha I's death in 1819, they again congregated where foreigners with valuable goods had arrived, but *not* in the bustling harbor area. New attractions drew the aliʻi to settle here—the missionaries' religion certainly, but more importantly, the literacy and the education that came with it.

The aliʻi lived across King Street, in front of where Honolulu Hale, the city hall, now stands to our right, and on what is now the lawn of the state library, directly before us, and the grounds fronting ʻIolani Palace, to our left. In the mid-1820s, when the bodies of Kamehameha II and Queen Kamāmalu were returned to Honolulu after their fatal journey to London, they were placed in a mausoleum, now marked by that fenced-in compound in the makai (ocean-side) corner of the palace grounds. These and other remains would be moved to Mauna ʻAla, the Royal Mausoleum in Nuʻuanu Valley, when construction was completed in 1865.

As the harbor and Merchant Street became primarily, though not entirely, the center of commerce and trade, here at Kawaiahaʻo the aliʻi created the political center of the kingdom. The number and the functions of buildings multiplied. Education was a major spur. In the early 1830s, the Oʻahu Charity School began operating where Aliʻiōlani Hale, the imposing building behind the Kamehameha Statue that we just walked past, now stands. This school taught Hawaiian and hapa-haole children in English; most of the children .

were related to foreign merchants and officials operating near the harbor. In 1839, the Chiefs' Children's School began to provide the heirs of the highest-ranking aliʻi a Western Calvinist education. Erected on what are now the palace grounds and run by missionaries Amos Starr and Juliet Montague Cooke, this boarding school instructed all five mōʻī who would in turn succeed Kauikeaouli (Kamehameha III) after his death in 1854: Alexander Liholiho (Kamehameha IV); Lot Kapuāiwa (Kamehameha V); William Charles Lunalilo, whose parents Kekāuluohi and Charles Kanaʻina also lived on the palace grounds; David Kalākaua; and Liliʻuokalani. Alexander Liholiho's consort Queen Emma went to school there as well, as did Bernice Pauahi, heir to the estates of so many aliʻi, which together became the endowment for Kamehameha Schools.

Now let's walk back to the Kamehameha Statue (**8**), and look mauka at ʻIolani Palace. The building in front of you is the second to occupy the site. The first one, a wooden building with a stone foundation, was built in 1845. Because at that time the center of governance was wherever Kamehameha III happened to be, when he was on Oʻahu, that palace was it. Other substantial aliʻi residences were close by. Victoria Kāmamalu, the sister of Kamehameha IV and V, and eventually the kuhina nui, or coruler of the kingdom, lived in a house called Mililani, where we are standing, with her kahu, or guardian—the same John Papa ʻĪʻī who wrote about the harbor when Kamehameha I lived there. The building behind the statue is Aliʻiōlani Hale, an emphatic statement that here, and not Merchant Street, was where the Kingdom of Hawaiʻi would be governed. Kamehameha V laid the cornerstone in 1872 but did not live to see its completion in 1874, when the legislative, judicial, and administrative branches of government, then housed in the old courthouse where we started, migrated to this space close to the residence of the mōʻī.

Although American troops threatened ʻIolani Palace from a position just facing the palace to our right during the overthrow of the kingdom in January 1893, the "Committee of Safety," that handful of haole businessmen who plotted and carried it out, read the declaration of their usurping government from the back steps of Aliʻiōlani Hale to virtually no one. Throughout the territorial period, this building housed Hawaiʻi's most prominent courtrooms. The trial of the murderers of Joseph Kahahawai, a defendant in the notorious Massie rape case that drew all of America's attention in 1931 and 1932, took place here. Today it houses the Hawaiʻi State Supreme Court and the fictional police headquarters used in TV's latest *Hawaii Five-0*.

From the moment of its construction, however, the second ʻIolani Palace, David Kalākaua's declaration of the kingdom's sovereignty in the face of domestic and external pressures, has been the centerpiece of the Capitol

District. It was more a monument than a home; Kalākaua preferred sleeping in a modest bungalow on the grounds. Washington Place, Liliʻuokalani's residence before she became mōʻī, lies on the other side of the palace, across Beretania Street.

Because the palace embodied the authority and responsibility of the constitutional ruler of the islands, stripping it of its royal status was not surprisingly a priority after the overthrow in 1893. The conspirators took possession of it, and then during the Hawaiian Republic (1894–98), they used it to conduct the military tribunal that condemned patriots, including Liliʻuokalani, who had tried but failed to overthrow the overthrowers and restore the kingdom. After her sentencing, her palace became her prison. After 1900, the palace housed the territorial legislature, and after 1959, the state legislature. In a similar move, after Liliʻuokalani's death in 1917, Washington Place was first turned into the residence of the territorial governor, and later the governor of the state. In 2002 it became a museum devoted to Liliʻuokalani; the governor has a new mansion on the same site.

After the new state capitol building was completed in 1969, restoration of ʻIolani Palace to its status as a symbol of the Kingdom of Hawaiʻi steadily progressed. With the important exception of the room where Liliʻuokalani was imprisoned, the exterior and interiors are now as they were during the reign of Kalākaua. Mass demonstrations and commemorations regarding the Hawaiian Kingdom and the Hawaiian nation take place on the palace grounds, at the state capitol behind it, or both.

Let's consider now these and some of the other buildings surrounding the palace. Taken together, they embody the many historical debates over who should wield power in Hawaiʻi. If the wooden mission houses were a model of what civilized living should look like in the 1820s, Kawaiahaʻo Church, with its lack of adornment, its open yet heavy interior, and its massive coral blocks, makes an austere 1840s Congregationalist spiritual claim to Hawaiʻi. In the 1870s, Aliʻiōlani Hale declared that the kingdom was substantial, functional, and stable; ten years later, the second ʻIolani Palace proclaimed the power and cultural sophistication of the mōʻī. A major feature of Victorian institutional architecture, the gothic elements of both ʻIolani and Aliʻiōlani invoke medieval European precedents. Saint Andrew's Cathedral, next to Washington Place on Beretania Street, would eventually feature even more elements. Not surprisingly, Alexander Liholiho, Kamehameha IV, preferred British Anglicanism, with its respect for monarchy, to the missionaries' republican-leaning Congregationalism. The king translated the Book of Common Prayer himself, invited a bishop from England to preside over the new church, and planned a cathedral that would challenge Kawaiahaʻo architecturally. (Built at the same time as Kawaiahaʻo, the ornate Cathedral Basilica of Our Lady of Peace on Fort Street was seen as a similar Roman Catholic challenge.)

The famous Kamehameha statue, placed between the Palace and Aliʻiōlani Hale during Kalākaua's 1883 coronation, was another statement of continuity and royal power. As public venues for the arts, humanities, and civic life, the New Music Hall and Arion Hall to our left, built in the late 1870s and 1880s, embodied the mōʻī's civilized and cosmopolitan tastes. They became, however, sites of struggle. When Robert Wilcox and his supporters occupied ʻIolani Palace in 1889 in an attempt to restore the full royal authority Kalākaua had lost because of the extorted Bayonet Constitution of 1887, troops fired guns and threw bombs into the palace grounds from the upper stories of the New Music Hall. And on the day of the overthrow in 1893, the American troops marched from Brewer's Wharf at the harbor to Arion Hall, then set up their artillery, aiming it at the palace.

Both Arion Hall and the New Music Hall are gone, replaced by what is now called the King David Kalākaua Building. Built during the territorial period, it still houses a post office, but it used to contain the U.S. Customs Service and the federal courts. Like the Merchant Street police station, its tiled roof and stucco exterior invoke California and the American Southwest, asserting Hawaiʻi's status as a territory of the United States. Buildings making a similar statement through architecture include the huge Honolulu Hale (city hall) built in 1926, across King and Punchbowl Streets to our far right; the Hawaiʻi State Library (1913), just to our right, one of the many public libraries across America partially funded by American steel baron and philanthropist Andrew Carnegie; and Julia Morgan's YWCA, mauka and to our left, facing the Richards Street gate of the palace.

The most ponderous example, however, stands to our right next to Aliʻiōlani Hale. If naming a federal post office after David Kalākaua seems crass, naming the territorial building after Mataio Kekūanāoʻa, the governor of Oʻahu and the father of two mōʻī—Alexander Liholiho [Kamehameha IV] and Lot Kapuīwa [Kamehameha V]—and one kuhina nui (Victoria Kamāmalu) seems sadistic. The name of an aliʻi who helped to create and administer the Hawaiian Kingdom for over forty years appears prominently on a building made possible by that kingdom's destruction.

We end our tour by carefully crossing King Street on the crosswalk just to our left and walking mauka through the palace grounds to the statue of Queen Liliʻuokalani (**9**), facing the state capitol behind ʻIolani Palace. Unlike many other states, Hawaiʻi's capitol building did not use the U.S. Capitol in

Seals of the Kingdom of Hawai'i, the Hawaiian Republic, the territory of Hawai'i, and the state of Hawai'i.

Washington, DC, as a template. In fact, it has no historical dimension at all. Instead, the 1969 building invokes Hawai'i's geographical features. The surrounding pool represents the ocean. The legislative chambers suggest volcanoes; the columns look like palm trees. Open to the wind, rain, and sun, the capitol also features a skylight. At the building's exact center, you can gaze up into the heavens, the offices of legislators, the governor, and other state officials rising in tiers on all four sides.

As state capitols go, it certainly insists on Hawai'i's distinctiveness. But let's return to the statue of the queen. Although Washington Place and Saint Andrew's Cathedral are off to her left, what hangs right in front of her is the state of Hawai'i seal, suspended from the back wall of the capitol. Like everything else on this tour, this gigantic medallion is historically stratified. The current version is a 1959 modification of the 1900 territorial seal, which was a modification of the 1894 seal of the Hawaiian Republic, which was itself an extensive revision of the seal of the Kingdom of Hawai'i. Commissioned by Kamehameha III in the 1840s, the first version featured the ali'i Kamanawa and Kame'eaumoku flanking a crown, a symbol of monarchy and of the kingdom that these two warrior uncles of Kamehameha I helped to create.

Beneath the images run the famous words Kamehameha III spoke on July 31, 1843, at the ceremony returning the kingdom to his control after its unauthorized seizure by a British admiral: "Ua mau ke ea o ka aina i ka pono." Usually rendered as "The life of the land is perpetuated in righteousness," many Hawaiians today translate it as, "The life of the land is perpetuated in sovereignty."

The Republic of Hawai'i substituted a rising sun for the crown; stuck an American star dead centerz; replaced the two ali'i with Kamehameha I and the Spirit of Liberty; and added a phoenix, the mythical bird that arises alive out of the ashes of its own pyre. The words "Republic of Hawai'i" and the date "1894" are imposed on top, but Kauikeouli's words still curve around the bottom of the seal.

Those words were still on the seal after the supposed annexation, when *Territory* replaced *Republic*, and *1894* was changed to *1900*. And they remain there, even after *State* replaced *Territory*, and the date was changed to *1959*.

When alive, Lili'uokalani saw all of these versions except the last, which her statue now gazes at while it hangs from a building designed to stress geography over history, but which nevertheless sits uncomfortably amid the concentration of historical monuments, traces, and erasures that make up downtown Honolulu and the Capitol District of Hawai'i nei.

Tina Grandinetti

Unearthing 'Auwai and
Urban Histories in Kaka'ako

Beneath an unassuming concrete pathway in Kaka'ako, a quiet rush of fresh
water flows from mau ka to ma kai (mountain to ocean)—a forgotten 'auwai,
or traditional irrigation waterway running under the city—shaded from the
hot Hawaiian sun. The 'auwai is a remnant from another time. In the 1800s,
a fishpond, fed by an artesian well, thrived where the Neil Blaisdell Center
currently stands. Overflow from the fishpond was diverted into the 'auwai
and used to irrigate lo'i kalo (wetland taro terraces) along its path; fish from
the reef would swim up the 'auwai and into the fishpond, where they were
fattened for harvest. Records indicate that in 1931, as Honolulu urbanized,
culverts were built over the 'auwai, and eventually, as the city grew around
it, the memory of the water was lost. Decades later, in January 2015, during an archeological survey of the area, developers from the Howard Hughes
Corporation lifted a manhole and were surprised to find not storm runoff or
sewage but clear running water, still flecked with small fish swimming against
its gentle current.

For a time, Howard Hughes Corporation considered raising the 'auwai and
making it a central feature of its master-planned community, Ward Village.
The 'auwai could bring "a bit of old Hawai'i to the urban area" and conveniently, much of it runs along the area where Howard Hughes was already
planning to construct a promenade and water feature connecting two of its
main residential properties.[1] Where the water diverged from this path, the
developer considered the possibility of rerouting it to suit the preplanned
landscaping, or simply building a new stream to "honor" the original.

This 'auwai speaks to the layered histories of urban Honolulu, still present all around us, though sometimes buried under a few layers of soil and

concrete. Walking through Kakaʻako, you'll pass trendy bars, bustling coworking spaces, hip boutiques, and vibrant murals. You'll hear a cacophony of construction noises—the sound of money being made. At sunset, you can look up at towering construction cranes silhouetted against the bright pink sky alongside luxury high-rises, their glass facades reflecting the searing colors of the setting sun. In Kakaʻako, young Hawaiian millennials, along with large-scale corporate developers, are experimenting with their own, often competing, visions of island urbanism. But just across Ala Moana Boulevard, the failures of this urbanism are evident in the tents and blue tarps that line the sidewalk and shelter a shifting community of houseless men, women, and children, most of whom are of Kanaka Maoli or Pacific Islander descent. During the peak of Kakaʻako's rapid redevelopment, this encampment swelled to a population of nearly five hundred people who were subjected to constant city sweeps and raids. As you walk through Kakaʻako, remember the water flowing under your feet and consider the ways in which our city, built upon Kanaka Maoli land, works to include some, and exclude others, from Hawaiʻi's urban spaces.

From Wetland to Working Class

The place we now know as Kakaʻako sits in the moku (district) of Kona, in the ahupuaʻa (land division) of Waikīkī, and along the coastal edge of the neighboring ʻili (smaller land divisions) of Kaʻākaukukui and Kukuluāeʻo. The area, along with as much as one-third of the Honolulu plain, was once home to wetland environments that helped to sustain abundant fishponds and agricultural production. But things started to change in the late 1800s, when massive dredging projects transformed the environment to make way for wharves and harbors. After the overthrow of Queen Liliʻoukalani, the illegal provisional government's Board of Health declared that the remaining wetlands of Honolulu posed a health risk as a breeding ground for mosquitos. Throughout the early twentieth century, subsequent in-filling brought irreversible change to the abundant environment, displacing the loʻi kalo and rice fields that provided livelihoods for Hawaiian and Asian settler families. Waste from Honolulu was transported to Kakaʻako to be incinerated, and the resulting ash was used as in-fill, creating twenty-nine acres of new land within the Kaʻākaukukui seawall in Kewalo Basin.

Throughout the late nineteenth and early twentieth centuries, the landscape was also changing across Oʻahu as plantation owners diverted water from streams and ʻauwai to feed thirsty sugarcane fields. Many Hawaiian kalo (taro) farmers were forced to give up farming and move into the city, and by the 1920s Kakaʻako had become a thriving multiethnic, working-class neighborhood. People lived in clusters of small houses called "camps," which were named after their landlords, the street they were located on, or sometimes the dominant ethnic group—mostly Portuguese, Hawaiian, Chinese, Japanese, and Filipino. Most residents had never lived in an urban setting before; many Hawaiians had previously lived in the countryside, and most households of other ethnic backgrounds had moved to Kakaʻako from the plantations, transitioning from plantation labor to industrial jobs at Kakaʻako's ironworks or tuna cannery.

While the neighborhood had a rough-and-tumble reputation, it also fostered a vibrant public life and a strong sense of community. During the day, children would head to the docks, showing off elaborate moves as they dove for coins thrown overboard by visiting tourists. In the evenings, Japanese households might have outdoor *ofuro*, or baths, that neighbors could use for a small fee. The streets often were filled with people who gathered to listen to political candidates address the district. And, along the shoreline, urban Kānaka Maoli created makeshift shelters and formed a community known as Squattersville. There, people could work in the city while maintaining their traditional ways of living by fishing or harvesting the limu (seaweed) that was still abundant in those waters. One former Kakaʻako resident reflected on his childhood home: "I don't care who that lived in Kakaʻako, all say they love Kakaʻako . . . because we knew all the people . . . we knew the place. I don't know, we'd sort of got a feeling that that's where we belong."

Kakaʻako's working-class community thrived for three decades or so, but in the post–World War II era, things began to change. As land prices increased in downtown Honolulu, the territorial government designated Kakaʻako as an industrial zone in order to absorb businesses that were priced out of the central business district. Scores of residents were evicted from the neighborhood, and the community slowly deteriorated.

Shaping the City

By the 1970s, Hawaiʻi was in the throes of a prolonged post-statehood economic boom that saw rapid development across Oʻahu, and a doubling of the island's population between 1950 and 1975. In 1976, the legislature passed Act 153, which designated Kakaʻako as a special district slated for renewal and created the Hawaiʻi Community Development Authority (HCDA), a public corporation sanctioned to redevelop Kakaʻako by facilitating partnerships with businesses in the private sector. At first, the act seemed to be a step toward responding to Honolulu's rapidly increasing housing demand. It implemented progressive inclusionary zoning measures that required that developers ensure that a certain number of units in each new development would be affordable to low-income and working-class families. But as Honolulu grew, land values skyrocketed, and Kaka'ako became prime real estate. The district's landowners, eager to cash in, were wary of inclusionary zoning. "They want prestige buildings and don't want the stigma of public housing," said Ali Sheybani, a planner with the Office of Council Services, in an article in the *Honolulu Observer*.

When the first development plan for Kaka'ako was released in 1981, it described a city of soaring high-rises, elevated walkways, and luxury condos. It was lavish, beautiful, and expensive. At the time, however, a staggering 75 percent of O'ahu households could not buy housing without some kind of assistance. The HCDA had decided that effective development would be defined by profit and investment rather than community need, even though it knew that this would bring drastic changes to the neighborhood. In fact, the final Environmental Impact Statement for the plan bluntly stated that the growing market for luxury condos was already transforming the community and that displacement was occurring along ethnic and class lines. The EIS noted that while the existing community in Kaka'ako was a mixed plate of Japanese, Chinese, Hawaiians, and Filipinos, the two new condo towers housed predominantly haole (white) residents and a large number of Japanese residents.

This was not a coincidence. It was a trend that was projected to continue as development progressed: "New Kaka'ako residents are expected to be predominately Caucasian and Japanese . . . . Because they tend to have lower incomes, part-Hawaiians, Filipinos, and most other ethnic groups are *not expected to be represented in proportion to their share of Oahu's population.*"[2] Kaka'ako's planners had effectively decided that a successful development was a profitable one, and in doing so they had deemed Kanaka Maoli and working-class families as undesirable.

Kaka'ako Today

While the HCDA's plans for Kaka'ako stagnated in response to a downturn in the global economy, today development is back with a bang. As many as thirty new high-rises are slated to be built within the next twenty years, and it seems that each day brings news of more penthouse apartments set at prices of upward of $30 million. This development means different things to different people. With so much investment concentrated in one place, some artists and small-business owners have found exciting opportunities to fund their projects, build new networks, and create spaces that benefit many within the community. Galleries, pop-up restaurants, artists' markets, and community events are found all over Kakaʻako and each is the product of Hawaiʻi entrepreneurs using the resources available to them in order to make their vision of urban Hawaiʻi a reality.

Meanwhile, public officials and advocacy groups have struggled immensely with the growing epidemic of houselessness. Efforts to address houselessness have ranged from providing more services to criminalizing houselessness to implementing raids on houseless encampments. All have stopped short of addressing the broader issue of economic inequality, and many have treated people experiencing houselessness as the source of economic hardship, rather than the victims of it. In response to pressures from developers and business owners who view the presence of houseless people as a detriment to their business operations, the state and the city have often resorted to measures that wage war not on poverty, but on the poor. Between 2013 and 2015, the city and county of Honolulu spent $1,875,000 enforcing ordinances that prohibited people from sitting, lying down, or storing property on sidewalks. And despite admitting that they had criminalized people living on the streets without giving them anywhere to go, the city continues attempts to expand these kinds of policies, calling them "compassionate disruption."[3]

The disparity between rich and poor is extreme in Kakaʻako, and it cannot be ignored because in many ways it is a cross section of the inequality that spans across the paeʻāina (archipelago). In 2018, a minimum wage earner in Hawaiʻi would have to work 109 hours a week to afford a market rate one-bedroom apartment. As housing costs continue to outpace wages, an estimated 58 percent of families are housing cost burdened, meaning they spend more than 30 percent of their monthly income on shelter. And roughly one of every three households in Hawaiʻi faces a severe housing cost burden, meaning they spend more than *half* of their income simply to keep a roof over their heads. This financial burden has real impacts on our island community. A 2016 Hawaiʻi Housing Planning Study reported that 30 percent of people expecting to move away from the islands cited housing prices as their main reason for leaving; meanwhile, nearly 30 percent of all condominium units are owned by people from outside the state of Hawaiʻi. When you understand these figures in the context of settler colonialism, the failure to provide affordable housing continues a legacy of pushing Indigenous people to the margins while creating more and more space for settlers.

With so many families struggling to get by, it can be difficult to stomach developers' obsession with luxury. The HCDA points to its inclusionary zoning measures in order to ameliorate concerns about affordable housing. This measure requires 20 percent of units in any new development to be set aside as "reserved housing," for sale or rent to households making no more than 140 percent of area media income (AMI).

A closer examination of these numbers has led many to argue that current regulations simply do not do enough to alleviate the burden that local families face. First, although the conventional measure of affordability is that housing costs amount to no more than 30 percent of household income, HCDA defines affordability (of for-sale units) at 33 percent of a household's income. This slight increase may seem minimal on paper, but it can be a heavy burden on households that are already struggling to make ends meet. Second, these regulations do not engage with the long-term implications of Hawai'i's housing crisis. While rental units in Kaka'ako are regulated for thirty years, for-sale units are only required to remain affordable for ten years, which does little to curb speculation in Honolulu's wildly profitable housing market. Third, by setting the reserved housing requirement to target households earning higher incomes of up to 140 percent AMI, the HCDA effectively excludes a large portion of Hawai'i's population that is in desperate need of housing. In 2018, 100 percent AMI amounted to $96,000 for a family of four, and 140 percent AMI amounted to $134,400. Meanwhile, many essential workers, from rookie police officers to experienced teachers, fall decidedly within the low-income category, which is unaccounted for in HCDA's requirements. In fact, roughly 75 percent of housing demand comes from low-income households, meaning they are not served by the HCDA's reserved housing program and are left out of the growing community in Kaka'ako.[4]

'Auwai and Waiwai in Kaka'ako

Through all of the changes that have taken place in Kaka'ako, it is remarkable that the gentle gurgle of the 'auwai has continued, quiet and unnoticed, under its streets. As Howard Hughes reviews options for what to do with the water flowing under its properties, one plan under consideration is to uncover the 'auwai, augment its flow, and wind its route throughout the grounds of Ward Village's Central Plaza, a four-acre, privately-held public-access park. While the future of the 'auwai remains undecided, we can imagine that, if it is brought to the surface, its path might be marked with signposts detailing its history, the history of Ka'ākaukukui and Kukuluāe'o, and the history of ancient Hawai'i. Maybe it will be an opportunity to teach new residents about the sophisticated irrigation and agricultural systems that Kanaka Maoli developed on this land over generations.

But even if the ʻauwai becomes a central feature of the Ward Village community, what will certainly be lost is the fact that this ʻauwai is not merely a symbol of Hawaiian culture or Hawaiʻi's past. It is a small part of a once expansive system that viewed water as vital to life, and it is a reminder that this system persists even today, despite years of colonization and erasure. In ʻōlelo Hawaiʻi, the word for water is wai, and the word for wealth and well-being, waiwai. Without a deep understanding of this worldview, developers will celebrate this ʻauwai, which survived so many decades of changes, by capturing its flow and sending it to trickle purposelessly through landscaped lawns. Where this water once contributed to building waiwai, it may soon be reduced to creating profit.

This veneer of cultural respect and "authenticity" is thin but prominent in Kakaʻako, and is used not just by HHC—a mainland corporation—but also by Kamehameha Schools and the Office of Hawaiian Affairs, two Native Hawaiian institutions that own large tracts of land in the district. Howard Hughes's ultraluxury high-rise is named "Waiea," or "water of life," and boasts a penthouse set at the cost of $36 million. One Kamehameha Schools' development is called Salt, after the salt pans that once dominated the land upon which it is built. As the buildings go up, construction sites are enclosed by barriers adorned with images of Oʻahu's natural beauty.

Expressions of Hawaiian culture are co-opted by developers that seek to attract buyers and investors with the promise of a unique and "authentic" consumer experience, but each element is handpicked according to its ability to produce returns. Packaging Hawaiian culture in this way allows developers to claim that they are being respectful of Hawaiʻi's past while retaining their monopoly on Hawaiʻi's future. Hawaiian art and artifacts are incorporated within Kakaʻako developments while houseless Kanaka Maoli living on the ma kai side of Ala Moana Boulevard are villainized and powerful histories of Hawaiian resistance are removed from the district's cultural narrative. But for Kanaka Maoli, cultural expression is not branding. It is, in itself, an act of resistance and a claim to survival and self-determination. And in Kakaʻako, the politics of colonialism and urban development are inseparable.

Even in the case of Kamehameha Schools and the Office of Hawaiian Affairs, Hawaiian culture in Kakaʻako is treated primarily as a means of maximizing profit, which officials claim funds Indigenous projects in other spaces. At one public meeting, when asked how development in Kakaʻako serves Kamehameha's mission "to improve the capability and well-being of people of Hawaiian ancestry," Elizabeth Hokada, Kamehameha Schools' vice president for endowment, stated that the endowment fund develops real estate and

The Anaha residences' glass-bottom pool overlooks Auahi Street. Penthouses in Howard Hughes Corporation's Anaha Tower are priced between $1 million and $14 million. *Photograph by Tina Grandinetti.*

expands its global portfolio "so that Pauahi's money is put to work around the world to earn money to support the mission of Kamehameha Schools."

This statement speaks to the limits of corporate-led urban development. Even if we assume that developers have the best of intentions, we must begin to question their lack of imagination surrounding the future of our city: Why does Kakaʻako have to be a place that funds Indigenous well-being in other spaces? Can't we create well-being *within* our cities as well as outside of them?

Choosing Our Urban Future

Just as the ʻauwai persisted through so much change, Kānaka Maoli have persisted within Hawaiʻi's cities, creating possibilities for an urban future that is centered not around profit, but around community and ʻāina. Just outside of the official bounds of the Kakaʻako district, and just across street from the source of the ʻauwai's water, sits Thomas Square Park. Shaded by the expansive branches of gnarled banyan trees, the park has become an important site of grassroots resistance in Honolulu, and each year, on July 31, Kānaka Maoli gather here for Lā Hoʻi Hoʻi Ea, or Sovereignty Restoration Day. The holiday (unrecognized by the state but celebrated by the Hawaiian lāhui) commemorates the day that sovereignty was restored to the Hawaiian Kingdom after a rogue British officer staged an illegal overthrow of the King Kauikeaouli. Upon learning of this act, British Admiral Richard Thomas sailed to Hawaiʻi and joined Kauikeaouli at the square to restore sovereignty to the kingdom. There, the British flag was lowered, and the Hawaiian flag was raised. Later that day, Kauikeaouli declared, "Ua mau ke ea o ka ʻāina i ka pono" ("The sovereignty of the land is perpetuated in righteousness"). In honor of the British officer who did what was pono, Kauikeaouli named the site Thomas Square Park and designated it as the first public park in the kingdom.

In recent years, the park been used for everything from antiwar rallies to Hawaiian independence events, and it has become a gathering place for Honolulu's houseless. But, as Kakaʻako undergoes its redevelopment, Thomas Square Park, too, has been caught in the wake of urban renewal. In 2016, the state announced plans to renovate the park and open it to commercial activities in order to increase revenue. Community members expressed concern that certain public uses—and users—of the land would no longer be permitted and that cultural and political events held there would be exploited as profit-driven ventures.

Soon after the announcement of these plans, hundreds of Kānaka Maoli gathered at the park to celebrate Lā Hoʻi Hoʻi Ea. The celebration spanned two days and served as a reminder that the sovereignty of the Hawaiian King-dom is still intact. One of the highlights of the event was an imu, or under-ground oven, dug into the hard earth at Thomas Square Park. Community members were invited to bring food to share. Hundreds of pounds of ʻulu (breadfruit), kalo, and puaʻa (pork) were lowered into the ground, covered with maia leaves, and cooked long and slow by hot stones in warm earth. The imu reiterated the presence of Kanaka Maoli within Honolulu's urban bounds and highlighted the presence of Indigenous geographies in the past and present. Digging beneath the manicured, landscaped surface of Thomas Square Park to feed the lāhui demonstrated that Indigenous geographies and Kanaka Maoli sovereignty have never been extinguished and persist within the city of Honolulu and the settler colonial state of Hawaiʻi today. While the food cooked, people talked, organized, and celebrated. And then they ate from earth that many have forgotten still has the power to feed. The imu became a regular and loved feature of subsequent celebrations.

La Hoʻi Hoʻi Ea and the community imu speak to how our cities might look, feel, and function differently if they were designed with people in mind and if Indigenous knowledge served as the foundation upon which they were built. While the digging of the imu and the sharing of food were not acts of protest against the state's plans for the park, or of the HCDA's management of Kakaʻako, they can teach us much about the kind of city we wish to live in. Whereas the state seeks to "revitalize" public space at Thomas Square Park through commercialization, the organizers of La Hoʻi Hoʻi Ea choose to rein-vigorate the space by enacting self-determination, involving community, and sharing food harvested from their lands. In doing so they demonstrated that cities can indeed be spaces that nurture our connection to ʻāina and to each other. If Kakaʻako is to be a vision of Hawaiʻi's urban future, how can we shape that vision to ensure that it includes everyone within our community? Per-haps one day, Hawaiʻi's urban lands will once again nourish Hawaiʻi's people, and the ʻauwai that was uncovered beneath Kakaʻako will be used not just as a decorative feature in a luxury development, but as a true water source, sustaining ʻāina that creates not profit, but waiwai.

Notes

1   Christine Hitt and Lurline Mcgregor. "Unpaving Paradise," *Kakaako Magazine*, 2015.
2   Hawaii Community Development Authority, "Draft Environmental Impact Statement for the Kakaʻako Community Development District Plan," (Honolulu: State of Hawaiʻi, Hawaiʻi Community Development Authority, and U.S. Department of Housing and Urban Development, 1982).

3   See Melika Lincoln, "Mayor Suspends Kaka'ako Homeless Sweeps, Says They're 'Not Solving the Problem,'" *Hawaii News Now*, May 11, 2015, http://www.hawaiinewsnow .com/story/29037667/mayor-ends-kakaako-homeless-sweeps-says-theyre-not -solving-the-problem; and Natanya Friedheim, "Caldwell Wants a Sidewalk Sit-Lie Ban Everywhere on Oahu," *Honolulu Civil Beat*, April 6, 2018. http://www.civilbeat.org /2018/04/caldwell-wants-a-sidewalk-sit-lie-ban-everywhere-on-oahu/.

4   SMS Research and Marketing Services, "Hawai'i Housing Planning Study 2016," prepared for the Hawai'i Housing Finance and Development Corporation, 2016, https://dbedt .hawaii.gov/hhfdc/files/2016/12/State_HHPS2016_Report_111416-FINAL-122216.pdf.

Resources

To learn more about the process of urbanization in Hawai'i, read *Nā Kua'āina: Living Hawaiian Culture*, by Davianna McGregor (Honolulu: University of Hawai'i Press, 2007).

For oral histories about life in Kaka'ako, see "Remembering Kaka'ako 1910–1950," volume 1, by the Center for Oral History at the Social Science Research Network (Honolulu: University of Hawai'i at Mānoa, 1978), http://scholarspace.manoa.hawaii.edu/handle/10125 /30142/.

For in-depth information about the state of housing in Hawai'i, see the "Hawai'i Housing Planning Study 2016" by SMS Research and Marketing Services, prepared in 2016 for the Hawai'i Housing Finance and Development Corporation, https://dbedt.hawaii.gov/hhfdc /files/2016/12/State_HHPS2016_Report_111416-FINAL-122216.pdf.

DISPLACED KAKA'AKO

A SELECTION OF PAVED-OVER PLACES

PUNUI

punchbowl st

south st

'AUWAIOLIMU

pohukaina st

halekauwila st

ilaniwai st

MAGOON BLOCK
DEMOLISHED, 1950
Mixed-use tenement with dozens of shops, flats, and cottages.

ATKINSON PARK
DEMOLISHED, 1930s
Pohukaina School playground and 5-acre home of Kaka'ako Sons barefoot football team.

PA'AKAI

KA'ĀKAUKUKUI

auahi st

SPF PROJECTS
2013 - 2015
Artist-run gallery

HONOLULU IRON WORKS
1899 - 1973

ala moana blvd

keawe st

coral st

cooke st

ilalo st

SQUATTERSVILLE *EVICTED, 1927*
Early 20th century beachcomber community of 700 Kanaka Maoli living in makeshift hale on public land.

olomehani st

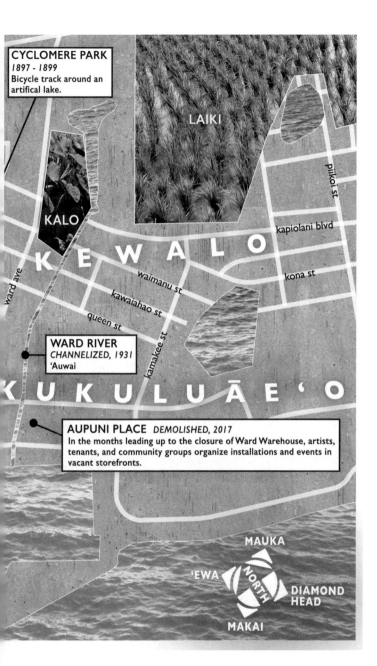

CYCLOMERE PARK
1897 - 1899
Bicycle track around an
artifical lake.

LAIKI

KALO

KEWALO

piikoi st

kapiolani blvd

waimanu st

kona st

ward ave

kawaiahao st

queen st

kamakee st

WARD RIVER
CHANNELIZED, 1931
'Auwai

KUKULUĀE'O

AUPUNI PLACE *DEMOLISHED, 2017*
In the months leading up to the closure of Ward Warehouse, artists,
tenants, and community groups organize installations and events in
vacant storefronts.

MAUKA

'EWA

NORTH

DIAMOND
HEAD

MAKAI

Adele Balderston.

Noenoe K. Silva

What's under the Pavement in My Neighborhood, Pūowaina

I live in a neighborhood where the sacred sites and place-names have been buried under pavement. The project of excavating those wahi pana began during a class I taught on contemporary Kanaka politics. I invited students to join me in researching the neighborhood, and three students accepted: Marissa Fong, Matthew Keoni Guss, and Ryan Murayama. (The remainder of the class was assigned to research other neighborhoods in a similar way.) I live in a building attached to the ma kai (ocean) side of Pūowaina directly ma uka of the state capitol and ʻIolani Palace. Pūowaina was renamed "Punchbowl" by foreigners, and that is now its official name. When I first moved in, I knew very little about the area and wanted to learn about it. At the same time, I want students to grapple with the reality of settler colonialism by gaining their own knowledge of sites significant to Kanaka in, on, or beneath the current built environment. I endeavor to teach the importance of rediscovery and use of our ancestors' names for the places around us. Erasure of those names by replacement with English ones is a common and powerful tool of settler colonialism. Recovery and use of the ancestral names is thus also a powerful tool of Indigenous resurgence.

My students and I first researched the cultural and historical significance of Pūowaina, the prominent volcanic crater that rises above Honolulu, and the area around it, and that is how I start here. I then take you through the tour as the students designed it, beginning in front of my building on Prospect Street, winding around Pūowaina, and ending at the top at the lookout point.

Cultural and Historical Significance of Pūowaina

Pūowaina lies in the second largest ahupuaʻa (land division) of Honolulu, between Pauoa and Waikīkī, in the moku of Kona on the island of Oʻahu. The smaller land division, the ʻili, of ʻAuwaiolimu lies to its west and north, and Kewalo lies to the northeast and runs all the way to the shore. These land division boundaries would sometimes change over time, but maps like the 1897 one referenced here can be helpful in rediscovering how our ancestors organized themselves politically and named and used the ʻāina (land).

At the top of Pūowaina was the pinnacle of a series of heiau (sites of religious ceremonies) in Kanaka ʻŌiwi times. Its name is said to be a contraction of Puʻu o ka waiho ʻana, Hill of the offering (my rough gloss). The imu ahi (underground pit for burning) or heiau puhi kanaka (corpse burning site) there was also called Pūowaina. According to Samuel Kamakau, the eminent nineteenth-century Kanaka historian, any person who violated the "kapu akua Alii" (aliʻi deity kapu) might be killed and offered in the rare burning ceremony. The heiau complex included Poʻouahi, on the eastern slope of Pūowaina; Mana heiau, now the site of a park named Dole Playground, presumably after the president of the provisional government that took power after overthrowing Liliʻuokalani; Kaʻakopua, which was the site of Aliʻi Nui Ruth Keʻelikōlani's home and is now the location of Central Intermediate School; Kānelāʻau, where Alapaʻi joins Kīnaʻu Street; and a pond near shore in Kewalo where the kapu violators were drowned.

Aliʻi nui of the past chose to live in the ahupuaʻa of Kewalo, including on the slopes of Pūowaina. Liliʻuokalani, for example, opens her autobiography as follows: "The extinct crater or mountain which forms the background to the city of Honolulu is known as the Punch-Bowl. . . . Very near to its site, on Sept. 2, 1838, I was born. My father's name was Kapaakea, and my mother was Keohokalole; the latter was one of the fifteen counselors of the king, Kamehameha III, who in 1840 gave the first constitution to the Hawaiian people." As mentioned above, Aliʻi Nui Ruth Keʻelikōlani made her home a little farther ma kai, and farther ma kai still is ʻIolani Palace, residence of the mōʻī (kings, queens) from Kamehameha III (r. 1820–54) through Liliʻuokalani (r. 1891–93).

During the era of Ko Hawaiʻi Pae ʻĀina (the independent nation of Hawaiʻi), until 1893, the top of Pūowaina was used as an observation point and a military installation called Pāpū (Fort) Pūowaina, which was designed for defense. Kamehameha I had heavy guns installed here for use in defending the island. These guns were sometimes fired in celebration of holidays, aliʻi births, and so on. For example, in 1843, when Hawaiʻi's sovereignty was returned after being temporarily snatched by a rogue British sea captain, "ua

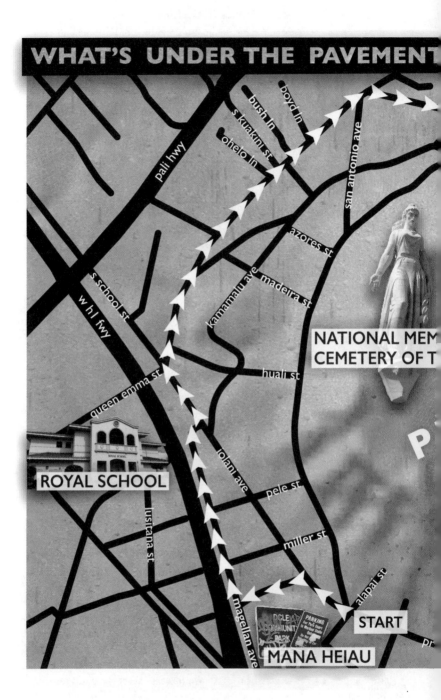

NATIONAL MEM
CEMETERY OF T

ROYAL SCHOOL

START

MANA HEIAU

pali hwy
boyd ln
bush ln
s kuakini st
ohelo ln
san antonio ave
azores st
kamamalu ave
madeira st
s school st
w h1 fwy
huali st
queen emma st
iolani ave
pele st
lusitana st
miller st
alapai st
magellan ave

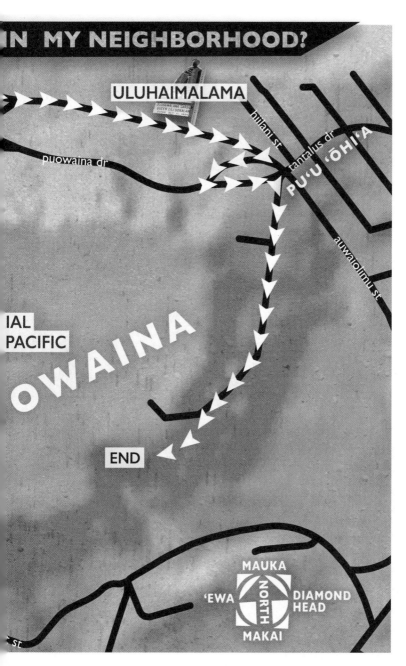

Map of Pūowaina. Map by Adele Balderston.

Queen Lili'uokalani. *Courtesy of the Hawai'i State Archives.*

kau ia ko Hawaii nei hae . . . a mauka hoi kekahi ma ka puu o puawaina [*sic*]; a ua ki nui mai na pu aloha mai o a o" ("Hawaiʻi's flag was raised [at the fort] and also on Puawaina; and many guns of aloha were fired everywhere"). And when Alexander Liholiho and Emma Rooke were married, "Ki aku na pu ma Puowaina me ka leo nui, a nani loa ka hele ana o keia poe hanohano" ("Guns were fired on Pūowaina very loudly, and the procession of these illustrious people was very beautiful").

The Walking Tour

The tour begins at the corner of Alapaʻi Street, ʻIolani Avenue, and Prospect Street. Alapaʻi Street was named for the aliʻi nui who was a companion of Nāhiʻenaʻena, child of Kamehameha I and Keōpūolani, and sister to Kamehameha II and III. Alapaʻi was the wife of Keoniana, also known as John Young II. ʻIolani (royal hawk) Avenue was most likely named for Liholiho, Kamehameha II, or Alexander Liholiho, Kamehameha IV, both of whom were also called ʻIolani. The hawk is one of the highest-flying birds in Hawaiʻi and so represents the highest-ranking aliʻi. To the east one block is Emerson Street, named for Dorothea Lamb Emerson, who was married to Joseph S. Emerson, brother of Nathaniel B. Emerson, both of whom were sons of the first missionaries who resided in Waialua on Oʻahu's north shore.

▸ **Liliʻuokalani**

Liliʻuokalani was the last mōʻī of Hawaiʻi. Born on the slopes of Pūowaina in 1838 to Keohokalole, her mother, who was a member of the founding House of Nobles, and Kapaʻakea, her father. She ascended to the throne in 1891, when her brother Kalākaua died. She inherited the unworkable and racist Bayonet Constitution, and she was overthrown when she attempted to replace it in January 1893. She was a noted composer.

Walk a half block west on ʻIolani and descend the Frear Street stairs, continuing to the corner of Frear and Magellan Avenue. You are now at Dole Playground, the site of Mana heiau, where it is said that the kāhuna prepared themselves for the burning corpse ceremony. Then follow Magellan Street west and continue west on ʻIolani until you reach Queen Emma Street, named for Emma Naea Rooke, granddaughter of John Young and daughter of George Naea and Fanny Kekelaokalani Young. She married Alexander Liholiho, and when he ascended the throne as Kamehameha IV, she became Queen Emma. After Liholiho's death, she ran for the office of mōʻī herself. She established the Queen's Hospital (now Queen's Medical Center), among many other remarkable achievements. As you look down Queen Emma Street, you'll see Royal School to the left, named for the Royal Chiefs' Children's School, which originally was nearer ʻIolani Palace.

Farther ma kai on the right, one might glimpse Central Intermediate School, the previous site of Kaʻakopua heiau and Ke Aliʻi Nui Ruth Keʻelikōlani's house. Ruth Keʻelikōlani was a remarkable leader and politician. She refused to speak English, cleaving always to her Native tongue. She served as the governor of Hawaiʻi Island, among other illustrious offices.

Now turn right and walk down Lusitana Street, which was named for a Portuguese immigrant welfare society whose members were mainly from the Azores. A significant part of the neighborhood here had been designated for Portuguese immigrants, and so you might also observe nearby street names such as Madeira, Azores, Concordia, and San Antonio. After a short while, you will see Kuakini Street on the left, named for Ke Aliʻi Nui Kuakini (who also took the name John Adams), a brother of Kaʻahumanu and governor of Hawaiʻi Island. He is said to have been one of the first aliʻi to learn to read and write in both Hawaiian and English. The famed historian and genealogist Davida Malo began his career as an advisor to Kuakini.

Next to Kuakini Street is Bush Lane, named for John Ailuene Edwin (or Edward) Bush, a member of the Hale ʻAhaʻōlelo Aliʻi (House of Nobles), a newspaper editor, governor of Kauaʻi, and Kalākaua's special envoy to Sāmoa. Next to Bush Lane is Boyd Lane, named for Robert N. Boyd, one of the young Kānaka that Kalākaua sent to Europe for an education. The most famous of them was Robert Kalanihiapo Wilikoki (Wilcox), who led two armed rebellions against the oligarchy that first deprived Kalākaua of his power and that six years later overthrew Liliʻuokalani's government.

At ʻAuwaiolimu Street, turn right. This street is said to be named for the long hair of a moʻo woman who bathed there in an ʻauwai (offshoots of streams that often irrigate loʻi). On the right in a short while is Whiting Street, named for Judge W. A. Whiting, who presided over the military tribunal that in 1895 tried and convicted Liliʻuokalani for misprision of treason, along with hundreds of her supporters over the course of a year or so.

Within the block on the left is Uluhaimalama, once the site of Queen Liliʻuokalani's garden, planted with plants and trees symbolic of her hoped-for

John Ailuene Bush. *Courtesy of the Bishop Museum.*

return to the throne by her supporters in 1894. It was later sold and became a cemetery. Its original significance has never been forgotten, however, and Hālau I Ka Wēkiu hula school, under Kumu Karl Veto Baker and Michael Lanakila Casupang, has recently been caring for the site and replanting some of the original plants.

Walk down ʻAuwaiolimu toward town, then turn right at and ascend Hoʻokuʻi Street, which means "collision"; it was perhaps named for the many car accidents that occurred there. At the top, turn left on Pūowaina Drive, walk to where it turns into the National Cemetery, and stop. Look to your left and you will see Papakōlea, one of the urban neighborhoods of Hawaiian Homelands. In that direction, Pūowaina Drive turns into Tantalus Drive, named for the mountain area there that was originally called Puʻu ʻŌhiʻa (ʻōhiʻa lehua hill). Students at Punahou School renamed it after the Greek myth of Tantalus, who was condemned to forever reach for but never grasp hanging fruit. We should call it Puʻu ʻŌhiʻa now; if we do, eventually that name will again come into common use, and the misnomer Tantalus could fade into memory.

Continue up Pūowaina Drive to the very top. You are now in the National Cemetery of the Pacific, a war memorial and cemetery where commemorations of World War II and other military commemorations are frequently held. At the very top lookout, facing ma kai and south, you have a breathtaking view of Honolulu and a great deal of the entire southern area of the island of Oʻahu. As you look down, you can see that both the state capitol building and ʻIolani Palace are in a direct line with this summit.

Here we stop to contemplate what Pūowaina looked and felt like during Kanaka ʻŌiwi times. In 1850, the first Mormon missionaries went to Pūowaina to pray and start their mission in Hawaiʻi. In 1865, in *Ka Lahui Hawaii*, a person named Nihiaumoe wrote an account of an early morning walk that included a trip up to the summit of Pūowaina.[1] Nihiaumoe reported only that the sound of the goats bleating deafened them, so they continued on their way. Ten years later, in *Ke Au Okoa*, a person named H. Kanaka recorded their walk to the summit and reported that Kalākaua had had trees planted and that the place looked beautiful; pine, mango, and kamani trees were surrounded by a wooden fence, with houses for caretakers in the middle.[2] In 1906, Kahikina Kelekona, author of *Kaluaikoolau*, wrote of ascending to the summit in the cold morning air and stopping at a platform where one of the guards who operated the cannon there once lived.[3] He gazed back at the high peak of Konahuanui "me he la e kaena mai ana no ka ui o kana punua i ka nuku lihipali o Nuuanu" ("that seemed as if it were boasting of the beauty of his fledgling at the cliff edge of the summit of Nuʻuanu"). He then took in the sights of Kaʻala in the west and Lēʻahi in the south, "ku hiehie oniole no iloko o na oehukai" ("which stood unmoving and elegant in the blustery sea"). He then began overhearing two spirits reminiscing as they looked down into Pauoa and Honolulu; they were regretting the loss of what was once green with loʻi kalo (taro fields) and filled with the houses of people they knew, among whom were Samuel Kamakau and John Bush. They remembered many people fishing in the stream, probably ʻAuwaiolimu, for ʻoʻopu (goby fish) and ʻōpae (shrimp). He writes that they spoke "na huaolelo piha naauaua" ("words filled with intense grief") over the changes that had befallen their town. Kelekona seems to grieve with them, writing, "O ke kahua ihikapu o na ʻLii ua pau ka hie a me ke kapu, a o ka hae kalaunu aole ia, he hae kahakahana okoa loa ia aʻu e ike aku nei" ("The dignity and sanctity of the sacred grounds of the Aliʻi are over, and the crown flag is gone; it is a very different striped flag that I see"). On the basis of Nihiaumoe's and Kelekona's experiences, and in spite of Kalākaua's attempts to make it into a tree-filled

> **John Ailuene Bush**

John Ailuene Bush was born in 1842 in Honolulu. In 1880 Kalākaua appointed him Kuhina Kālaiʻāina, or minister of the interior. Bush served as minister of finance as well. In 1886 he led the diplomatic mission to form an alliance with Sāmoa, which did not succeed. After Kalākaua was virtually overthrown with the Bayonet Constitution, Bush cofounded and was the elected president of Hui Kālaiʻāina, which attempted to rectify the wrong. After the overthrow of Liliʻuokalani in 1893, Bush cofounded and was a vice president of Hui Aloha ʻĀina, which attempted to reinstate her and prevent annexation to the United States. Bush was the founder and editor of the important newspapers *Ka Leo o ka Lahui* and *Ka Oiaio*.

NANI O PUOWAINA.

E KA LAHUI HAWAII;—*Aloha oe :*

Ua pii au maluna o Puowaina i kekahi la i hala iho nei, a ua mahalo au no ka hana maikai i hoala ia e ko kakou Moi. He oiaio ua nani no, a ina e holopono ka ulu ana o na mea kanu e like me ka manaolana o na makaainana, alaila, he pomaikai nui keia. He mau makahiki loihi ka waiho wale ana o kela kula i hele a panoa i ka wela o ka la, a ua lehulehu na Moi o kakou iloko o ia wa, aole nae hookahi o lakou i hoao e hoolilo i ua kula nei i ululaau, o Kalakaua wale no. Nolaila, he nani keia hana. Ua makaikai au i na mea i hana ia malaila. Nui no na laau i kanu ia, ke paina, ka manako, ke kamani, a pela aku a lehulehu wale. Ua pa ia me kekahi pa laau poepoe a puni, a e ku ana he mau hale mawaena; ua hai ia mai ia'u no ka poe kiai ia hale. He punawai kekahi malaila, a he mahuahua iki no ka wai a'u i ike aku ai. Ua ike no hoi au malaila i ke ku o ka paila omole. Lehulehu na omole e mokaki ana. Ua ane like me na omole a'u e ike nei maloko o na hale inu rama. Ua haohao au i ke kumu o ka lehulehu ana o na omole malaila. Ua noonoo au, a ua manao wale iho no he mau omole wai hoopulu mea kanu paha. Eia nae kahi mea kupanaha, ua manao au e hoopau i ko'u kuhihewa, nolaila, ua kau ae la i kekahi omole i ko'u puka-ihu, eia ka he wai io no, he wai, hoopulu nae i na pulapula ponoi o ka lahui, he waiona—auwe! Aole paha e ae ka Moi "Hooulu Lahui" i keia ano wai e lawe ia malaila. I ko'u ike a hoomaopopo ana i ke ano o ua mau paila nei, pe'a ae la ko'u mau lima ma ke kua a huli hoi mai la, me ka nalu wale iho no o loko no kela mau omole.

H. KANAKA.

Honolulu, Apr. 27, 1875.

Article written by H. Kanaka about Pūowaina.

Source: H. Kanaka, "Nani O Puowaina," Ka Lahui Hawaii, April 29, 1875, 3.

park, it seems that Pūowaina was a kind of sad place, not one where a person might feel invited to enjoy the view with pleasure. Now that it is the site of a U.S. war memorial and cemetery, it is an even more grief-filled place.

Famous People Who Lived in the Pūowaina Area
Kahikina Kelekona's essay gives us most of the names of famous people from the area that I pass on here. John Ailuene Bush, mentioned earlier, lived near Hotel and Punchbowl Streets ma kai of this neighborhood. Simona Kaʻai, aliʻi nui, served as a member of both the Hale ʻAhaʻōlelo Aliʻi and Hale ʻAhaʻōlelo Lunamakaʻāinana (House of Representatives); he was also a writer for the Hawaiian-language newspapers. G. B. Kalaaukane served as a Lunamakaʻāinana. Samuel M. Kamakau was the most famous Kanaka historian of the nineteenth century. Kapaʻakea and Keohokalole were aliʻi nui and the birth parents of Kalākaua, Liliʻuokalani (both mōʻī), Likelike, and Leleiōhoku. J. W. Keawehunahala served as a Lunamakaʻāinana for numerous terms. N. Kepoʻikai, J. Komoikeehuehu, P. Naone, and D. L. Naone also served as Lunamakaʻāinana.

This is the end of the tour. My neighborhood was once the chosen home of many aliʻi nui and rulers of the whole archipelago. It was also the site of a rare and what seems today horrifying human sacrifice ceremony that required violators of the divine aliʻi kapu to be drowned and their corpses subsequently burned in a place where all Oʻahu could see the smoke. It became a site of observation and weaponry of war, though there was never enough of either to prevent our country being taken by the United States. It is now a place that commemorates U.S. victories in war with the firing of guns and aerial acrobatics of fighter jets.

Pūowaina is also where many of us have relatives buried or their ashes interred; they are those who were drafted or chose to serve in the U.S. military, and many of them lost their lives doing so. It is worth a visit on Memorial Day, when the specifically Hawaiian version of that very American day produces the sight and scent of acre upon acre of tropical flowers, a sea of red ginger, heliconia, and birds of paradise.

The names of the streets, the sites where heiau had been, and especially Pūowaina itself are telling their stories of our ancestors' ways of life, their modes of governance, our loss of governing our own country, and our current efforts at resurgence. Tours such as this one help us to hear those stories embedded in the landscape all around us.

Notes

1   Nihiaumoe, "Ka ea kakahiaka nui," *Ke Au Okoa*, October 16, 1865, 2.

2   H. Kanaka, "Nani O Puowaina," *Ka Lahui Hawaii*, April 29, 1875, 3.

3   Kahikina Kelekona (John G. M. Sheldon), "He Haawina Pahaohao," In *Kaluaikoolau,
    ke kaeaea o na Pali Kalalau a me na Kahei O Ahi o Kamaile* (Honolulu: n.p., 1906),
    115–120.

Bibliography

Arista, Denise Noelani Manuela. "Davida Malo: Ke Kanaka O Ka Huliau—David Malo:
    A Hawaiian of the Time of Change," Master's thesis, University of Hawaiʻi, 1998.

"Halau I Ka Wekiu - Wahine to Dance at Merrie Monarch about Uluhaimalama," *Hawaii
    News Now*, K5 website. Accessed February 27, 2017. http://www.k5thehometeam.com
    /story/14202912/halau-i-ka-wekiu.

"Ka Hoihoi ana o ke Aupuni," *Ka Nonanona*, August 8, 1843, 25.

Kamakau, Samuel M. "Ka Moolelo o Hawaii nei." *Nupepa Kuokoa*, June 22–October 7, 1865.

"Ka Mare ana o ka Moi," *Ka Hae Hawaii*, June 25, 1856, 66.

Kanahele, George S. *Emma: Hawaiʻi's Remarkable Queen: A Biography*. Honolulu: Queen
    Emma Foundation, 1999.

Kanaka, H. "Nani o Puowaina." *Ka Lahui Hawaii*, April 29, 1875, 3.

Kelekona, Kahikina. "He Haawina Pahaohao," appended to *Kaluaikoolau: ke Kaeaea o na
    Pali Kalalau a me na Kahei O Ahi o Kamaile: Piilani, ka Wahine i Molia i ke Ola, ke Kiu
    Alo Ehu Poka: Kaleimanu, ka Hua o ko laua Puhaka, ka Opio Haokila iloko o na Inea:
    he Moolelo Oiaio i Piha me na Haawina o ke Aloha Walohia*. Honolulu: Keena Puuku o
    ka Teritore o Hawaii, 1906.

Liliuokalani. *Hawaii's Story by Hawaii's Queen*. Rutland, VT: Charles E. Tuttle, 1964 [1898].

Monsarrat, M. D. *Honolulu, Hawaiian Islands* [map]. n.p. 1897. Accessed February 27. 2017.
    http://www.avakonohiki.org/maps-kona.html.

Nihiaumoe. "Ke Ea Kakahiaka Nui," *Ke Au Okoa*, October 16, 1865, 2.

Nogelmeier, Puakea. *Pūowaina*. Honolulu: Hawaiian Studies Institute, The Kamehameha
    Schools/Bernice Pauahi Bishop Estate, 1985.

Sterling, Elspeth, and Catherine C. Summers. *Sites of Oahu*, rev. ed. Honolulu: Bishop
    Museum, 1978.

Candace Fujikane

Mapping Wonder in Lualualei on the Huakaʻi Kākoʻo no Waiʻanae Environmental Justice Bus Tour

Puʻu Heleakalā in Waiʻanae rises up in massive, ridged brown columns above the kula pili, the yellow, grassy plains below. When I look at it, I imagine Māui lassoing the sun's rays, muscles straining as he struggles to break the kukuna o ka lā, the rays of the sun, to slow his traversal across the sky so that Māui's mother Hina can dry her kapa (bark cloth). The land shimmers with the heat of the sun that has teeth in Lualualei, the sun that bites my feet. Behind me flows Ulehawa Stream. As I stand looking at this great hill, the curved columns sharpen into view as the thighs of Hina from whence Māui is born. The waters of Ulehawa then appear as the birth waters flowing to the sea, where Māui fished up the islands with his fishhook Mānaiakalani to join the moana kahiko, the ancient seas.[1]

On April 26, 2010, I entered the land struggles in Waiʻanae through a play about the Māui moʻolelo (stories/histories) for an American Friends Service Committee (AFSC) Hawaiʻi chapter fundraiser organized by Kyle Kajihiro and Terrilee Kekoʻolani. At the end of the performance, Alice Kaholo Greenwood, a descendant of the nineteenth-century intellectual and political leader John Papa ʻĪʻī, rose with her cane and spoke to the audience about the ongoing struggle in Lualualei Valley to protect Māui's birth sands, the place where he was born. A developer, Tropic Land LLC, had begun a process to petition the State of Hawaiʻi Land Use Commission for a boundary amendment to reclassify ninety-six acres of land from an agricultural district to an urban district for a light industrial park.

Greenwood invited the audience to take the Huakaʻi Kākoʻo no Waiʻanae Environmental Justice bus tour organized by the Concerned Elders of Waiʻanae (an organization of more than two hundred kūpuna, elders, and cultural practitioners), KĀHEA: The Hawaiian-Environmental Alliance, and the AFSC. The bus tour would make it possible for residents of Waiʻanae to expand their base of support by teaching people across the island about the threatened wonders of Lualualei and encouraging them to share these struggles and testify at the upcoming Land Use Commission hearings, the first of which was slated for that September. As a teacher of moʻolelo at the University of Hawaiʻi, I went on this bus tour to learn about the ways that people of Waiʻanae have shared the wonder of the moʻolelo to organize their communities against environmental racism and settler colonial injustices.

The stories of Māui's gifts are particularly important in Nānākuli, Lualualei, and other places along the Waiʻanae coast, which have been depicted in the media as arid wastelands both geographically and culturally, places of poverty, houselessness, substance abuse, and violence, despite the abundance of those farming communities and the waiwai (wealth) of their knowledges, cultural practices, and social relationships. Waiʻanae is a distinctively Hawaiian place because Hawaiian Homestead lands were established there by the State of Hawaiʻi to move Kānaka ʻŌiwi away from the increasingly lucrative land markets in Honolulu. Because the only municipal landfill and the only construction and demolition landfills have been situated in Waiʻanae, it has also been made into an environmental hotspot for illegal dumping activities, with devastating effects for the people of Waiʻanae, who consequently suffer from the highest rates of health problems, including cancers and respiratory diseases.[2]

The Environmental Justice Bus Tour took us on a huakaʻi, a physical, spiritual, and intellectual journey, to the place of Māui's birth. So many of us have grown up alienated from the land in the urban environments where we live, and huakaʻi is the piko, the umbilicus, that provides a way for people to reconnect past, present, and future generations through the lessons of the moʻolelo. The huakaʻi helps us to grow aloha ʻāina, a love for places on the land that takes root in our hearts, and one through which undercurrents of Kanaka ʻŌiwi national consciousness flows today.

Moʻolelo are also critical to the lāhui, the nation and the cultivation of a Hawaiian national consciousness. On these huakaʻi, moʻolelo are a part of the

▶ **Alice Kaholo Greenwood**

"What had happened was that I was doing a lot of land research, and I had the land deeds for cultural sites in Waiʻanae. Then, at a meeting, Lucy was talking about the cultural impact statement that mentioned Kaolae and when she said that name, I turned around and said, 'Oh, that's the land where Māui was born at!' And I showed her the land deed I was working with. LCA [Land Commission Award] 3131 was given to Kuapuu, and Kaolae is on the Ewa [east] side of it."—Alice Kaholo Greenwood

Alice Kaholo Greenwood on the bus tour sharing photos she has collected during her research. *Photograph courtesy of Christina Aiu.*

resurgence of Kanaka ʻŌiwi (Native Hawaiian) ways of knowing, and moʻolelo have critical decolonial effects as they teach us about Kanaka economies of abundance that restore "wastelands" to ʻāina kamahaʻo (wondrous land) and ʻāina momona (abundant land), growing not only the food that physically nourishes people but also what Cristina Bacchilega describes as the wonder that spiritually and intellectually sustains us. Although ʻŌiwi have a genealogical connection to land that others do not, all people who live in Hawaiʻi have the capacity to grow aloha ʻāina and to take on the responsibilities of protecting wahi pana and wahi kapu, celebrated and sacred places in Hawaiʻi.

Two weeks after the Kumu Kahua play, many of us boarded a bus at MAʻO Organic Farms in Lualualei Valley, where KĀHEA community outreach coordinator Shelley Muneoka handed out a fact sheet on urban development and the "Purple Spot." The sheet explained that in previous Waiʻanae Sustainable Communities Plans, the community had been adamant that urban development should not be allowed to intrude into the agricultural district and instead should be focused around already existing urbanization along Farrington Highway. The 2009 version of the sustainability plan, however, featured a purple spot representing the proposal for a light industrial park deep in the green agricultural district of the valley.

From the outset, the Concerned Elders of Waiʻanae and their attorney from KĀHEA, Marti Townsend, were aware that the urbanization of one spot would pave the way for an industrial/urban corridor into the agricultural lands of Lualualei Valley. In effect, urban spot zoning makes urban creep possible. Developers purchase inexpensive agricultural land and speculate on rezoning it to urban land so that they can flip it for a profit. Once a spot is rezoned, other developers use it to rezone adjacent lands on the basis of the argument that their proposed urban use is "consistent" with existing urban uses. Townsend had found a proposal in the city and county of Honolulu's Waiʻanae Sustainable Communities Plan to build a secondary access road through Pōhākea Pass in the mountains that rise up inland behind the Purple Spot, and Kajihiro located that road as Project 57 in the Oahu Regional Transportation Plan 2030. As Lucy Gay, one of the elders, pointed out on the bus tour, the Purple Spot was part of a larger vision of urban development. It took on a life of its own in community organizing against urban spot zoning, helping to symbolize visually the dangers of settler colonial urban spot zoning taking place all over the islands.

The core planning group of Concerned Elders of Waiʻanae included Alice Greenwood, Lucy Gay, Walterbea Aldeguer, Lori and John Nordlum, Cynthia Rezentes, Pat Patterson, Kapua Keliʻikoa-Kamai, Johnnie-Mae Perry, Fred Dodge, Karen Young, Georgette Meyer, Jack Defeo, and Elizabeth Stack, as well as Kajihiro and Kekoʻolani from the AFSC and KĀHEA coordinators Marti Townsend, Shelley Muneoka, Lauren Muneoka, and Miwa Tamanaha. As those of us on the bus tour traveled along a roadmap of the Concerned Elders' activism over the years and their ongoing struggles, Lucy focused on environmental impacts and community organizing, Alice spoke about social justice and her advocacy for the people of Waiʻanae, and Walterbea recounted for us the stories of her childhood and the moʻolelo of Lualualei. On the bus, as the three voices moved in and out of the storytelling, they wove together a description of the exploitative political and corporate forces they face as they stand for the land in community organizing inspired by the moʻolelo of Lualualei. They wove a lei from strands of the past and the present, from the actions of kūpuna (ancestors, elders) in times past to people's struggle against environmental injustices today.

▶ **Lucy Gay**

"A line on a map is never just a line. It represents the dreams and desires, the vision of the developer. So what we call the 'Purple Spot' that marks the development project isn't on the map in isolation—it's connected to the line on the map that now represents the developers' desire for a road. And when you have roads, you also have the other things that roads attract: gas stations, restaurants, housing, people. And over time, these roads become urban and industrial corridors into rural or agricultural communities."—Lucy Gay

Lucy Gay speaking on the bus tour. *Photograph courtesy of Christina Aiu.*

The bus took us down Farrington Highway, with the deep blue sea on our right and the small businesses and homes along our left. We entered Lualu-alei Valley along Māʻiliʻili Road and drove into the agricultural valley of two-acre truck farms fronted with farmers' homes. The bus first stopped on the bridge over the shallow waters of the concretized channel of Māʻiliʻili Stream (once known as Māʻiliʻiliʻi), where the elders described their efforts against decades of settler colonial militarization and environmental racism that has led to both legal and illegal dumping in Waiʻanae. Alice tells us how they went out with cameras and binoculars to photograph and document what turned out to be their own city's illegal dumping of concrete into the Māʻiliʻili Stream in 2008 and 2009. As a result of the Concerned Elders' efforts, the city was forced to pay $1.3 million in fines that were used for removing the illegal fill and new projects to restore Waiʻanae watersheds.

We then stopped at the quarry on Paʻakea Road, where we saw the dou-bled exploitation of land. There, the land is first excavated for the extrac-tion of resources, hollowed out, then later presented as emptied spaces for landfills. Paʻakea means "white hardness" and is a word used for limestone, sedimentary rock made up of the skeletal fragments of marine life. In the Kumulipo, the creation chant that traces the genealogy of Kanaka ʻŌiwi to the creation of the world, one of the very first ancestors of the Kanaka ʻŌiwi is the uku koʻakoʻa, the coral polyp. As we look out over the white limestone quarry, the makai (seaward) area of Lualualei that was once a coral bed, we see the exposed bones of the land that are ground up and used as an ingredient in concrete for the high-rise hotels in Waikīkī. Lucy explains how developer Henry J. Kaiser anticipated the build-up of hotels in Waikīkī after statehood in 1959, and because at that time cement was shipped in from the continent, he was able to get a permit for a quarry and cement plant in Lualualei. In 2005, neighboring farmers reported that toxic bottom ash, the residue from burning coal for energy, was being dumped in quarry cells, where water levels rose and fell with the tides, and the toxic materials were being carried out to the sea. When the owner of the quarry proposed to repurpose the quarry as a landfill, the Concerned Elders raised their concerns about the bottom ash, and as a result, the Department of Health did not renew the landowner's permit for accepting bottom ash, and the quarry was not made into a landfill.

The tour then stopped at the birthplace of Māui, the proposed Purple Spot at the foot of Puʻu Heleakalā. It is also a place that provides us with a portrait of Hawaiʻi's history of U.S. occupation. In 1848, when the Māhele privatized land in Hawaiʻi, Lualualei Valley was designated as crown lands, and after the overthrow in 1893 and illegal annexation in 1898, Land Grant 4751 was sold in 1903 to H. M. Von Holt, who was associated with the Committee of Safety that overthrew Queen Liliʻuokalani. That land was later purchased by Lincoln McCandless, whose heirs leased seventeen acres to Tadashi and Kazuto Araki. The Araki brothers farmed an abundance of produce on that land from 1967 to 1978, at which time they were forced to leave when the McCandless heirs proposed to increase their rent and take a percentage of their crop yields. Ryoei and Nancy Higa then moved onto the land and farmed it from 1978. In 1988, the land was sold to Kabushiki Kaisha Oban, one of many Japanese corporations that sought to develop golf courses in Hawaiʻi. The Higas were given a notice of eviction, which ignited a firestorm of protest in the context of other historical cases of the eviction of farmers from places such as Kalama Valley and Waiāhole-Waikāne Valleys. Waiʻanae communities rallied at the Higas' farm,

> ▶ **Walterbea Aldeguer**

> "In 2009, I was reading the Kumulipo, and I came across the story of Māui's hatching from the egg and his mother hearing him coo, how he became a full-grown rooster, and then how his mother Hina referred to him as her 'brave child.' And I started to see how it's in our landscape. Keaulumoku was the haku [composer] who created this chant. And I thought, how wise, how knowledgeable this person was to have known that this story actually exists. The features, everything, is in Waiʻanae still."—Walterbea Aldeguer

Walterbea Aldeguer telling the moʻolelo of Māui's birth on the bus tour.
Photograph by Candace Fujikane.

where Ryoei Higa told everyone, "No can eat golf balls!" These words were quickly emblazoned on thousands of t-shirts and continue to echo in the collective memory to the present. The community won that battle, but in 2005 Tropic Land purchased the land and proposed to develop it into a light industrial park.

To help bus riders to see the land as the kūpuna once did, Walterbea pointed out that the birth of Māui is visible over and over again as one paddles in a canoe or drives along Farrington Highway toward Kaʻena, the moʻolelo unfolding along the ʻōmoʻomoʻo (ridgeline) of Puʻu Heleakalā against the hot blue skies of Lualualei. Walterbea directed our attention to the mountains that rise up at the back of Lualualei in order to show us the fluid metamorphosis of the moʻolelo. She began by pointing to the great brown dome of Puʻu Heleakalā, the egg from which Māui emerges. As we traveled along the coast, we saw the land shifting, and from the composite of mountain ridges twin peaks appear as a beak emerges from the side of the egg, a chick hatching from the egg. As we turned off the coast mauka, toward the mountains, up into the Princess Kahanu Estates on Hawaiian Homestead

Profile of Māui as a handsome man. *Photograph by Candace Fujikane.*

lands, the beak and the body shift again as the ridgeline of Puʻu Heleakalā, extending to Palikea, becomes the silhouette of a beaked man with a wattle. As we continued up Hakimo Road, the silhouette finally transforms into the rugged facial planes of a handsome man with waved hair, a high forehead, strong brow, and angular jaw. Walterbea's recovery shows us how the features of the land evoke the memories of these moʻolelo and ensure that these stories continue to be told into the present, grounding the people of Lualualei in the stories of their kulāiwi, the ancestral bones of their Native lands.

The huakaʻi ended with a story of regeneration at MAʻO Organic Farms. MAʻO is an acronym for Māla ʻAi ʻŌpio, which has a double meaning: "the youth food garden" and "the place that grows young people." Although the developer's environmental impact statement describes the soil of the land as "unsuitable for cultivation," the young people of Waiʻanae learn that Lualualei vertisol soil, when irrigated, is among the richest soils for planting in the world. Social Enterprise Director Kamuela Enos described how MAʻO developed the two-year Youth Leadership Training College Internship program through which interns learn the moʻolelo of Lualualei Valley, the names of its mountains and other land formations, the winds and rains, and the akua (deities that are the elemental forms) associated with different places, which helps them to engage in sustainable leadership and farming skills rooted in ʻŌiwi knowledges.

What allows wonder to grow from aloha ʻāina to a sense of kuleana (responsibility, purview, privilege) and direct action is the way that Walterbea, Alice, and Lucy opened up a space for those who are not kamaʻāina (Native to or born and raised in a place) to Waiʻanae to join them in testifying at the

Land Use Commission hearings against the boundary amendment. The bus tours continued for nine months, and at hearings during that time, residents of Waiʻanae, nā kūpuna, cultural practitioners, farmers, environmental justice activists, demilitarization activists, young people interning at MAʻO Organic Farms, university professors, and cultural experts on the Māui moʻolelo in Hawaiʻi and across the Pacific all testified to the significance of this land because they had traveled to it on the bus tours.

We won the battle by one vote. Yet this land struggle was about much more than the industrial park. It was about educating entire communities about the wonders of Lualualei, both those of the Māui moʻolelo and those of the power of ʻŌiwi activism and community organizing.

The bus tours have continued, and Alice Greenwood, Lucy Gay, Walter-bea Aldeguer, and I tell the moʻolelo of Māui in order to map wonder on the ground. The people of Waiʻanae, like Māui, have been incredibly resource-ful not only in protecting land in Waiʻanae but in offering their own gifts to future generations in Waiʻanae. The Kumulipo describes Māui's gifts with a beautiful word; they are referred to as ua (rain), which was translated by Queen Liliʻuokalani as "showers." The people of Waiʻanae today offer the ua of new moʻolelo, ones that tell of their transformative activism and organizing for future generations, moʻolelo that fall upon the land like rain for renewed abundance.

Notes

1   A longer version of this essay was published as "Mapping Wonder in the Māui Moʻolelo: Growing Aloha ʻĀina through Indigenous and Affinity Activism," in "Rooted in Wonder: Tales of Indigenous Activism and Community Organizing," ed. Bryan Kamaoli Kuwada and Aiko Tamashiro, special issue, *Marvels and Tales* 30, no. 1 (2016): 45–69. A longer version will also appear in my forthcoming book, *Mapping Abundance: Indigenous and Critical Settler Cartography in Hawaiʻi.*

2   D. Krupitsky, F. Reyes-Salvail, Kramer K. Baker, and A. Pobutsky, *State of Asthma, Hawaiʻi 2009* (Honolulu: Hawaiʻi State Department of Health, 2009), 7.

Resources

Bacchilega, Cristina. *Fairy Tales Transformed? Twenty-First Century Adaptations and the Politics of Wonder.* Detroit: Wayne State University Press, 2013.

KĀHEA: The Hawaiian-Environmental Alliance website. http://www.kahea.org/issues /environmental-justice.

Kamakau, Samuel Mānaiakalani. *Tales and Traditions of the People of Old/Na Moʻolelo a ka Poʻe Kahiko.* Translated by Mary Kawena Pukui. Honolulu: Bishop Museum Press, 1991.

Kelly, Marion. "Notes on the History of Lualualei and Honouliuli." In *Research Design for an Archaeological Survey of Naval Magazine, Lualualei; Naval Communication Area Radio Transmission Facility, Lualualei; and Naval Air Station, Barber's Point, Oʻahu, Hawaiʻi*, edited by Alan E. Haun, 35–36. Honolulu: Department of Anthropology and Bernice Pauahi Bishop Museum, 1984.

Kumulipo. *He Pule Hoolaa Alii: He Kumulipo Ka I-imamao, a ia Alapai Wahine*. Honolulu: Paʻiia e ka Hui Paʻipalapala Elele, 1889.

The Kumulipo: An Hawaiian Creation Myth. Translated by Queen Liliʻuokalani. Honolulu: Pueo Press, [1897] 1978.

MAʻO Organic Farms. https://www.maoorganicfarms.org/.

McGrath, Edward J., Kenneth M. Brewer, and Bob Krauss. *Historic Waianae: A Place of Kings*. Honolulu: Island Heritage Limited, 1973.

PART IV. **Hawai'i beyond the Big Eight / New Mappings**

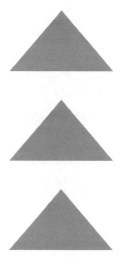

Maps offered in guidebooks locate places through longitude and latitude, coordinates that fix places in space, use an abstract concept of scale to substitute for the real thing, and help people imagine travel to and across unknown geographies. In guidebooks, Hawai'i is most often illustrated and mapped through its largest and most touristic islands: Hawai'i Island, Maui, O'ahu, Kaua'i, Moloka'i, and Lana'i. While Ni'ihau and Kaho'olawe round out the "Big Eight," they are less known because the former is privately owned and restricted to Native Hawaiian families, and the latter is uninhabited because of decades of military weapons testing.

But Hawai'i is more than its geographic location. Hawaiians have always voyaged, by choice and by force, beyond the shores of the islands. As David A. Chang notes, Kanaka 'Ōiwi have a long tradition of voyaging and have themselves been part of explorations and migrations that have crisscrossed the Pacific and beyond. Challenging the notion that Natives "stay" and others "go," Chang's historical mapping of the routes Hawaiians have long traveled is an important corrective to assumptions that Indigenous peoples are fixed both in place and in time. Hawaiians and their companions continue to voyage with purpose and mission. Linda H. L. Furuto's experiences on the worldwide voyage of the Hōkūle'a illuminates how Hawai'i has much to share with a world that struggles with the legacies of colonialism, the damage of rampant capitalism, and the consequences of human impacts on land and sea. When we travel, we carry our culture on our canoe. The Hōkūle'a embodies how communally powered huakaʻi is about the exchange of manaʻo (ideas) and ʻike that seek to transform the world and all of us who live upon it.

At the same time, Hawaiians have been forced to move because of political, economic, and social conditions beyond their control. Sonny Ganaden tracks the extension of the archipelago through a prison industrial system that has systematically exported disproportionate numbers of Kānaka ʻŌiwi to the arid lands of Turtle Island. In this new carceral mapping, a discriminatory legal system disperses the family and the community, and strains the ties that bind us to homelands and each other. As described in essays throughout the volume, forced dislocations have moved many peoples to Hawaiʻi—from labor-based migrations to contemporary flows of Oceanic peoples seeking refuge from military testing in their homes, rising oceans, and stunted economies. Hawaiʻi plays a key role in the Pacific region that both solidifies and challenges what it means to be island people.

Echoed across this expanded map of Hawaiʻi and the multiple diasporas that shape it is the strident call for stewardship. Kekuewa Kikiloi's contribution on Papahānaumokuākea extends the archipelago beyond the Big Eight. Reconnected with the Northwestern Hawaiian Islands, he emphasizes the kind of stewardship that is needed if we are going to co-create alternative futures.

David A. Chang

Where Is Hawai'i?
Hawaiian Diaspora and Kuleana

Where is Hawai'i? The answer is not as simple as it might seem. Of course, Hawai'i is an archipelago in the central Pacific, and we all know how to find the islands on a map. But Hawai'i is also a lāhui—it is a nation in the sense of a people. Hawaiians have been moving and settling around the globe since the end of the 1700s. The Hawaiian diaspora is a central fact of Hawai'i's past and its present. This means that Hawai'i (in the sense of the Hawaiian lāhui) is now located in sites across the globe. It remains rooted in the Hawaiian Islands, but Hawai'i can be found around the world.

For Kanaka (Native Hawaiians) and others who care about Hawai'i, this diasporic reality can shape how we understand our kuleana. Kuleana—our roles, our rights, our responsibilities—derive from our specific genealogies. They also derive from our relationship to specific lands. So how does diaspora affect kuleana? To find some specifics, let's take a tour (or rather, a detour). Let's visit a few of the sites around the world where many Kānaka landed and think about what their lives can tell us about kuleana.

We start in the early years of Hawaiian diaspora, in the first half of the nineteenth century. Labor on sea and on land brought an enormous number of Kānaka—mostly men, but a few women—to other Pacific islands and the Pacific and Atlantic coasts of the Americas. By 1845, the Hawaiian government estimated that one-fifth of young Kanaka men were working overseas. This is an astronomically high number. It dramatically reverses expectations about Hawai'i: that tourists from far away will travel across the globe to visit a tropical paradise, and that Native Hawaiians will remain on the islands to receive them, lei in hand, with aloha. Instead, one in five young Hawaiian men left the islands in the early decades of the nineteenth century. Why? Most were sailing laborers, often on whaling ships. Many worked in Pacific ports, like the four hundred Kānaka who lived in Papeete, Tahiti, or the fifty living in Paita, Peru. Hundreds more worked for fur-trading companies, like the five hundred who lived and labored in the Columbia River area in what is now called the Pacific Northwest. Meanwhile, the American whaling fleet, which was based in New England, brought many other Kānaka all the way around Cape Horn to the cold waters of New England. By mid-century, hundreds could be found in Nantucket, New Bedford, New London, and along the coast to Long Island. And all this was before the 1848 discovery of gold drew thousands of Kānaka to California, a place the United States was in the process of seizing at that very moment.

What happened to these men and women? Most probably eventually returned to Hawai'i, but an untold number did not. Many died—victims of disease, overwork, and abusive and dangerous labor conditions. Noelani Arista, Ikaika Hussey, and Lehuanani Yim have composed a mele kanikau (mourning chant) for the Kānaka who died at the New England whaling outpost of Nantucket, "nā hoa holo mamao me ke koholā lele" (those who traveled far with the leaping whale). In an oli lei (a chant for the offering of lei) for these ancestors, they tell them, "Ho'omaha 'ia mai 'oukou i kō 'oukou hā'awe / I ke aloha o kō 'oukou hoa" (You are relieved of your burden / In the love of your companions).[1] The sad loveliness of this song reminds us of the thousands of others around the world who died, unable to return home. It is right to remember their deaths.

But this powerful mele reminds us that it is also right to remember their lives. Though many died far from home, they did not disappear without a trace. Many labored for years overseas—loading and unloading ships in port, making rope, processing furs, panning and digging for gold, fishing—all of which are tasks that the exploding colonial capitalist economy of the nineteenth century demanded. Far from Hawai'i, they made lives. And they also made families, and from those families come lineages of mamo Hawai'i (branches and offshoots of Hawai'i) that live on to our times.

The nineteenth-century movement of wage laborers and gold-seekers out of Hawai'i was largely comprised of men, and when they made new homes far from Hawai'i, they often did so in relationship with local women. Tahitian and Marquesan women and 'Ōiwi men made families in the Pacific. In doing so, they knit back together lines of genealogy that had separated centuries before, as the ancestors of the Hawaiians left the archipelagoes to the south to settle in Hawai'i. A Kanaka named Pu'u, for example, married into a family from Fatu Hiva sometime around 1850. Before long, members of that family had come to Hawai'i, connecting to Hawaiians (and also to missionaries) there. Along the Pacific Coast of North America from Alaska to California, 'Ōiwi men made families with Indigenous North American women and joined their communities. Ioane Keaala came to California in the 1840s and married a Concow Maidu woman named Su-my-neh. They became ancestors to generations of Maidu people. Kānaka who made their way to New England and stayed there mostly joined neighborhoods that whites and officials often simply called "black." The men who made families mostly made them with women who were called "black." And the men who were buried in Nantucket were interred in a part of the cemetery for people who were called "black." That term was imprecise: it hid the fact that 'Ōiwi men were entering into families and communities that already reflected a mixture of African, Native American, and European ancestries—communities more precisely known as "people of color."

'Ōiwi men in the diaspora left descendants, of course, some of whom know about their Hawaiian ancestors. American Indian people all along the Pacific Coast of North America know they have Hawaiian roots. In Oregon, Cowlitz Indian residents of Kalama know that their town is named for John Kalama from Kula, Maui, and that he and many other Kānaka came and settled among the Native people there long ago. They also know that many of the residents descend from those Kānaka 'Ōiwi. The same can be said in a

▶ **People of Color**

How did diasporic Kānaka fit into racial hierarchies where they settled? How did those hierarchies shape their lives? When we look at three of the places mentioned here (Fatu Hiva, Northern California, and New England), we notice a trend: Native Hawaiians were living among, joining into, and casting their lots with people around the globe whom today we would call "people of color"—other Pacific Islanders, Native Americans, people of African descent. The term *people of color* obviously refers to skin color. It reminds us that the Western racial (and racist) system decreed that anyone who did not fit its category of "white" was a person of color.

But race in the nineteenth century (like today) was about much more than skin color or other physical markers. Race was a question of power, and it meant that whites had the power to enslave and that dark-skinned people were in danger of enslavement. Race meant whites had the power to seize land, and dark-skinned people might see their land stolen. Race meant whites had the power to seize political power, and dark-skinned people might see their homelands colonized. So when 'Ōiwi made their lives and cast their lots with American Indians, with other Pacific Islanders, and with black people in New England, it implied a racial position for Kānaka: they also were "people of color." (In contrast, note that historian Jean Barman finds that Kānaka in British Columbia could and did take on the legal privileges of whiteness.) Of course, when Hawaiians entered into the category "people of color," it was not a choice purely of their own making. Whites called Kanaka black and brown and dark and tawny, and whites had the power to define race in places like California and New England. But when these 'Ōiwi made their lives with people of color, they implicitly made a declaration of loyalty to them.

number of Native communities all along the coast. Similarly, in New England, some Wampanoag with Hawaiian ancestry have preserved the knowledge of this heritage. And some members of communities like these have reconnected with Hawai'i. Henry Azbill, a Concow Maidu with Hawaiian ancestors who lived in the Sacramento area, became deeply involved in learning about and preserving Hawaiian traditions in the 1960s and 1970s. Farther north, in Oregon, Washington, and British Columbia, American Indians with 'Ōiwi ancestors have all reconnected with Hawai'i. Sometimes these connections have taken place around genealogy. Sometimes they have centered on shared (but differing) canoe traditions. But always these connections have asserted that the shared heritage matters.

Many Kānaka moved overseas long after these early emigrants of the mid-nineteenth century. Among those are the many Hawaiian Mormons who traveled to Utah, the global center of their church. Beginning in 1889, one group of these migrants settled in a town called Iosepa. In a hamlet in Skull Valley, they made a village that struggled, strived, and survived until 1915, when the head of the Mormon Church (Joseph F. Smith) declared that a temple would be established in Lā'ie, on O'ahu. That temple would become the new center for Mormon Hawaiian life. Iosepa was (reluctantly) abandoned, as many Hawaiian Mormons gathered at Lā'ie. But more Hawaiians arrived in Utah over the years, and the state became a center of the Hawaiian diaspora. There, Kānaka built a strong community (especially in the West Valley area) and strong ties to other Polynesian Mormons who had come to Utah.

Many other 'Ōiwi have relocated to the continental United States since then, especially since the 1960s and 1970s. In some form, many of these people can be considered economic refugees. Hawai'i's economy had little room for them. The flourishing military-tourist economy of Hawai'i created a service sector that dominated the state. Waiting tables, cleaning hotel rooms, maintaining grounds, guiding tours—these were the only kinds of jobs that many 'Ōiwi were offered. Even college-educated people often found themselves working in this service economy. And while service-sector jobs are poorly paid almost everywhere, in Hawai'i they were paired with a skyrocketing cost of living, especially for housing. The same hotel/military/retirement-in-Paradise boom that was creating service-sector jobs was also swallowing up land and housing and pushing the cost of living through the roof. And so thousands upon thousands of Kānaka, finding themselves priced out of their homeland, sought options elsewhere.

Many (perhaps most) landed in the American West. Portland, Seattle, Anchorage, Oakland, Los Angeles, Las Vegas, Salt Lake City—all became centers of life in the Hawaiian diaspora. The particular shape of Hawai'i's economy was causing many Native Hawaiians to abandon their native land. This was a profound result of colonialism, and it is an ongoing reality.

A great irony is that when a U.S. colonial economy forces Kānaka out of their homeland, it pushes them onto the homelands of other Indigenous peoples subject to the U.S. empire. 'Ōiwi leave occupied Hawai'i and land in occupied Duwamish land, and Klamath land, and Ohlone land, and Goshute land, and Juaneño land, and the lands of dozens of other Native nations across the United States. Refugees from their own homeland, they become what could arguably be called settlers on somebody else's.

Of course, this is not a first for Kānaka. As we have seen, in the early and mid- nineteenth century, 'Ōiwi were leaving Hawai'i and making homes on the lands of Tahitians and Marquesans and Indigenous people of North and South America. But something has changed: in most of those places, Native people are a much smaller fraction of the population than they had been in the 1840s and 1850s. At that time, Kānaka frequently lived among and made their lives with Indigenous communities. Many entered those communities in various ways, often by forming families, having children, and settling down. In migration since the 1960s, and certainly today, this is not nearly as likely. When a person moves from Maui (pushed out by the overdevelopment of the tourist complex there) to Portland or Oakland or Orange County or Chicago, they will not automatically find themselves among many Native American people.

And this is where the question of kuleana really comes to the fore. As Indigenous people of one land who are living on the lands of other Indigenous people, what is the kuleana of 'Ōiwi in diaspora? What are their obligations, born of their genealogy and of their connections to place? Pehea lā e pono ai—what is the right way to act in such circumstances? For Kānaka in diaspora, the question is a real one.

Of course, it is not up to me to tell people what their kuleana is. But for my own purposes, it is helpful to look back to the kūpuna (ancestors) who traveled overseas long ago. Even in 1850, it was not a given that Kānaka would enter into Native communities and implicitly declare their loyalties to them. They could have worked to set themselves apart, and some presumably did. Yet many, partly by choice and partly under the constraints of racism, did make a commitment to the Native people of the lands upon which they settled. They did this so much so that they left descendants among those people.

And here we return to the dual nature of kuleana—it derives from genealogy and from a relationship to land. In very literal ways, genealogy ties Kānaka to many American Indian communities because of intermarriage in the past. Ties between the lāhui and Native nations live on in descendants of unions between ʻŌiwi and Native North American people. More figuratively, though, a shared genealogy (in the broader sense of history) ties Kanaka and other Indigenous people together. It ties them to histories of land: lands that were lost, lands they were forced from, and lands they find themselves on in the context of colonialism.

For me, as I think about my own kuleana as a Kanaka living in Minnesota, this is where genealogy and land come together. Together, they add up to a need to be connected and responsible to the American Indian people among whom I live. To be in diaspora could simply mean to be a settler. To a certain extent, there is no escaping that. But I hope that by thinking through kuleana in diaspora, there can be a way for me to arrive at a more ethical way to act in colonial circumstances by committing to Indigenous communities and their needs.

One more crucial thing: when Kānaka made connections with people of color in New England, they were not just connecting to other Indigenous people in the context of colonialism. They were connecting to other racialized people in the context of racism. The Kānaka who settled in New England among the people of color cast their lot with the racialized, binding their fates. To me, this is a heritage to look to and to claim. It is a heritage to act upon through solidarity with antiracist movements such as Black Lives Matter and in solidarity with other colonized and dispossessed peoples. After all, the colonialism that occupied Hawaiʻi is inseparable from the colonialism that occupied the lands of other racialized people. It is inseparable from the colonialism that forced the migration of other people in the bellies of slave ships, across border rivers, through refugee camps, and across seas in rubber boats.

Seen in this light, where is Hawaiʻi? It is in the Pacific, in the homeland of the Hawaiian people. It is a homeland that has, like those of so many other peoples, suffered the onslaught of Western colonialism over centuries. And Hawaiʻi is also in the descendants of the many Hawaiians who left the islands in the context of our long and ongoing colonial age and its crushing difficulties. Following the trajectories of those emigrants and their descendants helps us to understand that Hawaiʻi, for all its distinctions, is deeply tied to other colonized spaces, Indigenous peoples, and racialized communities. And from that can emerge a sense of kuleana that spreads outward across the Hawaiian diaspora and far beyond.

Note

1   Noelani Arista, Ikaika Hussey, and Lehualani Lim, "Oli lei for the Offering of Leis to Our *kupuna kane* at the African Cemetary of Nantucket" and "He Mele Kanikau, no nā make 'ana i Nanatukete o nā kupuna kane Hawai'i (Mourning Chant in Honor of the Deaths in Nantucket of the kupuna kane of Hawai'i)," in Frances Karttunen, *The Other Islanders. Part I: Nantucket's First Peoples of Color* (Nantucket, MA: Nantucket Historical Society, 2002), appendix 2, 62–64.

Linda H. L. Furuto

_____

We Never Voyage Alone

We Can Always Change Our Sails

We cannot control the winds, but we can always change our sails. When we change our sails, we often arrive not necessarily where we think we need to be, but exactly where we are supposed to be. The winds and other signs from the universe carry the voices of our ancestors, teachers, and navigators, who speak to us, if we will listen. They have taught us how to exist in the world today and sail with Indigenous wisdom while engaging twenty-first century connections as we reflect, observe, and live.

Hōkūle'a, star of gladness, is internationally renowned for the role she has played in rekindling the oceanic voyaging tradition of non-instrument wayfinding techniques based on celestial navigation. When she was built and first launched in the 1970s, it had been more than six hundred years since the last traditional voyaging canoe. Over the past forty years, the dream of reviving the legacy of exploration, courage, and ingenuity that brought the first Polynesians to the archipelago of Hawai'i is alive and flourishing. The story of _Hōkūle'a_ is about uniting people of diverse backgrounds and professions, Native Hawaiian and non-Native Hawaiian alike. This is possible because _Hōkūle'a_ is more than a voyaging canoe. She represents the common desire shared by the people of Hawai'i, the Pacific, and the world to protect our most cherished values and places from disappearing. In the words of Nainoa Thompson, Polynesian Voyaging Society (PVS) executive director, "The story of Hōkūle'a is a story of survival, rediscovery, and the restoration of pride and dignity. It is a story of a society revaluing its relationship to its island home. It is a story that is crucially important as the world's populations struggle with the ability to live in balance with our island that we call earth. It is a story that is still being written for our children and all future generations" (PVS 2018, 1).

Our kūpuna (elders) who have guided us on this voyage include Pwo (master navigator) Pius "Mau" Piailug from the Carolinian island of Satawal. Papa Mau was our visionary first teacher who navigated the 1976 maiden voyage of *Hōkūle'a*, a voyaging canoe many times bigger than his own in Micronesia, with a crew he had never met. While known for his navigational ability to wayfind and his skills as a consummate mariner, Papa Mau was especially a noble teacher dedicated to passing on this sacred knowledge to the next generation. Papa Mau taught us the importance of knowing who we are and the traditions of where we come from.

Edward Ryon Makuahanai "Eddie" Aikau is one of the most respected names in surfing and will always be remembered for his efforts to perpetuate his Native Hawaiian heritage. He was the first lifeguard hired by the city and county of Honolulu to work on the North Shore of O'ahu, and not one life was lost while he served as a lifeguard at Waimea Bay. The saying "Eddie would go" refers to his aloha and ability to rescue in impossible situations. In 1978, on the second voyage of *Hōkūle'a* from Hawai'i to Tahiti, the canoe developed a leak in one of the hulls and capsized in stormy weather. In an attempt to save his crew and *Hōkūle'a*, Eddie bravely paddled toward Lāna'i on his surfboard and was never seen again. Eddie showed us the true meaning of courage in the face of fear. His plaque on the front of *Hōkūle'a* reads, "No greater love hath a man than this, that he lay down his life for his friends."

Myron Bennett "Pinky" Thompson provided leadership as PVS president for almost two decades before his passing in 2001. Uncle Pinky was a social worker, a community leader, and a force for the betterment of Native Hawaiians and all of Hawai'i's people. Uncle Pinky provided the counsel of leadership through challenging situations and reminded us that 90 percent of voyaging is planning. If we don't have a plan, we don't sail; if we don't sail, we don't move forward.

Another kupuna who understood the trials we face and the role of education in overcoming them was Colonel Lacy Veach. Raised in Hawai'i, Lacy was an astronaut with NASA and saw the close connections between the frontiers of space and ocean science. Lacy was an optimist, but he also felt a great concern over the imbalance between human needs and the limited resources of our small planet. He urged us to think about the future, stating, "You don't know how beautiful island earth is until you see it from space. Hawai'i needs to become the laboratory and the school to help us relearn how to live well on islands" (PVS 2018, 2).

The founders of PVS—Native Hawaiian artist Herb Kawainui Kāne, anthropologist Ben Finney, and waterman Tommy Holmes—not only inspired us but held us accountable to our visions. Their names are engraved on *Hōkūleʻa*, with the reminder that we are part of a story strengthened by individuals who sailed in solidarity. Founded on a legacy of Pacific exploration, PVS seeks to perpetuate the art and science of traditional voyaging and the spirit of exploration through educational programs that inspire students and their communities to respect and care for themselves, each other, and their natural and cultural environments. This vision is open to all who are invested in these principles and philosophies.

Our kūpuna, Native Hawaiian and non-Native Hawaiian alike, have shown us how to make transformative decisions and follow the winds to new destinations. With their guidance, *Hōkūleʻa* has come to represent a common symbol shared by people around the world to protect our values, cultures, and places through changing times and tides. Our kūpuna provide ever-present direction from the past with concomitant hope for the future.

Mālama Honua Worldwide Voyage: Stories of Landings

Over the past four decades, *Hōkūleʻa* has sailed more than 160,000 nautical miles, including the most recent 2013–17 Mālama Honua Worldwide Voyage. The mission of mālama honua—to care for island earth—is to connect Indigenous wisdom with innovative twenty-first century learning in an effort to map a course for the future. The Mālama Honua Worldwide Voyage sail plan included more than 150 ports, 20 countries and territories, and 8 United Nations Educational, Scientific and Cultural Organization (UNESCO) Marine World Heritage sites. During the voyage, we visited communities across the Pacific, Indian, and Atlantic Oceans.

In 2014, I became a crew member on the first international leg, from Hawaiʻi to Tahiti, and participated in subsequent legs to American Samoa, Samoa, Olohega (Swain's Island), Aotearoa (New Zealand), South Africa, Virginia, Washington, D.C., Mannahatta (New York City), and back to Hawaiʻi. My kuleana (responsibilities, obligations, authority) on and off the canoe are apprentice navigator and education specialist. For me, voyaging contains some fundamental questions: In the defining moments when the winds shift, how do we frame our paradigms and practices? What are we willing to sail for on land and sea? What guides our internal compasses throughout the journey, and how do we know we have arrived? Given my kuleana, the stories of landings in particular are moments of meaningful and lasting exchange.

American Samoa

I initially thought the job of the apprentice navigator was to arrive at a specific destination within the parameters of the plan. On the Mālama Honua Worldwide Voyage around the Samoan Islands, we planned to visit a number of locations, but we were not able to because of directional winds. Instead, we returned early to Tutuila, the main island in American Samoa, where we were able to interact with about twenty elementary, middle, and high schools.

While at Matatula Elementary School, in the eastern district of Tutuila Island, I had an experience that redirected the vision of my journey. After our educational presentation, the class expressed their appreciation, and an eight-year-old child stood up and started speaking in the *matai* (chiefly language), which was translated for me. At the end he said, "Thank you for teaching us what is not written in our textbooks." I was deeply and profoundly moved, and I responded, "Mahalo nui loa and fa'afetai tele lava to your tua'a [ancestors] who bravely sailed from the Navigator Islands of Samoa to Hawai'i. It is because of you we are here today, and it is because of you we are able to sail around the world."

As we work to protect cultural and environmental resources for our children's futures, our Pacific voyaging traditions teach us to venture beyond the horizon in order to connect and learn with others. Voyaging is a means by which we engage in bridging traditional and new technologies to live sustainably, while sharing, learning, creating global relationships, and discovering the wonders of this place we all call home. The children remind us why we do the things we do, and together we are writing anew the textbooks of island earth.

South Africa

Hōkūle'a arrived in Cape Town, South Africa—approximately halfway around the world from her home in Hawai'i—at the end of 2015. The experiences provided the background text of peace, war, colonialism, postcolonialism, and postapartheid, some of which is written in history books but much of which is not. During our time in South Africa, *Hōkūle'a*'s crew members visited Robben Island with a former political prisoner who showed us the cell where Nelson Mandela was held for eighteen years. We journeyed to Mossel Bay, where the origin of human civilization dates back 162,000 years, and we ascended 3,500 feet to the top of sacred Table Mountain, where we supped on the precipice of one of the seven new natural wonders of the world. There

Kamehameha Schools and Hālau Kū Māna children from Hawai'i engaging in cultural exchanges with children from St. Mary's School in South Africa. *Photograph by Linda Furuto.*

we saw and felt the palpable physical, cultural, and spiritual relationships from mountain to sea.

At a rural township school, we watched as children from South Africa and Hawai'i engaged in intercultural exchanges as part of educational outreach. After a group of Kamehameha Schools and Hālau Kū Māna children shared mele (songs) and hula (dance) from Hawai'i, children from St. Mary's School in South Africa asked if they could borrow the pahu (drum) and then proceeded to wrap us in a lei of beauty, power, and emotion in the rhythms they created. Nainoa Thompson and I leaned back on a parked car taking it all in, then he exhaled and quietly said, "Now I know what world peace looks like." The children know who they are and where they come from, and they are writing their own histories in pulsating beats. We must listen to the construction of their words and songs to hear messages of equity, justice, reverence for life, and love of humankind.

An excerpt from "Ho'oheno kēia no 'Akipīhopa Desmond Mpilo Tutu" (2015), a haku mele (poetic text) composed for Archbishop Desmond Mpilo

Tutu by Randie Kamuela Fong, states, "Ubuntu ē, ubuntu ho'i, Ubuntu ke aloha o ka mauli ola . . . Ho'oheno ē" ("Ubuntu—a quality that includes the essential human virtues—compassion and humanity—is the very essence of life . . . let it be cherished"). The Kamehameha Schools and Hālau Kū Māna children performed this in recognition of Archbishop Desmond Mpilo Tutu's dedication to advancing human rights in his homeland and for people around the world. When we work for peace, we must recognize that we are more often alike than we are different.

U.S. East Coast

These words echoed in my mind as *Hōkūle'a* made her way back to the U.S. and I rejoined the PVS crew from Virginia to Washington, D.C., to Mannahatta (New York City) in May–June 2016. The crew members were filled with excitement, engaging keiki (children) to kūpuna in educational outreach; paying homage to the First Nations; and interacting with sights, sounds, and wonders on this historic leg. It inspired us to consider how far we have come and how much we have yet to explore.

En route to Mannahatta, the crew members requested permission from the First Nations to enter their lands in the Chesapeake Bay. As *Hōkūle'a* approached from the distance, the original stewards gathered at the dock waiting for her arrival. Chief Billy Tayac of the Piscataway Nation and Chairman Francis Gray of the Piscataway Conoy Tribe gave the signal that allowed the PVS crew members to join them ashore, and then they extended an invitation to participate in a solemn ceremony. The Hawai'i delegation entered with traditional genealogy chants, mele, and hula, acknowledging respect for our Native American hosts. Pwo Kālepa Baybayan formally requested permission to enter the Piscataway land and reflected on the mission of the Mālama Honua Worldwide Voyage. To seal the ceremony, Chief Tayac resolutely expressed, "You are the second vessel to enter this area in four hundred years, and you are the first to ask for permission. It is our great hope that together we will be able to reverse some of the damage that was caused by the first vessel."

Requesting permission to enter lands continued as *Hōkūle'a* arrived in Mannahatta, where she was welcomed by thousands of supporters. Through our interactions with the Indigenous peoples of each of the communities we visited, we engaged with them in a way grounded in the spirit and nature of the people who first settled these lands. The arrival event began with a traditional ceremonial welcome by Native American tribes including the Ramapough Lenape Nation, Delaware Nation at Moraviantown, Shinnecock Indian Nation, Unkechaug Indian Nation, Mohegan Tribe, and Haudenosaunee

Hōkūleʻa arriving into Mannahatta. *Photograph by Naʻalehu Anthony.*

Confederacy. As each PVS crew member disembarked *Hōkūleʻa*, a Native American smudging protocol and smoke ritual was performed for spiritual and physical cleansing. A traditional Hawaiian ʻaha ʻawa, or ʻawa ceremony, was held and hula hālau (hula groups/schools) from New York and Hawaiʻi offered performances. From the heart of Mannahatta, the Ramapough Lenape Nation stated, "We have come home. You have inspired the next generation of our navigators to know who they are and where they come from" (PVS 2018, 1).

The educational stories of hope we encountered are powerful. On the one hand, we observed the realities of sea level rising in Cape Town, the coastline eroding in the Chesapeake Bay, and oyster populations declining at Governor's Island in Mannahatta. On the other, we learned how comprehensive, integrated stewardship plans are being developed for agricultural operations, forests, shorelines, wetlands, reserves, and wildlife preservation. Around the world, stories of hope highlight the work being done to intimately connect students with experiential, place-based learning. For example, through monitoring water quality, the Chesapeake Bay has become a classroom for real-world applications such as determining when an algal bloom is going to occur, measuring oxygen levels, and examining the effects of high bacterial counts. Students, teachers, and community members analyze data from both the present and the past in order to make predictions about the future (Chesapeake Bay Foundation 2018). These are lessons that will save our collective home.

Navigating Our Kuleana

The experiences circumnavigating the globe bring us back to Hawaiʻi and navigating our kuleana through collective impact in sustainable educational transformations. As a teacher, I have thought deeply about what this means in our schools, communities, and places we call home. Now on land, I bring the lessons of the *Hōkūleʻa* to the classroom by addressing issues of equitable and quality education through the field of ethnomathematics, which is grounded in diverse cultural systems and ways of knowing. In the process, students and teachers experience rigorous, relevant, and sustainable examples of mathematics that bridge Indigenous wisdom and twenty-first century learning. For example, students learn about proportions and ratios of sails, ocean currents, and wind dynamics through technology and build canoes using natural resources from their environment. They then use their model canoes to perform experiments, such as researching water quality and collecting marine debris, in their school communities. These discoveries promote the type of holistic education envisioned by our kūpuna Papa Mau, Eddie Aikau, Uncle Pinky Thompson, Colonel Lacy Veach, Herb Kāne, Ben Finney, and Tommy Holmes.

A key aspect of the work in ethnomathematics is that it is guided by PVS values: mālama (to care for), aloha (to love), ʻimi ʻike (to seek knowledge), lokomaikaʻi (to share with each other), naʻau pono (to nurture a deep sense of justice), and olakino maikaʻi (to live healthy). Values-based education enriches the classroom by cultivating students who engage in learning through a sense of purpose and a sense of place. Similar to experiences in Samoa, South Africa, Mannahatta, and the Chesapeake Bay, we have worked to develop contextualized and relevant mathematics lessons by building on the strengths of students. In the process, we provide practices that challenge, engage, and empower their identities as authors of mathematics. As students solve rigorous and worthwhile mathematical tasks, ethnomathematics amplifies their voices and mathematical ideas, supports collaborative classroom communities, and leverages mathematics as a sense-making tool for personal and social change. One teacher commented that "taking an ethnomath approach means that you are not only having students do abstract math on a chalkboard, or read about scientific theories in a textbook. They

Children building models of *Hōkūleʻa* through ethnomathematics lessons before departure on the first international leg of the Mālama Honua Worldwide Voyage in Hilo, Hawaiʻi. *Photograph by Linda Furuto.*

are also having experiences solving technical problems hands-on. Students gain conceptual understanding of an idea, and develop the kinds of relationships that Hawaiians and other Indigenous cultures know to be essential . . . the relationships are there, waiting to be reclaimed."[1]

With the support of community organizations and research institutions, we have developed the world's first academic program in ethnomathematics at the University of Hawaiʻi at Mānoa. As we work to become a model Indigenous-serving University of Hawaiʻi System (UHS), a new academic graduate-level program focused on preparing teachers as leaders to provide ethnomathematics instruction in their schools and communities strengthens the educational pipeline from early childhood education through graduate studies. As stated by UHS President David Lassner, "The new ethnomathematics program will become a model for other programs interested in creating alternate pathways towards traditional academic goals."[2] Former president of the International Commission on Mathematical Instruction, Ferdinando Arzarello, adds, "Its creation opens new paths for research, where mathematics can be looked at from fresh and exciting standpoints. It will certainly promote international cooperation within different communities of researchers, from mathematics to anthropology through a long list of intertwined disciplines."[3]

The opportunity to fulfill my kuleana as an education specialist and apprentice navigator is clear. I belong to a strong genealogical line of voyagers on land and sea who have gifted me with the knowledge and responsibility to teach the next generation. Our children inherit the world we create and give them. In the defining moments when the winds shift, our paradigms and practices are solidified as we adjust accordingly.

Reflections

About ten years ago, when I first started voyaging, my teacher Pwo Bruce Blankenfeld asked me a question while we sailed on *Hōkūleʻa* on a clear, moonlit evening: "How many people do you think are on *Hōkūleʻa*?" I looked around and counted the crew members. "Thirteen," I replied. He then firmly and compassionately counseled, "No . . . there are thousands of people on *Hōkūleʻa*. They are checking lines, watching the sails, walking around the deck, and making sure we get to where we're supposed to be." I have learned that once we learn to find our way, we can never be lost no matter where we go.

Hōkūleʻa's legacy and vision stand as witnesses that each of us was born with purpose and meaning to step up, imagine, and innovate through our internal compasses in all kinds of weather. We honor this legacy by continuing to voyage and by connecting the classroom to the ecological, cultural, historical, and political contexts in which schooling takes place. We know we have a lot of work ahead of us, but we also have calls to action; a global network of educators; and healthy, vibrant stories of inspiration. We hold to the sacred knowledge that we are never alone and that we sail the oceanic highways with past, present, and future generations.

Notes

1   Quote from an unnamed teacher participant at Mālama Honua Fair and Summit homecoming on June 18, 2017.

2   David Lassner letter to the Hawaiʻi Teacher Standards Board in support of the addition of ethnomathematics as a field of licensure, April 21, 2017.

3 Ferdinando Arzarello, in a University of Hawai'i System News story video, January 11, 2019, accessed March 15, 2019, https://www.hawaii.edu/news/2018/01/14/first-ethnomathematics-academic-program/.

References

Fong, R. "Ho'oheno Kēia No 'Akipīhopa Desmond Mpilo Tutu." Honolulu: Kamehameha Schools, 2015.

"How We Save the Bay." Chesapeake Bay Foundation. 2019. Accessed March 8, 2019. http://www.cbf.org/.

Kyselka, Will. An Ocean in Mind. Honolulu: University of Hawai'i Press, 1987.

Low, Sam. Hawaiki Rising. Honolulu: Island Heritage, 2013.

"The Story of Hōkūle'a." 2019. Polynesian Voyaging Society (PVS). Accessed March 8, 2019. http://www.hokulea.com/voyages/our-story/.

Sonny Ganaden

Law of the Canoe

Reckoning Colonialism and Criminal Justice in the Pacific

Everything looks different from the seat of a canoe. From that vantage point outside Kewalo Basin, Honolulu looks like a far smaller town than it does from land, fronting an endless southern sea, as if the opposite vertices of the Polynesian triangle are merely paddling distance just over the horizon. This practice is typical for our canoe club Ānuenue (named after the Hawaiian word for rainbow): a short run to the buoy outside of the surf break at Bowls, and then a sprint to the buoy a kilometer off Lēʻahi, Diamond Head—where watermen such as Duke Kahanamoku and Tom Blake tested their mettle and created a contemporary global culture of surfing and outrigger canoe racing nearly a century ago—then circle the buoy and return to Kewalo. Honolulu traffic hums and pulses in the late afternoon. The waves for today's practice are coming in choruses too, and soon the workday is forgotten, overtaken by the focus of physicality and the ephemeral joy of the sunset sea.

A few weeks earlier and a world away, I saw the proverbial end of the rainbow in the Sonoran desert. I was driving to see a client at Saguaro Correctional Center, run by a corporation called Core Civic, a private prison an hour's drive southeast of Phoenix, Arizona. Saguaro presently holds nearly two thousand of Hawaiʻi's citizens. Almost all the men incarcerated in Saguaro are Hawaiian or Pacific Islanders, housed on lands once controlled by the Oʻodham peoples, in what is now the town of Eloy in Pinal County, Arizona. Eloy is known for its federal, state, and private prisons, as well as its chest-caving heat. The sunsets, also spectacular, appear like they do on postcards of the American southwest.

To get there we drove past the strip malls of Casa Grande, the nearby town named after the ruins of thirteenth-century structures created by the

Hohokam peoples. I recognized saguaro cacti from Western movies, some four-story-tall desert giants, and paloverde trees, their trunks and branches the same pea green as their leaves, as if the creator was allowed only a solitary palette. Tumbleweeds piled along the windward side of fences that stretched past the horizon. We passed several of the private prison's black-painted transport buses, lined up as if in a funerary procession. A thought coursed through me: this prison is so far from the sea, so far banished from the community these pa'ahao (prisoners) come from. Only an absurd and unjust legal system could maintain this arrangement; a perverse remapping of Hawai'i through the capitalist carceral system. Another wave of thought: the ideologies that justify this arrangement, rooted in the legal fictions which supported colonialism in the 19th century, can only be changed by decolonizing the law in the 21st century.

A decolonized concept of the law could demolish and reconstruct criminal justice. Hawai'i has a troubled, overcrowded prison system, which includes four prisons and four jails on the islands, and the private prison contracts on the continent. The state of Hawai'i has housed inmates in corporate prisons since 1994, when it entered into a contract with Corrections Corporation of America (CCA), which later rebranded itself as Core Civic. The CCA was allowed to choose whom it housed from among the state's male and female inmate populations, choosing healthy inmates with long sentences, shuttling them across facilities in Alabama, Arizona, California, Colorado, Florida, Minnesota, Mississippi, Montana, and New Jersey. In 2008, the women who were sent to private prisons were brought home after lawsuits regarding sexual assault by guards. Most of the male pa'ahao were eventually consolidated in Saguaro. Core Civic also operates numerous immigrant detention centers and has seen its stock ascend since the beginning of the Trump administration.

The private prison contract resulted from decades of structural inequality in the United States and Hawai'i. The American drug war, initiated by the Nixon administration and expanded through the 1980s, included mandatory federal sentences for crimes and was subsequently adopted by states. At the same time, economic disparity on the islands increased. Land speculation expanded. In the early 1990s, the price of residential land throughout Hawai'i increased exponentially. A methamphetamine crisis exploded. Hawaiians were disproportionately affected. The war on drugs combined with these economic stressors lead to overcrowding in O'ahu Community Correctional Center and Hālawa Detention Center, and to numerous problems with failing infrastructure, guards, health concerns, lawsuits, and deaths. A 1993 lawsuit by the American Civil Liberties Union led to a consent decree with the state, which mandated basic requirements in these facilities but provided no state funds to develop them. From the perspective of a private prison corporation that could sell the state a contract to house its prisoners without actually fixing its issues, Hawaiʻi was the perfect customer. Because facilities have deteriorated in Hawaiʻi since 1994, the contract has expanded under every state governor since its inception.

Several audits and state task force reports have slammed the private prison arrangement. The Native Hawaiian Justice Task Force Report was submitted to the legislature in January 2013. Nine members representing the criminal justice system were appointed to the task force, and 157 people testified, including legislators, judges, activists, the formerly incarcerated, and current paʻahao. I was the "lead writer" and, with a team from the Office of Hawaiian Affairs, compiled much of the research and testimony into a narrative form. A unanimous recommendation was that "prisoners held out of state should be returned. The State should make the return of inmates a top priority . . . and inmates should be returned as soon as practicable, consistent with public safety." Like other state-sponsored, well-intentioned documents, it was ignored. Recent task forces criticize the practice of pretrial detention and the development of a new Oʻahu Community Corrections Center without the development of best practices, as the current facility will be demolished in anticipation of the Honolulu rail transit system and the continuing gentrification of urban Honolulu. Death, sex assault, riots, and criminal behavior by guards have become common in local news. Despite decades of data, in 2014, legislative bills were passed to allow for a new facility to be built on Oʻahu by a private prison contractor for the amount of $498 million. Core Civic lobbied aggressively for this option.

Nothing will change unless our most deeply held concepts of justice are reformed. From the perspective of Indigenous peoples and people of color in America, the criminal justice system is broken. Mass incarceration is and has been used as a tool of oppression. With the overthrow of the Hawaiian Kingdom came a restructuring of Hawaiʻi's law: everything about being Hawaiian became de facto illegal, including access to the sea, communal ownership of land, and the ability to practice traditional forms of dance and sport. Poverty continues to be criminalized throughout the islands, with draconian laws regarding bail, and state and county ordinances that attack the survival behavior of those with the fewest resources. The lawful practice of banishing Hawaiʻi's inmates to private prisons is the ultimate expression of American colonialism in the twenty-first century. It is the result of centuries of systemic oppression of Indigenous communities, their cultures, and their displacement from their lands. The law must change.

Despite, or possibly because of, alienation from land, family, and culture, the Native men in Saguaro have created their own practices of resiliency. In preparation for the annual Makahiki celebration, they practice hula, chant, and Indigenous forms of leadership. Men prepare meals together, worship together, and support each other's progress. These programs are not funded or state sanctioned. When their cultural implements were confiscated without due process in 2012, several inmates sued with the assistance of the nonprofit organization Native Hawaiian Legal Corporation. They eventually won. A Hawai'i Supreme Court case did not outlaw the use of private prisons, but it did extend the rights of the Hawai'i Constitution to pa'ahao and preserved their right to cultural and religious practices. The stories of the men and women who have been shuttled across the Pacific Ocean and part of the United States, shackled in corporate buses and forced to survive violence, banishment, and maltreatment, are as numerous as they are abhorrent. The Native Hawaiian Justice Task Force Report is filled with them, as are several recent film documentaries and works of journalism. The systemic racism inherent in American mass incarceration has historical roots in the racist disenfranchisement of African American communities after the Civil War. This history has become common knowledge as a result of difficult, diligent work by academics, cultural practitioners, and artists. The parallel interrogation of mass incarceration in the Pacific is currently underway.

Any legal argument validating the present situation must be cast in the light of historical context and evaluated against the lived experience of the diverse peoples of the Pacific. Lessons from around the world are unanimous: mass incarceration does not work to make communities safe. What does work are collaborative, community-based restorative justice programs; evidence-based models for rehabilitation; addiction treatment; job training; the zealous preservation of due process; and traditional cultural practices that perpetuate a sense of belonging and pride. In communities where basic human needs are met, crime is rare. For the small percentage of people who are a legitimate danger to society, municipalities should maintain small, well-managed prisons. Much else is colonialism embedded in criminal law.

To decolonize criminal law, we articulate a demand for human rights. In doing so, we return to the canoe, and to the first law of the nation of Hawai'i, which comes from canoe culture. Kamehameha I established Ke Kānāwai Māmalahoe (the law of the splintered paddle) as the first royal edict or law upon the unification of the Hawaiian Islands under his reign. Historians explain that Native Hawaiians had developed an endogenous concept of human rights on the islands over the course of centuries. As the story goes, Kamehameha I was a kolohe (mischievous) young warrior when he chased a commoner who, in self-defense, struck Kamehameha with a canoe paddle, shattering it upon his head. As a divine king years later, while developing Hawai'i's original jurisprudence, Kamehameha reflected on that moment. He established the law from this experience: "E hele ka 'elemakule, ka luahine, a me ke kama a moe i ke ala," or "let every elderly person, woman and child lie by the roadside in safety." As the first law of the nation of Hawai'i, it became the law of the territory of Hawai'i, and then of the state of Hawai'i. Under the modern Hawai'i Revised Statutes, "The state retains the power to provide for the safety of the people from crimes against persons and property." Ke Kānāwai Māmalahoe sets principles of human rights and public safety as the foundation of Hawaiian law.

Legal structures can both build and destroy. As the Kānāwai illustrates, the law is also built of metaphors. They shape the way we conceptualize our most deeply held values. Most of the personal protections articulated in the U.S. Bill of Rights and subsequent constitutional amendments are similar reactions to violence and subjugation. The same can be said for nation-states that overtly decolonized during the twentieth century. Decolonizing the law in the twenty-first century, then, is tied up in the intentional use of legal metaphors and what exactly the political state is allowed to do with our bodies.

The canoe has guided decolonial visions of the law before and could again, as it did during the Hawaiian renaissance and the 1978 Hawaii Constitutional Convention. The young state, made up of a diverse populace born of Native Hawaiians and the descendants of plantation labor, expected jurisprudence that reflected communal values. In 1973, William S. Richardson, Hawai'i's first Native Hawaiian chief justice since the overthrow, developed water rights unique to the United States by putting the resource under the management of the state, in trust for its residents. The Hawai'i Supreme Court described the public trust doctrine as "the right of the people to have the waters protected for their use [which] demands adequate provision for traditional and customary Hawaiian rights, wildlife, maintenance of ecological balance and scenic beauty, and the preservation and enhancement of the waters." It was an act of judicial activism: by citing the laws of the Kingdom of Hawai'i, Chief Justice Richardson connected the health of humanity on the islands to the health of its environment and to the rights of Indigenous people. Pacific legal traditions, which intersect human and environmental protections, predate by centuries the embrace of capitalism and the tourism industry by the state of Hawai'i. In the law of the Kingdom, the sea was largely public domain, up to the high tide mark on land, where one could park a canoe safely. After a century of the application of American law, this legal right was restored by the Hawai'i Supreme Court under Chief Justice Richardson. Modern legal scholars cite those decisions as the work of a "decolonized" mind.

State politicians have all the reports, data, and narrative necessary to radically change criminal law. What is necessary is the collective power to do so. Like paddling a canoe, envisioning a new legal future through decolonization is an act of movement and dreaming. It is both process and physical methodology. Exerting labor on a canoe with others is a form of collective movement on the sea. No metaphor is perfect, and canoe paddling is fraught with the same shortcomings as American baseball. But as a living symbol of the actual practices of the Pacific, it retains metaphoric merit. A tenet of decolonial thought is the importance of Indigenous and endemic culture for developing policies that are relevant and actionable.

A more radical, jurisdictional concept of the canoe is necessary. A decolonial discussion of the law would adapt and broaden concepts from the diversity of the Pacific, with an emphasis on the human rights articulated in founding documents. We must borrow from all legal disciplines and from minds outside the law, from Judge Learned Hand to writer Epeli Hau'ofa. From the Anglo-American common law of torts we ask, Who has breached the duty to create a fair criminal justice system? What are its specific causes? What is the damage? From Pacific models of restorative justice practices we broaden the questions: How do we right historic wrongs without the bitterness of blame and create a healing criminal justice system that works for the historically disenfranchised, all while honoring those who came before us and those who will follow? Articulating collective trauma is necessary as a baseline of understanding, but it is too depressing as a point of community organizing. We can instead hold forth a communal metaphor of the canoe, take lessons from all the places the culture of the canoe alights, and look to those communities for best practices and shared strategy.

The metaphor of the canoe implicates our bodies and how our bodies can be used in concert for the greater good. From afar, paddling can be mad boring to watch. But the perspective within the canoe is entirely different: one of focused labor, of breathing, of muscles contracting and expanding. Time contracts to the rate of the stroke and stretches to the expanse of the ocean. Most of what I know about the Pacific—the diverse peoples of Oceania and the ocean itself—I know from experiences in and around these vessels. ʻŌlelo noʻeau, ubiquitous proverbs of Hawaiʻi compiled by Mary Ka-wena Pukui—which include traditional common sayings such as "Pupukahi i holomua" (Unite to move forward) and "E lauhoe mai na waʻa; i ke ka, i ka hoe; i ka hoe, i ke ka; pae aku i ka ʻāina" (Paddle together, bail, paddle; paddle, bail; paddle toward the land)—make sense only when you're stuck with five sort-of friends trying to get back to the parking lot without flipping onto the sharp reef after a sprint to the buoy.

For the men in Saguaro prison, their families, and the victims of crime, working together has been an organic necessity because of a lack of govern-mental support in the form of adequately funded programs, services, and culturally appropriate models. As a community organizer, I have learned les-sons the hard way. In a canoe, an overbearing individual can be a hindrance if she or he is not working with the crew. A less powerful group, if entering the water together and exiting the water together, breathing in unison, can be fast, efficient, and beautiful to watch.

I can speak only for what has worked for me: Use your body in advo-cacy, put your physical self in places where you will change and evolve with others, taking a seat in government, a canoe, a classroom, or a boardroom. Forgive yourself and others often when working together. The laws of Hawaiʻi will improve for the entire community if we promote utopian visions and legal concepts that support open and civil societies developed from our rich and contentious history. Criminal law will become equitable. Private prisons will be illegal. Despite seemingly overwhelming waves of resistance, we will reach calmer seas with our heads up, working together, reaching out farther toward the horizon.

Kekuewa Kikiloi

Reconnecting with Ancestral Islands

A Guide to Papahānaumokuākea
(the Northwestern Hawaiian Islands)

The manu o kū bird (literally "bird of Kū" or white tern; *Cygis alba roths-childi*) flew overhead and the wind rushed against my face as the traditional double-hulled voyaging canoe *Hōkūle'a* was nearing the island of Ni'ihau, making its way back toward our home. As the canoe moved with amazing speed, I could feel the rise and fall of its weight riding the crests of the waves as it traveled across the open ocean. We had a sense of empowerment and achievement: we had just spent the past few days at sea traveling to a distant island called Nihoa, in the northwest, past our main chain. Nihoa is part of the Northwestern Hawaiian Islands and is the first of ten smaller islands that extend past the main Hawaiian chain and have been largely forgotten over the past century. This 2003 voyage marked a new age of exploration for us, rediscovering the extents of our homeland. Stretching roughly 1,200 miles, the Northwestern Hawaiian Islands is a vast oceanic region with open blue waters and sky as far as the eye can see. We were full of pride because this was the first time Native Hawaiians had voyaged to these islands using traditional noninstrumental navigation in the past hundred years. We had reengaged our ancestors through traditional ceremonies on these islands and began the process of spiritual reconnection. These actions would shape the trajectory of the Hawaiian movement, solidifying Native interest in reclaiming this part of our homeland and securing long-term protection of the resources of this magnificent place.

Hōkūle'a, a traditional double-hulled Hawaiian voyaging canoe created in the 1970s, has been a symbol of hope and cultural revitalization for our people. It has had many achievements over the past two decades, voyaging successfully to all the various corners of the Pacific and making important connections with our oceanic cousins. This trip into the Northwestern Hawaiians Islands, however, allowed us to understand our home and a greater aspect of ourselves as Native Hawaiians as we reconnected with a region associated with the spirits of our ancient gods and ancestors. Halealoha Ayau, a Hawaiian cultural practitioner, organized the voyage, traveled on the canoe, and conducted traditional ceremonies on the island. While in transit back home to Oʻahu, he reflected, "I was totally humbled to watch them navigate at night, and totally blown away to wake up the next morning and see Nihoa without the use of any instruments. I mean, talk about ancestral connection when you are using the moon . . . the stars . . . when you are keenly observant of everything—the wind, the motion of the waves, everything that is happening. To me that is ancestral connection, because those are our ancestors." This voyage was a catalyst for community activism that would fight for the protection of this region.

We grew up in Hawaiʻi, and the roots of our miseducation can be linked to normalization of Western worldviews in American colonial schools that taught us that our own homeland was an island chain limited only to the eight main Hawaiian Islands. This idea of "eight main islands" is strikingly peculiar when one considers that our "main" chain actually comprises eleven islands (some of which are smaller islets, like Molokini, Lehua, and Kaʻula, but are still culturally significant and substantial enough to not be ignored). Also, when you geographically expand past these "main" islands and include all the atolls, shoals, banks, and coral reefs that extend to the northwest, this total number climbs to *twenty-one* main islands that make up our homeland. The entire Hawaiian archipelago represents the longest and oldest chain of islands on Earth. Existing over 70 million years, it represents the full range of geological stages of an island's life cycle, from birth to death, each island being created one by one on a relatively fixed hotspot underlying a tectonic plate slowly moving northwest.

The Northwestern Hawaiian Islands are made up of ten landforms along this linear trail that are much smaller; they are known by the names Nihoa, Necker (Mokumanamana or Haena), French Frigate Shoals (Lalo), Gardner Pinnacles (Onu-nui and Onu-iki), Laysan Island (Kamole), Lisianski Island (Kapou), Maro Reef (Ka Moku o Kamohoaliʻi), Pearl and Hermes (Manawai), Midway Atoll (Kuaihelani), and Kure Atoll (Holani-ku). These islands represent the latter half of the geological life stages, as they are subsiding and eroding, changing from high volcanic island fragments that are rocky with

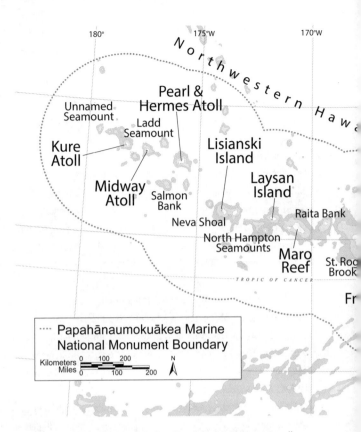

Map of the Hawaiian Islands and the location of the Northwestern Hawaiian Islands (Papahānaumokuākea Marine National Monument). *Courtesy of the National Oceanic and Atmospheric Administration.*

poor soil development to low-lying, sandy atolls with complex mazes of reefs and banks.

Together, the islands in this section alone span about 1,200 miles, and their surrounding nearshore, offshore, and open waters comprise an enormous 350 million acres of ocean that is teeming with marine and avian wildlife; high rates of endemism; and an underwater world comprising submerged reefs, sunken islands, banks, and over 215 seamounts. This region is entirely wild, with birds, fish, and other marine life that have had little or no interaction with humans or the impacts associated with us. With the

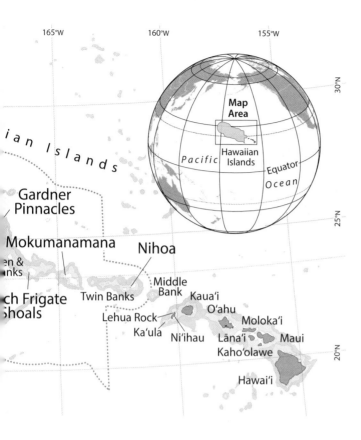

Northwestern Hawaiian Islands encompassing such a vast area and having such rich natural resources, how could our community forget it?

Culturally, this region was significant because it was tied to Hawaiian origins and cosmological stories of creation. The region was considered sacred and a place of primordial darkness from which all life sprang and to which all spirits return after death. The Hawaiian archipelago was understood to be made up of two realms: pō, a place reserved for the ancestral gods and spirits of the deceased (the Northwestern Hawaiian Islands); and ao, the realm of the living (the main Hawaiian Islands). Two of the islands centrally located in the middle of the archipelago—Nihoa and Mokumanamana—were in a unique position as the axis between the worlds of the supernatural and the living.

Mokumanamana. *Photograph by Kekuewa Kikiloi.*

These two islands worked together, with Mokumanamana primarily used as a religious site at which to petition the gods. Its landscape is dominated by thirty-four individual heiau (temples) and were used for ritual purposes. Nihoa served as an annex where elites could rest and gain provisions. Our ancient chiefs would access this region as a rite of passage to commemorate the source of origins and mana (power), and of authority as derived by the ancestral gods. The occupation and use of these islands represent one of the earliest signs of Hawaiian religious activity. For over four hundred years (ca. AD 1400–1815) the islands were used as a ritual center of power supported by an extensive voyaging interaction sphere that supported long-term settlement of the islands.

From the time of Western contact, several falsehoods have been created, perpetuated, and ingrained in our consciousness over time. One of the most damaging is the portrayal of this region in the context of mystery and abandonment. This myth began early as soon as European ships traveled through this region on transit between continents. They assumed that the Northwestern Hawaiian Islands were abandoned before Western contact, as they saw physical evidence of human settlement, such as cultural sites and remains, but the islands appeared to be void of people. These concepts are dangerous because they imply that this area was just empty space for the taking or that we had somehow relinquished claim to it or do not belong to it anymore. Throughout the post-contact period (after AD 1793), the Hawaiian Islands emerged as a nation-state, forming into the Kingdom of Hawai'i. Several of the remote Northwestern Hawaiian Islands were formally claimed as territory and annexed. In 1893, however, the Kingdom of Hawai'i was overthrown by the provisional government, which later consolidated title of the archipelago and then ceded it to the United States without a formalized treaty of annexation.

Through the early 1900s, these myths became even more prevalent within anthropology and archaeology as researchers from local museums did research on the region, furthering this idea of mystery. When looking at the material record left behind by the past, they began to cast doubt on whether the historic remains even belonged to Native Hawaiians. They often speculated on whether they could have originated from early migrant Pacific Islanders from the Society Islands or the Marquesas Islands. In 1928, Kenneth P. Emory, widely regarded as the forefather of modern Pacific Archaeology, once said, "[It was] insufficient to determine who these early occupants were or why they were there except that some early culture, differing remarkably in some respects from the known Hawaiian culture, was represented."[1] Statements like these further alienated our people from their cultural past and solidified our dispossession.

Throughout the 1900s, the Northwestern Hawaiian Islands became a site for U.S. military expansion and resource extraction. For Native people whose identity is tied to the land, sky, and sea, these activities only added to the emotional stress and trauma associated with dispossession. Over time, the slow transformation of the landscape started to erode any recollection of the past and any sense of identity for this region. After enactment of the 1900 Organic Act that formed the Territory of Hawai'i, these islands underwent heavy construction. Midway Atoll was built up and transformed almost entirely into a military base, known widely as the famous location of the Battle of Midway in World War II. Another two U.S. Coast Guard LORAN stations were built, one on French Frigate Shoals and another on Kure Atoll.[2] Historically, from the late 1800s into the 1900s, the islands' resources were heavily exploited as seal hunters, whalers, feather hunters, pearl divers, and guano miners all had their turn stripping the islands and waters of their resources, often resulting in environmental damage from which they have never fully recovered. During this period, very few Native Hawaiians accessed this remote region.

The voyaging canoe *Hōkūleʻa* passing Nihoa Island. *Photograph by Naʻalehu Anthony.*

In the 2000s, a cultural revival began in the Northwestern Hawaiian Islands as Native Hawaiians became interested in and wanted to organize and sail traditional voyaging canoes or use modern vessels to rediscover these islands. During 2003–5, the *Hōkūleʻa* took three main trips to Nihoa, to Mokumanamana, and up the entire chain to Kure and back.

It was through the acts of voyaging and visiting these islands, and sailing these seas, that we began to recover an active memory of our past. Cultural research efforts in historical archival work, archaeology, and ethnography simultaneously began to inform this reconnection process. The revival of ritual practice was at the forefront of these spiritual quests, as ceremonies were held on the islands in a similar manner as the ancient chiefs did in the past.

As an offshoot of these cultural efforts, the Native Hawaiian community started to organize and play a key leadership role in driving the public process to design, establish, and properly manage this region. In 2001, the Northwestern Hawaiian Islands Ecosystem Reserve was established under Executive Orders 13178 and 13196 in response to Native Hawaiian fishers and cultural practitioners seeing the need for greater protective measures. Led by esteemed kupuna (elder) Uncle Buzzy Agard, along with other Hawaiian leaders such as Vicky Holt-Takamine, William Aila, Isaac Harp, and Tammy Harp, this group went to Washington, D.C., to lobby for more resources, thereby creating one of the largest marine conservation areas in the world at that time. Soon after, the state of Hawaiʻi also recognized the region's cultural significance when it established the Northwestern Hawaiian Islands State Marine Refuge in 2005. In 2006, the islands reached an important milestone when they became a Marine National Monument. Throughout this process, the Native Hawaiian community self-organized and formulated the Native Hawaiian Cultural Working Group. This body comprised Native Hawaiian cultural practitioners, scholars, educators, activists, and kūpuna who have strong historical ties to the region, ensuring that Native Hawaiian input is incorporated into all management actions.

Culture became strongly linked to the monument soon after its establishment, and the name "Papahānaumokuākea" was given to the region through a naming process. This process was led by the Native Hawaiian Cultural Working Group and drew inspiration from ancient Hawaiian traditions and original islands names documented by early Native elders. The name represented the union of the names "Papahānaumoku" and "[W]ākea," who are known in Hawaiian traditions as "Earth Mother" and "Sky Father." The merging of these names acknowledged the importance of our ancestral past and the union of these two people in symbolically "birthing" the archipelago, as told in our ancient stories, and creating us as a people. Naming the monument Papahānaumokuākea has helped to sustain a Hawaiian identity for this region and has reemphasized the importance of the genealogical connection between people and nature as the foundation of our culture.

In 2010, Papahānaumokuākea received global recognition as a UNESCO World Heritage site because of its outstanding natural and cultural universal value. It became the world's first cultural seascape owing to its continuing connection to living Indigenous people. As with every other protection effort, Native Hawaiians were directly engaged throughout this nomination process, the monument's design, and in advocacy. Finally, in 2016, Native Hawaiians helped lead the Expand Papahānaumokuākea Coalition, a diverse community-driven effort that included kūpuna, fishers, educators, cultural practitioners, scientists, conservation organizations, veterans, and other community groups that pushed for the monument's expansion in order to reestablish it as one of the largest conservation areas in the world. Expansion was achieved, allowing for the broadest regional and holistic protection of an entire seascape against any extractive, commercial, or industrial activities that are incompatible with a Hawaiian cultural worldview.

The National Wildlife Refuge at Nihoa Island. *Photograph by Kekuewa Kikiloi.*

Over the years, Papahānaumokuākea has become a model for conservation around the world through its integration of culture into its operations and management. Its foundation is built on Native Hawaiian values and integrates culture into five dimensions: education, access, research, policy, and management. The innovations in management have had far-reaching effects on marine conservation worldwide, serving as a model for other management areas. Since its establishment, more than ten nations have created large-scale marine protected areas and many have integrated knowledge and cultural values into their frameworks.

Through this process of reconnection, important steps have been taken to position ourselves as Native people in order to help shape the direction of the management and stewardship of the Northwestern Hawaiian Islands. Early cultural efforts to go on spiritual quests and voyaging considerable distances in traditional canoes to conduct ceremonies helped to build a sense of community for the region and were a catalyst for political organizing and collective action. Since the establishment of these protections, access to the region has opened for our people; at least eight ongoing cultural activities have occurred on twenty-seven separate expeditions to this remote region. The management structure and rules allow for Native cultural practices to effectively thrive while all exploitative activities and impacts are limited. Other important achievements are how culture has been integrated into the management and operations of the monument and representation has been solidified through dedicated seats on the Reserve Advisory Council and through the Native Hawaiian Cultural Working Group. In addition, through the expansion process, the Office of Hawaiian Affairs is now a co-trustee with the state of Hawai'i, the Department of the Interior, and the Department of Commerce, affording us some level of decision making, control, and empowerment.

As we were on the canoe coming back from the historic voyage to Nihoa Island, I started to realize the importance of reconnecting to these ancestral islands. An entire second half of the Hawaiian archipelago had historically been taken away from us and erased from our memory. Now we were reclaiming it. Recovering a sense of homeland is essential to recovering identity, health, and well-being for Native people. It was now our kuleana to return home and let our Hawaiian communities know of the importance of this region.

Notes

1   Kenneth P. Emory, *The Archaeology of Nihoa and Necker Islands*. (Honolulu: Bishop Museum Press, 1928), 3.

2   M. Rauzon, *Isles of Refuge: Wildlife and History of the Northwestern Hawaiian Islands* (Honolulu: University of Hawai'i Press, 2002).

Resources

Kerr, Joni, Paul DeSalles, Sylvia A. Earle, Kekuewa Kikiloi, Rick MacPherson, Sara M. Maxwell, Robert Richmond, Callum M. Roberts, Narissa P. Spies, U. Rashid Sumaila, and Angelo Villagomez. *Pu'uhonua: A Place of Sanctuary—The Cultural and Biological Significance of the proposed expansion for the Papahānaumokuākea Marine National Monument*. June 2016. Accessed February 25, 2019. http://expandpmnm.com/wp -content/uploads/PMNM06142016.pdf.

Kikiloi, Kekuewa. "Rebirth of an Archipelago: Sustaining a Hawaiian Cultural Identity for People and Homeland." *Hūlili: Multidisciplinary Research on Hawaiian Well-being* 7, no. 1 (2010): 73–115.

Kikiloi, Kekuewa, Alan M. Friedlander, 'Aulani Wilhelm, Nai'a Lewis, Kalani Quiocho, William 'Āila Jr., and Sol Kaho'ohalahala. "Papahānaumokuākea: Integrating Culture in the Design and Management of One of the World's Largest Marine Protected Areas." *Coastal Management* 45, no. 6 (2016): 436–51.

MacKenzie, Melody Kapilialoha, and B. Kaiama. *Native Hawaiian Claims to the Lands and Natural Resources of the Northwestern Hawaiian Islands.* Report to the Office of Hawaiian Affairs, Honolulu, 2003.

Yamase, Dennis K. "State-Federal Jurisdictional Conflict over the Internal Waters and Submerged Lands of the Northwestern Hawaiian Islands." *University of Hawaiʻi Law Review* 4 (1982): 139–80.

Hōkūlani K. Aikau and
Vernadette Vicuña Gonzalez

With this volume we have shared only a small fraction of the decolonial projects taking place in Hawaiʻi and beyond, by Kānaka and non-Kānaka alike. As we close this book, we cannot stress enough that this work is not finished—ʻaʻole i pau. There is more work to do, more stories to uncover and tell, more songs about our ʻāina to be written and sung, and more mālama ʻāina to cultivate and share.

The process of restoring ea is ongoing, collective, and generative. Our contributors, and all those unnamed souls standing beside them, collectively strive for a future of their own—our own—making. These stories reflect our imagination, a possible future we create together. It is our hope that this volume inspires, models, births other projects not just in Hawaiʻi, but in other places where the work of decolonization is ongoing. The future is open and awaiting us.

ʻAʻole i pau . . .

Glossary of Terms

The Hawaiian alphabet (and this glossary) follows this standard order:
a e h I k l m n o p u w

For additional information about terms in the glossary and in the volume, please refer to wehewehe.org. The definitions here are meant to assist the reader with basic or most common meanings especially as related to the usages in this book, but cannot encompass the rich multiplicity of meaning that ʻōlelo Hawaiʻi embodies.

ʻāʻā: dumb, silent, still; to stutter and stammer

ʻaha: meeting or assembly

ʻaha hoʻohanohano: ceremony and protocol

ahu: stone altar

ahupuaʻa: traditional land division that corresponds to a watershed, sometimes from mountain to sea, but also sometimes smaller land divisions such as ʻili

aikāne: intimate companions and lovers

ʻāina: land, or that which feeds

ʻāina kamahaʻo: wondrous land

ʻāina momona: fat or abundant land

akua: gods; deities in their elemental forms

ʻalaea: water-soluble, colloidal, ocher-colored soil used for coloring salt

alakaʻi: leaders

ʻalamihi and ʻaʻama: two types of black crabs

alanui: road

aliʻi: ʻŌiwi chiefly leadership

aliʻi ʻai moku: district chiefs

aliʻi holo moana: voyaging chiefs

aliʻi nui: high-ranking chief or leader

aloha: love, affection; greeting

aloha ʻāina: love for the land; patriot

alo i alo: face-to-face

ʻamaʻu: fern belt

ao: light, day, also cloud

ʻaʻole: no, not, never; to be none, to have none

āpaʻa: dryland forest and grassland ecosystems

au: ocean currents; period of time

aumoe: late at night, around midnight

ʻauwai: passageway through which ocean water flows in and out of the loko iʻa

ʻawa: kava; bitter, poisonous, sour

ea: life, breath, sovereignty

hā: breath; stalk of the kalo plant

haʻahaʻa: humble

haʻi ʻōlelo: Hawaiian-language oratory

hau: a lowland tree; ice, frost, dew, snow

haumāna: students

haumea: the Earth Mother (also known as Papa or Papahanaumoku)

haku mele: poet; to create a poetic text, song, chant

halalū: young scad or akule fish

hālau hula: hula schools

hālau waʻa: canoe house

hale: house

Hale ʻAhaʻōlelo Aliʻi: House of Nobles

hale kiaʻi: guardian outposts

hale kipa: visitor house

hana kaulike: justified work

hānau: to give birth

heʻe: octopus

heiau: temple; traditional rock-built religious structures

hewa: curse; wrong, incorrect; mistake, fault, error

hipa: sheep

hōʻailona: sign, symbol, omen

hōʻao: to stay until daylight

hoa kipa: guests

hoa waʻa: waʻa friends

hoe uli: steering paddle on a canoe

honu: sea turtle

hoʻokupu: offerings, gifts

hoʻolewa: funeral

huakaʻi: cultural field service trip; a physical, spiritual, and intellectual journey

huakaʻi hele: to go on a field trip or journey

hukilau: communal seine net fishing

ʻike: knowledge

ʻike Hawaiʻi: Hawaiian knowledge

ʻike kupuna: ancestral knowledge

ʻili: land division smaller than an ahupuaʻa

ʻili kupono: an ʻili land division within an ahupuaʻa with some independence from the chief of the ahupuaʻa, but paying tribute to the ruling chief

ʻili ʻāina: land inheritance

ʻimi ʻike: to seek knowledge

imu: underground oven

iwi: bones

iwi kupuna: ancestral bones

kaʻao: tale, legend

kaha: writing

kahakaha: writing pad

kahakai: the area near sea often referred to as the strand or beach

kāhili: feather standards

kahuna: priest, sorcerer

kaiāulu: community

kālaiʻāina: chiefly redistribution of ʻāina

kalo: taro

kamaʻāina: children of the land; native to or born and raised in a place

kanaka/kānaka: human person (singular/plural forms); Hawaiian, when capitalized

Kanaka Maoli: Native people of Hawaiʻi

Kanaka ʻŌiwi: Native Hawaiian

Kanaloa: god of the ocean, a name for Kahoʻolawe Island

Kāne: the god of fresh water and sunlight; men; male

kani ka pila: to play music

kanikau: dirge, lamentation

kao: goats

kapa: bark cloth

Ka pae ʻāina Hawaiʻi: the Hawaiian archipelago

kapu: prohibition or ban; prohibited; restrictions

kapu aloha: a restriction on the language and behavior of activists on Mauna a Wākea in their commitment to nonviolent civil disobedience

kauhale: housing compound

kaulana mahina: lunar calendar

kauwela: summer; hot, dry season

kāwele: conversational style of chanting

keiki: child

kiaʻi: guardians

kiaʻi loko: fishpond caretakers/guardians

kīhāpai: small land division; garden

kiʻi: carved wooden image

kilo: active observers

kino: body; form

kinolau: plant-body form of akua

kīpuka: oasis of forest in lava flow; an opening into a different state of being

koholā: humpback whale

koʻihonua: genealogical chant (e.g., Kumulipo)

kōkua: help; to be helpful

kolohe: mischievous

konohiki: ahupuaʻa-based resource manager; traditional steward

Kū: god of war

kuapā: walls of a fishpond

Kuhikuhi Puʻuone: master architect and engineer

kuhina nui: co-ruler

kukui: candlenut tree

kukuna o ka lā: the rays of the sun

kula: plains; fields; arid coastal lands upland from the sea

kulāiwi: homeland; the plain where the bones of one's ancestors are buried

kula pili: the yellow, grassy plains

kuleana: right to access; responsibility, rights, roles; obligation; authority

kumu: teacher

kumu hula: hula teacher

kumulipo: a koʻihonua or genealogical chant that documents the origin of the Hawaiian universe up to the birth of David Kalākaua

kupa: native

kupua: shapeshifter

kupuna/kūpuna: elder, ancestor (singular/plural forms)

kupunakāne kualua: great-great-grandfather

kuʻu pē: my child

lāhui: people; nation

lamakū: large torch traditionally using kukui nuts for light

lau: leaves

lauhala: pandanus tree

laulima: many hands; cooperation; to work together

lawaiʻa: fisherpeople

Leina/Leina ka ʻuhane: place where spirits jump into the afterlife

lepo ʻai ʻia: edible mud

limu: seaweed

loʻi kalo: wetland taro fields

loʻi paʻakai: salt bed

loko iʻa: fishponds

lokomaikaʻi: generosity

loli: sea cucumber

lololo: new insights, deep thinking

lūʻau: large family gatherings

luna: a locational term for high, upper, above

maiau: neat and careful in work; skillfull, ingenious, expert, thorough, meticulous

mahaʻoi: nosey, presumptuous

makai (also ma kai): a directional phrase referring to "toward the ocean"

makau liʻi liʻi: small fishhooks

mākāhā: gate

makahiapo: firstborn

Makahiki: ancient festival beginning about the middle of October and lasting about four months, with sports and religious festivities with a kapu on war

makana: gift

makaʻāinana: people of the land, commoner

makua/mākua: parent/parents (singular/plural forms); parents' generation

māla: cultivated area; garden

mālama: to care for

mālama ʻāina: to care for the land

mālama honua: to care for island Earth

malihini: visitors, foreigners, strangers

maluhia: peace, serenity; safety

Mamo Hawaiʻi: branches and offshoots of Hawaiʻi

mana: spiritual, divine, and political power

mana wahine: female power

manawa: time, turn, season

mana'o: thinking, wisdom

manini: surgeonfish, convict tang

manu o kū: white tern

mauka (also ma uka): a directional phrase referring to "toward the mountains"

mauliauhonua: descendant of old chiefs of a land

mele: song; a type of chant

mele kāhea: chant requesting entry

mele kanikau: mourning chant

mele ko'ihonua: genealogical chant

mele komo: chant calling out to guests to enter

mele wahi pana: chant or song written about a place

menehune: legendary race of small people who worked at night building fish ponds, roads, temples

moana kahiko: the ancient seas

moananuiākea: the vast, deep ocean

moe aku, moe mai: sleeping there and here; a poetical saying about a person who has many lovers

moku: district or land division larger than ahupua'a

mō'ī: kings, queens, rulers

mo'o: reptile of any kind; dragon, serpent; water spirit

mo'o 'āina: narrow strip of land smaller than an 'ili

mo'okū'auhau: genealogy

mo'olelo: story, tale, history

mo'olelo 'āina: histories of the land

moʻolelo haʻi waha: oral traditions

moʻopuna: grandchildren

naʻau: gut, intuition

naʻau pono: a deep sense of justice; upright

nāhele: forest, grove, wilderness

nānaku: the native bulrush

naupaka: Native species of shrubs found in mountains and near coasts, with white or light-colored "half" flowers

nehu: anchovy

nīʻau: midrib of the coconut leaf

ʻoama: young goatfish

ʻohana: immediate and extended family

ʻōhiʻa lehua: flower of the lehua tree

ʻōhiki: sand crab

ʻōhua: baby fish

ʻōiwi: Native person

okea: white sand or gravel

olakino maikaʻi: to live healthy

ʻōlapa: dancer

ʻōlelo Hawaiʻi: Hawaiian language

ʻōlelo hou: say it again

ʻōlelo noʻeau: poetical sayings; words of wisdom

oli: a type of chant

oli kāhea: a chant requesting permission to enter

oli lei: a chant for the offering of lei

ʻōmoʻomoʻo: ridgeline

one hānau: birthplace or birth sands

ʻoni: to move; movement

ʻono: delicious

ʻōʻō: digging stick

ʻoʻopu: goby fish

ʻōpae: shrimp

ʻōpakapaka: blue snapper

ʻōpelu: mackerel

ʻopihi: limpets

ʻōpua: cumulus clouds

paʻahao: prisoners

paʻakai: salt

pahikaua: sharp, serrated objects; swords; a type of shellfish

pāhoehoe: smooth lava

pahu: drums

paʻipaʻi: slapping the water

palaoa: sperm whale

pālau: wrasse

palekana: to ward off, safe

palena: place boundaries; a protected place

pali: cliffs

paniolo: cowboys

paukū ʻāina: a parcel of land

piko: umbilical cord; navel; place of convergence

pili: to cling or stick to

pilina ʻāina: intimate connection to lands

pipi: Hawaiian pearl oysters; cattle

pipipi: small mollusks

pō: generative, ancestral blackness

pōhaku: stone, rock, boulder

pōhaku kiʻi: petroglyphs

pono: goodness, uprightness,

poʻe: people

poʻe hula: hula practitioners

pua: baby fish

puaʻa: pig

pueo: owl

puna: well, spring

pūnawai: source of fresh water

pūʻali aliʻi: chiefly warrior

puʻu: hill

puʻuhonua: place of refuge, sanctuary

pwo: master navigator

tūtū: grandparent

tūtū nui: great-grandparent

ua: rain

uē: to weep, to cry, to mourn

uhau humu pōhaku: dry stack rock masonry

uku koʻakoʻa: coral polyp

ulu: breadfruit

ʻupena: fish nets

wā: period of time, epoch, era

wai: water (other than sea water)

wai kai: a mix of fresh water and saltwater

waikū: secondary well

waiwai: wealth

wao akua: a remote upland region reserved for the gods

wahine: woman; female

wahine koa: courageous women

wahi kapu: sacred or restricted places

wahi pana: sacred places

wana: urchin

waʻa: canoe

waʻa kaulua: double-hulled voyaging canoe

waʻapā: short canoe

weke: goatfish

Select References

Arista, Denise Noelani Manuela. "Davida Malo: Ke Kanaka O Ka Huliau—David Malo: A Hawaiian of the Time of Change." Master's thesis, University of Hawaiʻi, 1998.

Bartholomew, Gail, and Bren Bailey. *Maui Remembers: A Local History*. Taiwan: Mutual Publishing, 1994.

Cajete, Gregory. *Native Science: Natural Laws of Interdependence*. Santa Fe, NM: Clear Light Publishers, 2000.

Casey, Edward. "How to Get from Space to Place in a Fairly Short Stretch of Time: Phenomenological Prolegomena." In *Senses of Places*, edited by Steven Feld and Keith Basso, 13–52. Santa Fe: School of American Research, 1996.

Chernin, Ted. "My Experiences in the Honolulu Chinatown Red-Light District." *The Hawaiian Journal of History* 34 (2000): 203–18.

Coffman, Tom. *The Island Edge of America: A Political History of Hawaiʻi*. Honolulu: University of Hawaiʻi Press, 2003.

Dorrance, William H. *Fort Kamehameha: The Story of the Harbor Defenses of Pearl Harbor*. Shippensburg, PA: Beidel Printing House, 1993.

Emory, Kenneth P. *The Archaeology of Nihoa and Necker Islands*. Honolulu: Bishop Museum Press, 1928.

Fanon, Frantz. *The Wretched of the Earth*. New York: Grove Press, 1973.

Ferguson, Kathy E., and Phyllis Turnbull. *Oh, Say, Can You See? The Semiotics of the Military in Hawaiʻi*. Minneapolis: University of Minnesota Press, 1999.

Genz, Joseph H., Noelani Goodyear-Kaʻōpua, Monica C. La Briola, Alexander Mawyer, Elicita N. Morei, John P. Rosa. "Indigenous Responses, Resistance and Revitalization." In *Militarism and Nuclear Testing in the Pacific*. Teaching Oceania Series, vol. 1, edited by Monica C. LaBriola. Honolulu: Center for Pacific Islands Studies, University of Hawaiʻi-Mānoa, 2018. http://hdl.handle.net/10125/42430/.

Gonzalez, Vernadette Vicuña. *Securing Paradise: Tourism and Militarism in Hawaiʻi and the Philippines*. Durham, NC: Duke University Press, 2013.

Goodyear-Kaʻōpua, Noelani. "'Now We Know': Resurgences of Hawaiian Independence." *Politics, Groups, and Identities* 6, no. 3 (2018): 453–65.

Goodyear-Kaʻōpua, Noelani, Ikaika Hussey, and Erin Kahunawaikaʻala Wright, eds. *A Nation Rising: Hawaiian Movements for Life, Land, and Sovereignty*. Durham, NC: Duke University Press, 2014.

Goodyear-Kaʻōpua, Noelani, and Bryan Kamaoli Kuwada. "Making ʻAha: Independent Hawaiian Futures." *Dædalus, the Journal of the American Academy of Arts and Sciences* 147, no. 2 (2018): 49–59.

Handy, E. S. C., and E. G. Handy. *Native Planters in Old Hawaii: Their Life, Lore, and Environment*. Honolulu: Bishop Museum Press, 1972.

Hoʻokano, Pauahi. "Aia i Hea ka Wai a Kāne (Where Indeed Is the Water of Kāne?)." In *A Nation Rising: Hawaiian Movements for Life, Land, and Sovereignty*, edited by Noelani Goodyear-Kaʻopua, Ikaika Hussey, and Erin Kahunawaiklaʻala Wright, 220–31. Durham, NC: Duke University Press, 2014.

Jung, Moon-Kie. *Reworking Race: The Making of Hawaii's Interracial Labor Movement*. New York: Columbia University Press, 2006.

Kajihiro, Kyle. "Moananuiākea or 'American Lake'? Contested Histories of the U.S. 'Pacific Pivot.'" In *Under Occupation: Resistance and Struggle in a Militarised Asia-Pacific*, edited by Daniel Broudy, Peter Simpson, and Makoto Arakaki, 126–60. Newcastle upon Tyne, UK: Cambridge Scholars, 2013.

Kajihiro, Kyle. "Resisting Militarization in Hawaiʻi." In *The Bases of Empire the Global Struggle against U.S. Military Posts*, edited by Catherine Lutz, 299–332. London: Pluto, 2009.

Kamakau, Samuel. *Hawaiian Annual*. Honolulu: Thomas G. Thrum, 1932.

Kamakau, Samuel. *Tales and Traditions of the People of Old/Nā Moʻolelo a ka Poʻe Kahiko*. Honolulu: Bishop Museum Press, 1991.

Kanahele, George S. *Emma: Hawaiʻi's Remarkable Queen: A Biography*. Honolulu: Queen Emma Foundation, 1999.

Kauanui, J. Kēhaulani. "A Sorry State: Apology Politics and Legal Fictions in the Court of the Conqueror." In *Formations of United States Colonialism*, edited by Alyosha Goldstein, 110–34 Durham, NC: Duke University Press. 2014.

Kent, Noel. *Hawaii: Islands Under the Influence*. Honolulu: University of Hawaiʻi Press, 1983.

Kikiloi, Kekuewa. "Rebirth of an Archipelago: Sustaining a Hawaiian Cultural Identity for People and Homeland." *Hūlili: Multidisciplinary Research on Hawaiian Well-being* 7, no. 1 (2010): 73–115.

Kuwada, Brian Kamaoli. "'Na Moolelo o Kou Aina Makuahine': Our Kūpuna on Sovereignty and Overthrow," KE KAUPU HEHI (blog), January 17, 2017. https://hehiale.wordpress.com/2017/01/17/ha-moolelo-o-kou-aina-makuahine-our-kupuna-on-sovereignty-and-the-overthrow/.

Kyselka, W. *An Ocean in Mind*. Honolulu: University of Hawaiʻi Press, 1987.

Liliuokalani. *Hawaii's Story by Hawaii's Queen*. Rutland, VT: Charles E. Tuttle, [1898] 1964.

Liliʻuokalani, Queen of Hawaiʻi, 1883–1917. *The Kumulipo: An Hawaiian Creation Myth*. Kentfield, CA: Pueo Press, 1978.

Low, S. *Hawaiki Rising*. Honolulu: Island Heritage, 2013.

McDougall, Brandy Nālani. "The Second Gift." In *The Value of Hawaiʻi 2: Ancestral Roots, Oceanic Visions*, ed. Aiko Yamashiro and Noelani Goodyear-Kaʻōpua, 250–53. Honolulu: University of Hawaiʻi Press, 2014.

McGrath, Edward J., Kenneth M. Brewer, and Bob Krauss. *Historic Waianae: A Place of Kings*. Honolulu: Island Heritage Limited, 1973.

McGregor, Davianna Pomokaʻi. *Nā Kuaʻāina: Living Hawaiian Culture*. Honolulu: University of Hawaiʻi Press, 2007.

Nogelmeier, Puakea. *Pūowaina*. Honolulu: Hawaiian Studies Institute, The Kamehameha Schools/Bernice Pauahi Bishop Estate, 1985.

Osorio, Jonathan Kay Kamakawiwoʻole. *Dismembering Lahui: A History of the Hawaiian Nation to 1887*. Honolulu: University of Hawaiʻi Press, 2002.

Pukui, Mary Kawena. *Ōlelo Noʻeau: Hawaiian Proverbs and Poetical Sayings*. Honolulu: Bishop Museum, 1983.

Pukui, Mary Kawena, and Samuel Elbert. *Hawaiian Dictionary: Hawaiian-English, English-Hawaiian*. Honolulu: University of Hawaiʻi Press, 1986.

Pukui, Mary Kawena, Samuel H. Elbert, and Esther T. Mookini. *Place Names of Hawaiʻi*, revised and expanded edition. Honolulu: University of Hawaiʻi Press, 1974.

Rauzon, Mark J. *Isles of Refuge: Wildlife and History of the Northwestern Hawaiian Islands*. Honolulu: University of Hawaiʻi Press, 2002.

Rosa, John P. *Local Story: The Massie-Kahahawai Case and the Culture of History*. Honolulu: University of Hawaiʻi Press, 2014.

Saranillio, Dean Itsuji. "Colliding Histories: Hawaiʻi Statehood at the Intersection of Asians 'Ineligible to Citizenship' and Hawaiians 'Unfit for Self-Government.'" *Journal of Asian American Studies* 13, no. 3 (October 2010): 283–309.

Silva, Noenoe K. *Aloha Betrayed: Native Hawaiian Resistance to American Colonialism*. Durham, NC: Duke University Press, 2004.

Silva, Noenoe K. "I Kū Mau Mau: How Kanaka Maoli Tried to Sustain National Identity within the United States Political System." *American Studies* 45, no. 3 (2004): 9–31.

Simpson, Audra. "Consent's Revenge." *Cultural Anthropology* 31, no. 3 (2016): 326–33.

Simpson, Audra. *Mohawk Interruptus: Political Life across the Borders of Settler States*. Durham, NC: Duke University Press, 2014.

Simpson, Leanne. *Dancing on Our Turtle's Back: Stories of Nishnaabeg Re-creation, Resurgence and a New Emergence*. Winnipeg, Manitoba: Arbeiter Ring, 2011.

Simpson, Leanne. *Islands of Decolonial Love*. Winnipeg, Manitoba: Arbeiter Ring, 2013.

Smith, Linda Tuhiwai. *Decolonizing Methodologies: Research and Indigenous Peoples*. 2nd ed. London: Zed Books, 2017.

Stannard, David E. *Honor Killing: How the Infamous "Massie Affair" Transformed Hawai'i*. New York: Viking, 2005.

Sterling, Elspeth, and Catherine C. Summers. *Sites of Oahu*, rev. ed. Honolulu: Bishop Museum, 1978.

Trask, Haunani-Kay. "Settlers of Color and 'Immigrant' Hegemony: 'Locals' in Hawai'i." *Amerasia Journal* 26, no. 2 (2000): 1–24.

Vizenor, Gerald. "Aesthetics of Survivance: Literary Theory and Practice." In *Survivance: Narratives of Native Presence*, ed. Gerald Vizenor, 1–28. Lincoln: University of Nebraska Press, 2008.

West, Paige. *Dispossession and the Environment: Rhetoric and Inequality in Papua New Guinea*. New York: Columbia University Press, 2016.

Yamase, D. K. "State-Federal Jurisdictional Conflict over the Internal Waters and Submerged Lands of the Northwestern Hawaiian Islands." *University of Hawai'i Law Review* 4 (1982): 139–80.

Contributors

HŌKŪLANI K. AIKAU is Kanaka ʻŌiwi, born in Honolulu, and raised in Navajo, Ute, and Goshute territories. She is an associate professor in the divisions of gender studies and ethnic studies at the University of Utah. She is the author of *A Chosen People, a Promised Land: Mormonism and Race in Hawaiʻi* and mother to Sanoe, ʻĪmaikalani, and Hiʻilei.

MALIA AKUTAGAWA is Kanaka ʻŌiwi, born and raised on the island of Molokaʻi. She is an associate professor of law and Hawaiian studies with the Hawaiʻinuiākea School of Hawaiian Knowledge–Kamakakūokalani Center for Hawaiian Studies and the William S. Richardson School of Law–Ka Huli Ao Center for Excellence in Native Hawaiian Law. She is part of Hui ʻĀina Momona, a consortium of scholars throughout the university community charged with addressing compelling issues of Indigenous Hawaiian knowledge and practices, including the legal regime and Native Hawaiian rights associated with mālama ʻāina (caring for the land), and with a focus on cross-disciplinary solutions to natural and cultural resource management, sustainability, and food security.

ADELE BALDERSTON is a place-based storyteller from Oʻahu specializing in new media and psychogeography. She is the founder of 88 Block Walks, a series of unconventional walking tours in Kakaʻako. Working at the intersection of geography, art, and activism, Adele promotes awareness of socio-spatial inequality and advocates for community agency through personal narratives, mapping, and interaction with urban environments.

KAMANAMAIKALANI BEAMER is an associate professor at the Center for Hawaiian Studies in the Hui ʻĀina Momona Program at the University of Hawaiʻi at Mānoa, with a joint appointment in the Richardson School of Law and the Hawaiʻinuiākea School of Hawaiian Knowledge. He has revitalized and maintained loʻi kalo (taro ponds), providing himself and his children opportunities to mālama ʻāina, deepen connections with cultural traditions, and derive leadership lessons from the land. In 2014 he published *No Mākou ka Mana: Liberating the Nation*, which received multiple awards including the Samuel M. Kamakau Book of the Year Award from the Hawaiʻi Book Publishing Association.

ELLEN-RAE CACHOLA is a lecturer for the Department of Ethnic Studies at the University of Hawai'i at Mānoa and the evening supervisor and archives manager at the University of Hawai'i School of Law Library. Ellen-Rae is also the cofounder of Women's Voices Women Speak, an O'ahu-based organization committed to building women's leadership to organize for peace and demilitarization across Oceania.

EMILY CADIZ is a graduate of the Natural Resources and Environmental Management Department at the University of Hawai'i at Mānoa; she has a background in marine biology. Emily is program director for the Hui Maka'āinana o Makana in Hā'ena, Kaua'i, and an active member of Nā Kilo 'Āina, a hui dedicated to helping community members to become active observers and caretakers of their sources of sustenance.

IOKEPA CASUMBAL-SALAZAR is Kanaka 'Ōiwi and a professor of Native American and Indigenous Studies in the Center for the Study of Culture, Race, and Ethnicity at Ithaca College in New York.

DAVID A. CHANG is a Kanaka Maoli historian at the University of Minnesota who is deeply interested in the intersections of American Indian and Kanaka Maoli histories, politics, and present circumstances. His most recent book is *The World and All the Things upon It: Native Hawaiian Geographies of Exploration*.

LIANNE MARIE LEDA CHARLIE is Tagé Cho Hudän (Big River People), Northern Tutchone–speaking people of the Yukon in northern Canada. She is a political science instructor at Yukon College in Whitehorse, Yukon, and a PhD candidate in the Indigenous Politics program at the University of Hawai'i at Mānoa.

GREG CHUN is a Kanaka Hawai'i social scientist whose professional experience is in organizational development, land use, and historic preservation. Greg is currently an associate specialist at the University of Hawai'i at Mānoa, managing a program of training and practice in community engagement with a focus on supporting complex resource management and scientific research projects requiring broad community involvement.

JOY LEHUANANI ENOMOTO recently finished two master's degrees in library and information science and in Pacific Island studies. Joy is also a mixed-media visual artist and social justice activist whose work engages with climate justice, extractive colonialism, and other issues currently affecting Pacific peoples. Her artwork and scholarship have been featured in the Routledge Postcolonial Handbook series, *Finding Meaning: Kaona and Contemporary Hawaiian Literature*, the *Amerasia Journal*, *Bamboo Ridge: Journal of Hawai'i Literature and Arts*, and *Hawai'i Review*.

S. JOE ESTORES, a Pearl Harbor survivor, graduated from St. Louis, Honolulu, in 1952. He received a bachelor's degree in political science from the University of Nebraska and a master's in international relations from the University of Arkansas. Joe spent twenty years in the U.S. Army and is now a retired Lieutenant Colonel; he was a helicopter pilot in Vietnam. Joe spent thirty-five years in the Federal Civil Service; five years at the Drug Enforcement Agency headquarters in Washington, D.C.; fifteen years with the U.S. Army

Corps of Engineers in Europe; and fifteen years as a civilian working at the Department of the Army. Joe is now based at home, in Pupukea.

NICHOLAS KAWELAKAI FARRANT is a Kanaka Maoli raised in Paumalū, Oʻahu. He strives to serve his home community as the outreach coordinator for the North Shore Community Land Trust and through his current graduate studies in the Department of Natural Resources and Environmental Management at the University of Hawaiʻi at Mānoa.

JESSICA KAUʻI FU is a Native practitioner hailing from the North Shore of Kauaʻi and currently resides in Kīlauea. She comes from a family of avid fishermen and teachers. She paddles at Hanalei Canoe Club and sails with her keiki at Waipā. She and her cousin Billy Kinney organized the interview process that led to the piece "Kahaleʻala, Haleleʻa," about an area where their ʻohana has roots in Kalihikai.

CANDACE FUJIKANE is a Japanese settler ally in Hawaiʻi and professor of English at the University of Hawaiʻi. She was born in Honolulu and grew up in Pukalani, Maui. She is currently working on a book titled *Mapping Abundance for a Planetary Future: Kanaka Maoli and Critical Settler Cartographies in Hawaiʻi.*

LINDA H. L. FURUTO is an education specialist and apprentice navigator with the Polynesian Voyaging Society, professor of mathematics education at the University of Hawaiʻi at Mānoa, and director of the world's first program in ethnomathematics. She was raised in Hauʻula, Koʻolauloa, Oʻahu, where she currently resides with her family. Her work has been published by the International Congress on Mathematical Instruction, Oxford University Press, and National Council of Teachers of Mathematics.

SONNY GANADEN is a lawyer, writer, artist, and teacher. In 2012, he was the lead writer of the Native Hawaiian Justice Task Force Report, delivered to the Hawaiʻi state legislature in 2013. In 2017, he was named "Best Single Writer" by the Hawaiʻi chapter of the Society of Professional Journalists for work in magazines. He is an instructor in the Ethnic Studies Department at the University of Hawaiʻi at Mānoa, and an active member of the Honolulu Printmakers and Ānuenue Canoe Club.

CHERYL GESLANI hails from the north side of Chicago, and she is thankful to raise her family in the mist of Mānoa Valley on Oʻahu. After finishing her PhD at the University of Hawaiʻi at Mānoa, Cheryl began working as an energy analyst for the State of Hawaiʻi Department of Business, Economic Development, and Tourism. She hopes to bridge efforts between the state government, the University of Hawaiʻi system, and those who speak on behalf of the land and fresh water.

VERNADETTE VICUÑA GONZALEZ is a Filipina settler ally in Hawaiʻi, born and raised on the island of Negros in the Philippines. She is an associate professor of American studies and the director of the Honors Program at the University of Hawaiʻi at Mānoa. She is the author of *Securing Paradise: Tourism and Militarism in Hawaiʻi and the Philippines.* She lives in Pālolo Valley on Oʻahu.

NOELANI GOODYEAR-KAʻŌPUA is a Kanaka Maoli, born and raised on Oʻahu. A professor of Hawaiian and Indigenous politics at the University of Hawaiʻi at Mānoa, Noe is the author of *The Seeds We Planted: Portraits of a Native Hawaiian Charter School*. Her coedited books on Hawaiian social movements include *A Nation Rising: Hawaiian Movements for Live, Land and Sovereignty* (2014) and *Nā Wāhine Koa: Hawaiian Women for Sovereignty and Demilitarization* (2019). Noe serves on the board of Hui o Kuapā, a community nonprofit organization whose mission is to restore fishponds on Molokaʻi.

TINA GRANDINETTI is a biracial Uchinaanchu (Okinawan) settler from Mililani. She currently lives and works on the lands of the Boonwurrung and Wurrundjeri peoples in Australia, where she is a PhD candidate at RMIT University. Her research and activism focus on issues of urban justice, settler colonialism, and militarism in Hawaiʻi.

CRAIG HOWES is the director of the Center for Biographical Research, the coeditor of *Biography: An Interdisciplinary Quarterly*, and a professor of English at the University of Hawaiʻi at Mānoa. He is the coeditor of *The Value of Hawaiʻi: Knowing the Past, Shaping the Future*, and a coproducer of the *Biography Hawaiʻi* television documentary series.

AURORA KAGAWA-VIVIANI was raised in ʻAuwaiolimu on Oʻahu and grew up listening to her mom light up when remembering her visits with family on Kauaʻi. Aurora is currently a PhD candidate in the Geography Department at the University of Hawaiʻi at Mānoa and still has never seen a live upapalu.

NOELLE M. K. Y. KAHANU is a Native Hawaiian writer, curator, and artist with over twenty years of experience in the museum field, including fifteen years at Bishop Museum. She is currently an assistant specialist of Public Humanities and Native Hawaiian programs at the American Studies Department of the University of Hawaiʻi at Mānoa.

HALEY KAILIEHU is a Kanaka ʻŌiwi artist born and raised in the ʻili ʻāina of Kukuipuka, a beautiful puʻuhonua in the ahupuaʻa of Kahakuloa, on the island of Maui. Haley is a professional artist and educator. She is invested in creating community- and ʻāina-centered experiences that allow current and future generations of Kanaka ʻŌiwi to (re)learn and assert our kuleana, (re)establish connections to our moʻolelo and kūpuna (ancestors), and (re)affirm our rightful place in our homelands.

KYLE KAJIHIRO, formerly the program director for the American Friends Service Committee, Hawaiʻi Area Program, coordinates Hawaiʻi DeTours, an educational project of Hawaiʻi Peace and Justice. He is a PhD candidate in geography at the University of Hawaiʻi and is studying the social and environmental effects of the military and community resistance to militarization.

HALENA KAPUNI-REYNOLDS is a graduate student and museum scholar in the Department of American Studies at the University of Hawaiʻi at Mānoa. He is committed to preserving the history of his community, the Hawaiian Homestead of Keaukaha.

TERRILEE KEKO'OLANI is a long-time Kanaka Maoli activist who has been involved in Native Hawaiian land and independence struggles, environmental justice activism, and demilitarization and antinuclear movements, ranging from local sites, such as Kaho'olawe and Mōkapu, to international networks, such as the International Women's Network Against Militarism. She coordinates Hawai'i DeTours for Hawai'i Peace and Justice.

KEKUEWA KIKILOI is an associate professor at the Hawai'inuiākea School of Hawaiian Knowledge at the University of Hawai'i at Mānoa. His research interests include Hawaiian resource management, Indigenous knowledge, traditional society, genealogies, cultural revitalization, and community empowerment. His research spans the main Hawaiian Islands, the Northwestern Hawaiian Islands, and greater Polynesia.

WILLIAM KINNEY is from northern Kaua'i. Billy was raised in a ranching and fisher family. He spent most of his early years with the mākua of Hanalei and Hā'ena. Currently an undergraduate in English at Mānoa, he is interested in contemporary stories as they connect people, places, and resources in order to enrich advocacy.

FRANCESCA KOETHE was born and raised in Mililani, O'ahu, and completed her master's degree in natural resources and environment management at the University of Hawai'i in 2017. She currently works at O'ahu Resource Conservation and Development Council helping local producers through sustainable agriculture.

KAREN K. KOSASA, a third-generation Japanese settler, is an associate professor and director of the Museum Studies Graduate Certificate Program in the Department of American Studies at the University of Hawai'i at Mānoa. For thirteen years she taught in the visual arts in Hawai'i and in the continental U.S.

N. TRISHA LAGASO GOLDBERG is a curator, public art administrator, and artist. She holds a master of arts in art history from San Francisco State University and a bachelor of fine arts in New Genres from the San Francisco Art Institute. Lagaso Goldberg works as a public art project management consultant, leading large-scale commissioned art projects for government agencies. As an independent curator and organizer of public programs, her work has been presented at the Bishop Museum, the Honolulu Museum of Art, the Luggage Store Gallery, San Francisco Museum of Modern Art, and Southern Exposure.

KAPULANI LANDGRAF is an artist who examines historical and contemporary issues and their impact on the culture of the Hawaiian people. Her sixth book, *Ē Luke Wale Ē* [Devastation upon Devastation], a collection of photographs and Hawaiian verse, chronicles the wahi pana destroyed by the construction of O'ahu's H-3 freeway.

NANEA LUM, a Native Hawaiian painter, is deeply connected to her love for the land and waters of her environment. "No O'ahu mai au, ke noho nei au i ku'u 'aina hānau a mau." Her paintings are abstract representations that contemplate spaces inside the body as well as deep spaces of the atmosphere. Her materials vary from oil paints to inks, acrylics, earth, and water gathered from specific geographies, as well as her own hair on raw canvas surfaces. The process of creation is visceral for Nanea Lum. She studies at the University

of Hawaiʻi at Mānoa in the masters of fine arts program and exhibits her research at www
.nanealumpaintings.com.

LAURA E. LYONS is a professor of English and interim dean of the College of Languages,
Linguistics, and Literature at the University of Hawaiʻi at Mānoa. She is coeditor of and a
contributor to the volume *Cultural Critique and the Global Corporation*.

DAVID UAHIKEAIKALEIʻOHU MAILE is a Kanaka ʻŌiwi scholar, activist, and practitioner from Maunawili, Oʻahu. He is an assistant professor of Indigenous politics in the Department of Political Science at the University of Toronto. He is also an organizer with the
Red Nation, a coalition centered on Indigenous liberation.

BRANDY NĀLANI MCDOUGALL is an associate professor specializing in Indigenous
studies in the American Studies Department at the University of Hawaiʻi at Mānoa. She
is the author of *The Salt-Wind/Ka Makani Paʻakai*, a collection of poetry, and *Finding
Meaning: Kaona and Contemporary Hawaiian Literature*, which was awarded the 2017 Bea-
trice Medicine Award for Scholarship in American Indian Studies. She was raised on the
slopes of Haleakalā on Maui and now lives in Makiki, Oʻahu.

DAVIANNA PŌMAIKAʻI MCGREGOR is a professor and founding member of the Department of Ethnic Studies at the University of Hawaiʻi at Mānoa and the director of the department's Center for Oral History. Her ongoing research endeavors focus on the persistence
of traditional Hawaiian cultural customs, beliefs, and practices in rural Hawaiian communities on the main Hawaiian islands. This work is featured in her book *Kuaʻaina: Living
Hawaiian Culture* (2007). She lives in Kaiwiʻula on the island of Oʻahu and in Hoʻolehua on
the island of Molokaʻi. As a member of the Protect Kahoʻolawe ʻOhana, she helps provide
stewardship of the island of Kanaloa Kahoʻolawe.

LAUREL MEI-SINGH was born and raised near Lēahi (Diamond Head) and is an assistant
professor of ethnic studies at the University of Hawaiʻi at Mānoa. She is currently writing
a book that develops a genealogy of military fences and grassroots struggles for land and
livelihood in Waiʻanae.

P. KALAWAIʻA MOORE is an associate professor and the director of Hawaiian studies
at Windward Community College, where he teaches Hawaiian mythology, history, genealogy, and traditional Hawaiian house and rock wall building and runs a Hawaiian cultural
garden.

SUMMER KAIMALIA MULLINS-IBRAHIM is a full-time mother to her two children and
is a Kanaka Maoli cultural practitioner, activist, educator, and community organizer with
generational ties to Kaʻena and Mākua.

JORDAN MURATSUCHI is from Kāneʻohe, Oʻahu, and recently completed his master's
degree in natural resources and environmental management. He currently works on pollution issues and community improvement in Hawaiʻi.

HANOHANO NAEHU is a Kanaka Maoli born and raised on the east end of Moloka'i. He has been a kia'i loko (fishpond guardian) at Keawanui for over fifteen years. A storyteller and rapper who goes by the name Paniolo Prince, Hanohano released his debut album, *The Tip of the Spear: Songs of Hawaiian Independence*, in 2018. He is a fierce advocate of aloha 'āina and Hawaiian sovereignty.

MALIA NOBREGA-OLIVERA is from Hanapēpē Valley, Kona, Kaua'i. She is currently the director of strategic partnerships and community engagement at the Hawai'inuiākea School of Hawaiian Knowledge and also the director of a program called Loli Aniau, Makaala Aniau (Climate Change, Climate Alert). Malia is a makuahine, Native Hawaiian educator, kumu hula, salt maker, cultural practitioner, filmmaker, community organizer, and advocate of Indigenous rights at all levels: local, regional, and international.

KATRINA-ANN R. KAPĀ'ANAOKALĀOKEOLA NĀKOA OLIVEIRA, a Kanaka raised on O'ahu and Maui, is a professor of Hawaiian at the University of Hawai'i at Mānoa. She is the author of *Ancestral Places: Understanding Kanaka Geographies*.

JAMAICA HEOLIMELEIKALANI OSORIO is a Kanaka Maoli wahine poet, activist, and scholar born and raised in Pālolo Valley to parents Jonathan and Mary Osorio. Heoli earned her PhD in English (Hawaiian literature) upon the completion of her dissertation entitled, "(Re)membering 'Upena of Intimacies: A Kanaka Maoli Mo'olelo Beyond Queer Theory." Currently, Heoli is an assistant professor of Indigenous and Native Hawaiian politics at the University of Hawai'i at Mānoa. Heoli is a three-time national poetry champion, a poetry mentor, and a published author. She is a proud past Kaiapuni student, Ford Foundation fellow, and a graduate of Kamehameha, Stanford (BA), and New York University (MA).

NO'EAU PERALTO is an 'Ōiwi scholar and community organizer in his kulāiwi of Hāmākua Hikina, Hawai'i. He holds a PhD from the Indigenous politics program at the University of Hawai'i at Mānoa and currently serves as the executive director of Hui Mālama I ke Ala 'Ūlili, a grassroots community organization based in Pa'auilo.

NO'U REVILLA is an 'Ōiwi queer feminist poet and educator from the island of Maui. She is an assistant professor of creative writing at the University of Hawai'i at Mānoa. She has performed throughout Hawai'i and in Canada, in Papua New Guinea, and at the United Nations. Her work has been published in *Literary Hub*, *Poetry*, *Black Renaissance Noire*, *The Missing Slate*, and Poem of the Week by Kore Press.

KALANIUA RITTE is a Native-born son of Moloka'i nui a Hina. He is the lead kia'i loko (fishpond guardian) at Keawanui, where he has been working since 2001. Kalaniua and Hanohano previously hosted and produced a local television program called "Hemowai Brothers," which provided education about political issues affecting Hawaiian lands, waters, and communities. As a hunter and community leader, Kalaniua continues to be an advocate and practitioner of aloha 'āina.

MAYA L. KAWAILANAOKEAWAIKI SAFFERY, Kanaka from Kailua, Oʻahu, is the curriculum specialist for Kawaihuelani Center for Hawaiian Language at the University of Hawaiʻi at Mānoa. Her scholarly work is grounded in the kanaka-ʻāina relationships and is largely influenced by her continued practice of traditional hula as a graduated ʻōlapa and kumu hula from Hālau Mōhala ʻIlima.

DEAN ITSUJI SARANILLIO is an associate professor in the Department of Social and Cultural Analysis at New York University. His teaching and research interests are in settler colonialism and critical Indigenous studies, Asian American and Pacific Island histories, and cultural studies. His book titled *Unsustainable Empire: Alternative Histories of Hawaiʻi Statehood* (Duke University Press, 2018) examines the complex interplay between various Asian American groups, Native Hawaiians, and whites within historical flashpoints of interaction shaped by opposing versions of history.

NOENOE K. SILVA, Kanaka Hawaiʻi from Kailua, Oʻahu, is a professor of Indigenous politics and Hawaiian language at the University of Hawaiʻi at Mānoa. She is the author of *Aloha Betrayed: Native Hawaiian Resistance to American Colonialism* and *The Power of the Steel-tipped Pen: Reconstructing Native Hawaiian Intellectual History*.

TY P. KĀWIKA TENGAN is an associate professor of ethnic studies and anthropology at the University of Hawaiʻi at Mānoa. He is the author of *Native Men Remade: Gender and Nation in Contemporary Hawaiʻi*.

STEPHANIE NOHELANI TEVES, Kanaka Maoli from Ewa Beach, Oʻahu, is an assistant professor of women's studies at the University of Hawaiʻi at Mānoa. She is coeditor of *Native Studies Keywords* and author of *Defiant Indigeneity: The Politics of Hawaiian Performance*.

STAN TOMITA is now retired. From 1979 to 2015 he taught photography for different periods at the University of California at Berkeley, Honolulu Community College, and the University of Hawaiʻi at Mānoa.

MEHANA BLAICH VAUGHAN is a mother of three, teacher, writer, assistant professor, and community member from Namahana and Kalihiwai, Kauaʻi. She is dedicated to enhancing community capacity to care for sustaining places and is the author of *Kaiāulu: Gathering Tides*.

WENDY MAPUANA WAIPĀ is a kamaʻāina of the Hawaiian Homestead of Keaukaha. She is the director of Ke Ana Laʻahana Public Charter School and the vice president of the Keaukaha Community Association.

JULIE WARECH is an academic from South Florida and is of Eastern European Jewish and Romani heritage. She received her BA in sociology and anthropology from Swarthmore College and her MA in cultural anthropology from the University of Hawaiʻi at Mānoa. Her research focuses include Native Hawaiian politics, settler colonialism, indigenizing and decolonizing anthropology, and settler alliances in activism and academia.

Index

Castle Memorial Building, 171

Casumbal-Salazar, Iokepa, 121–22, 200–210

Casupang, Michael Lanakila, 335

Cathedral Basilica of Our Lady of Peace, 311

C. Brewer and Company, 8–9, 286–90, 304

Central Maui Hawaiian Civic Club, 53

CEPA Gallery (Buffalo, New York), 147

Chang, David A., 352, 355–61

Charlie, Lianne Marie Leda, 18, 94–95, 96–106

Chief's Children's School, 309

Chinatown (Honolulu), 252–53

Chinese in Hawai'i, 252–54, 256, 286

Christianity: Hawaiian conversions to, 214–15; in Honolulu, 308–14

Chun, Gregory, 121, 182–92

citizenship, Hawaiian national opposition to, 55

Cleghorn, Archibald, 70–71

Cleghorn, Victoria Kawēkiu Ka'iulani Kalaninuiahilapalapa (Princes Ka'iulani), 18, 67–75, 299, 309–10

climate change, place boundaries and, 24–25

Cold War, Hawaiian tourist sites and, 53–54

Committee of Safety, 309, 345

Concerned Elders of Wai'anae, 248, 340–48

Concrete Industries, 37

Congregational Mission Church, 308

contract labor, 7–9

Cook, Captain James, 1, 7, 143, 176

Cooke, Juliet Montague, 309

Core Civic, 373–79

Corrections Corporation of America (CCA), 374

Cortes Torres, Primitivo, 293

criminal justice, decolonization and, 373–79

cultural practices: of imprisoned Hawaiians, 373–79; revival of, 10–11

Customs House (Honolulu), 305

Darrow, Clarence, 253

da Silva, Kahikina, 142–43

da Silva, Māpuana, 135

Davies Pacific Center, 307

decolonization: aloha and, 120, 125–31; criminal justice in Pacific and, 373–79; cultivation of ea (breath and sovereignty) and, 3–5; postcard project for, 147–48; projects relating to, 120–22; refusal protests and, 198; sovereign space and, 132–45

Deedy, Christopher, 253

deer hunting, 240

Defeo, Jack, 343

deoccupied love, 125–31

Department of Conservation and Resource Enforcement, 275–76

Department of the Interior (DOI), 193–98

Department of Land and Natural Resources (DLNR), 206–7, 271, 275–77

DeTours Project, 246, 249–59, 283–90

development: in Kaka'ako (Honolulu), 315–24; land use and, 183–92

diaspora, kuleana and, 355–61

didactic art, 147

Dillingham Transportation, 307

dispossession: DeTours' exploration of, 284–90; of fishermen, 274–76; history of Hawai'i and, 7–9

diversity in Hawai'i: labor movement and, 287–90; propaganda and stereotypes of, 53–54, 126–31, 247–48

Dochin, Mahi'ai, 83

Dodge, Fred, 343

Dole, James Drummond, 86, 89–90

Dole, Sanford, 89

Dole Food Company, 86–87

Dole Pineapple Cannery, 307

Dole Playground, 329, 333

Doughty, Andrew, 97, 99

Drayton, Richard Harry, 174

Durest, James Alanan, 197

Land Grant 4751, 345

land use: ahupua'a (land division), 132–33; ahupua'a boundaries and, 19–25, 30–36, 92–93; development and, 184–92; environmental justice and, 343–48; on Kanaloa Kaho'olawe, 265–70; kuleana (responsibility) for, 108–9; on Moloka'i, 155–57; resource subzones and, 203–10; settlement patterns and, 186–88; U.S. imperialism and, 89–90, 286–90; by U.S. military, 253–59. *See also* Homelands leases; sacred land

Laulima (cooperation), 215–19

Lawai'a (fisherpeople), 236, 271–82

Lawai'a Action Network, 272–82, 274–76

Laysan Island (Kamole), 381

Lehua Island, 381

Lehuanani Enomoto, Joy, 121, 173–81

Lē'ahi (Diamond Head), 284

Leisure Estates, 37

Lihikai Park, 117

Likelike, Miriam, 71

Lili'uokalani, Lydia (Queen), 8–9, 32, 68, 329–30, 333; coup against, 248, 251–52, 310, 334, 345; monuments and streets in honor of, 71–72, 311, 314; "Queen's Prayer" composed by, 299

Lisianski Island (Kapou), 381

Lloyd, John "Jack," 289–90

Local 5 labor group, 288–90

lo'i (salt bed), 224–29

lo'i kalo (wetland taro fields), 258–59, 284; destruction in Honolulu of, 316–17

loko i'a (fishpond), 230–43, 284

lololo (observation), 267–68

Lono (Hawaiian deity), 268–69

Lualualei Valley, 340–48

lū'au (large family gatherings), 114, 153

Lum, Nanea, 120, 123

Lum, Verdelle, 100

Lunalilo, William Charles, 309

Lyon, Harold, 173

Lyon Arboretum, 173

Lyons, Laura E., 18, 86–93

Macfarlane (Colonel), 69

Māhele land division, 7–9, 166; Lualualei Valley and, 345–48; Pa'auilo plantation town and, 30–36

Mā'ili'ili Stream, 344

Mā'ilikūkahi, 21

maiau (excellence), 215, 217–19

Maile, C. B., 194–95

Maile, David Uahikeaikalei'ohu, 9

mākāhā (sluice gates), 235–39

Makahiki (Hawaiian deity), 268–69

Makahiki celebration, 21–25, 376

Makapu'u Lighthouse, 165

Mākua (O'ahu), 247

Mākua Military Reservation, 276–79

Mālama Honua Worldwide Voyage, 364–70

mālama 'āina (care of the land), 16, 209–10, 215–19

Mālama Kailua Festival, 135, 138

Mālama Mākua, 278–79

malihini (visitors), 116–17, 132–33, 158

"Mall at Pearl Harbor," 256

Malo, Davida, 334

Malo 'ohana (family), 111

Managauil, Joshua Lanakila, 204–5

Mana heiau, 333

Manu 'Ō'ō, 129–31

Maoli Arts Month, 168

MA'O Organic Farms, 341–48

mapping technology: Hawaiian culture and, 17, 58–66, 352–53; plant identification and, 173–81

Mapuana Waipā, Wendy, 18, 107–18

Marine National Monument project, 239, 387

Maro Reef (Ka Moku o Kamohoali'i), 381

Marquesas Islands, 384

martial law, imposition of, 252–53

Marx, Karl, 92

Kahoʻolawe resistance to, 263–70; labor movement and, 287–90; on Lānaʻi, 86–93; at Mauna Kea, 200–210; on Molokaʻi, 157–63; postcards and, 147–48; responsible tourism negotiations, 153–63; sacred places and, 17; transformative practices and, 10–11

Townsend, Marti, 342, 343

transformative practices of journeying, 10–11

Trask, Lākea, 194

tribal recognition, refusal of, 121–22

Tropic Land LLC, 340

Tutu, Archbishop Desmond Mpilo, 366–67

Tutuila (American Samoa), 365

Uahikeaikaleiʻohu Maile, David, 121–22, 193–99

"Ua Like no a Like" (Everett), 128–29

uhau humu pōhaku (dry stack rock masonry), 212–19

ʻŪlei Pahu i ka Moku hula, 143–45

ʻUmi-a-Līloa, 32, 35

United Public Workers Union, 288

United States: Hawaiian relocation to, 355–61; Hōkūleʻa voyage to, 367–68

University of Hawaiʻi (UH), 202–10

University of Hawaiʻi System (UHS), 370

urban renewal, development and, 317–24

U.S. Army Museum, 284–85

U.S. Bill of Rights, 377

U.S. imperialism: aloha and, 126–31; Hawaiian diaspora and, 355–61; Kaʻiulani's haunting of, 67–75; Kepaniwai Heritage Gardens as image of, 54–56; legacy in Oʻahu of, 247–48; on Molokaʻi, 155–56; in Pacific, 256–59; tourism and, 283–90

U.S. Indo-Pacific Command, 254

U.S. military presence in Hawaii, 54–56, 77–84, 126–31, 247; Hawaiian archipelago and, 385–89; history of, 253–54, 284; on Kahoʻolawe, 262–70; Mākua

Military Reservation, 277–79; sexual harassment and, 288–90; tourism and, 249–59; in Waikīkī, 284–90

Vaughan, Mehana Blaich, 18, 96–106

Veach, Lacy, 363

Vicuña Gonzalez, Vernadette, 391

violence, of place-making, 17

Von Holt, H. M., 345

wāhine koa (women warriors), 70

wahi pana (storied places), 16, 18, 45–49; decolonization projects and restoration of, 136; Kahoʻolawe as, 263–70; in Keaukaha, 108–18; mapping of, 58–66; restoration of, 182

Wai, Leandra, 277

Waiʻanae Sustainable Communities Plans, 340–47

Waiheʻe III, John, 265

wai kai (brackish water), 239

Waikīkī: ghost tours of, 68; history of, 283–90; legacy of U.S. imperialism in, 247–48; mapping of, 63–64; presence of Princes Kaʻiulani in, 67–75

waikū (secondary well), 224–25

Wailuku River, diversion of, 56

waiwai, in Kakaʻako, 320–24

Wākea (Hawaiian deity), 126–31, 209–10, 217

Walker Park, 300–302

Wallace, George, 54

Wall Street Journal, 86, 90

Wanini, 98–106

Wanini stream, 101

Ward Village planned community, 315, 320–24

Warech, Julie, 122, 230–43

War Memorial Stadium and Gym, 55

water diversion projects, 56–57, 156; fishpond restoration and, 230–43; in Kakaʻako (Honolulu), 315–24; in Waikīkī, 72, 74–75, 286–90